COMPLETELY FREE

Completely Free

THE MORAL AND POLITICAL
VISION OF JOHN STUART MILL

John Peter DiIulio

PRINCETON UNIVERSITY PRESS

PRINCETON & OXFORD

Published by Princeton University Press
41 William Street, Princeton, New Jersey 08540
99 Banbury Road, Oxford OX2 6JX

press.princeton.edu

Library of Congress Control Number 2021950444
ISBN 978-0-691-21122-0
ISBN (e-book) 978-0-691-21123-7

British Library Cataloging-in-Publication Data is available

Editorial: Matt Rohal
Production Editorial: Jill Harris
Jacket Design: Pamela L. Schnitter
Production: Erin Suydam
Publicity: Alyssa Sanford and Charlotte Coyne
Copyeditor: Joseph Dahm

Jacket image: Everett Collection / Shutterstock

This book has been composed in Miller

Printed on acid-free paper. ∞

Printed in the United States of America

10 9 8 7 6 5 4 3 2 1

For my father, who introduced me to *On Liberty* in my youth, and who has in all ways embodied its deepest teachings

I should have loved freedom, I believe, at all times, but in the time in which we live I am ready to worship it.

—ALEXIS DE TOCQUEVILLE

Offensively lucid.

—FRIEDRICH NIETZSCHE ON MILL

CONTENTS

IN MY EARLY years of studying Mill—long before I made the naïve decision to write a book on him—I came across the following lines from Murray Rothbard: Mill "was the quintessence of soft rather than hardcore, a woolly-minded man of mush in striking contrast to his steel-edged father," and his "enormous popularity and stature in the British intellectual world was partially due to his very mush-headedness."[1] And I had seen friendlier but comparable sentiments from some of his most notable progeny, like Isaiah Berlin. The conventional wisdom seemed to be that despite his palpable brilliance and focused insights, Mill was a thinker of far too many parts and all too many contradictions.

To many, Mill's practical philosophy has all sorts of problems: a confused, abstruse hedonism; a perplexed, hesitant Utilitarianism; a jerry-built, gimcrack liberalism; a shaky attempt to synthesize Bentham with his other influences, like the Romantics and the Greeks; an ambiguous, faltering posture toward democracy; and the list goes on.[2] Countless attempts to reconcile or reinterpret the moving parts in Mill's thought have, in turn, generated a litany of scholarly debates, none of which have yet settled even the most fundamental issues: "Whether Mill is better read as advocating a *eudaimonistic* or hedonistic conception of the good is still a live issue, as is how this theory of value relates to his account of morality."[3] Moreover, the attempt to dispel these mysteries has, in each case, generated a plethora of clashing interpretations. The literature on Mill's doctrine of the higher pleasures, for instance, abounds with so many idiosyncratic readings that one gets the sense that many scholars are basically just "testing" different approaches.

Now, at the time, Mill's reputation was troubling to me. While I could certainly feel Mill's work pulling me hither and thither, I also felt that there was a profound method to his madness, and that he was actually a cogent and capable moderate, in the deepest, capital-M sense of the word: immune to one-sided doctrines or ideologies, weaving together various

1. Rothbard, *Classical Economics*, 277.
2. See Gray, "John Stuart Mill," 7–35.
3. Macleod and Miller, "Preface," xvii.

strands of philosophy, showing how some of our most intransigent battles are actually being fought between different aspects of the same holistic truth. There was a disconnect, I believed, between Mill the philosopher, whose works are nothing if not lucid, and Mill the scholarly subject, whose works are supposedly filled with knotty frictions. As I began exploring the secondary literature, I discovered that many authors regarded Mill with an attitude similar to my own, and that there was a revisionist tradition of Mill scholarship. And yet, while I found myself tremendously stimulated and encouraged by the key strands of this tradition, I still felt rather frustrated, and I thought at least one more attempt should be made to make sense of Mill's practical philosophy. It was at that moment this book was conceived.

My initial intention was to write an all-embracing work, covering *all* the elements of Mill's thought: not just morals and politics, but also literature, history, economics, and so on. But I soon realized this was a two- or three-book task. What I "settled" for, then, was an original interpretation of Mill's core practical philosophy: his theory of happiness, morality, liberty, and freedom. This will carry us from the nature of "the good," to the nature of "the right," to the nature of a liberal society, to the nature of a free polity. And what I want to show, if nothing else, is that Mill's practical philosophy is not only a seamless tapestry but also profoundly resistant to accusations of "mush-headedness."

Before I commence, I would like to express my deepest thanks to the individuals and organizations without whose invaluable counsel, generous aid, and cherished friendships this book would not have been possible: Matt Rohal, for navigating, advising, and encouraging me at every juncture with indispensable wisdom and good cheer. My anonymous reviewers, for their insightful comments and criticisms. Joseph Dahm, for his graceful edits. My teachers and mentors: Jeff Green, Ellen Kennedy, Anne Norton, Rogers Smith, and Annie Stilz; and especially Philip Pettit, Melissa Lane, and Robby George. My colleagues: Paul Baumgardner, Gabby Girgis, Suzie Kim, Mary Kroeger, Bronwen McShea, and Tom Pavone. Princeton University: the Department of Politics and the University Center for Human Values; and especially the James Madison Program in American Ideals and Institutions, for their incomparable support and hospitality during the 2018–2019 academic year. The University of Pennsylvania: the Program for Research on Religion and Urban Civil Society; Fox Leadership International; and the Collegium Institute. The Matthews: Liz, Sean, Johnny, Teddy, and Joey. My brother, Daniel, for discouraging this project for all the right reasons. My mother, Rosalee, for all the discussions. And my father, John, for all the debates. And a special thanks to Jackie, for having to endure John Peter *and* John Stuart, and for doing so with boundless love and patience.

What is good in this book is due to those mentioned above. The rest, mea culpa.

COMPLETELY FREE

Introduction

Once More unto the Breach

Upon hearing I was writing this book, a colleague inquired, "What is there left to say about John Stuart Mill?" The question, or challenge, struck me as apt, certainly for a book on Mill's moral and political vision. Mill is widely considered to be "the most influential English language philosopher of the nineteenth century,"[1] and as having been a "quintessential public intellectual before the term was created." The mountains upon towering mountains of commentary on his practical philosophy, especially on seminal works like *Utilitarianism* and *On Liberty*, can quickly induce altitude sickness in the scholar. As Mill biographer Richard Reeves has said, "If the true measure of greatness is posthumous productivity, as Goethe suggested, Mill's status is assured."[2] So, indeed: *another* book?

Well, the simple fact is that despite continuous efforts by numerous scholars to come to terms with Mill, there still exists a remarkable number of basic disagreements about how to interpret and weave together the various strands of his thought. At the most basic level, scholars like John Gray have distinguished between what he calls the *traditional* and the *revisionist* interpretations of Mill.[3] While these schools are marked by their own internal disputes, the former tends to interpret Mill's work as being shot through with intractable philosophical difficulties, whereas the latter tends to interpret his work as being misunderstood by the former and characterized by a deeper philosophical harmony, albeit one that raises problems and puzzles of its own. What I develop in this book is

1. Macleod, "John Stuart Mill."
2. Reeves, "Mill's Mind," 3.
3. See Gray, "John Stuart Mill," 7–35.

what we might call a *new* revisionist reading of Mill, one that embraces the attitude or outlook of the revisionist school while also integrating the enduring insights of the traditional school.

One of the intriguing things about Mill is that he was much more than a mere public intellectual, and yet not at all purely a moral or political philosopher. He philosophized largely in response to the "hot" issues of his time: "There were many such things, too: parliamentary reform, the US Civil War and slavery, the Irish potato famine, religious freedom, inherited power and wealth, and women's rights, to name only the most obvious."[4] However, he also found in these issues, and in his private ruminations, an opportunity to explore, develop, and express independent, theoretical ideas. Indeed, more than anything else, Mill was what the Jesuits would call a contemplative in action, and his life was action-packed.

Mill's rich biography is the stuff of academic legend and great literary drama. Those familiar with Mill will probably already know the beats to the story: a rigorous, experimental education under the tutelage of James Mill, his imperious father; raised to carry the torch for the Utilitarian reform project of his father and godfather, Jeremy Bentham, the leading light of England's Philosophical Radicals; a nervous, near suicidal, breakdown at age twenty; recovery via Romantic poetry, which filled the sentimental and aesthetic void left in his soul by his exhausting, emotionally barren upbringing; meeting Harriet Taylor, the then-married love of his life, and carrying on a scandalous courtship with her; making deep and abiding friendships with many of his Conservative rivals; working at the East India Trading Company; his marriage to and intellectual partnership with Taylor; serving a storied spell in Parliament; and all the while pondering and scribbling away as he produced some of the most momentous and famous philosophical treatises of all time.

While there have been many wonderful biographies of Mill, my main interest lies in that last bullet point. Mill's philosophical writings have inspired and provoked countless readers since their earliest publication. Essays like *On Liberty* and *The Subjection of Women* triggered fierce storms of discussion and argument, storms that have still not abated. And many of Mill's most notable works, like *Utilitarianism*, were written as much or more for wide consumption as for esoteric study. And yet, most all of Mill's writings, from the breezy, loaded lines of *Utilitarianism* to the imposing rigor of *A System of Logic*, are composed with a distinctive acuity and intensity. As a whole, Mill's corpus is one of world literature's

---

4. Reeves, "Mill's Mind," 3.

greatest and most enduring displays of philosophical genius. However, Mill is as often noted for his inconsistency, illogic, and incoherence as he is for his unquestioned brilliance and profound influence. And that is what this book addresses.

A Surprisingly Difficult Writer

Harold Bloom, commenting on the panoramic richness of Shakespeare, once wrote, "You can bring absolutely anything to Shakespeare and the plays will light it up." Bloom was cautioning would-be interpreters to take care before assigning any particular ideas or sentiments to the Bard, for his works capture all too much; and however carefully we read his plays, "his plays will read us more energetically still."[5]

A similar word of warning has often been expressed in relation to Mill. Scholars have consistently noted the challenging, maze-like breadth and depth of Mill's thought. As George Kateb remarks, *On Liberty* is "restless," "almost unmanageably instructive," and "when we think we have learned all its lessons, we may be mistaken."[6] Maria Morales believes that "labels are generally dangerous [with Mill] because counterexamples to one-sided interpretations can always be found in his corpus."[7] And as J. C. Rees declares, there "would be something profoundly unimaginative and unhistorical about any attempt to present [Mill's] entire output as all of a piece."[8] Indeed, the nature of Mill's work is almost paradoxical: he writes with unsurpassed clarity and frankness, and yet remains, in Alan Ryan's words, a "surprisingly difficult writer."[9]

In *On Liberty*, for instance, Mill claims to be advancing "one very simple principle," that "the sole end for which mankind are warranted, individually or collectively, in interfering with the liberty of action of any of their number, is self-protection." This principle—the Harm Principle— is based, Mill says, on utility "in the largest sense," and he then ostensibly proceeds to demonstrate the social benefits resulting from our adherence to this principle.[10] It sounds straightforward. And yet generations of scholarly attempts to come to grips with Mill's "simple principle" have generated endless controversy and no shortage of opposing views since

5. Bloom, *Shakespeare*, xxii, 9.
6. Kateb, "Reading of *On Liberty*," 28–29.
7. Morales, "Rational Freedom in John Stuart Mill's Feminism," 47.
8. Rees, *John Stuart Mill's* On Liberty, 9.
9. Ryan, *Making of Modern Liberalism*, 257.
10. Mill, *On Liberty*, 223–224, *CW* 18.

the essay's publication—so much so that *On Liberty* "has ever since been hard to see for the smoke of battle." Scholars appear to agree on one thing only: *On Liberty* "is a liberal manifesto"—but "*what* the liberalism is that it defends and *how* it defends it remain matters of controversy."[11]

While the controversies surrounding Mill are indeed too many and too difficult to squeeze into a single book, my intention is to step into the breach and make one more attempt at reconstructing the "spinal column" of Mill's practical philosophy: his theory of happiness, morality, liberty, and freedom. At the crux of this reconstruction is an old challenge: reading together what are, perhaps, the alpha and the omega of Mill's corpus—his 1861 essay *Utilitarianism* and its classic counterpart, his 1859 essay *On Liberty*. The former gives us the fullest and most renowned statement of Mill's value and moral theory, and the latter gives us the fullest and most renowned statement of Mill's social and political theory. One issue Mill is traditionally perceived to have is that *Utilitarianism* places absolute value on the general happiness, whereas *On Liberty* places absolute value on individual liberty: "What intellectual enterprise could be more misconceived, or more doomed to failure?"[12] As Alan Ryan declares, "Mill cannot wish both to espouse happiness as the only ultimate value and to defend liberty on absolute terms as well."[13] I argue that he can. And as C. L. Ten remarks, Mill must either subordinate liberty to utility, in which case liberty is violable whenever optimal; or subordinate utility to liberty, in which case utility is ancillary and, when push comes to shove, irrelevant.[14] I argue that push does not (*cannot*) come to shove.

Nonetheless, given how stubborn the many troubles and enigmas posed by Mill's writings have been, it would behoove any interpreter to take very seriously the warning of scholars like Rees, and thus to make sure that they are not distorting anything or papering over any of the difficulties standing between the reader and a unified interpretation of Mill's practical philosophy. Mill's thought is like a hedge maze, and where you enter, and which ways you turn, raises certain problems and avoids others; and the problems you avoid will just be questions left unanswered unless your navigation really was pure and true at every intersection. To interpret Mill is to embark on a hazardous quest!

---

11. Ryan, *Making of Modern Liberalism*, 292.
12. Gray, *Mill on Liberty*, ix.
13. Ryan, *J. S. Mill*, 131.
14. See Ten, "Mill's Defence of Liberty," 213–222.

A Unified Interpretation

Yet, despite my trepidation, my overarching contention is that the core components of Mill's practical philosophy present us with *one* seamless and comprehensive picture of happiness, morality, liberty, and freedom. For all his complexity and capaciousness, Mill maintains an essential unity of thought and vision.

Most scholars, when they attempt to unify Mill's practical thought, treat the steps in his philosophy—his value theory, his moral theory, his liberal theory—as if they were different cities that need to be connected by interpretive bridges: How does Mill's concept of individual happiness fit alongside his moral theory? How does Mill's liberal theory, especially as represented by the Harm Principle, square with his Utilitarianism?

However, what I argue is that each step in his thought is actually just a different layer of *the exact same city*. Mill's value theory describes a conception of happiness divided between the higher pleasures of individuality and sociality. Thus, the question becomes: what basic balance should (or *must*) the individual strike between individuality and sociality? The answer is provided by Mill's moral theory, which takes up *precisely* where his value theory leaves off. Mill argues that the hedonic *value*-sense theory by which we discern these twin spheres of happiness is, when converted into a hedonic *moral*-sense theory, also the means by which we discern the extent to which sociality cannot be but *obligatory* to anyone likewise responsive to the realm of desirability. But, then, the question becomes: when, if ever, would justice allow society at large to interfere with individual liberty? Mill's liberal theory replies: in order to enforce an ideal balance between individuality and sociality—indeed, the very same basic degree of sociality that is morally obligatory. And when we get to chapter 4 and Mill's principle of freedom as non-domination, we will see that freedom, properly understood, not only protects our liberty but also fortifies and enhances the ideal balance between individuality and sociality that we, as individuals, need to be happy, moral, and free.

Indeed, according to Mill, as long as society remains completely free, the well-developed person gains everything and loses nothing, at least nothing of intrinsic or ultimate worth. Mill is pluralistic in his value monism, but he *is* a value monist: he believes that all valuable things hang together. The deepest insight, for Mill, is that a happy life is a moral life; that a moral life is a liberal life; and that a liberal life is a life of total freedom.

My interpretation of Mill is based on a close reading of his most salient texts, particularly *Utilitarianism* and *On Liberty*, buttressed by regular appeals to his broader, quite bountiful corpus. While Mill's personal life and character, along with his historical situation and motivations, are important to understanding him fully, my reading is tightly focused on the writings Mill left behind. Needless to say, I make references to his personal or historical context, and certainly to his intellectual milieu, whenever helpful or necessary. But I want to see how far we can get, or where we end up, by considering what his words have to tell us—directly, now, in our own time and place—about some of the deepest, eternal questions: What is happiness? What is morality? What is justice? What is freedom?

In trying to make sense of Mill, I have been reminded constantly of a warning from George Kateb, which I encountered in the first paragraph of the first Mill commentary I ever cracked open. Referring to *On Liberty*, Kateb observes, "There is no reason to think that any account of the book will ever satisfy all who take the book seriously. Indeed, any single reader is likely to grow dissatisfied after a while with his or her own interpretation."[15] Kateb's reflection, applied to Mill as a whole, proved all too prophetic: God only knows how many crumpled outlines I rimmed off my recycling bin. Moreover, I am neither barmy nor smug enough to imagine that this will be the Mill book to end all Mill books. Indeed, Mill is highly resistant to any decisive, definitive treatment: "His goal to unite the philosophies represented in his own age by Bentham and Coleridge plays out throughout his philosophy as no less than an attempt to reconcile Enlightenment and Romanticism, liberalism and conservatism, scientific explanation and humanistic understanding."[16] I do not believe even Mill *himself*, were he alive today, would be able to devise a self-interpretation that would convince or appease *all* his readers.

Nonetheless, the final outline (spared a perilous flight across my office) was, to my mind, convincing and appeasing in ways that I thought worth sharing at length. What I have laid out in this book is, I think, a unified interpretation of Mill that not only feels truly fluid and organic, but also shows itself to be self-reinforcing. In the ensuing chapters, Mill's doctrines of happiness, morality, liberty, and freedom are not merely *reconciled*; rather, they actually *emanate* from one another, whether working forward or backward. Mill's liberal theory flows from his moral theory, which flows from his value theory; and Mill's value theory is implicit in his moral theory, which is implicit in his liberal theory. Properly understood, you can begin with *any* of Mill's doctrines and deduce the others.

15. Kateb, "Reading of *On Liberty*," 28.
16. Macleod and Miller, "Preface," xvii.

One thing I have assiduously tried to avoid is the temptation to bracket or highlight specific passages as being *the* definitive statement of this or that Millian theory. This temptation rears its head time and again in the literature. For instance, there are plenty of scholars who would like to reduce Mill's conception of happiness to what we discover in the second chapter of *Utilitarianism* or the third chapter of *On Liberty*.[17] Similarly, there is a tendency in the revisionist literature to reduce Mill's moral standard to a single passage from the fifth chapter of *Utilitarianism*: "Mill's conception of moral requirement is simple; he states it in a couple of sentences."[18] To put it mildly: *no*, he does *not*. On the contrary, his moral standard, while ultimately rather simple, takes no small degree of jigsaw-puzzle labor to piece together.

To wit, the true challenge in interpreting Mill is that *there is no* section, line, or passage where Mill expresses himself so definitively, so thoroughly, that *all other* sections, lines, or passages must be filtered and evaluated accordingly. This is not to say that certain sections, lines, or passages do not pronounce or evoke certain fundamental Millian ideas or principles; rather, this is just to say that there is no section, line, or passage that establishes an Archimedean point of interpretation. To interpret Mill effectively is to tell a story in which every section, line, and passage has its proper role and place, but in which *no* section, line, or passage takes on an outsized, domineering importance. A jigsaw puzzle indeed.

Why Mill?

None of this, though, illuminates why we ought to surrender our attention, here and now, to yet another book on Mill. Well, justifying Mill himself is easy enough: Mill has a richly deserved place in the philosophical pantheon; he is a brilliant, ageless, elevating thinker. When asked why he intended to scale Mount Everest, George Mallory replied, "Because it's there." A similar spirit ought to prevail in our study of the greatest minds that have ever lent themselves to the deepest human inquiries: What is valuable, and what is the nature of happiness? What is obligatory, and what is the nature of morality? What is freedom, and what is the nature of a just and good society? These are questions that should engage our interest whenever and wherever we find ourselves. Stranded on a deserted

17. Typically, the latter appeal is made in passing.
18. Brown, "Harm Principle," 420.

island, any contemplative castaway would be lucky to have Mill's collected works close at hand.

Moreover, the philosophy of Mill is remarkably well suited to our contemporary environment. We find ourselves in a secular, disenchanted age, when values and morals are struggling to establish themselves as something more than merely subjective. We find ourselves in an ever more interconnected mass society, where the relationship between the solitary individual and the powers that be, both social and political, is becoming an ever more pressing and challenging concern. We find ourselves in a social and political landscape where it is becoming ever less apparent what social or political values, if any, could or should unite us, and how we ought to understand any such values. Needless to say, Mill felt and saw *all* these developments in England and abroad, living through the mid-nineteenth century, a period of rapid and unprecedented transition. And while Mill's work is timeless, I think any sensible, sensitive reader will also find his philosophy to be strikingly timely.

However, the justification for *this* volume is threefold. First, for reasons that will become apparent throughout the following chapters, I found myself deeply engaged and enriched but ultimately dissatisfied with the extant scholarship on Mill. Standing on the shoulders of countless others, I thought I could see an even further horizon and took it upon myself to journey toward it. Personally, I also wanted to compose a book on Mill that preserves and even accentuates what makes his work so musical and vigorous. In this pursuit, I have doubtless traded some precision for style, but hopefully not at the expense of any substance.

In addition to this exegetical rationale, I wrote this book as a sympathetic account of Mill's uncommon common sense. Indeed, Mill is an empirical thinker who stretches the evidence of everyday life to dazzling and bracing philosophical heights; *anyone* can read Mill and be transported philosophically based on nothing more than their own experiences and observations. While valuable for plenty of other reasons, what was missing, I felt, from many other works on Mill was a *strong* or *thick* sense that Mill might actually be *right*; that we, too, should be Utilitarians and liberals of his persuasion. Mill is even alleged by many of his admirers to have regrettably weak theoretical foundations: the competent judge, the infamous "proof," the principle of liberty. However, when suitably represented, I think Mill makes a cogent, potent argument for his distinctive vision.

And finally, with liberalism reeling if not fading throughout the world, I believe it is a perfect moment to consider Mill afresh. For one thing,

Mill is a thinker for whom the term "liberal" is as much an adjective as a noun. Liberalism as a *noun*, or as a *thing*, refers to a set of principles and practices, typically having to do with things like individual rights and liberties, sociopolitical equality, and limited government. But liberal as an *adjective*—that is, the *modifying* liberal, in the sense of being *liberal-*minded, or having a *liberal* outlook, spirit, or method—refers to a more general capaciousness, humility, and generosity. Mill's philosophical approach is as much or more about *being* liberal in mind, heart, and soul as it is about liberalism itself. Thus, to return to Mill anew is to plant and nurture precious seeds that might grow and flourish despite the storms and surges of the wider world.

Indeed, good, healthy societies have guiding philosophies, not brittle ideologies; and if something is going to replace liberalism, it can still be a *liberal* version of whatever it turns out to be. To be sure, Mill defends certain institutions and policies as being best or ideally representative of liberty and freedom; but this does not mean that liberty and freedom must be totally forgone in their absence, or that nonliberal regimes cannot embrace liberty and freedom to a greater or lesser extent. In short, just as a robust liberalism should be mindful of and inflected by Sir James Fitzjames Stephen, whatever emerges next could be mindful of and inflected by Mill, which makes understanding Mill at his best of pressing importance—not least of all for possibly stemming any illiberal tides.

Mill's Value Theory

In chapter 1, I discuss Mill's value theory. What is intrinsically valuable or desirable? And what does Mill mean by happiness, or the good life? First, I assess Mill's so-called doctrine of the higher pleasures and argue that Mill successfully combines the hedonistic and qualitative aspects of his doctrine into a *supra*-hedonistic position that I call *high-minded hedonism*. This involves rejecting the most notable readings of Mill as a qualitative hedonist and proposing a new way of synthesizing his hedonistic and non-hedonistic claims. Second, I reconstruct Mill's empirical defense of the higher pleasures and develop what I call his hedonic value-sense theory. In so doing, I represent Mill's critique of psychological hedonism along the very lines defended by some of his most trenchant critics. Third, I highlight Mill's division between the higher pleasures of *individuality* and *sociality*. In a proof-by-demonstration of his aforesaid critique, I reveal how Mill rejects not only psychological hedonism, but also its progenitor, psychological egoism. And finally, I show how Mill's empirical approach to the higher pleasures pushes him beyond a merely aggregative conception of happiness to one that is more Aristotelian: *the activity of the higher faculties in accordance with the higher pleasures.*

Mill's Moral Theory

In chapter 2, I discuss Mill's moral theory. What are we obliged to do or refrain from doing? And what moral meaning and weight should we accord to things like utility, rules, and justice? First, I show how the entirety of *Utilitarianism* is devoted to "proving" *one* proposition: that the general happiness (or Utility) is the only morally relevant value. This involves separating Mill's moral standard, the Utility Principle, from the Benthamite directive to maximize the general happiness; and this also involves expanding Mill's "proof" of the Utility Principle beyond the unfairly maligned opening passage to the fourth chapter of *Utilitarianism*. Second, to bolster these other reflections, I disinter Mill's empirical defense of the Utility Principle and develop what I call his hedonic moral-sense theory. In so doing, I repurpose the evidence given for what is often called Mill's Sanction Utilitarianism. Third, I dissociate Mill's Utilitarianism from the most famous brand of Utilitarian ethics and the school in which Mill was raised; namely, Benthamism. Drawing on his hedonic moral-sense theory, I argue that Mill has a much less "totalizing" vision of morality than Bentham. Fourth, by reconstructing his theory of *morality as impartiality*, I explain how Mill actually intends for us to interpret the demands of the Utility Principle. This will prompt me to introduce a figure lurking in the background of his moral theory: the *impartial observer*. Fifth, I compare Mill to the classic debate between Act and Rule Utilitarianism. While affirming that Mill makes moral judgments entirely on the basis of moral rules, I argue that the Act versus Rule dichotomy is, for Mill, incoherent and needless. And finally, I address Mill's concept of justice, which focuses on the natural emergence of perfect duties. This will provide an opportunity to interrogate the relative inattention Mill pays to *imperfect* duties.

Mill's Liberal Theory

In chapter 3, I discuss Mill's liberal theory. What principle ought to govern the relationship between the individual and society? When is it permissible for society to interfere with the individual? First, I motivate the discussion by explicating the general value Mill places on what is known as *liberty as non-interference.* I argue that Mill both echoes and exceeds the core Benthamite reasons for valuing liberty. Second, I address the meaning of the so-called Harm Principle. My core contention is that to "harm," for Mill, is to act "unjustly," which merges Mill's liberal theory with his moral theory. However, I maintain that the *other* main stream of scholarship, which assigns to Mill a more common or colloquial concept of harm, is *also* essential. As I contend, Mill uses an *ordinary* concept of harm in order to underscore the inviolability of what I label *inward liberty*. Third, I reconstruct Mill's absolutist defense of intellectual liberty. In short, I show how the second chapter of *On Liberty* is, at core, a painstaking, step-by-step Utilitarian defense of freedom of thought, speech, and discussion. Fourth, I do the same for Mill's absolutist defense of ethical liberty. This will involve paying special attention to Mill's conception of *individual originality*, and how it deepens and refines his theory of happiness. And finally, I press Mill on the issues of liberal civility and anti-paternalism, and consider how his liberalism at once succeeds and fails in handling the challenge of uncivil or immature citizens.

Mill's Republican Theory

In chapter 4, I discuss Mill's republican theory. What principle ought to direct or frame the relationship between individuals and the sociopolitical institutions that govern them? What should be the individual's relationship to social or legal power? First, I distinguish between what I call the *libertarian* and *republican* concepts of freedom: the former is *liberty as non-interference*, whereas the latter is *freedom as non-domination*. In so doing, I give a theoretical account as to why Mill, based on his empirical teleology, would naturally reject the libertarian view of freedom and endorse the republican theory. Second, I provide a republican reading of Mill's concept of freedom. While other scholars have looked to *The Subjection of Women* to make this argument, I look to *On Liberty* instead and show how that famously libertarian text is actually republican to its core. Third, I taxonomize Mill's various reasons for *valuing* freedom as non-domination over and above, and, indeed, often at the expense of, mere liberty as non-interference. Several scholars have remarked that Mill sees in domination the tendency to keep the dominated in the immaturity of their faculties; but, in fact, he has a litany of principled reasons for opposing domination. And finally, I touch upon the significance Mill places on civic participation. As we will see, civic participation is necessary not only to secure non-domination, but also to ensure and enhance individual and social flourishing.

Mill and His Critics

In chapter 5, having worked my way through Mill's practical philosophy, I consider a few general lines of criticism—not a comprehensive review of any and all relevant critiques, but a meditation on several pointed concerns one might have with Mill's oeuvre. The questions are as follows: First, is Mill *too libertarian*? Here we encounter *the* classic conservative critique of Mill. Second, is Mill *too progressive*? Here we encounter the *other* notable conservative critique of Mill, one stemming from the revisionist tradition. Third, is Mill *too conservative*? Here we encounter what might be the most resonant progressive critique of Mill. And finally, is Mill *too communitarian*? Here we encounter the question of moral motivation and ask whether or not Mill can account for the *whole* of morality. In short, I argue that Mill's practical philosophy, while certainly not immune from error or criticism, can withstand these inquiries.

Footnotes

All my footnotes to Mill correspond to *The Collected Works of John Stuart Mill*. They reference the title of the work, the page number(s), and the volume of the collection. For instance, "Mill, *On Liberty*, 217, *CW* 18" means page 217 of volume 18. Similarly, all my footnotes to Bentham (with some exceptions) correspond to *The Works of Jeremy Bentham* and follow the same structure. For example, "Bentham, *Principles of Morals and Legislation*, 14, *W* 1." For the sake of keeping the footnotes clean, I include the volume reference only the first time a work is cited in each chapter. Both collections are available at the *Online Library of Liberty*: https://oll .libertyfund.org.

Also, all emphases in quotations are from the original source unless otherwise noted in the corresponding footnote.

CHAPTER ONE

Noble Pleasures

MILL ON DESIRABILITY AND HAPPINESS

*He courageously faces the difficulty by pronouncing in favour of a
difference in kind or quality among pleasures; which difference he
expands on through two or three eloquent pages, which I believe have
received more attention from critics on the other side than all the rest
of the book put together.*

—ALEXANDER BAIN ON MILL'S *UTILITARIANISM*

*The first question in regard to any man of speculation is, what is his
theory of human life?*

—MILL, "BENTHAM"

IN THIS CHAPTER, we examine the nature and foundations of Mill's value
theory—his theory of the good life. Unlike many contemporary liberal
theorists, Mill grounds his entire practical philosophy on a definite theory
of what constitutes human well-being. As a Utilitarian, Mill regards happiness as the *summum bonum*. But what *is* happiness for Mill? And how
does he *defend* his conception of happiness?

The study of Mill's value theory revolves around the issue of what his
fundamental attitude is toward the nature of the good. In general, there
have been two opposing schools of thought on this question. The traditional view says that Mill, like Bentham, defends some version of what
can be called *value subjectivism*: the value of an object or end is merely a
matter of subjective attitude, feeling, or preference. Most commonly, those
who read Mill along these lines associate his theory of the good life with
hedonism, the view that objects or ends are valuable only insofar as they

cause pleasant feelings or sensations. Other scholars in this family associate his theory with *desire-satisfaction*, the view that objects or ends are valuable only insofar as they fulfill subjective wants or needs.[1]

Now, unless all else fails, it would be wise to sideline desire-satisfaction. In *Utilitarianism*, the focal point of this debate, Mill appeals to desires as *evidence* of what is valuable, not as ends unto themselves. And indeed, it is precisely on this evidential basis that many *non*traditional, or revisionist, scholars have read Mill as an exponent of *value objectivism*: an object or end is valuable insofar as it embodies or exhibits certain properties, features, or attributes that are inherently worthy or desirable. From the position of a value objectivist, it could very well be reasonable to declare that you *ought* to value or desire a given object or end, even if you experience *no* subjective inclination toward it, and vice versa.

The central passage in this debate is from the second chapter of *Utilitarianism*, where Mill proclaims his doctrine of the higher pleasures. For some traditional scholars, this doctrine is a workable if not welcome, albeit possibly abstruse, qualitative amendment to Bentham's quantitative hedonism. However, for revisionist scholars, with this doctrine Mill sails into an altogether different ethical realm from Bentham, where it becomes impossible to call Mill a hedonist, and where a reader must look between and around the lines in order to comprehend what he *actually* believes and why. In short, the core controversy is over what significance pleasure has in Mill's theory of the good life.

My first contention in this chapter is that the revisionist interpretation is *right* to dissociate Mill from hedonism, but *wrong* to go looking for excuses to abjure, or reasons to amend, his affirmation of pleasure as the end of life. Pleasure *is* the proper end of life for Mill, yet in a *non*-hedonistic sense. Mill's unambiguous appeal to pleasure—far from being confused, coy, or obscure—is perfectly in keeping with his value objectivism. Indeed, what I offer below is a new revisionist reading of Mill's value theory, one that vindicates his value-objectivist commitment to pleasure, and that thereby avoids coherent but erroneous value-subjectivist readings interpreting Mill as a qualitative hedonist.

However, my subsequent and overarching thesis is that Mill's theory of the good life is better explained and more cogently justified by turning away from his doctrine of the higher pleasures and toward his psychology of human desire. As we will see, Mill develops and defends his value theory by examining our psychological experience of the good; he

1. See Jenkins, "Desire and Human Nature in J. S. Mill," 219–234.

contends that we desire only what is attractive to our mind's eye, and that we are attracted to certain goods or activities *because* they are inherently worthy or desirable. With this empirical approach, he ultimately advances a conception of happiness that embraces both individuality and sociality in a more-Aristotelian-than-not vision of human flourishing.

Again, the role of pleasure is fundamental here. If Mill's doctrine of the higher pleasures is his testament to pleasure as the *final good* of a noble life, then Mill's psychology of human desire is his meditation on pleasure as the *first evidence* as to what makes life noble. As we will see, Mill's theory is that the mind's eye takes *subjective* pleasure in the thought or idea of various goods or activities for *objective* reasons; that these hedonic reasons can withstand critical scrutiny; and that these goods or activities include both self-regarding (*individual*) and other-regarding (*social*) pursuits and ideals.

This distinction between individuality and sociality begs the question of what we are *morally* obliged to do or refrain from doing, which leads us into the thicket of chapter 2. However, we must first lay the seeds by tackling the first principal question of Mill's value theory: what, if anything, is generally desirable?

The Higher Pleasures

In the fourth chapter of *Utilitarianism*, Mill lays down the first principle of his practical philosophy: "The utilitarian doctrine is, that happiness is desirable, and the only thing desirable, as an end; all other things being desirable as means to that end."[2] Happiness is the *summum bonum*; the highest or ultimate good. When asked "Why do you eat chocolate?" or "Why do you listen to opera?" or "Why do you foster friendships?" the *final* answer, according to a Utilitarian, always is and/or should be the same: *happiness*. In the abstract, Mill's basic notion of happiness is the same as that of every ethicist from Aristotle to Bentham; namely, a life "inclusive of all that has intrinsic value."[3] An intrinsic value is a noninstrumental good: it is valued or valuable not as a means to an end but as an end unto itself; it is attractive or desirable for its own sake and thus constitutes a sufficient motive or reason for action. Thus, a happy life is one defined by the enjoyment of intrinsic values—the "ingredients of happiness."[4] But, of course, this begs the question: what is intrinsically valuable?

2. Mill, *Utilitarianism*, 234, *CW* 10.
3. Nussbaum, "Mill between Aristotle & Bentham," 61.
4. Mill, *Utilitarianism*, 235.

Mill develops his most famous (or infamous) answer in response to Bentham's hedonism. A hedonist believes that pleasure is not just *one* but the *only* intrinsic value (our sole raison d'être), and thus that happiness and pleasure are, in effect, synonymous. As Bentham declares, "benefit, advantage, pleasure, good, [and] happiness" all mean "the same thing."[5] (Chocolate, opera, and friendship are valuable only if and because they are pleasurable.) For Bentham, pleasure refers to any agreeable mental or bodily sensation: "No refinement, no metaphysics. . . . Pain and pleasure are what everybody feels to be such."[6] Pleasure is whatever feels good— indeed, whatever *feels* good, such that we would desire, on balance, to prolong, intensify, or repeat the experience. (Chocolate, opera, and friendship count as pleasures insofar as they produce appealing sensations.) In addition, or perhaps as a corollary to his hedonism, Bentham declines to evaluate pleasure by any standard that might be called *qualitative*. Rather, his evaluative criteria are strictly *quantitative*, such as intensity, duration.[7] To be happier is to have *more* pleasure; our helping of happiness is equivalent to "the sum total of [our] pleasures."[8]

By the time Mill wrote *Utilitarianism*, Bentham's hedonism was reviled by many as a rather unsavory creed: "To suppose that life has (as they express it) no higher end than pleasure—no better and nobler object of desire and pursuit—they designate as utterly mean and groveling; as a doctrine worthy only of swine." Mill is likely paraphrasing his friend Thomas Carlyle, who had spiritedly encapsulated this "inveterate dislike"[9] for "the monster Utilitaria"[10] by dismissing Bentham's dogma as "Pig Philosophy."[11] Aspersions aside, Carlyle cannot be accused of distorting Bentham's position. Bentham had frankly and repeatedly avowed that happiness *is* pleasure, and that all other goods or activities have merely an instrumental value: "Prejudice apart, the game of push-pin is of equal value with the arts and sciences of music and poetry. If the game of push-pin furnish more pleasure, it is more valuable than either." To assert the objective "pre-eminence" of the arts and sciences is to offer an "altogether fanciful" judgment—it is to reveal our prejudices.[12] Bentham derided all such

5. Bentham, *Principles of Morals and Legislation*, 1–2, *W* 1.
6. Bentham, *Theory of Legislation*, 3.
7. See Bentham, *Principles of Morals and Legislation*, 16ff.
8. Ibid., 2.
9. Mill, *Utilitarianism*, 210.
10. Carlyle, *Sartor Resartus*, 204.
11. Carlyle, *Latter-Day Pamphlets*, 315.
12. Bentham, *Rationale of Reward*, 253, *W* 2.

prejudices with "good-humoured contempt,"[13] declaring, for instance, that if "poetry and music deserve to be preferred before a game of push-pin, it must be because they are calculated to gratify those individuals who are most difficult to be pleased."[14] (Those who would rather pore over Pushkin than play push-pin are just being fussy hedonists!) Thus, Bentham was branded the advocate of a brazenly dissolute ideology.

Enter Mill, who argues that the assumed tension between Bentham and our Carlylean intuitions is needless and wholly contrary to Utilitarianism properly understood: "The comparison of the Epicurean life to that of beasts is felt as degrading, precisely because a beast's pleasures do not satisfy a human being's conceptions of happiness." Mill begins by parroting the crux of Bentham's creed: "pleasure and freedom from pain, are the only things desirable as ends," and "all desirable things" are "desirable either for the pleasure inherent in themselves, or as means to the promotion of pleasure and the prevention of pain." And yet, for Mill, Bentham's fundamental mistake had been to evaluate pleasure quantitatively to the exclusion of qualitative judgments. Utilitarians, Mill avers, can and must acknowledge higher gradations of hedonic desirability: "It is quite compatible with the principle of utility to recognise the fact, that some *kinds* of pleasures are more desirable and more valuable than others. It would be absurd that while, in estimating all other things, quality is considered as well as quantity, the estimation of pleasure should be supposed to depend on quantity alone." And these qualitative distinctions, once duly accounted for, will validate the intuitive conviction that certain pleasures, such as the arts and sciences, are of a qualitatively superior stock: "the pleasures of the intellect, of the feelings and imagination, and of the moral sentiments, [have] a much higher value as pleasures than [do] those of mere sensation." In fact, Mill theorizes that "the manner of existence which employs [our] higher faculties" boasts "a superiority in quality, so far outweighing quantity as to render it, in comparison, of small account."[15] In this way, Mill professes a hedonistic faith that essentially inverts the hedonism proclaimed by Bentham.

However, as countless scholars have remarked, Mill's revisionist account of hedonism—the doctrine of the higher pleasures, or qualitative hedonism—would appear to exceed the conceptual limits of hedonism. The puzzle is always the same: how can the higher pleasures be higher

13. Mill, "Bentham," 120, *CW* 10.
14. Bentham, *Rationale of Reward*, 254.
15. Mill, *Utilitarianism*, 210–211.

without being either *more* pleasurable or more than *merely* pleasant? To many, the answer is obvious: *they cannot*, and so Mill must either abandon hedonism or discard this qualitative dimension. Most of Mill's early critics argued that, logically, hedonism *cannot* weigh qualitative, and can include *only* quantitative, distinctions between pleasures; that by evaluating pleasure qualitatively, we necessarily "go to something *outside* pleasure," in which case "we have thrown over Hedonism altogether."[16] How, they queried, can a Mill-minded hedonist answer the question "What quality?" without naming a non-hedonic source of value? Qualitative hedonism was seen to be as self-contradictory as the avaricious but upstanding person who declares, "I care for nothing but money, but it must be honestly come by."[17]

MILL CONTRA HEDONISM

As we will see, this critique is far too hasty; qualitative hedonism *can* be rendered coherent. Nonetheless, the reality is that Mill bucks hedonism regardless. Mill's doctrine of the higher pleasures is not *non*-hedonistic (where pleasure is regarded with indifference or outright disdain), but it is *supra*-hedonistic, by which I mean that the value of the higher pleasures, while incorporating or even necessitating pleasure, cannot ultimately be reduced to pleasure; pleasure will be an essential byproduct of their pursuit or realization, but the higher pleasures are valuable principally and most significantly because they evince certain more-than-merely-hedonic characteristics.

To begin, Mill all but explicitly disowns hedonism by proclaiming the "intrinsic superiority" of the higher pleasures: they are "more desirable and more valuable"; they are "better" rather than "inferior"; they are perched atop "higher ground"; and they appeal to those with "high aspirations" and "a sense of dignity" as opposed to those who have either lost their passion for the "nobler feelings" or succumbed to an "infirmity of character." Such remarks strongly suggest a qualitative outlook that favors certain pleasures for supra-hedonic reasons. The higher pleasures are "more elevated" than either the "animal appetites" or any other "inferior type" of pleasure belonging to a "lower grade of existence." And Mill associates their "elevated" nature with the *kind-of-life-being-led* rather than the *type-of-pleasure-being-felt*: "It is better to be a human being dissatisfied than a

16. Bradley, *Ethical Studies*, 119–120.
17. Carritt, *Theory of Morals*, 21.

pig satisfied; better to be Socrates dissatisfied than a fool satisfied."[18] Mill is plainly appealing here to the ways of life to which different pleasures belong; he is not looking to the pleasures themselves. Mill would have us believe that Socrates awaiting his hemlock is happier than the fools who sentenced him to death, for Socrates knows what it means to live well and has lived a good life.

Furthermore, the lower pleasures are valued for their "mere sensation," whereas the higher pleasures are valued for something else entirely, what Mill dubs their "intrinsic nature."[19] Whether or not sensations can be properly understood as intrinsic to objects or experiences is beside the point; the point is that Mill, in distinguishing the higher pleasures, appeals to their "intrinsic nature" as something apart from and superior to any "mere sensation" they produce. To any hedonist of Bentham's ilk, this is tantamount to saying that the higher pleasures are valued for their supra-hedonic quality, whereas the lower pleasures are valued for their hedonic effects. Indeed, for Bentham, pleasure just *is* a "mere [agreeable mental or bodily] sensation." Thus, to elevate a pleasure for its "intrinsic [not-merely-felt] nature" is, for an errant Benthamite like Mill, to exalt it for a supra-hedonic reason.

Likewise, the lower pleasures are valued for their purely "passive" nature, whereas the higher pleasures are valued for their distinctively "active" nature.[20] But, again, pleasure *itself* simply *is* passive, in the sense that the feeling of pleasure could be replicated by a pleasure pill without losing any of its *hedonic* value.[21] Thus, to bracket and underscore the "active" employment given to the higher faculties by the higher pleasures is to distinguish these pleasures for their not-merely-felt, more-than-just-hedonic quality. The higher pleasures are loftier partly *because* they exercise the higher faculties. And this echoes the rest of Mill's corpus, where he evaluates activities, norms, and institutions almost exclusively by the extent to which they have successfully "called forth and invigorated the active faculties."[22] The specter of hedonism vanishes almost entirely.

We can also look to the only direct defense Mill offers for the existence of the higher pleasures: his appeal to those whom he dubs "competent judges." As Mill writes, "If I am asked, what I mean by the difference of quality in pleasures, or what makes one pleasure more valuable than

18. Mill, *Utilitarianism*, 210–213.
19. Ibid., 211.
20. Ibid., 215.
21. See Nozick, *Anarchy, State, and Utopia*, 42–45.
22. Mill, "Coleridge," 140, *CW* 10.

another, merely as a pleasure, except its being greater in amount, there is but one possible answer. Of two pleasures, if there be one to which all or almost all who have experience of both give a decided preference," then "that is the more desirable pleasure." And his contention is that the pleasures belonging to the higher faculties will prevail—indeed, that they always do: "Now it is an unquestionable fact that those who are equally acquainted with, and equally capable of appreciating and enjoying, both [types of pleasure], do give a most marked preference for the manner of existence which employs their higher faculties." This "verdict" of the competent judge conflicts with hedonism for several reasons.[23]

For one, Mill implies that the competent judge is promoting the higher faculties even at the *expense* of pleasure: "Few human creatures would consent to be changed into any of the lower animals, for a promise of the fullest allowance of a beast's pleasures; no intelligent human being would consent to be a fool, no instructed person would be an ignoramus, no person of feeling or conscience would be selfish or base." Lower, inferior beings seek fully to satisfy their hedonic proclivities (they want to be "content"), whereas competent judges prefer the "gratification" of their "highly endowed" nature despite the greater "discontent" that often accompanies this "very different" idea of happiness. Again, the impression one gets is unmistakable: the competent judge locates the higher pleasures on a worthier plane of intrinsic value. And this impression is deepened by the fact that competent judges can suffer from *akrasia*, or weakness of will: they can "fully appreciate" and be "perfectly aware" of the "intrinsic superiority" of the higher pleasures while being concurrently "addicted" to "sensual indulgences"; they can *degenerate*, like "a very tender plant, easily killed."[24] They are not just missing out on better pleasures; their lowly "manner of existence" offends their "sense of dignity" and thus inspires a proper sense of *shame*.

Moreover, Mill attributes a sort of epistemic *authority* to the *majority* of competent judges: "On a question which is the best worth having of two pleasures, or which of two modes of existence is the most grateful to the feelings, apart from its moral attributes and from its consequences, the judgment of those who are qualified by knowledge of both, or, if they

---

23. Mill, *Utilitarianism*, 211, 213. Importantly, competent preferences do not *constitute* but rather provide *evidence* for what is qualitatively superior. The higher pleasures are preferred because they are qualitatively superior; they are not qualitatively superior because they are preferred.

24. Ibid., 210–213. Mill writes, "full appreciation" and "addict."

differ, that of the majority among them, must be admitted as final."²⁵ However, this begs the question: how can the minority be *wrong* having acquired the requisite competence? The most plausible inference one can make is that Mill is defending a standard of supra-hedonic value that they are misapprehending or disregarding despite their hedonic experience.

And, as is often mentioned, the competent judge also reflects Mill's influences, specifically the supra-hedonistic doctrines of Plato, Aristotle, and Wordsworth. Mill's theory mirrors Book IX of Plato's *Republic*, where Socrates compares the pleasures of "wisdom-loving, victory-loving, [and] gain-loving" persons. Competent, "wisdom-loving" judges are "most experienced in all the pleasures of which we [are] speaking." Thus, we can be confident that "living more nobly" is equivalent to "living more pleasantly."²⁶ Similarly, the competent judge resembles the "good man" from Aristotle's *Nicomachean Ethics*, whose wisdom decides what is *truly* valuable and pleasant: "For each state of character has its own ideas of the noble and the pleasant, and perhaps the good man differs from others most by seeing the truth in each class of things, being as it were the norm and measure of them." The pleasures of the "bad man" are painful to those habituated to distinctively human activities.²⁷ Mill's competent judge attests to the same wisdom. And furthermore, the competent judge is willing to endure "acute suffering"²⁸ for the sake of the higher pleasures, which echoes Wordsworth's ethic of noble striving. In "Character of the Happy Warrior," Wordsworth describes a heroic soul, who, while "doomed to go in company with Pain," is rendered "happy as a Lover" by "high endeavors" and "glorious gain."²⁹ The "noble enjoyment" of Mill's "moral hero,"³⁰ that is, his "mere consciousness of well-doing,"³¹ recalls this theme. For the sake of "*real* happiness," or "well-being,"³² the competent judge prefers a life largely beset by painful "imperfections."³³

Now, there are certainly moments in Mill's corpus that could give the (mistaken) impression that he is indeed committed to hedonism. For

25. Ibid., 213. "Final" is a bit misleading: as Mill suggests in *Utilitarianism*, and as his other writings confirm, he has in mind a *contestable* finality, open to revision based on further experience—like a democratic law.

26. Plato, *Republic of Plato*, 581c–582a.

27. Aristotle, *Nicomachean Ethics*, III.4; X.6.

28. Mill, *Utilitarianism*, 212.

29. Wordsworth, *Major Works*, 320–322. See also Aristotle, *Nicomachean Ethics*, III.6.

30. Mill, *Utilitarianism*, 217.

31. Mill, *System of Logic*, 842, *CW* 8.

32. Mill, "Herschel's Preliminary Discourse," 285, *CW* 22, my emphasis.

33. Mill, *Utilitarianism*, 212.

instance, in his commentary on Plato's *Gorgias*, Mill says that Callicles could "easily have parried" Socrates's "dialectical" moves against hedonism. But is Mill thereby intimating that there is anything to the Calliclean ethic? Not at all. To concede that Callicles could have weathered the storm of Socratic inquiry is *not* to confess that this weathering would give any credence to his hedonism. On the contrary, it is merely to imply what Mill regularly avows: that ethical principles cannot be defended via logical analysis; that individuals can discern the supra-hedonic nature of the good only via their experience of the good. In other words, nothing anyone *argues* can bring Callicles around. In a Platonic spirit, Callicles must first come to *love* what is good: "*How* to live virtuously, is a question the solution of which belongs to the understanding: but the understanding has no inducements which it can bring to the aid of one who has not yet determined whether he will endeavour to live virtuously or no. It is impossible, by any arguments, to prove that a life of obedience to duty is preferable, so far as respects the agent himself, to a life of circumspect and cautious selfishness."[34] Callicles has either not experienced the good or been degraded or corrupted in his experience; he is, for Mill, in desperate need of an ethical rebirth that only the fuller and finer experiences of life can deliver.[35]

In sum, given the logic of his theory and the tenor of his prose, I believe we must conclude that the higher pleasures definitively outstrip the conceptual limits of hedonism. Mill's sphere of intrinsic (*human*) value comprises *higher* goods and activities. This should not be surprising to anyone familiar with Mill, considering that the vast majority of his works are characterized by a clear and keen supra-hedonistic ethos. In *A System of Logic*, Mill draws a thick line of demarcation between our lowlier desire for pleasure and our loftier desire for higher ends. As Mill says, happiness can be defined *either* "in the humble sense, of pleasure and freedom from pain," *or* "in the higher meaning," "such as human beings with highly developed faculties can care to have."[36] And what Mill in *On Liberty* calls the "largest" sense of "utility" is concerned with whatever aids or thwarts our "progressive" development toward "the ideal perfection of human nature."[37] As the rest of this chapter (and book) demonstrates, Mill's conception of happiness is not hedonistic but pluralistic and hierarchical: "His theory of value is pluralistic in that a diversity of things are desirable ingredients

34. Mill, "The Gorgias," 135, 148–149, *CW* 11.
35. Cf. Beaumont, "J. S. Mill on Calliclean Hedonism," 553–578.
36. Mill, *System of Logic*, 952.
37. Mill, *On Liberty*, 224, 278, *CW* 18.

of happiness. And it is hierarchical in that it ranks ingredients of the good life."[38]

Nonetheless, there have been numerous attempts to reconcile the doctrine of the higher pleasures with hedonism, or to explain why such a reconciliation is actually unnecessary. While some of these attempts largely succeed in establishing qualitative hedonism *itself* as a viable, consistent doctrine—and thus in overturning the stale assumption that qualitative judgments simply cannot mix logically with hedonism—they all still fail to salvage or justify a hedonistic reading of Mill. In what follows, I address what appear to be the three most prominent interpretations of Mill as a qualitative hedonist.

MILL CONTRA QUALITATIVE HEDONISM

Some scholars frame Mill as a qualitative hedonist by associating his concept of quality with the heterogeneity of pleasure. Recall that Bentham evaluates pleasure solely by its quantity—as if all pleasures could be reduced to "a single homogenous sensation"[39] that differs in degree but not in kind or feel. Mill's early critics argued that Bentham's strict adherence to quantitative hedonism is just a testament to his consistency; indeed, against Mill they maintained that weighing all pleasures *as if* they were homogenous is just a logical necessity for any true hedonist. As G. E. Moore writes, "Let us suppose [Mill] to mean that there are various kinds of pleasure, in the sense in which there are various kinds of colour—blue, red, green, etc. Even in this case, if we are to say that our end is colour alone," then "there can be no possible reason for preferring one colour to another, red, for instance, to blue, except that the one is more of a colour than the other."[40] Certainly no hedonist, Moore's only point here is that as long as Bentham is going to dismiss as fanciful the idea that some pleasures are inherently worthier than others, then he is correct in thinking that there can be nothing of import left to consider but their amount.

However, this conclusion runs afoul of everyday experience. First of all, to enjoy the pleasures of chocolate, opera, and friendship is to be at once disabused of the notion that there exists "a single homogenous sensation" into which all these pleasures collapse. As Alasdair MacIntyre remarks, the "pleasure-of-drinking-Guinness is not the

---

38. Hoag, "Happiness and Freedom," 195.
39. Nussbaum, "Mill between Aristotle & Bentham," 63.
40. Moore, *Principia Ethica*, §48.

pleasure-of-swimming-at-Crane's-Beach, and the swimming and the drinking are not two different means for providing the same end-state."[41] Pleasure is whatever *feels* good, and yet different pleasures feel essentially and irreducibly *different*, such that downing another pint can offer us more "pleasure-of-drinking-Guinness" but not more pleasure-full-stop. Mill concurs: "Neither pains nor pleasures are homogenous." Thus, a hedonist should be able to evaluate discrete pleasures not only as "means to a collective something termed happiness," but also for the distinctive hedonic qualities belonging to each of these pleasures respectively.[42]

On this basis, Mill *could* explain why a steadfast hedonist might choose the lesser of two hedonic quantities. Even if one pleasure outweighs another quantitatively, a hedonist can still prefer the hedonic qualities of the latter, perhaps so much so that the greater quantity of the former pales in comparison. For instance, I can prefer one scoop of vanilla ice cream to three scoops of strawberry *just because* the former is qualitatively more pleasing to my taste buds. And perhaps the pleasure of reading *Pride and Prejudice* can eclipse the pleasure of sipping lemonade *just because* the pleasant qualities of Jane Austen's prose—such as "wit," "beautiful syntax," and "exquisite delineation of character"—are preferred in kind to the taste of the beverage: "There is nothing to prevent [a hedonist] claiming that it would not matter how long the experience of enjoyable drinking could be prolonged: she would never enjoy it as much as she enjoyed the novel."[43] This rendering *could* ground Mill as a qualitative hedonist, for, on these terms, nothing seems to matter but pleasure: "If Mill is correct that there really are introspectively different feelings that are all varieties of pleasure and not of something else, then it is possible for these to be compared on the basis of their felt differences and for some to be preferable to others."[44] Indeed, favoring the unique sensations of some pleasures over others is, by definition, perfectly consistent with valuing nothing but pleasure as an end unto itself.

The problem, though, is that the feelings that characterize the higher pleasures just serve to reaffirm their supra-hedonic nature. Among the sensations caused by Austen's novel—sensations that testify to the "intrinsic superiority" of devouring *Pride and Prejudice*—are the *admiration* we have for its virtues as a novel and the *gratification* or *fulfilment* we derive from its literary splendor and edifying content. Anyone who appreciates

41. MacIntyre, *After Virtue*, 64.
42. Mill, *Utilitarianism*, 213, 235.
43. Crisp, "Hedonism Reconsidered," 633.
44. West, *Introduction to Mill's Utilitarian Ethics*, 71.

superlative "wit," "beautiful syntax," and "exquisite delineation of character" will surely derive pleasure from Austen's prose; but the better part of this pleasure will be taken *in*, or directed *toward*, these qualities in recognition of their supra-hedonic value. Plato's *Euthyphro* raises the right question: "When Euthyphro says that piety is what the gods love, Socrates asks if the gods love it because it is pious or is it pious because it is loved. The analogy here is that we can ask whether a pleasurable sensation is liked because it is pleasurable or it is pleasurable because it is liked."[45] And while one might insist on the former, the higher pleasures look to fall in line with the latter. What defines Mill's higher pleasures is the distinctive feeling of having done or experienced something of more-than-just-hedonic worth.

Other scholars frame Mill as a qualitative hedonist by associating his concept of quality with empirical, good-making properties. On this view, when Mill refers to "quality," he is appealing to constitutive elements that contribute to making certain pleasures more valuable: "In Mill's system, value or good is produced by the two basic good-making properties, quantity (intensity and duration) and quality (kind)." And the contention is that it would be "absurd" to hold that a hedonist cannot be interested in the "cause," "source," or "phenomenal" nature of pleasure.[46] Of course, the obvious retort is that to value a pleasure's good-making properties, at least its "cause" or "source," is to take a supra-hedonic interest *in* these properties. However, there is more to this interpretation of Mill:

> Consider . . . a *Bacchant*, i.e., someone who cares about wine *in itself* and not consequent pleasure, so is undeterred by, for example, the prospect of a hangover. Such a person cares about the quantity of wine—that is, they always want more wine rather than less, *ceteris paribus*—but they also care about its quality. . . . Although, other things being equal, they always prefer more wine to less, if we offer them a choice between a bottle of inferior wine and a glass of superior wine, it is possible that they will prefer the glass of superior wine. This does not seem strange.[47]

Not strange at all. A *Bacchant* can care about all the good-making properties of wine—e.g., its aesthetic features, like color, taste, and odor—without relinquishing this title.[48] Of course, we might protest: "This so-called *Bacchant* values aesthetics!" And while we would be right in a general

45. Ibid., 58.
46. Donner and Fumerton, *Mill*, 21, 24.
47. Saunders, "J. S. Mill's Conception of Utility," 61.
48. See Donner, *Liberal Self*, 83–91.

sense, we would be wrong in the relevant sense. A *Bacchant* cares about aesthetics *only* as it pertains to and enhances the value of wine, for wine is all a *Bacchant* cares about. And now just apply the same logic to pleasure (and the figure of the *Hedonist*) and qualitative hedonism is made perfectly coherent: "The crucial point is that, although wine's [or pleasure's] aesthetic [or qualitative] value has a basis in phenomenal properties," these "properties do not themselves constitute and are not identical with the value."[49] Nothing strange. These good-making properties have no independent integrity as values. Hedonic qualities contribute to, but are subsumed under, the ultimate interest of the *Hedonist*.

But the issue here is that the figure of the *Competent Judge* is just not akin to the *Bacchant* or the *Hedonist*. The latter two are looking for qualities that improve their chosen aims, whereas the former is identifying qualities that signify the existence of other, higher aims. Take Mill's repeated use of the concept *nobility*. The higher pleasures are "better" because they are "nobler," which implies that the pursuit or realization of these goods or activities contributes not only to a qualitatively more pleasurable life, but more essentially to a qualitatively superior "manner of existence," one befitting a "superior being."[50] The higher pleasures evince qualities by which they are enhanced not as pleasures but *as ends*. When a sommelier loses their taste for fine wines, it is a failure of the palate; but when a competent judge loses, or abandons, their capacity for the "nobler feelings," it is a failure of the soul and not simply of their sensitivity to the sub-hedonic properties of certain pleasures. The failure goes to something higher because the higher pleasures are *themselves* something higher.

Finally, some scholars frame Mill as a qualitative hedonist by reducing his concept of quality to quantity. There are many versions of this reading, arguing, for instance, that Mill's concept of quality is best interpreted as an extreme difference in quantity, like the qualitative difference "between a shout and a murmur";[51] that he associates the higher pleasures "with a *mode of life* that *quantitatively* outranks the mode of life with which the lower pleasure[s] [are] associated";[52] that he frames the higher pleasures as inexhaustible, "non-depletable sources of ever more lower-order pleasures";[53] that he gives the higher pleasures a greater "collective worth,"

---

49. Ibid., 85.
50. Mill, *Utilitarianism*, 212.
51. Sosa, "Mill's *Utilitarianism*," 163.
52. Long, "Mill's Higher Pleasures," 285.
53. Milligram, "Liberty, the Higher Pleasures, and Mill's Missing Science of Ethic Jokes," 340.

in that they promote the pleasure of "all or nearly all," whereas the lower pleasures do this for "only a few";[54] that he means to say that "a pleasure x is of higher quality than a pleasure y iff one unit of pleasure x gives more pleasure than one unit of pleasure y";[55] or that by *quantity* he just means "intensity," whereas by *quality* he just means any quantitative feature "distinct from intensity."[56]

The sheer range of these readings is indicative of their shared vice. In short, they posit mere possibilities that are difficult to refute exegetically but that fail to spring organically from an impartial reading of Mill. However, the deeper problem with these readings is that the reduction of quality to quantity simply "misses the whole spirit of Mill."[57] Between these concepts Mill all but digs a moat: "If one of the two is, by those who are competently acquainted with both, placed so far above the other that they prefer it, even though knowing it to be attended with a greater amount of discontent, and would not resign it for any quantity of the other pleasure which their nature is capable of, we are justified in ascribing to the preferred enjoyment a superiority in quality, so far outweighing quantity as to render it, in comparison, of small account."[58] Admittedly, it is *possible* that Mill was *really* trying to defend a higher kind of quantitative value all throughout his theory; but his testimony here, and everywhere, seems to push (or, indeed, shove) in the opposite direction.

Consider: had Mill been talking about a higher kind of quantity, he could (and likely would) have said so, especially as his distinction between quantity and quality was bound to create the exact impression it created, an impression shared (reluctantly!) even by Mill's acolytes.[59] And pay attention to Mill's language: "They would not resign what they possess more than [the fool, the dunce, or the rascal] for the most complete satisfaction of all the desires which they have in common with him. If they ever fancy they would, it is only in cases of unhappiness so extreme that to escape from it they would exchange their lot for almost any other, however undesirable in their own eyes."[60] This claim makes sense only if the competent judge is working with a *non*-quantitative notion of quality. If all pleasures are, at bottom, valued quantitatively, then what could make

54. Quincy, "Higher Pleasures & Their Quantification," 474.

55. Schmidt-Petri, "On an Interpretation of Mill's Qualitative Hedonism," 173.

56. Sturgeon, "Mill's Hedonism," 1715.

57. Donner, *Liberal Self*, 47.

58. Mill, *Utilitarianism*, 211.

59. See Bain, *J. S. Mill*, 113–114.

60. Mill, *Utilitarianism*, 211–212.

the exchanged for lifestyle "undesirable"? Indeed, how could *any* "lot" be "*un*desirable" on quantitative grounds, unless it suffers from a greater balance of *pain*, which, as Mill says, the "lot" of "the fool, the dunce, or the rascal" is far less beset by in general, and far, *far* less beset by in this particular case?

True, under the right conditions, the higher pleasures *will* furnish the competent judge with more pleasure in a purely quantitative sense. As Harriet Taylor penned to Mill, "It is for *you*—the most worthy to be the apostle of all loftiest virtue—to teach, such as may be taught, that the higher the *kind* of enjoyment, the *greater* the *degree*."[61] However, as Taylor is obviously suggesting, this superiority in degree does not define or establish but rather is a welcome byproduct of our loftier enjoyments. Taylor, whose "principal effect" on Mill was "to enlarge and exalt" his "conceptions of the highest worth of a human being,"[62] is said to have turned him toward a higher ideal of happiness, an ideal bound up with "the strengthening, exalting, purifying, and beautifying of our common nature."[63] This ideal can and should provide *more* pleasure in the quantitative sense for any number of reasons having to do with its "circumstantial advantages,"[64] as Epicurus would say. But the crucial point is that the higher pleasures are, indeed, *higher* for reasons having nothing to do with their quantitative returns.

In sum, Mill should not be read as a qualitative hedonist. His conception of happiness is chiefly concerned with the unfolding of "the elevated characteristics of human nature."[65] It is an ideal we "take pleasure *in*";[66] an ideal we find desirable for its own sake and thus direct our feelings *toward*. But herein lies a riddle: Why, then, does Mill retain the language of hedonism? Why are the higher pleasures classed as *pleasures* if they are valued, in essence, for their *supra*-hedonic nature? This is the eternal argument for anyone who insists on reading Mill as a hedonist: "*He* affirms hedonism; he does so unequivocally; and while he may say things that *sound* like they go beyond hedonism, *never* does he *definitively* break away from this, the crux of Bentham's creed." Indeed, this is forever the key challenge facing anyone who reads Mill as I have read him: "Explain yourself!"

61. Taylor, "On Marriage," 24.
62. Mill, *Autobiography*, 198, *CW* 1.
63. Mill, "Inaugural Address Delivered to the University of St. Andrews," 220, *CW* 21.
64. Mill, *Utilitarianism*, 211.
65. Mill, *Principles of Political Economy*, 209, *CW* 2.
66. Mill, "Bentham," 96, my emphasis.

HEDONISM FOR THE HIGH-MINDED

The easiest but weakest way to square this circle is to assert that Mill did not really mean what he said. Perhaps Mill was overcome by filial piety, such that he could not or would not openly dissociate himself from the dogma of his father and godfather.[67] Perhaps he was torn, whether philosophically or psychologically, between Bentham's ideas and those of his other influences, like Aristotle, and wanted to manage the delicate task of bringing them into a deeper harmony.[68] Perhaps he was not speaking for himself at all and was just defining Bentham's doctrine for the reader before amending it beyond recognition.[69] These are all possibilities, and they each ring true to a certain extent. However, the *filial piety* argument is hard to maintain, seeing as Mill proved eager to criticize his father and godfather in published works both before and after their deaths. And the *conflicted* and *messenger* arguments, while plausible and even rather persuasive, are ultimately conjectural. Thus, tabling these speculations, let us inquire into a more substantial account of Mill's hedonistic façade.

One path forward is to argue that, despite appearances, Mill does *not* actually endorse hedonism. There are two prominent versions of this thesis. The first argues that Mill drives a wedge between happiness and pleasure, and frames happiness, not pleasure, as the *summum bonum*: "If one looks closely at Mill's discussion, it seems more accurate to say that, rather than analyzing the concepts of pleasure and pain, Mill presented an analysis of the notion of *happiness* with which he was working, thereby indicating what, in the way of pleasures, was included in that idea."[70] On this view, Mill's conception of happiness is an *inclusive* end: a "higher-order" good that treats any other good, like pleasure, as "derivative and secondary,"[71] that is, as valuable *"insofar as it is a constituent of a person's happiness which has value."*[72] This reading gives pleasure a *substantive* but not an *explanatory* significance: the good life is made up of pleasures, but pleasure is not what makes the good life good.

This view comports with my own: Mill's conception of happiness is distinct from and superior to pleasure. But, alas, this still begs the question: why, then, does Mill endorse Bentham's doctrine in chapter 2, paragraph 2

67. See Loizides, "Mill on Happiness," 305–306.
68. See Nussbaum, "Mill between Aristotle & Bentham," 67–68.
69. See Hoag, "Mill's Conception of Happiness as an Inclusive End," 426–427.
70. Berger, *Happiness, Justice, and Freedom*, 37.
71. Hoag, "Mill's Conception of Happiness as an Inclusive End," 420–421.
72. Berger, *Happiness, Justice, and Freedom*, 38.

of *Utilitarianism*? In response, we might point to the next line from that paragraph: "To give a clear view of the moral standard set up by the theory, much more requires to be said; in particular, what things it includes in the ideas of pain and pleasure; and to what extent this is left an open question."[73] Some scholars have found this caveat revealing: "Now, if Mill meant to define happiness *merely* by saying it is a pleasure, it is not clear that anything more needs to be said at all."[74] However, this caveat gives no help, for Mill hastily assures us that "these supplementary explanations do not affect the theory of life on which this theory of morality is grounded— namely, that pleasure, and freedom from pain, are the only things desirable as ends."[75] Thus, while this reading gets Mill basically correct, it still leaves us wondering why Mill introduces himself as a hedonist.

The second version of this thesis says that *Utilitarianism* ascribes to "pleasure" a colloquial, non-hedonistic meaning, one that refers to goods or activities *directly* and agreeable sensations only *indirectly*, if at all— like when we say, "his greatest pleasure is playing hockey."[76] On this view, Mill's higher pleasures are *objective*: they do not bracket the mental states caused by objects; they bracket the objects themselves. Evidence for this view is strewn throughout *Utilitarianism*, where we find Mill appearing to *equate* the higher pleasures to things like health, music, virtue, and intellectual activity.[77] When Mill says the "ingredients of happiness are very various, and each of them is desirable in itself, and not merely when considered as swelling an aggregate,"[78] this reading infers that he is using a non-hedonic notion of pleasure; that he is referring to goods or activities, not to the feelings they generate.

Once again, this view is essentially correct. However, the problem (again) is that it fails to acquit Mill of inconsistency. Mill *does* assert hedonism in the offending lines: happiness *is* "pleasure, and the absence of pain." Even if Mill then *proceeds* with an objective notion of pleasure, he still weds himself in this first instance to pleasure itself. Moreover, Mill clearly believes that the *enjoyment* of objective ends is vital to happiness: an object cannot add to our happiness unless it gives us pleasure. And besides, while we often refer to objects as pleasures, it is perfectly reasonable (and predictable) for a hedonist to refer to pleasures as objects: "Mill's

73. Mill, *Utilitarianism*, 210.
74. Berger, *Happiness, Justice, and Freedom*, 37.
75. Mill, *Utilitarianism*, 210.
76. Brink, *Mill's Progressive Principles*, 52.
77. Brink, "Mill's Deliberative Utilitarianism," 73.
78. Mill, *Utilitarianism*, 235.

remarks are an appropriate and acceptable economy of expression to compensate for the absence of separate names for conscious states."[79] Like his father and godfather, Mill could just be utilizing the names of objects as a convenient proxy for the sensations that accompany them. Hence, we are still left wanting an account of Mill's supra-hedonistic ethos that explains his opening avowal of hedonism.

Let me step back. As I have intimated, the doctrine of the higher pleasures looks to be just a thinly veiled reference to those pleasures that supervene à la Aristotle on our loftier, characteristically human pursuits: "Whether, then, the perfect and supremely happy man has one or more activities, the pleasures that perfect these will be said in the strict sense to be pleasures proper to man, and the rest will be so in a secondary and fractional way, as are the activities."[80] Like Aristotle, Mill is claiming that pleasures are higher (virtuous) or lower (vicious or neutral) in relation to the ends (good, bad, or indifferent) to which they naturally belong. There would be nothing perplexing about Mill calling the higher pleasures "pleasures" as long as they were not *themselves* the ends of life but instead the "by-product of the passionate pursuit of other ends, considered worthy in themselves."[81] Why, then, might Mill have sowed pointless confusion by *equating* happiness to "pleasure, and the absence of pain"?

Aristotle offers a solution. For Aristotle, anyone who loves or desires an end will, on balance, take pleasure in the pursuit or realization of that end: "For pleasure is a state of *soul*, and to each man that which he is said to be a lover of is pleasant; e.g., not only is a horse pleasant to the lover of horses, and a spectacle to the lover of sights, but also in the same way just acts are pleasant to the lover of justice and in general virtuous acts to the lover of virtue." Moreover, such pleasure perfects, or "intensifies," our activity in accordance with said end.[82] Conversely, and critically for the argument at hand, whenever we find an end disagreeable or bothersome, its corresponding activity will naturally give us pain, even if similar activity gives pleasure to others.[83]

In this spirit, we can theorize that at the heart of Mill's enigmatic use of "pleasure" is the notion that our happiness cannot be enhanced by any good or activity that we do not love or desire, or that we do not come to love

---

79. Hoag, "J. S. Mill's Language of Pleasures," 256.
80. Aristotle, *Nicomachean Ethics*, X.5.
81. Anderson, "John Stuart Mill and Experiments in Living," 20.
82. Aristotle, *Nicomachean Ethics*, X.5.
83. Ibid., I.8.

or desire through practice or habituation.[84] Happiness cannot be understood "independently of all considerations of pleasure or pain."[85] If we are unable to derive pleasure from an end then we do not love or desire said end; and if we do not love or desire said end then we may as well be "a stock or a stone"[86] for all the difference this end will make to our *actual* well-being. Indeed, we can value chess for its own sake while also recognizing the fact that playing chess will add to a random April morning only if we are in such a mood for the game that it brings us pleasure. When Mill says "pleasure" he means "a good or activity that one derives pleasure from." And by exalting the *higher* pleasures, Mill is just affirming, albeit obliquely, "the judicious utilitarianism of Aristotle."[87]

From this perspective, the assertion that pleasure is our sole good makes total sense for Mill. In fact, it is even fitting. Suppose we are faced with a multiplicity of competent judges: what will constitute their various, respective paths to happiness? Not just *any* goods or activities, but rather the *specific* goods or activities that they find pleasurable *as individuals*; the goods or activities that appeal to *this* or *that* competent judge. To wit, Mill *does* affirm hedonism, but *only* for the high-minded: *once* you are competent *then* you can treat life *as if* pleasure is all that matters, because, at *that* point, there is *nothing* left to consider but *which* higher ends *please you*. At this juncture, we can hear echoes of *On Liberty*: there exists an indefinite plurality of "noble and beautiful" lifestyles, each of which is gratifying to *some* "well-developed" souls but not to *others*.[88] And just as the Mill of *On Liberty* defends freedom as the highest sociopolitical value, but not (yet) for children or barbarians, the Mill of *Utilitarianism* upholds pleasure as the highest ethical value, but not (yet) for "the fool, the dunce, or the rascal."

I believe the disconnect here is that we have always been reading Mill's doctrine of the higher pleasures *backward*. We have hitherto interpreted Mill as if he opens with a stark hedonism before offering a qualitative proviso. However, with respect to the structure of his theory, I would argue that Mill actually *begins* with this qualification. That is, when Mill defines happiness as "pleasure," he is *really* defining happiness as "whatever is pleasurable to a competent judge." Mill's subsequent appeal to the competent judge, then, is not a caveat to hedonism but rather a clarification to the effect that ethical competence is to be presupposed in his affirmation

84. See the discussion of "internal goods" in MacIntyre, *After Virtue*, 187ff.
85. Mill, "The Protagoras," 61, *CW* 11.
86. Mill, *Autobiography*, 145.
87. Mill, *On Liberty*, 235.
88. Ibid., 266–267.

of this ethos. Thus, Mill's position might be condensed like so: happiness is pleasure *provided* we are speaking *only* of well-developed persons. Mill's intended hedonists can be *truly* happy only insofar as they have *transcended* hedonism by cultivating a prevailing love or desire for the high-minded, *supra*-hedonic ends of life.

Of course, this, too, begs the question: if Mill walked the Aristotelian walk then why was his Aristotelian talk so confused or confusing? I think the best answer is that the Mill of *Utilitarianism* was navigating an existing dispute that was itself framed in rather perplexing and unhelpful terms. As we can see in chapter 4 of *Utilitarianism*, the debate between the Utilitarians and their rivals, the Intuitionists, was framed as an either/or between *pleasure* and *virtue*. This stark dichotomy smacks of the Hellenistic conflict between the Epicureans and the Stoics: whereas the former believed that "pleasure is the beginning and end of a blessed life," the latter maintained that "virtue alone was necessary and sufficient for happiness" and "also the only real good." What is arguably lacking here is the earlier, synoptic vision of Aristotle, who saw pleasure and virtue as two integral components of a broader, deeper story. As Anthony Kenny writes, Aristotle identifies happiness

> not with the exercise of a single dominant virtue but with the exercise of all the virtues, including not only understanding but also the moral virtues linked with wisdom. Activity in accordance with these virtues is pleasant, and so the truly happy man will also have the most pleasant life. For the virtuous person, the concepts "good" and "pleasant" coincide in their application; if the two do not yet coincide then a person is not virtuous but incontinent. The bringing about of this coincidence is the task of ethics.

The "supreme good" is *also* the "supreme pleasure," and the virtuous life is not *truly* virtuous unless it is *also* a life of sublime satisfaction. Therefore, Aristotle, like Mill, "entitles himself to be called a hedonist," but "of a very unusual kind," for while pleasure is essential and ultimate, it is not *itself* the *summum bonum*.[89] However, in tackling the Utilitarian/Intuitionist dichotomy (his own version of the Epicurean/Stoic divide) on its own dubious terms, Mill just plumps for his ancestral camp. And again, it is well that he does so; for as we just discussed, that which generates pleasure for a competent *individual* is that which best, or most specifically, defines their *unique* expression of the good life.

89. Kenny, *New History of Western Philosophy*, 219–220, 223.

Similarly, Mill favors the Socrates of Plato's *Protagoras*, who, according to Mill, argues "that Pleasure and the absence of Pain are the ends of morality,"[90] over the non-hedonistic Socrates of Plato's *Gorgias*. Yet, far from espousing or upholding hedonism proper, what Mill is doing here and elsewhere is defending pleasure against the sometimes-Socratic impulse to dismiss pleasure as extrinsic to the good life. Again, Mill would concur with Aristotle: "Those who say that the victim on the rack or the man who falls into great misfortunes is happy if he is good are, whether they mean to or not, talking nonsense." And indeed, as we have seen, happiness itself can be regarded as pleasure, for pleasure is the culminating sign that the good has been actualized: "And for this reason all men think that the happy life is pleasant and weave pleasure into their ideal of happiness."[91]

THE HIGHER PLEASURES AS IDEALS

Having thus divorced the higher pleasures from (genuine) hedonism, we can now ask: What exactly *are* the higher pleasures? How, conceptually, might we encircle the sphere of higher pleasures? The short answer is that Mill consistently identifies the higher pleasures as *ideals*: each one is an abstract, "ideal end,"[92] composed of an unlimited range of concrete goods or activities. For instance, studying Plato is one way of seeking the higher pleasure of *knowledge* or *wisdom*; and helping others is one way of engaging the higher pleasure of *love* or *benevolence*. Ironically, there is an overlap here between Mill and one of his most biting, scathing critics, G. E. Moore, who, as an Ideal Utilitarian, avoids the deepest pitfalls of Mill's alleged hedonism by replacing *pleasure* with *ideal*.[93] In any event, which ideals are included among the higher pleasures?

Predictably, Mill does not propose a list of higher pleasures, and countless references to the higher pleasures appear throughout his works, making it difficult to give any clean, crisp summary of their scope. Nonetheless, Mill's most prized ideals—from *individuality* to *wisdom* to *benevolence* to *nobility* to *impartiality*—are the gods of world thought and culture. Those who have encountered Mill's various influences—the Greeks, the Christians, the Romantics—or who have been exposed to the humanities should have a good sense of where Mill is coming from. For example, Mill

90. Mill, "Grote's Plato," 391, *CW* 11.
91. Aristotle, *Nicomachean Ethics*, VII.13. Socrates is happy unto death because, as he explains in Plato's *Phaedo*, his passing is not a "great misfortune" but either a wash or a boon.
92. Mill, "Bentham," 95.
93. See Moore, *Principia Ethica*, §110–135.

marks one higher pleasure we might call *sublimity*, which refers to all that is "sublime and elevating," that is, to "ideal conceptions grander and more beautiful than we see realized in the prose of human life."[94] Under this ideal falls the goods or activities of rhetoric, music, and all subjects of grand reflection, including "the objects of nature, the achievements of art, the imaginations of poetry, the incidents of history, the ways of mankind past and present, and their prospects for the future."[95] Those who exhibit a passion for and sensibility to the sublime in all its forms can be said to have developed a strong "internal culture,"[96] something that Mill believes himself to have been denied in his upbringing.

Now, some scholars define the scope of the higher pleasures by relying on Mill's distinction between "mental" (higher) and "bodily" (lower) pleasures.[97] This division has led to many readings of Mill as drawing a line between the intellectual or cerebral pleasures (like studying Plato) and the physical or sensual pleasures (like food and sex). But this is just erroneous; Mill's "mental" pleasures are those goods or activities that exercise and gratify the higher faculties (the faculties of the human mind or soul), and they can be intellectual *or* physical. For instance, while casual sex might be a lower pleasure, making love is a higher pleasure; and while actively engaging with Plato is a higher pleasure, hastily skimming his dialogues for an exam is (in my experience) not a pleasure at all. And this ties back into our discussion: making love and studying Plato are attractive to the higher faculties because these activities embody certain ideals, such as *intimacy* and *wisdom*.

Other scholars, having come this far, define the scope of the higher pleasures as *whatever* exercises the higher faculties: "The exercise of one's higher capacities is the one and only intrinsic good, things are good insofar as they exercise higher capacities, and happiness consists in the exercise of higher capacities."[98] However, this is far too broad. Many things exercise the higher faculties that take no part in Mill's theory of the good life. Some are pointless (like counting blades of grass), while others are immoral or dissolute (like harming others or debasing oneself). On Mill's view, the higher pleasures *cannot* be meaningless or debauched, for they include *only* those goods or activities that inspire the approval or admiration of other competent judges. Indeed, it is not *just* the exercise of the higher

94. Mill, "Utility of Religion," 419, *CW* 10.
95. Mill, *Utilitarianism*, 267.
96. Mill, *Autobiography*, 147.
97. Mill, *Utilitarianism*, 211.
98. Brink, *Mill's Progressive Principles*, 63.

faculties, but, crucially, the higher ideals that attract and guide their activity, that give their exercise its supra-hedonic quality. This is not to imply that all "active" pleasures that inspire disfavor are lower pleasures; rather, those of them that inspire disfavor for reasons having to do with their iniquity or depravity could be what we might dub *higher pains*—a foreshadowing of next chapter.

And finally, the most perceptive attempts to delineate the higher pleasures can be folded into our discussion. Scholars have argued that the lower pleasures are "the sensations themselves," whereas the higher pleasures are "the grand ideas" that "the sensations [give] rise to";[99] that the lower pleasures are all "sensory," whereas the higher pleasures are all "attitudinal," meaning that they are "taken in suitably 'higher' objects";[100] and that the higher pleasures are "basically the Greek virtues weakly expressed in order not to lose [their] empirical grounding."[101] These readings present different ways of interpreting the higher pleasures as ideals: our "grand ideas" are *of* ideals; our "attitudinal" pleasures are taken *in* ideals; and "the Greek virtues" just *are* ideals. And indeed, once we establish that Mill's higher pleasures are *ideals*, it makes it nigh impossible to interpret them as sensations, which makes it all the more implausible to interpret Mill as any kind of authentic hedonist.

THE LOWER PLEASURES

One classic puzzle remaining regards the value or status of the lower pleasures. Mill thinks the competent judge will have a "marked" preference for the higher pleasures. But when, if ever, will the life of a high-minded hedonist include lower pleasures, or *merely* agreeable ends? Mill's stated reply is that the higher pleasures should enjoy a "decided predominance."[102] Pure pleasure, while certainly not verboten for Mill, should not prevent us from paying sufficient mind to the higher pleasures.[103] What does it mean to give the higher pleasures their due? Mill does not say. Still, we can easily imagine the competent judge ruling on whether our ratio of higher to lower pleasure is neglecting the former or overindulging in the latter—anyone who has felt guilty for binge-watching "that stupid show" *again* rather than dusting off *Middlemarch* knows what this means.

99. Feagin, "Mill and Edwards on the Higher Pleasures," 249.
100. Feldman, *Pleasure and the Good Life*, 73.
101. Williams, "Greek Origins of J. S. Mill's Conception of Happiness," 13.
102. Mill, *Utilitarianism*, 215.
103. See Holbrook, *Qualitative Utilitarianism*, 103.

This sounds reasonable enough. And yet, there might seem to be a paradox lurking beneath the surface. Question: Can *any* quantity of lower pleasure *ever* be more valuable than even *one* helping of higher pleasure? Could the pleasures of an oyster, if enjoyed for all eternity, be deemed more desirable than a single, passing moment of joy experienced by Haydn as a composer?[104] If the answer is *no* then there might appear to be no good reason *ever* to make time for the lower pleasures: "On this reading, we should be tireless and pure in our pursuit of higher pleasures, never admitting any lower ones, no matter how pleasurable, so long as there is no opportunity cost to them, however modest, in terms of higher pleasures."[105] Every needless break from the higher pleasures is thus a lapse in virtue, and Mill's appeal to "decided predominance" just becomes an ad hoc concession to what might look to be the more intuitively satisfying position. But if the answer is *yes* then the qualitative barrier between the higher and lower pleasures might appear to collapse, the argument being that the lower pleasures can outrank a higher pleasure only if we are dealing with a single value scale that admits of large quantitative gaps but that rejects any qualitative discontinuities.

However, this is a false dilemma. The question above is framed in terms of what pleasures we select on a moment-to-moment basis rather than what pleasures best define our "manner of existence." Mill's ethical standard is the inclusive end of happiness, which is evaluated by the latter and not the former. For the sake of argument: no barrels of cheap wine can surpass the value of sipping a Château d'Yquem; no marathon of amusing B movies can eclipse the value of delving into *Citizen Kane*; no crowd of friendly acquaintances can exceed the value of one true friend à la Aristotle. In each of these pairings, there is a qualitative barrier between the latter and the former. And yet, it would be perfectly rational in each case to make room or time in our lives for the former; for all that this qualitative barrier signifies is that the latter is higher for *higher* reasons, and thus for reasons the former cannot outweigh or overcome simply by multiplying its *own* reasons for being chosen.[106] But the former *can* be chosen for the highest reason of all: that a happy life calls for more than *just* the higher things; that a competent judge will prefer a healthy balance of the mental and the bodily; of the rational and the appetitive; of supra-hedonic activity and hedonic recreation.

104. See Crisp, *Reasons and the Good*, 112.
105. Brink, *Mill's Progressive Principles*, 50. See also Miller, *J. S. Mill*, 58.
106. See Riley, "Interpreting Mill's Qualitative Hedonism," 411–417.

Needless to say, there are certainly *some* lower pleasures that Mill regards as being beyond the pale. Mill thinks the "unwillingness" of competent judges to forgo the higher pleasures is best explained by their "sense of dignity, which all human beings possess in one form or other, and in some, though by no means in exact, proportion to their higher faculties, and which is so essential a part of the happiness of those in whom it is strong, that nothing which conflicts with it could be, otherwise than momentarily, an object of desire to them."[107] Thus, if a lower pleasure is either damaging, diluting, or degrading to our higher "manner of existence," then it will be categorically rejected by the competent judge. Unless suffering from *akrasia* or *acedia*, a high-minded hedonist will avoid things like "sexual profligacy"[108] and "moral depravity,"[109] for instance.

However, as I end this section, the elephant in the room is sounding its trunk: why is anything Mill says *correct*? The competent judge, while a key piece of evidence for what Mill thinks about happiness, does not prove much of anything in a philosophical sense: "The philosopher who is a half-hearted sensualist cannot estimate the attractions of a debauched existence, any more than the sensualist flicking through the pages of Hume can estimate the pleasures of philosophy."[110] While the higher pleasures reveal Mill's break with Bentham, there is likely nothing in this doctrine that would induce Bentham to break with himself. The preferences of the competent judge would be mere pretenses to Bentham (mere prejudices), and nothing Mill says rebuts that retort. Even if the overwhelming majority of competent judges share these preferences, this does not prove anything, least of all for Mill: the ignorance, bigotry, and incoherence of majoritarian opinions is one of his great themes. Thus, Mill must say something more if he wants to provide a compelling theory; he must *defend* the "higher ground" of his competent judge. To see him do this, we must begin afresh.

To wit: what is intrinsically valuable?

Desire unto Desirability

Mill is a disciple of empiricism, an epistemology holding that all knowledge is derived from experience or observation. Mill sees himself as the latest in a long line of empirical thinkers from Bacon down to Bentham: "We see no ground for believing that anything can be the object of our

107. Mill, *Utilitarianism*, 212.
108. Mill, *Auguste Comte and Positivism*, 311, *CW* 10.
109. Mill, "Nature," 389, *CW* 10.
110. Ryan, *J. S. Mill*, 111.

knowledge except our experience, and what can be inferred from our experience by the analogies of experience itself; nor that there is any idea, feeling, or power in the human mind, which, in order to account for it, requires that its origin should be referred to any other source."[111] This a posteriori theory—which excludes all intuitive, mystical, or other a priori claims to knowledge—lies at the heart of the natural and social sciences. But what about the science of intrinsic value? What can an empiricist tell us about the nature of the good life?

Mill begins as follows: "Questions of ultimate ends are not amenable to direct proof. Whatever can be proved to be good, must be so only by being shown to be a means to something else admitted to be good without proof in the ordinary acceptation of the term."[112] Intrinsic values are first principles, not in the way of being self-evident (like a geometric postulate), but in the sense that their status as intrinsic values cannot be deduced from antecedent truths. As with any of the "disputed questions of philosophy," the question of intrinsic value defies "intuition" and appeals instead to "our senses" (i.e., experience and observation) and our "internal consciousness" (i.e., reflection and analysis). To arrive at any sort of "proof" of intrinsic value, we cannot look to a priori insights; we must depend entirely on the study of what human beings in fact value. As Mill declares, "the sole evidence it is possible to produce that anything is [attractive or] desirable, is that people do actually desire it."[113] Desire is the only evidence we have, subject to reflection and analysis, that is relevant to the issue of desirability. Thus, the question becomes: what does human desire reveal about the good life?

PSYCHOLOGICAL HEDONISM

The key to Bentham's philosophy is the idea that human beings desire— that they are hardwired to desire—pleasure and pleasure alone: "Nature has placed mankind under the governance of two sovereign masters, *pain* and *pleasure*," which "govern us in all we do, in all we say, in all we think: every effort we can make to throw off our subjection, will serve but to

---

111. Mill, "Coleridge," 128–129.

112. Mill, *Utilitarianism*, 207–208, 234. The clause "in the ordinary acceptation of the term" is from a later discussion (234) in which Mill is recalling his earlier point (207–208).

113. Ibid., 208, 234. In response to this last sentence, many scholars have charged Mill with an "is-ought" fallacy "of the most appalling kind" (Ryan, *J. S. Mill*, 117). But this is a baseless accusation: "Mill here is simply bringing in empirical evidence that bears on the subject. He is saying that only things actually desired are plausible candidates for being desirable as ends" (Donner, *Liberal Self*, 30).

demonstrate and confirm it."[114] For Bentham, this is just a brute psychological fact: all we desire is pleasure; non-hedonic ends are desired only ever as means to this ultimate end. We *are* hedonists: natural-born individual utility-maximizers. This latter-day declaration of psychological hedonism was classically espoused by Epicurus: "Pleasure is our first and kindred good. It is the starting-point of every choice and of every good thing."[115] Bentham, though, is likely drawing his inspiration from the *philosophe* Claude Adrien Helvétius: "Corporeal pleasure and pain are the real and only springs of all government."[116]

Now, we might protest: What about non-hedonic ends, such as love, or wisdom, or beauty? Are we not regularly attracted to these and other ideals for their own sake? Bentham replies with a resounding *nay*: "In words a man may pretend to abjure their empire: but in reality he will remain subject to it all the while."[117] If this doctrine holds water then Bentham has all the evidence he needs to reduce happiness to pleasure; for if pleasure is the only thing we *can* desire then it must be our only intrinsic value; and if pleasure is our *only* intrinsic value then it is, in effect, tantamount to happiness. And as we saw, this is precisely what Bentham concludes: "happiness, good, and pleasure" all come to "the same thing."

However, to advance this theory is to run headlong into a puzzle that Henry Sidgwick dubbed "the fundamental paradox of Hedonism," which states that pleasure can be obtained only by seeking *non*-hedonic ends as ends unto themselves: "The impulse towards pleasure, if too predominant, defeats its own aim. This effect is not visible" in "the case of passive sensual indulgences. But of our active enjoyments generally" it "may certainly be said that we cannot attain them, at least in their highest degree, so long as we keep our main conscious aim concentrated upon them."[118] In other words, in order to have a pleasurable life, we must live for everything or anything *other* than pleasure.

In *Autobiography*, Mill makes a similar observation: "The enjoyments of life" are "sufficient to make it a pleasant thing, when they are taken *en passant*, without being made the principal object. Once make them so, and they are immediately felt to be insufficient. They will not bear a scrutinizing examination. Ask yourself whether you are happy, and you

114. Bentham, *Principles of Morals and Legislation*, 1.
115. Laertius, *Lives of Eminent Philosophers*, X, §128–130.
116. Helvétius, *Treatise on Man*, 148.
117. Bentham, *Principles of Morals and Legislation*, 1.
118. Sidgwick, *Methods of Ethics*, 48–49.

cease to be so."[119] That is, the person bound to achieve the *least* pleasure is the self-conscious hedonist. This reality is often most evident in the most stereotypically hedonistic cases: "The more a man tries to demonstrate his sexual potency or a woman her ability to experience orgasm, the less they are able to succeed. Pleasure is, and must remain, a side-effect or by-product, and is destroyed or spoiled to the degree to which it is made a goal in itself."[120] But the claim holds true for anything, and for anyone, such as Sidgwick's artist: "In all kinds of Art," the "exercise of the creative faculty is attended by intense and exquisite pleasures: but it would seem that in order to get them, one must forget them: the genuine artist at work seems to have a predominant and temporarily absorbing desire for the realisation of his ideal of beauty."[121] The same tale can be told about the scientist, the musician, the baker, the politician—their desired pleasures can be (fully) realized only by focusing on their respective non-hedonic objects.

For psychological hedonists, and hedonists proper, the fact that the only thing we can, or ought to, desire cannot be pursued directly, but only indirectly via non-hedonic dummy-ends, should appear, well, rather paradoxical. However, for certain critics of the hedonist tradition, the hedonistic paradox is *not* a paradox at all, but rather a reflection of the fact that we are actually inclined to desire anything *but* pleasure: "Man does *not* strive for happiness; only the English do that."[122] Despite Nietzsche's barb, the most renowned formulation of this view belongs to the English bishop Joseph Butler. In the eleventh of his *Fifteen Sermons*, Butler argues that we cannot derive pleasure from an object without assuming a desire for the object itself: "That all particular appetites and passions are towards *external things themselves*, distinct from the *pleasure arising from them*, is manifested hence; that there could not be this pleasure, were it not for that prior suitableness between the object and the passion."[123] Every feeling of pleasure entails an antecedent attraction to the source of the pleasure: "An external thing causes pleasure only if there is a desire for that thing."[124] To derive pleasure from love, wisdom, or beauty shows that we desire love, wisdom, or beauty *itself*.

119. Mill, *Autobiography*, 147.
120. Frankl, *Man's Search for Meaning*, 122.
121. Sidgwick, *Methods of Ethics*, 49.
122. Nietzsche, *Twilight of the Idols*, 6.
123. Butler, *Fifteen Sermons*, XI, §6.
124. Sober, "Hedonism and Butler's Stone," 99.

While Butler may have "overstated his case,"[125] his point is generally well taken, especially as it pertains to "the moral, intellectual, or other ideal pleasures." There are myriad instances in which psychological hedonism falls into a "hysteron-proteron," a placing of the cart before the horse, where "the imagined pleasantness is created by the desire, not the desire by the imagined pleasantness." As Hastings Rashdall observes, "To the mind that does not desire knowledge, knowledge is not pleasant," just as benevolence "does not give pleasure to people who are not benevolent."[126] Only those who take an interest in the well-being of others will derive pain from the act of harming them; only those moved by satire itself will derive pleasure from Austen's gibes. Indeed, if a friend fails to take pleasure in reading *Pride and Prejudice*, we might surmise, as one possibility, that our friend lacks an appreciation for Austen's rapier wit. But this hypothesis is intelligible only because the pleasure of wittiness depends on an antecedent attraction to wittiness itself. In an Aristotelian spirit, Butler regards pleasure as the feeling that *supervenes* on our realized desires: "pleasure consists in the satisfaction of just these 'disinterested' impulses."[127]

Butler's wisdom can be grasped via introspection, where we often find that our desires precede our pleasures, or that the satisfaction of our desire is what generates our pleasure. We desire various things, and we typically expect to derive pleasure from life by getting what we want. In fact, in most cases, all a pleasure pill *could* induce would be the feeling of having obtained a desired object. Consider the pleasure of earning a promotion, or wedding your true love, or winning a decathlon. These pleasures are taken *in* the realized desire itself—the position, the marriage, the victory— and thus could be produced only by a pleasure pill that creates the illusion of having *done* these things.[128] It is really only the purely *sensual* pleasures that could be replicated by a pleasure pill without relying on this illusion—the mere sensations of food, sex, or drink. Only in such cases as these would it ever be right to say that what the individual *really* desires is pleasure despite the paradoxical need to pursue the food, sex, or drink itself. Hence hedonism's swinish reputation.

---

125. Sidgwick, *Methods of Ethics*, 44. Sidgwick continues: "For many pleasures,— especially those of sight, hearing and smell, together with many emotional pleasures,—occur to me without any perceptible relation to previous desires, and it seems quite *conceivable* that our primary desires might be entirely directed towards such pleasures as these" (45).

126. Rashdall, *Theory of Good and Evil*, 15–16.

127. Sidgwick, *Methods of Ethics*, 44. Sidgwick is explaining Butler's argument.

128. Again, see Nozick, *Anarchy, State, and Utopia*, 42–44.

Regardless, the most relevant evidence, for us, for Butler's view is advanced by F. H. Bradley and G. E. Moore. As Bradley argues, psychological hedonism rests on "the confusion between a pleasant thought and the thought of a pleasure; between an idea of an objective act or event, contemplation of which is pleasant, and of which I desire the realization, and the idea of myself as the subject of a feeling of satisfaction which is to be."[129] The pleasure that drives our behavior (and which thus satisfies Bentham's psychological claim) can spring from a "mere idea" that strikes the mind's eye as pleasant, in which case the object of our desire is *whatever* good or activity is contained in this thought. As Moore explains, "it is the object of the thought—that which we are thinking about—which is the object of desire and the motive to action; and the pleasure, which that thought excites, may, indeed, cause our desire or move us to action, but it is not our end or object nor our motive."[130] Psychological hedonism simply elides the distinction between a plausible premise concerning the governance of our actions and an implausible conclusion regarding the object of our desires. If this analysis is correct then the scope of our desires is, in theory, limitless: we can take pleasure in, and thus form desires for, the "mere idea" of virtually *anything*.

In the fourth chapter of *Utilitarianism*, Mill appears to endorse, if not psychological hedonism, then at least psychological utilitarianism. His goal is to show "not only that people desire happiness, but that they never desire anything else."[131] This chapter is notorious for its ambiguity as to what Mill means by *happiness*: Does he mean just "pleasure," in which case he is upholding psychological hedonism? Or does he mean happiness in the *inclusive* sense, in which case he is endorsing psychological *utilitarianism* and just arguing that we do not desire anything unless it can be regarded as constitutive of happiness? There is no denying Mill's indistinctness in this chapter; and, as with chapter 2, his use of "pleasure" can be disorienting. Nonetheless, I think it is safe to say that Mill is indeed still speaking the same language: happiness here is an inclusive end. Against the intuitive, a priori theorists, who claim that certain ends can be desired for themselves, sans any relationship to happiness, Mill argues that *nothing* can be desired unless it is one of the "ingredients of happiness."

This reading will be most clearly borne out by scrutinizing Mill's critique of psychological hedonism. The reception of Mill's psychological

129. Bradley, *Ethical Studies*, 258.
130. Moore, *Principia Ethica*, §42.
131. Mill, *Utilitarianism*, 234.

theory has been nothing if not ironic. Though a staunch critic of psychological hedonism, Mill has been interpreted (and attacked) as a psychological hedonist by many scholars, including Bradley and Moore. Not only that, Mill's critique of psychological hedonism is essentially *the same* as that of Bradley and Moore. And scholars have often since felt that they must explain away Mill's avowals of psychological hedonism by pointing to his associationism, whereas, in reality, Mill makes *no* such avowals, and whereas associationism is actually the most relevant argument *against* the Mill-Bradley-Moore consensus.

MILL CONTRA PSYCHOLOGICAL HEDONISM

In "Remarks on Bentham's Philosophy," Mill declares that our actions are "wholly determined by pleasure and pain." One might immediately assume that Mill is following Bentham. However, Mill quickly dismisses Bentham's inference that "all our acts are determined by pleasures and pains *in prospect*, pains and pleasures to which we look forward as the *consequences* of our acts." On the contrary, Mill holds that the "pain or pleasure which determines our conduct is as frequently one which *precedes* the moment of action as one which follows it." According to Mill, we are often governed by the pleasure or pain we take in the "very thought" of an object or ideal, irrespective of the pleasure or pain we expect to derive from its pursuit or realization.[132] As Mill elaborates in *Utilitarianism*,

> I believe that . . . desiring a thing and finding it pleasant, aversion to it and *thinking of it* as painful, are phenomena entirely inseparable, or rather two parts of the same phenomenon; in strictness of language, two different modes of naming the same psychological fact: that *to think of an object* as desirable (unless for the sake of its consequences) and *to think of it* as pleasant, are one and the same thing; and that to desire anything, except in proportion *as the idea of it* is pleasant, is a physical and metaphysical impossibility.[133]

This passage has often been construed as an *endorsement* of psychological hedonism, and it is easy to see why. At first glance, Mill looks to be drawing a strong association between what we desire and what we find pleasant. However, as the italicized phrases suggest, what we *really* have here is the far less contentious, and perhaps even intuitive, claim that human

132. Mill, "Remarks on Bentham's Philosophy," 12, *CW* 10.
133. Mill, *Utilitarianism*, 237–238, my emphases.

beings desire only what they find attractive, and that they find attractive
only what is pleasing to their mind's eye. Mill is just stating what is, for
him, an indubitable fact: that our desires are naturally attached to objects
that we think of "in a pleasurable light, or of [their] absence in a painful one." This is why he is able to follow this passage with what would
otherwise be a patently absurd wager: "So obvious does this appear to me,
that I expect it will hardly be disputed."[134] Otherwise absurd indeed. Take
Sidgwick, who, aware of Butler's stature, is baffled by how Mill could say
something so outlandish: "It is rather curious to find that one of the best-
known English moralists regards the exact opposite of what Mill thinks so
obvious, as not merely a universal fact of our conscious, but even a necessary truth."[135] But, alas, Sidgwick's understated amazement is rooted in a
basic misreading of Mill.

In truth, Mill's theory of desire is strikingly similar to that of Bradley and Moore: a potential object comes before our mind's eye; we take
pleasure in the "mere idea" of this object; and this mental pleasure creates "that state of incipient activity, which is called 'desire.'"[136] Pleasure
designates without necessarily *constituting* the object of our desire; we
can, in principle, form a desire based on the "mere idea" or "very thought"
of *anything*. For instance, a righteous man "recoils" from "perpetrating
[a] crime" not because of "the fear of pain *consequent* upon the act," but
because "the *idea* of placing himself in such a situation" is "painful"—
because of "the feeling of duty," which compels him to abstain from crimi-
nality "merely because it is wrong."[137] Likewise, the thought of individuality is "animating," less as a means to pleasure and more as "a noble and
beautiful object of *contemplation*."[138] The pain we take in the "mere idea"
of crime reflects our desire for uprightness; and the pleasure we take in
the "very thought" of individuality reflects our desire for self-realization.
While every desire may stem from "a pleasant thought," not every pleasant
thought is "the thought of a pleasure." Thus, Mill, too, explodes the limit to
the variety of ends that might appeal to the human psyche: the "prevailing
error of Mr. Bentham's views of human nature" is that "he supposes mankind to be swayed by only a part of the inducements which really actuate
them."[139] Mill's critique of Bentham reflects a hedonic value-sense theory:

134. Ibid., 238–239.
135. Sidgwick, *Methods of Ethics*, 44.
136. Moore, *Principia Ethica*, §42.
137. Mill, "Remarks on Bentham's Philosophy," 12–13, my emphasis.
138. Mill, *On Liberty*, 266, my emphasis.
139. Mill, "Remarks on Bentham's Philosophy," 16–17.

the mind's eye perceives the value or disvalue of various goods and activities and thus experiences a reactive pleasure or pain.

As with the higher pleasures, Mill does not provide a comprehensive list of human desires. However, he occasionally offers concentrated bursts of insight into their diverse content, like in the following passage from his second of two essays on Bentham's philosophy:

> Man is conceived by Bentham as a being susceptible of pleasures and pains. . . . And here Bentham's conception of human nature stops. . . . Man is never recognised by him as a being capable of pursuing spiritual perfection as an end; of desiring, for its own sake, the conformity of his own character to his standard of excellence, without hope of good or fear of evil from other source than his own inward consciousness . . . and neither the word *self-respect*, nor the idea to which that word is appropriated, occurs even once, so far as our recollection serves us, in his whole writings. Nor is it only the moral part of man's nature, in the strict sense of the term—the desire of perfection, or the feeling of an approving or of an accusing conscience—that he overlooks; he but faintly recognises . . . the pursuit of any other ideal end for its own sake. The sense of *honour*, and personal dignity—that feeling of personal exaltation and degradation . . . the love of *beauty*, the passion of the artist; the love of *order*, of congruity, of consistency in all things, and conformity to their end; the love of . . . making our volitions effectual; the love of *action*, the thirst for movement and activity . . . the love of ease. . . . Even under the head of *sympathy*, his recognition does not extend to the more complex forms of the feeling—the love of *loving*, the need of sympathising support, or of objects of admiration and reverence.[140]

Here, Mill lays out each "aspect" of human life: "*moral*," "*aesthetic*," and "*sympathetic*."[141] This division pops up repeatedly in Mill's writings and will be central to understanding the dynamic he envisions between happiness and morality. But, overall, Mill gives the impression that the scope of human desire is quite extensive. In *Utilitarianism*, he includes "music" and "health";[142] in *Autobiography*, he discusses "poetic culture";[143] and in "On Genius," he isolates "wisdom and virtue,"[144] each of which plays a

140. Mill, "Bentham," 94–96.
141. Ibid., 112.
142. Mill, *Utilitarianism*, 208, 235.
143. Mill, *Autobiography*, 115.
144. Mill, "On Genius," 330, *CW* 1.

leading role in *On Liberty* and *Utilitarianism*, respectively, with "wisdom" recast as "truth"[145] in the former. And, for Mill, perhaps no other desire is as integral to well-being as freedom: "the love of liberty and personal independence."[146] As we will discuss in later chapters, freedom not only emerges as the deepest part of happiness for Mill but also grounds our realization of happiness more generally.

Mill's critique of psychological hedonism is highly intuitive and, I think, verified by everyday experience. There exists an indefinite plurality of goods and activities, of objects and ideals, that strike the mind's eye as attractive and thus pleasant. Consequently, Bentham is rebuked by Mill for being utterly blind to the richness of human nature: "Man, that most complex being, is a very simple one in his eyes." What Bentham rejects as a sign of "despotism in the moralist," Mill attributes to the higher mind's eye; what Bentham belittles as mere "idiosyncrasies of taste," Mill esteems as "the deeper feelings of human nature"; and whereas Bentham would dismiss all such feelings as "vague generalities," Mill thinks they comprise "the whole unanalysed experience of the human race." Bentham's complete lack of "self-consciousness" and total failure at "deriving light from other minds" resulted in an account of human desire that embodies nothing more than "the empiricism of one who has had little experience."[147] According to Mill, the will to pleasure cannot even begin to comprehend the vast array of desires exhibited by mindful individuals.

MILL CONTRA ASSOCIATIONISM

However, some scholars tell a different story: they say that Mill *does* affirm psychological hedonism, but that he then *overcomes* it via associationism; they maintain that, for Mill, non-hedonic ends can be desired *as ends* only insofar as they have been *associated* with pleasure. The fourth chapter of *Utilitarianism* frames virtue in these terms:

> To illustrate this farther, we may remember that virtue is not the only thing, originally a means, and which if it were not a means to anything else, would be and remain indifferent, but which by association with what it is a means to, comes to be desired for itself, and that too with the utmost intensity. . . . Virtue, according to the utilitarian conception, is a good of this description. There was no original desire of it,

145. Mill, *On Liberty*, 229–231.
146. Mill, *Utilitarianism*, 212.
147. Mill, "Bentham," 90, 92, 96.

or motive to it, save its conduciveness to pleasure, and especially to protection from pain. But through the association thus formed, it may be felt a good in itself, and desired as such with as great intensity as any other good. . . .[148]

The lesson often drawn is that virtue, like anything else, is made attractive only via association: "Originally we desire virtue as a means to happiness, but through psychological association virtue becomes pleasurable and so a component of happiness."[149] And indeed, Mill often speaks this way: "the strongest natural attraction, both of power and of fame, is the immense aid they give to the attainment of our other wishes; and it is the strong association thus generated between them and all our objects of desire, which gives to the direct desire of them the intensity it often assumes, so as in some characters to surpass in strength all other desires."[150] The despot and the celebrity once sought power and fame, respectively, for the sake of certain pleasures; but, as time wore on, these means took on a life of their own; they became so entangled with pleasure that they came to be desired as ends unto themselves.

However, there are two problems with leaving the story here. First, this reading does *not* explain why Mill would characterize non-hedonic desires as *authentic* facts; for, on this reading, our non-hedonic desires are just artificial, often delicate, illusions. To wit, these "associative links" could always "come apart."[151] And second, the fact is that Mill's psychological theory travels far beyond the bounds of associationism. While Mill always recognized the power of association, he identified the theory of association*ism* as the chief threat to his theory of human desire, and sought to counter it as such. As one Mill biographer remarks, and as we will see, this was a deeply personal departure: "Mill felt trapped by one element of his youthful creed, the 'associationist' psychology of Hartley, which implied that everyone is shaped by their circumstances into the person they are destined to remain."[152]

In response to the Mill-Bradley-Moore consensus, a psychological hedonist could argue that all our non-hedonic pleasant thoughts are really just thoughts of means that we *associate* with hedonic ends. This idea was central to the Benthamite worldview and was impressed upon a

148. Mill, *Utilitarianism*, 235–236.
149. Donner and Fumerton, *Mill*, 25.
150. Mill, *Utilitarianism*, 236.
151. Ten, "Liberal Self," 328.
152. Reeves, "Mill's Mind," 5. Reeves is referring to eighteenth-century English philosopher David Hartley.

young Mill by his father: "My course of study had led me to believe, that all mental and moral feelings and qualities" were "the results of association; that we love one thing and hate another, take pleasure in one sort of action or contemplation, and pain in another sort, through the clinging of pleasurable or painful ideas to those things, from the effect of education or of experience." On this account, the pleasant "contemplation" of any non-hedonic object can be reduced to an "artificial" link between that object and our desire for pleasure.[153] As James Mill writes, it is "to be observed that Wealth, Power, and Dignity, afford perhaps the most remarkable of all examples of that extraordinary case of association, where the means to an end, not only engross more of our attention than the end itself, but actually supplant it in our affections."[154] Thus, a miser can desire pleasure alone and yet take pleasure in the "very thought" of wealth insofar as the "mere idea" of wealth has "clung together" with his basic hedonic drive. And the psychological hedonist can hypothesize that "the effects of association" often lack durability and will thereby gradually fall prey to the "dissolving influence of analysis"—unless, that is, these "effects" have become "so intense and inveterate" as to defy all hedonic scrutiny.[155] In sum, Mill is being misled, as Bentham would say, by "fictitious entities,"[156] the factual "roots" or "foundations"[157] of which are, in *all* cases, hedonic in nature.

This rejoinder cuts to the core of what psychological hedonism really *is*. The first premise of every psychological hedonist from Epicurus to Helvétius to Bentham—and even some critics of psychological hedonism, like Mill—is that human beings are purely hedonistic in their nascent and unaffected condition: pleasure is our "first and kindred good";[158] the only desire we take "from the hand of nature";[159] the sole impetus of our "natural constitution";[160] and the crux of all our "primitive desires."[161] The will to pleasure is uniquely inborn. The central tenet, then, of psychological hedonism is that human beings either cannot or do not subsequently acquire or develop other, non-hedonic desires: "Psychological hedonism is, at bottom, the claim that the intrinsic desires that play [a] role in the adult

153. Mill, *Autobiography*, 141.
154. Mill, *Analysis of the Phenomena of the Human Mind*, 172–173.
155. Mill, *Autobiography*, 141–143.
156. Bentham, *Fragment on Ontology*, 196, *W* 8.
157. Bentham, *Table of the Springs of Action*, 211, *W* 1.
158. Laertius, *Lives of Eminent Philosophers*, X, §128–130.
159. Helvétius, *De l'espirit*, 245.
160. Bentham, *Principles of Morals and Legislation*, 2.
161. Mill, *Autobiography*, 236.

are essentially the same as the intrinsic desires of the infant."[162] In defense of this view, a psychological hedonist can proceed inductively by attempting to show that any seemingly non-hedonic desire we possess can be better understood or more intuitively explained as part of the "unfolding"[163] of our "original and inherent"[164] desire for pleasure. For James Mill especially, association is *the* crux of this inductive agenda: even our most cherished ends—such as love, or wisdom, or beauty—are nothing more than ideals "associated with a hundred times as many pleasures as another," making them "a hundred times more interesting."[165]

Again, Mill readily grants the influence of hedonic association. In fact, he often testifies to its pervasive effects on our behavior: "As we proceed in the formation of habits, and become accustomed to will a particular act or a particular course of conduct because it is pleasurable, we at last continue to will it without any reference to its being pleasurable."[166] Nonetheless, Mill would argue that his father's reductive inductivism fails for two reasons. First, our non-hedonic pleasant thoughts often endure even *after* our "practised," habit-breaking "habits of self-consciousness and self-observation" have loosened our associative knots.[167] While a non-hedonic pleasant thought may *begin* as an "artificial creation," it can thereafter "harmonize" with a supra-hedonic "department of our nature"[168] and thus become attractive to us "independent of the native elements from which [it is] formed."[169] This "mental chemistry,"[170] through which a supra-hedonic desire emerges from the interaction of hedonic and non-hedonic elements, is particularly obvious in human maturation: what the child initially desires in anticipation of carrots or sticks, the child-turned-adult comes to desire for chiefly "disinterested"[171] reasons. As we will see, this applies most emphatically to our other-regarding ends: those goods or activities that fall under ideals like *generosity, altruism, benevolence.* Childhood ought to be in large part a process of socialization, whereby children learn to treat other persons in an empathetic, impartial manner; the family should be "a school of sympathy, tenderness, and loving

162. Harman, *Reasoning, Meaning, and Mind,* 70.

163. Helvétius, *D l'espirit,* 248–249.

164. Mill, "James Mill's *Analysis of the Phenomena of the Human Mind,*" 220, *CW* 31.

165. Mill, *Analysis of the Phenomena of the Human Mind,* 164.

166. Mill, *System of Logic,* 854.

167. Mill, *Utilitarianism,* 214, 237.

168. Ibid., 230–231. See also ibid., 235–237.

169. Mill, "James Mill's *Analysis of the Phenomena of the Human Mind,*" 220.

170. Mill, *System of Logic,* 854.

171. Mill, "James Mill's *Analysis of the Phenomena of the Human Mind,*" 220.

forgetfulness of self."[172] Very few individuals, having been thus socialized, would ultimately deem their other-regarding habits to be hollow or arbitrary, even upon recognizing their associative roots. Rather, these habits weather the storm of scrutiny; they prove enduringly valuable to us insofar as the ends they serve appear intrinsically desirable.

And second, our non-hedonic pleasant thoughts often arise spontaneously, without any associative origin story to speak of: "Those who have studied the writings of the Association Psychologists, must often have been unfavourably impressed by the almost total absence, in their analytical expositions, of the recognition of any active element, or spontaneity, in the mind itself."[173] It is this "active element," this "spontaneity," which Mill thinks accounts historically for most of our nobler desires: it is from "representations" of persons "whose actions and sentiments were of a more generous and loftier order" that "the noblest minds in modern Europe derived what made them noble" and "even the commoner spirits what made them understand and respond to nobleness."[174] The doctrine of the higher pleasures is Mill's testament to the fact that non-hedonic thoughts can strike the mind's eye as pleasant even when these ideas are associated with relatively little pleasure or even great pain.[175] Moreover, Mill's writings are bursting with allusions to desires that we acquire or develop not from association, but simply from the exercise of our higher faculties. Most importantly, Mill believes we can come to desire, or to recognize the desirability of, hitherto undesired ends by way of deliberation—discussing, reading, practicing, ruminating. This is one of the central themes of *On Liberty*. It is also a key part of Mill's life, during which he "obtained in the natural course of [his] mental progress, poetic culture of the most valuable kind, by means of reverential admiration for the lives and characters of heroic persons; especially the heroes of philosophy." Indeed, Mill reports that his adoption of a higher ideal of happiness was due most particularly to having that ideal placed in a pleasant light by Harriet Taylor: "My conception of the highest worth of a human being, was immeasurably enlarged and exalted" by "the *direct operation* of her intellect and character upon mine."[176] Again, this is all highly intuitive and verified by

172. Mill, *Subjection of Women*, 289, *CW* 21.

173. Mill, "Bain's Psychology," 354, *CW* 11.

174. Mill, "Ware's Letters from Palmyra," 460, *CW* 1.

175. This would likely be Mill's response to Sidgwick's idea that the strength of our "ideal" desires can always be reduced to their "degree of [hedonic] productiveness" (Sidgwick, *Methods of Ethics*, 401).

176. Mill, *Autobiography*, 115, 622–623, my emphasis.

everyday experience: our desire for love, wisdom, and beauty can often be traced to our direct, active encounters with these ideals. The higher faculties, when well cultivated and freely exercised, are sensible and naturally responsive to attractive ends of all shapes, sizes, and colors.

Associationism's deep inadequacy as a comprehensive theory of human desire was brought home to Mill in a very personal, very acute way. In "a dull state of nerves," a young Mill posed himself the following question:

> "Suppose that all your objects in life were realized; that all the changes in institutions and opinions which you are looking forward to, could be completely effected at this very instant: would this be a great joy and happiness to you?" And an irrepressible self-consciousness distinctly answered, "No!" At this my heart sank within me: the whole foundation on which my life was constructed fell down. All my happiness was to have been found in the continual pursuit of this end. The end had ceased to charm, and how could there ever again be any interest in the means? I seemed to have nothing left to live for.[177]

Scholars have routinely construed Mill's epiphany as being the source of his disillusionment with Benthamism. For instance, as Isaiah Berlin says, Mill's "No!" impelled him to inquire, "What, then, [is] the true end of life?" However, Mill's discontent with Bentham's philosophy *as a philosophy* emerged later, and even then only gradually. What Mill was realizing here, at this critical juncture in his life, was that he had no genuine *desire for* "the noble Benthamite ideal of universal happiness."[178] He was not yet questioning *anything* about the Benthamite worldview. Rather, he was recognizing his own insensibility to its objects, namely, the objects of the Philosophical Radicals: moral, social, and political reform along Benthamite lines. Mill had been trained to associate all his hopes for pleasure with the realization of these objects. And for some time, he pursued these objects happily. However, armed with a dangerously well-developed analytical intelligence, but lacking the "internal culture" that could convert associative impulses into *authentic* desires, this young reformer's aims could not and did not survive the slightest examination: "I was thus, as I said to myself, left stranded at the commencement of my voyage, with a well-equipped ship and a rudder, but no sail; without any real desire for the ends which I had been so carefully fitted out to work for: no delight in virtue or the general good, but also just as little in anything else."[179] The

---

177. Ibid., 137–139.
178. Berlin, "John Stuart Mill and the Ends of Life," 220–221.
179. Mill, *Autobiography*, 143.

young Mill was not yet in want, at least not consciously, of a new theory of life, but was instead in desperate need of a "sail," that is, an "internal culture" that could catch the wind of pleasant ideas and thus propel him toward desirable ends—indeed, desirable ends such as "virtue" and "the general good."

Fortunately, Mill encountered poetry, most notably that of Wordsworth, who rescued Mill from himself: "Mill's experiences in reading Wordsworth's poetry" awakened him "to the higher sentiments, which enabled him to take lasting pleasure in things seen to be intrinsically valuable, apart from the merely 'casual' associations they had with external pleasures." In short, we might say that associationism fails by failing to explain Mill's "depression and manner of recovery."[180] Through poetry, Mill first realized that individuals could form lasting desires simply from having objects placed before their mind's eye in a pleasant light: "Where the sense of beauty is wanting, or but faint, the understanding must be contracted: there is so much which a person, unfurnished with that sense, will never have observed, to which he will never have had his attention awakened."[181] Such objects do *not* need to be previously linked with pleasure. Association can plant the seeds of enduring desire; but valuable objects can also appeal directly to the higher faculties by virtue of their inherent qualities. What Mill learned in a deeply personal way was that human behavior is not merely the product of antecedent forces that *push* us hither and thither— what Aristotle calls *efficient* causality. Indeed, he realized that human beings also strive after ideals that *pull* us toward them, that exhibit a sort of magnetic attraction—what Aristotle calls *final* causality.[182]

FROM DESIRE TO DESIRABILITY

Thus far, we have been coming to grips with the idea of intrinsic value in terms of *attractiveness*: what, as a matter of psychological fact, *do* we desire? But what we really want to elucidate is the idea of intrinsic value in terms of *desirability*: What, as a matter of normative value, *should* we desire? What is *worthy* or *deserving* of our interest? As we saw before, the question of desirability is, for Mill, bounded by the question of attractiveness: "the sole evidence it is possible to produce that anything is desirable, is that people do actually desire it." What, then, can or does the *is* of desire tell us about the *ought* of desirability? Indeed, we might wonder whether hedonism might

180. Anderson, "John Stuart Mill and Experiments in Living," 17, 19.
181. Mill, "Writings of Junius Redivivus," 376, *CW* 1.
182. See Aristotle, *Physics*, II.3; and *Metaphysics*, V.2.

reassert itself here as an evaluative doctrine. As Hastings Rashdall notes, "we may hold that it is, as a matter of psychological fact, possible to desire other things besides pleasure, but that pleasure is the only proper or rational object of desire." An individual who pursues more than just pleasure may very well be "a fool for his pains."[183] This brings us back full circle: Can or does the data of human desire affirm Carlyle's "swine" objection and thereby confirm that certain ends are either becoming or unbecoming of a well-developed person? Or can or does the data of human desire lend support to the desirability of a hedonistic "manner of existence," its piggishness notwithstanding?

Mill's response is implicit in much of what I have already said: the desirability of a given end is evinced by our desire for said end insofar as we desire said end *because* said end is desirable. For Mill, the *fact* of desirability springs from the inherent qualities of the good or activity itself; certain objects strike the mind's eye as pleasant in light of their desirability and thus "excite in [the] mind the feeling of approbation."[184] None of this is a matter of intuition or a priori insight: we *experience* particular ends not only as attractive but also as desirable, such that it feels natural for us to declare "either that man *should*, or that he *should not*, take pleasure in one thing, displeasure in another."[185] Were Mill asked to account for the desirability of a given end on experiential grounds, he would "justify his approbation"[186] by dubbing the end "beautiful or noble";[187] "loveable or admirable";[188] or "morally right."[189] A sommelier is able to tell the difference between fine and pedestrian wines; likewise, to be endowed with higher faculties is to be naturally capable (in a teleological sense) of recognizing and appreciating the superior worth of what Mill calls the higher pleasures.

Bentham rejects the concept of desirability altogether, except as it pertains to getting what we find attractive, or pleasurable. Any appeal to what *ought* to be desired is regarded by him as nothing more than an "internal sentiment," a subjective feeling posing as an objective fact, and thus, in effect, "a cloke, and pretence, and aliment, to despotism."[190] What we *feel* to be the august model of "Socrates dissatisfied" is just our mere whimsy. For

183. Rashdall, *Theory of Good and Evil*, 7.
184. Mill, *System of Logic*, 949.
185. Mill, "Bentham," 96, my emphases.
186. Mill, *System of Logic*, 949.
187. Mill, "Thoughts on Poetry and Its Varieties," 374, *CW* 1.
188. Mill, *Autobiography*, 197.
189. Mill, *Utilitarianism*, 219.
190. Bentham, *Principles of Morals and Legislation*, 8 (note to §14). Bentham writes, "internal sentiments."

Mill, though, "internal sentiment" poses no problem. In fact, Mill's entire point is that our non-hedonic pleasant thoughts, which *are* "subjective feelings," often stem from our encounters with objective, supra-hedonic values: "the imaginative emotion which an idea when vividly conceived excites in us, is not an illusion but a fact, as real as any of the other qualities of objects." Mill argues that the "feeling of the beauty of a cloud lighted by the setting sun" gives us reason to think that the cloud *is* beautiful.[191] And the same goes for the sentiments linked to the desirability of love, or wisdom, or beauty: "What is there to decide whether a particular pleasure is worth purchasing at the cost of a particular pain, except the feelings and judgment of the experienced?" Needless to say, the influence of "internal sentiment" can lead to all kinds of dubious claims: "Mankind are always predisposed to believe that any subjective feeling, not otherwise accounted for, is a revelation of some objective reality."[192] And yet, as long as our shared feelings endure and deepen under mutual reflection and analysis, then they are scarcely less dependable as sources of knowledge than is our collective experience of the concrete world. Mill's position is that desirability is a basic feature of the world; it radiates from the higher pleasures no less than redness bounces off the skin of an apple. Indeed, we might say that Bentham carries an a priori bias against a particular empirical reality: the experience of desirability.

Let me unpack this point. The challenge for Mill is to demonstrate empirically (without relying on any intuitive, a priori insight) that certain goods or activities can be deemed *objectively* desirable; that at least *some* claims regarding what we either *should* or should *not* take pleasure in—or what we have *reason* to value or desire—are *more* than just arbitrary, prejudiced assertions. But, frankly, this is a relatively simple task for Mill. We call various things *desirable*, just as we call some apples *red*, because we *experience* them that way: we take pleasure in the thought or idea of pursuing certain goods or activities *because* they are desirable and thus worthy or deserving of our interest; we feel we have *reason* to value or desire certain objects *because* they are enriching, edifying, ennobling. In truth, we have, from one angle, as much occasion to believe in desirability on empirical grounds as we do in red apples; for whereas nothing you do can help *me* see redness through *your* eyes (and nothing you do can *reveal* redness to a blind person), there is a great deal you can do to help *my* mind's eye appreciate what *your* mind's eye views as desirable in

191. Mill, *Autobiography*, 157.
192. Mill, *Utilitarianism*, 213, 240.

a particular end. This goes back to Mill's emphasis on discussing, reading, practicing, ruminating—all of which employ "the faculty by which one mind understands a mind different from itself, and throws itself into the feelings of that other mind."[193] In other words, just as a decisive preponderance of clear-sighted persons see certain apples as red, a decisive preponderance of well-developed persons—free from the distorting, deadening influence of prejudice, dogma, or fanaticism—will, through the enduring impressions of either prior habituation (association) or later experience (deliberation), find an indefinite range of goods and activities desirable by virtue of their participation in various ideals: *individuality, wisdom, benevolence, nobility, impartiality.*

Naturally, we often find ourselves at loggerheads over *which* goods or activities truly manifest these ideals; and different ideals will rise or fall in the estimation of different persons or peoples depending on their social or cultural context. But as to the desirability of the ideals themselves, there can be little dispute on empirical grounds. Indeed, these and other ideals (let us not forget *love* and *beauty*) lie at the heart of our shared experience: the humanities are motivated by them; our ethical discourse is framed by them; across epochs and oceans we find them exerting a gravitational pull on the human soul in often foreign but universally intelligible ways; their light can be dimmed by tyranny, or chaos, or decadence, but it cannot be extinguished for good. Mill's theory of desire unto desirability is a profound attempt to embrace our common humanity, which is exemplified in various, partial ways in the matrices or systems of value of our various, familial cultures and civilizations. What counts as part of the good—and thus as part of our common humanity—is whatever is beheld by the universal mind's eye as "a noble and beautiful object of contemplation."[194] And Mill would ardently insist that there *is* this universal mind's eye: that is what allows different individuals or cultures to empathize with and appreciate one another regardless of their respective idiosyncrasies of attitude or outlook; that is why the humanities, though overflowing with tension and diversity, are able, in direct proportion to their manifold treasures, to broaden, deepen, and cultivate a single mind and soul.[195]

Of course, Mill also says that ends are desirable only insofar as they contribute to happiness. Is not *happiness*, then, the well from which our ideals draw their value? Well, yes, but this is only a manner of speaking. As

193. Mill, "Bentham," 91.

194. Mill, *On Liberty*, 266.

195. A parallel can be drawn here to Isaiah Berlin's value pluralism. For a general overview, see the essays in Berlin, *Crooked Timber of Humanity*.

I have argued, happiness is an *inclusive* end for Mill: it is "not an abstract idea, but a concrete whole,"[196] concretized in various abstract ideals. For instance, Mill asserts that "character itself should be, to the individual, a paramount end, simply because the existence of this ideal nobleness of character" would "go further than all things else towards making human life happy."[197] At first glance, this looks circular, for one of the very things that well-developed persons "can care to have" *is* this "nobleness of character." But all Mill is really saying is that "nobleness of character" is one of the "essential *constituents* of human well-being."[198] Happiness is an inclusive end, and nobility is one of its "parts."[199] Again, the closest analogy we can draw is to Aristotle's *eudaimonia*. Just as the Aristotelian virtues specify a plurality of ways in which a human being can flourish as a creature with a particular telos, the Millian higher pleasures include an indefinite plurality of ideals, each of which is constitutive of "the ideal perfection of human nature."

However, this conclusion introduces another problem: If we desire only what contributes to *our* happiness, then where does that leave *others* in our estimation? Are we *selfish* beings? Ethicists of the a priori persuasion wanted (*want*) to insist that other-regarding actions (especially of the *moral* variety) can and ought to be done "disinterestedly."[200] In this, Mill fully concurs; he is committed to a truly other-regarding brand of Utilitarianism. And yet, if the "utilitarian doctrine is, that happiness is desirable, and the only thing desirable, as an end," are we not dealing with a necessarily egoistic creed? Hardly. The solution is for altruism itself to be constitutive of happiness: to desire happiness is to desire all desirable things; and to desire all desirable things is to desire the good of others. A simple solution, but one that unveils the first move Mill makes toward his moral and political theory: the distinction between *individuality* and *sociality*.

Individuality and Sociality

Mill attacks egoism and defends altruism in what is, in essence, a proof-by-demonstration of last section's theory of human desire. Indeed, Mill argues that we exhibit other-regarding desires; that these desires both withstand scrutiny and emerge spontaneously; and that we desire the good of others *because* the good of others is desirable—we desire the good of others for

196. Mill, *Utilitarianism*, 236.
197. Mill, *System of Logic*, 952.
198. Mill, "Guizot's Essays and Lectures on History," 269, *CW* 20, my emphasis.
199. Mill, *Utilitarianism*, 236.
200. Ibid., 235.

supra-hedonic reasons. Therefore, altruism is constitutive of happiness. More broadly, though, what Mill does below is divide the universe of desirable ends between individuality (the sphere of *self*-regarding ends) and sociality (the sphere of *other*-regarding ends). This division between individuality and sociality will carry us to the brink of Mill's moral and political philosophy; for out of this distinction, Mill will develop his moral theory and, consequently, his theory of liberty and freedom.

PSYCHOLOGICAL EGOISM

While Mill does not provide a complete list of human desires, he does make a critical distinction between individuality and sociality. The desires of individuality are directed toward the good of the self; they "appertain to man as a mere individual"; they are the ends of "the mere intellect, and those of the purely self-regarding desires."[201] Individuality is about "pursuing our own good in our own way."[202] Conversely, the desires of sociality are directed toward the good of others; they "relate to the feelings called forth in a human being by other individual human or intelligent beings," including "the *affections*, the *conscience*, or feeling of duty, and the love of *approbation*."[203] Sociality embraces "the feelings and capacities which have the good of others for their object,"[204] which are often altruistic, but which also include reciprocal goods or activities, such as friendship. *Utilitarianism* houses Mill's most focused and extensive catalog of our social drives: the "impulse to promote the general good"; the "desire to be in unity with our fellow creatures"; the "feeling that the interests of others are [our] own interests"; and the "want that there should be harmony between [our] feelings and aims and those of [our] fellow creatures."[205] Thus, Mill identifies two spheres of human desire, mapping onto the "individual & social"[206] parts of human nature.

By recognizing individuality *and sociality*, Mill is rejecting not only psychological hedonism but also *psychological egoism*. Bentham, while not as resolute in his psychological egoism, depicts us as predominantly self-serving creatures: "In every human breast," "self-regarding interest is predominant over social interest: each person's own individual interest,

201. Mill, *Essays on Some Unsettled Questions of Political Economy*, 319, *CW* 4.
202. Mill, *On Liberty*, 226.
203. Mill, *Essays on Some Unsettled Questions of Political Economy*, 319.
204. Mill, *On Liberty*, 267.
205. Mill, *Utilitarianism*, 218, 231, 233. Mill writes: "wants."
206. Mill, "To Harriet Taylor," 9, *CW* 14.

over the interest of all other persons taken together."[207] In this way, Bentham presents Mill with a fresh challenge: even if we are not hedonists at heart, we are surely egoists at heart, such that *whatever* we desire, we tend to desire for the sake of our *own* welfare or benefit. As Mill explains, Bentham thinks that egoism, like hedonism, is made evident by our behavior: "the moment he has shown that a man's *selfish* interest would prompt him to a particular course of action, he lays it down without further parley that the man's interest lies that way," and "the conclusion which is always brought out is, that the man will act as the selfish interest prompts."[208] On Bentham's view, we can expect to extract other-regarding behavior *from* the individual only insofar as "the good of others" stands out as "the greatest and surest source" of pleasure *for* the individual.[209] This is why Bentham's moral theory is dependent for its binding force on artificial sanctions, both external (i.e., carrots, sticks) and internal (i.e., association). The *truly* happiest life is that of an unchecked, selfish appetite, and thus the goal of the Benthamite reformer—egoistically driven by the "pleasure of sympathy with human beings"[210]—is to bring self-interest to heel by artificially aligning the individual's interests with the interests of society at large. Hence Mill's early education and eventual mental crisis.

Psychological egoism has been met with less reflexive skepticism than its hedonistic progeny. In fact, the idea that we are driven chiefly if not exclusively by selfish motives was "at one time almost universally accepted by political economists, philosophers, and psychologists."[211] And indeed, psychological egoism seems to have an intuitive strength that psychological hedonism maybe lacks. There are numerous shallow but seductive reasons to think that egoism lies at the heart of everything. For instance, there is the notion that we always act *for* ourselves *as* ourselves: "Every action of mine is prompted by motives or desires or impulses which are *my* motives and not somebody else's. This fact might be expressed by saying that whenever I act I am always pursuing my own ends or trying to satisfy my own desires."[212] And similarly, there is the fact that individuals tend to get pleasure from their altruistic deeds, which "has suggested to many people that what we really want in every case [of other-regarding activity]

207. Bentham, *Book of Fallacies*, 482, W 2.
208. Mill, "Remarks on Bentham's Philosophy," 14.
209. Mill, *Autobiography*, 143. Mill writes: "surest sources."
210. Ibid., 143.
211. Feinberg, "Psychological Egoism," 183.
212. Duncan-Jones, *Butler's Moral Philosophy*, 96, quoted in Feinberg, "Psychological Egoism," 184.

is our own pleasure."[213] (This view advances a limited, altruism-denying psychological hedonism.) What are we to make of these assertions?

To begin, the *pleasure-seeking* argument runs headlong into Butler's analysis from the last section. Altruistic persons can (and often do) take pleasure *in* other-regarding ends because they have a desire for the ends *themselves*. Suppose Abe Lincoln rescues a sow's litter from drowning, but then poo-poos the apparent altruism of his act by confessing, "I should have had no peace of mind all day had I gone on and left that suffering old sow worrying over those pigs. I did it to get peace of mind, don't you see?"[214] However, Lincoln's explanation—that he simply wanted to realize a certain mental state—cannot endure Butler's inspection:

> The very fact that he did feel satisfaction as a result of helping the pigs presupposes that he had a preexisting desire for something other than his own happiness. Then when *that* desire was satisfied, Lincoln of course derived pleasure. The *object* of Lincoln's desire was not pleasure; rather pleasure was the *consequence* of his preexisting desire for something else. If Lincoln had been wholly indifferent to the plight of the little pigs as he claimed, how could he possibly have derived any pleasure from helping them? He could not have achieved peace of mind from rescuing the pigs, had he not a prior concern—on which his peace of mind depended—for the welfare of the pigs for its own sake.[215]

What prompts Lincoln to save the pigs is the pain he takes *in* the thought or idea of letting them drown. His pangs of conscience and eventual peace of mind are directed *toward* the true object of his desire: the well-being of the litter. What Lincoln fears in this instance is *allowing* his egoistic desires (perhaps for relaxation) to quash his altruistic interests. Moreover, we can easily identify scenarios in which individuals can act, and have acted, for altruistic ends without any real prospect of selfish gain—the classic case being the soldier who dives on an active grenade to save his comrades. Or as Hume inquires, "What interest can a fond mother have in view, who loses her health by assiduous attendance on her sick child, and afterwards languishes and dies of grief, when freed, by its death, from the slavery of that attendance?" Obviously, a psychological egoist *could* reframe all such cases so as to reaffirm the egoist outlook (e.g., the soldier was *actually* driven by the praise he would receive for his bravery).

213. Feinberg, "Psychological Egoism," 184.
214. Sharp, *Ethics*, 75, quoted in Feinberg, "Psychological Egoism," 186.
215. Feinberg, "Psychological Egoism," 186.

But, at that point, we are simply faced with a non-falsifiable farce and should thus feel at liberty to reject "the selfish hypothesis" as "contrary to common feeling and our most unprejudiced notions," and to accept the "thousand" instances of altruism implying "a general benevolence in human nature, where no *real* interest binds us to the object."[216] Indeed, the reductionism of the psychological egoist is pure ideology: what could be said to reframe *all* these cases so as to *persuade* Hume, or us, that psychological egoism is valid?

Next, what about the *self-regarding* argument? Simply, this thesis elides the distinction between all desires being self-*referential* and all desires being self-*regarding*. Again, the psychological egoist trips over Butler:

> Every particular affection, even the love of our neighbour, is as really our own affection, as self-love; and the pleasure arising from its gratification is as much my own pleasure, as the pleasure self-love would have from knowing I myself should, be happy some time hence, would be my own pleasure. And if, because every particular affection is a man's own, and the pleasure arising from its gratification his own pleasure, or pleasure to himself, such particular affection must be called self-love. According to this way of speaking, no creature whatever can possibly act but merely from self-love; and every action and every affection whatever is to be resolved up into this one principle.[217]

For Butler, psychological egoism takes a faulty leap of logic between the fact that we always do what *we* want to do and the idea that we always aim at our *own* good: "The ploy, notoriously, confuses the subject of the motivation (*who* has the desire) with the object of the motivation (*what* is desired)."[218] Every desire we have is, indeed, *our* desire. But this is just a self-referential truism that in no way challenges the veracity of our other-regarding objects. Mill charges Bentham with this very crime: "In laying down as a psychological axiom, that men's actions are always obedient to their interests, Mr. Bentham did no more than dress up the very trivial proposition that all persons do what they feel themselves most disposed to do."[219] Bentham is asserting either that all our actions are directed toward selfish ends (which is evidently false) or that all our actions are directed

216. Hume, *Enquiry Concerning the Principles of Morals*, appendix II.
217. Butler, *Fifteen Sermons*, XI, §7.
218. Snare, *Morals, Motivation, and Convention*, 119.
219. Mill, "Remarks on Bentham's Philosophy," 13.

toward desired ends (which is triflingly true). The "selfish theory"[220] is either wrong or vacuous. Nonetheless, let us delve into Mill's analysis, an application of his critique of psychological hedonism.

MILL CONTRA PSYCHOLOGICAL EGOISM

Having brushed aside Bentham's psychological egoism, Mill faces the open question of sociality and discerns that one side of our psyche is attracted to other-regarding ends: "There are, there have been, many human beings, in whom the motives of patriotism or of benevolence have been permanent steady principles of action, superior to any ordinary, and in not a few instances, to any possible temptations of personal interest. There are, there have been, multitudes, in whom the motive of conscience or moral obligation has been thus paramount."[221] In addition to observing that many persons exhibit a variety of other-regarding impulses, Mill is also alluding to the inner tension we experience between our self-regarding and other-regarding desires. In a Platonic sense, this would imply that there are *two* overarching principles in the human soul: one of them is selfish, and thus pulls one way, whereas the other is altruistic, and thus pulls the other way. Again, this squares with our ordinary experience and goes toward explaining Lincoln's inner *struggle* while observing the pigs.

But, for Mill, there is a larger sense in which our "motives" or "principles of action" are beside the point. Mill thinks we can *recognize* sociality as attractive, nay, as desirable, even if we do *not* possess a dependably altruistic character. Ultimately, we are not egoists for the same reason we are not hedonists. Like all our non-hedonic desires, the "very thought" of acting for the sake of others strikes our mind's eye as pleasant: a "noble mind," infected with a "sympathetic contagion," "assimilates other minds to itself";[222] the propensity "to love one's neighbour as oneself" is beheld as a "beautiful [and] exalted development of human nature";[223] and the idea that "Socrates, or Howard or Washington, or Antoninus, or Christ, would have sympathised with us" provides us with a "strong incentive to act up to [our] highest feelings and convictions"[224] concerning the good of others. High-minded hedonists regard sociality as "*loveable*"; it speaks

220. Mill, "Sedgwick's Discourse," 71, *CW* 10.
221. Mill, "Remarks on Bentham's Philosophy," 15.
222. Ibid., 16.
223. Mill, *Utilitarianism*, 218–219. Mill writes, "what more beautiful and more exalted developments of human nature."
224. Mill, "Utility of Religion," 422.

to their "human fellow-feeling."[225] Sociality may not be *innate*, but it *is* natural: "if not a part of our nature, [it] is a natural outgrowth from it; capable, like them, in a certain small degree, of springing up spontaneously; and susceptible of being brought by cultivation to a high degree of development."[226]

And yet, just as before, the threat of associationism rears its head: what if our altruistic pleasant thoughts are really just thoughts of means that we *associate* with egoistic ends? Like the miser's love of wealth, the fact that we come "to identify [our] *feelings* more and more with [the] good [of others]" could signify nothing more than "an even greater degree of *practical* consideration for [their good]."[227] As Mill's father is wont to argue, the will to sociality can be reduced to the will to pleasure (or self-interest), such that if our hedonic (or egoistic) prospects change (e.g., if we are given the opportunity to wield power in a "relation of master and slave," and thus to pursue our own good with a totally egoistic vigor), then our behavior will change accordingly—unless, again, our other-regarding habits or customs have become so rooted and calcified as to render us "unable to conceive as possible" any alternative "state of things." And as Mill himself notes, many of our most basic altruistic impulses were initially established via association with the viability of the "social state" and the "healthy growth of society," both of which are essential to our own good, and both of which are "impossible on any other footing than that the interests of all are to be consulted."[228] Indeed, many psychological egoists would contend that our altruistic drives are largely if not wholly contingent on something akin to Bentham's program of artificial sanctions: "Children are made to acquire the civilizing virtues only by the method of enticing rewards and painful punishments. Much the same is true of the history of the race. People in general have been inclined to behave well only when it is made plain to them that there is 'something in it for them.' "[229] In short, while we may have reason to believe that human beings have *real* nonhedonic desires, we might still suspect that all these desires are *really* self-regarding.

However, the two replies Mill offered above to his father's reductive inductivism also apply here. First, our other-regarding pleasant thoughts

225. Mill, "Bentham," 112.
226. Mill, *Utilitarianism*, 230. Mill is speaking here of our "moral feelings," which are just a particular species of our social feelings. We discuss this at length in chapter 2.
227. Ibid., 231, second emphasis mine.
228. Ibid., 231.
229. Feinberg, "Psychological Egoism," 184. Feinberg goes on to reject this argument.

often endure even *after* our "practised," habit-breaking "habits of self-consciousness and self-observation" have loosened our associative knots. Many altruistic desires, even those that were originally the products of association, can be neither eradicated by the "dissolving influence of analysis" nor otherwise dismissed "as a superstition of education, or a law despotically imposed by the power of society." Under scrutiny, our other-regarding ideals will present themselves as neither "artificial" or "arbitrary" nor indelibly entrenched. For "those who have it," the passion for altruistic goods or activities "possesses all the characters of a natural feeling"; they grow to "cherish it," to "work with, and not against the outward motive to care for others," despite their "selfish feelings,"[230] and to embrace "sympathetic association, having its roots no longer in the instinct of equals for self-protection, but in a cultivated sympathy between them."[231] The will to sociality is beheld by self-conscious, self-observing persons as "an attribute which it would not be well for [them] to be without." The socialized individual "comes, as though instinctively, to be conscious of himself as a being who *of course* pays regard to others. The good of others becomes to him a thing naturally and necessarily to be attended to, like any of the physical conditions of our existence."[232] Once more, this is introspectively valid and certainly gels with our mature sentiments: my readiness to share with you, while induced in kindergarten by my desire for acclamation, now reflects a truer regard for your general well-being.

And second, our other-regarding pleasant thoughts can arise from the free play of our higher faculties; they are capable of "springing up spontaneously" via deliberation. Mill argues that this development, in which sociality strikes the mind's eye as pleasant seemingly ex nihilo, can often be attributed to the influence of loved ones, moral heroes, and sublime writers:

> The love of virtue, and every other noble feeling, is not communicated by reasoning, but caught by inspiration or sympathy from those who already have it; and its nurse and foster-mother is Admiration. We acquire it from those whom we love and reverence, especially from those whom we earliest love and reverence; from our ideal of those, whether in past or in present times, whose lives and characters have been the mirror of all noble qualities; and lastly, from those who, as poets or artists, can clothe those feelings in the most beautiful forms,

230. Mill, *Utilitarianism*, 230–231, 233.
231. Mill, *Subjection of Women*, 294.
232. Mill, *Utilitarianism*, 233.

and breathe them into us through our imagination and our sensations. . . . Plato, when he argues about [virtue], argues for the most part
inconclusively; but he resembles Christ in the love which he inspires for
it, and in the stern resolution never to swerve from it, which those who
can relish his writings naturally feel when perusing them.[233]

Carrots and sticks are all well and good, and needed for the inveterately
egoistic souls among us. But, in the end, it is the education of the character
via our direct encounter with goodness to which Mill entrusts the progress
of civilization: "Not what a boy or a girl can repeat by rote, but what they
have learnt to love and admire, is what forms their character."[234] Indeed,
Bentham's egoistic doctrine is, to Mill, an *obstacle* to social flourishing:
"Upon those who *need* to be strengthened and upheld by a really inspired
moralist—such a moralist as Socrates, or Plato," or "Christ; the effect of
such writings as Mr. Bentham's, if they be read and believed and their
spirit imbibed, must either be hopeless despondency and gloom, or a reck-
less giving themselves up to a life of that miserable self-seeking, which
they are there taught to regard as inherent in their original and unalter-
able nature."[235] Bentham's outlook does not (*cannot*) account for the *spiritual* impact of psychological egoism. To regard altruism as illusory can
be utterly disheartening *because* altruism is real and really desirable; the
mind's eye revels in altruism for supra-egoistic reasons.

Nonetheless, we still might think there is something implicitly egoistic about Mill's depiction of our altruistic desires. Again, the *summum
bonum* is happiness; namely, a life "inclusive of all that has intrinsic value."
And, based on our "social feelings,"[236] we can say that happiness is partly
defined as a life inclusive of doing good for others. However, this would
seem to imply that doing good for others is ultimately desirable *because* it
enlarges our contact with the sphere of intrinsic value, which sounds flatly
self-regarding. Is there a satisfying way to resolve this seeming paradox?

Recall what was said above: to desire happiness is to desire all desirable
things; and to desire all desirable things is to desire the good of others.
Now, by pursuing the good of others, we thereby contribute to our happiness; but this contribution is not an *effect* or *consequence* of sociality; it is
constituted by sociality itself. Also, even if this contribution *was* an effect
or consequence of acting for others, this is *not* what the individual would

233. Mill, "The Gorgias," 150.
234. Mill, "Ware's Letters from Palmyra," 460.
235. Mill, "Remarks on Bentham's Philosophy," 16.
236. Mill, *Utilitarianism*, 231; and *Auguste Comte and Positivism*, 310.

(or *could*) be aiming at. Consider what we might call the egoistic paradox: If Jack is pursuing Jill's good *because* it enhances his happiness, then Jack is not *actually* pursuing Jill's good and will thus *fail* to make himself happy. Jack will find happiness in sociality *only* if he pursues Jill's good for its own sake. And unlike the hedonist pursuing dummy-ends, this does *not* call for a counterfeit desire on Jack's part: Jill's good really *is* intrinsically valuable for Jack; otherwise, seeking her good would not make him happy. Thus, while the pursuit of happiness refers, by definition, to the good of the self, this does not entail an egoistic psyche—far from it.

The question that arises next is the gateway to Mill's moral and political thought: what kind of balance can, should, or must an individual strike between individuality and sociality? Mill does not believe (as some liberal thinkers have) that the conflict between the individual and society is a zero-sum game. As Mill argues in *On Liberty*, the pursuit of individuality can be *itself* other-regarding to the extent that society thereby "becomes rich, diversified, and animating, furnishing more abundant aliment to high thoughts and elevating feelings, and strengthening the tie which binds every individual to the race, by making the race infinitely better worth belonging to." Even so, it is certainly the case that the individual and society *can* conflict in theory and *do* conflict in practice. In certain moods, Mill even depicts the history of human society as a "struggle" between "spontaneity and individuality" on one side and "the social principle" on the other. This "struggle" is unavoidable: "No person is an entirely isolated being."[237] Anything that an individual does or fails to do can adversely affect society at large; and much if not most of the time that we spend on individual pursuits is time that *could* be spent serving others. Thus, Mill asks: to what extent, if any, are we *obliged* to forget ourselves for the sake of society? This distinctively *moral* inquiry is the focus of chapter 2.

Happiness Revisited

With all this in tow, we arrive at the final question of the chapter: *what is happiness?* While we have been studying Mill's conception of happiness all along, we have thus far discussed only what it *includes*, that is, its various ingredients. But what kind of stew are these ingredients being mixed into? Does Mill's conception of happiness take on a larger meaning when considered in relation to the totality of our life and character?

237. Mill, *On Liberty*, 264–266, 280.

This brings us to Mill's treatment of arete: virtue or excellence. Happiness in the higher sense is made up of many goods and activities, falling under many ideals. And while simply pursuing a higher pleasure is itself desirable, what ultimately defines happiness for Mill in the deepest sense is how, through repeated, deliberate activity, we can progressively absorb and eventually come to personify the higher pleasures. To be truly happy is to have cultivated a full range of virtues or excellences; and to live happily is to pursue goods or activities in accordance with these embodied ideals. In short, Mill echoes Aristotle: the "human good turns out to be activity of soul exhibiting excellence."[238] As Mill says, "It is only when our purposes have become independent of the feelings of pain or pleasure from which they originally took their rise, that we are said to have a confirmed character."[239] And it is the breadth and depth of this active character that determines the breadth and depth of our happiness.

HAPPINESS AS AGGREGATION

Bentham measures happiness by way of pure aggregation: every pleasure adds to happiness; every pain subtracts from happiness; we are only ever as happy as our current balance of pleasure over pain. The good *life*, then, is a measure not only of our extant pleasures, but also of our prospects for "future utility." Happiness is a mutable hedonic sum, and what gives pleasure in the moment may at any moment fail to please. This is why Bentham views childhood, with its absorbing pleasures and transitory pains, as quite often the happiest time of life: "The child who is building houses of cards is happier than was Louis XIV when building Versailles." And so, the best policy for achieving a lifetime of happiness is to avoid any "pretended delicacy" that dulls our "appetite" for childlike pursuits: ideally, once card houses cease to please, we will turn to "a game at *solitaire*."[240] Hedonic reliability is what made Bentham's program of reform ostensibly congenial to the happiness of each reformer: his Philosophical Radicals believed that a life devoted to activism was "the greatest *and surest* source" of pleasure.

Though he avoids Bentham's hedonistic trappings, Mill, too, is seen to measure happiness by aggregating value: an "existence made up of few and transitory pains, many and various pleasures, with a decided

238. Aristotle, *Nicomachean Ethics*, I.7.
239. Mill, *System of Logic*, 842–843.
240. Bentham, *Rationale of Reward*, 254–255.

predominance of the active over the passive," "has always appeared worthy of the name of happiness."[241] And indeed, for Mill, a happy life demands a plethora of opportunities for such goods and activities. For the competent judge, the good life is one in which we devote ourselves to as many goods and activities, falling under as many ideals, as possible. Naturally, these goods and activities should be well ordered; that is, we ought to have a working "plan of life"[242] that preserves us from the now hither, now thither wanderings of a dilettante. But, on the surface, Mill's understanding of happiness is quite similar to that of Bentham, reflecting what has been called an *additive* notion of happiness: "the more goods you have, the happier you should be."[243]

HAPPINESS AS FLOURISHING

However, while Mill's conception of happiness affirms the importance of simply enjoying a multiplicity of higher pleasures, it also has a deeper, developmental layer. Mill distinguishes between *experiencing* happiness and *being* happy. To study Plato's dialogues or to aid those in need is (hopefully) to experience the higher pleasure of wisdom or altruism; but such experiences make us *intrinsically* happy only insofar as we thereby *become* wise or altruistic. By pursuing the goods or activities belonging to a higher pleasure, we (can) thereby exercise our higher faculties in accordance with this higher pleasure; and by exercising our higher faculties in accordance with this higher pleasure, we (can) thereby develop our nature in the image of, and thus achieve true happiness with respect to, this ideal. Consider the contrast between Socrates and his interlocutors: the latter are generally just experiencing (*not* always enjoying) the pursuit of wisdom, whereas the former is wisdom incarnate.

According to Mill, the mind's eye fixes not only on *doing* but also on *being*—on cultivating the virtues or excellences by which we become increasingly *like* the higher pleasures. What strikes the mind's eye as pleasant is not just the ideals that people pursue, but, more deeply, the characters of those who embody these ideals. Thus, in *On Liberty*, Mill defines happiness in the words of Wilhelm von Humboldt: "the end of man" is "the highest and most harmonious development of his powers to a complete and consistent whole."[244] For instance, the individual is rendered

---

241. Mill, *Utilitarianism*, 215.

242. Mill, *On Liberty*, 262.

243. Annas, *Morality of Happiness*, 36, 393.

244. Mill, *On Liberty*, 261. See Humboldt, *Limits of State Action*, 10.

happy in relation to wisdom by the development of those excellences of speculative reason by which we not only seek wisdom but also *become* wise: Mill promotes "bold, vigorous, independent train[s] of thought" as the only means by which the individual can achieve "the mental stature which they are capable of."[245] Or consider morality as a good or activity. We are happy in relation to "the pure idea of duty" only insofar as we are "really virtuous," meaning we have cultivated a reliably moral character; we *become* moral to the extent that we behave properly without the need for "deliberation" on whether to do our duty.[246] This point applies to the higher pleasures in toto: "It really is of importance, not only what men do, but also what manner of men they are that do it. Among the works of man, which human life is rightly employed in perfecting and beautifying, the first in importance surely is man himself."[247] To cultivate an active love and capacity for nobility is to *become* noble. Virtuous or excellent qualities, or their opposites, "show us to *be* wise or a fool, cultivated or ignorant, gentle or rough, sensitive or callous, generous or sordid, benevolent or selfish, conscientious or depraved,"[248] and thus show us to *be* happy or unhappy in these various ways.

Hence, for Mill, the best way to serve the happiness of others is to animate and energize their self-development in accordance with the higher pleasures: "They should be forever stimulating each other to increased exercise of their higher faculties, and increased direction of their feelings and aims towards wise instead of foolish, elevating instead of degrading, objects and contemplations."[249] And the form of education that is most conducive to our happiness covers "whatever we do for ourselves, and whatever is done for us by others, for the express purpose of bringing us somewhat nearer to the perfection of our nature."[250] In this way, Mill loosens his final tie to Bentham's doctrine: having rejected psychological hedonism and psychological egoism (along with hedonism itself), Mill defines happiness in its profoundest sense as a state of active being rather than mere experience-accumulation.

In sum, true happiness is flourishing: the full flowering of the individual. The incongruity between this conception of happiness and hedonism has been underlined by many thinkers, including Aristotle, who contends

245. Mill, *On Liberty*, 242–243.
246. Mill, "Remarks on Bentham's Philosophy," 12.
247. Mill, *On Liberty*, 263.
248. Mill, "Bentham," 113, my emphasis.
249. Mill, *On Liberty*, 277.
250. Mill, "Inaugural Address Delivered to the University at St. Andrews," 217.

that a happy person is generally immune from the vagaries of fortune: the virtuous man "will be happy throughout his life; for always, or by preference to everything else, he will do and contemplate what is excellent, and he will bear the chances of life most nobly and altogether decorously"; and "nobility shines through, when a man bears with resignation many great misfortunes, not through insensibility to pain but through nobility and greatness of soul."[251] Those who are virtuous or excellent, and who engage in virtuous or excellent activity, are happy *full stop*, irrespective of the pains they suffer as a result. A virtuous or excellent person can even experience the pleasure of a noble pain: even those who "perish in the breach" fighting for a worthy cause "will draw a noble enjoyment from the contest itself, which [they] would not for any bribe in the form of selfish indulgence consent to be without."[252] Happiness will elude a well-disposed soul only under conditions hostile to human flourishing; only when their opportunities for desirable activity are so limited, or when their "sufferings and misfortunes" are so extreme, that all they are really left with is a tragic existence—one "suitable to beasts."[253]

As we will see in chapter 3, and as we alluded to above while elucidating Mill's doctrine of high-minded hedonism, Mill's theory of happiness takes on another, more individualistic significance when applied to specific persons. However, as far as humanity as a whole is concerned, the fullest, greatest happiness is to be found in the deep, bountiful joys of virtuous or excellent activity—indeed, in a life of noble pleasure.

251. Aristotle, *Nicomachean Ethics*, I.10.
252. Mill, *Utilitarianism*, 217.
253. Aristotle, *Nicomachean Ethics*, I.5.

CHAPTER TWO

Impartial Duties

MILL ON UTILITY AND MORALITY

*Another of our differences is, that I am still, & am likely to remain, a
utilitarian; though not one of "the people called utilitarians"; indeed,
having scarcely one of my secondary premises in common with them;
nor a utilitarian at all, unless in quite another sense from what perhaps
anyone except myself understands by the word.*

—MILL TO THOMAS CARLYLE

IN CHAPTER 1, we saw Mill defend the thesis "that man should, or should
not, take pleasure in one thing, displeasure in another."[1] But notice: this
is not a statement of *necessity*. While we ought to exercise our higher faculties in accordance with the higher pleasures, Mill has said nothing so far
to suggest that we *must* be so engaged. We are well-advised but not *compelled* to pursue "the ideal perfection of [our] human nature."[2] The higher
pleasures should be powerful "motives," but they have no immediate "binding force."[3] If we opt for a life of lower pleasures, Mill might dub us immature (if we are an incompetent judge) or weak-willed (if we are competent
but *akratic*), and he might find our lives puerile or pitiable as a result. But
this is not to accuse us of failing in our *duty*. To be duty bound is to have
a certain range of actions either *mandated* or *prohibited*. This takes us to
Mill's moral theory. Irrespective of our desires or preferences, what are we
obliged to do or refrain from doing?

1. Mill, "Bentham," 96, *CW* 10.
2. Mill, *On Liberty*, 278, *CW* 18.
3. Mill, *Utilitarianism*, 227, *CW* 10.

The study of Mill's moral theory revolves around the issue of what his moral theory actually *says* in the first instance. In general, there have been two distinct schools of thought on this question. The traditional view says that Mill, like Bentham, espouses *Classical Utilitarianism*: details notwithstanding, we are morally obliged to promote, or maximize, the general happiness. However, the later, revisionist view says that Mill's *actual* moral theory is more nuanced. First, it argues that Mill, like *any* true Utilitarian, espouses *Philosophical Utilitarianism*, the more generic view that the general happiness is the only thing of moral value or relevance; as John Skorupski phrases it, "the good is the well-being of all, impartially considered."[4] Then it argues that to establish what this entails morally for Mill in the way of concrete duty or obligation is to ascertain what duties or obligations it would be expedient for society to impose on individuals.[5]

In short, the traditional interpretation locates Mill's moral theory in our *individual* responsibility to society to promote, or maximize, the general happiness, whereas the revisionist interpretation associates his moral theory with the individual duties or obligations that *society* ought to compel for the sake of the general happiness. Now, these positions *could* converge in practice: perhaps it would best serve the general happiness, on the traditional reading, if individuals were to bind themselves to just a limited set of social rules or expectations and to spend the rest of their lives on self-regarding pursuits; indeed, perhaps *both* the traditional *and* the revisionist readings give "a utilitarian rationale for the protection of an area of moral indifference"[6]—and perhaps it is the *same* area. However, such a practical convergence does not determine what Mill's moral theory is or why it is persuasive.

This debate hinges on the meaning of what Mill designates the principle of utility, or what we can label the Utility Principle. For traditional scholars, the Utility Principle is unambiguously conveyed in chapter 2 of *Utilitarianism*, where Mill articulates what he dubs the Greatest Happiness Principle, which says, in essence, that actions are moral or immoral insofar as they tend to augment or diminish the general happiness—a seemingly Benthamesque conception. And yet, for revisionist scholars, the *real* Utility Principle is found in places like chapter 4 of *Utilitarianism*, where Mill looks to characterize the principle of utility in more generic terms: the general happiness is "a" moral good (the *only* moral good) and

4. Skorupski, *Why Read Mill Today?*, 24.
5. See Gray, "John Stuart Mill," 12–14.
6. Gray, *Mill on Liberty*, 27–28.

thus "one of the criteria" (the *only* criterion) of morality.[7] These scholars then shift their attention to chapter 5 of *Utilitarianism*, where Mill is said to be arguing that the moral sphere is *defined* by what society has an interest in *punishing* us for doing or not doing. The Greatest Happiness Principle, for its part, is just discounted or trivialized.[8]

My overarching thesis in this chapter is that the revisionist interpretation is *right* to dissociate Mill from Classical Utilitarianism, but *wrong* to abjure the Greatest Happiness Principle, and *wrong* to associate Mill with a sanction-based moral standard. Indeed, what I defend below is a new revisionist reading of Mill's moral theory, one that I believe captures his true moral approach and embraces the totality of his moral thinking.

The key to understanding Mill's moral theory is to see how it emanates directly from his value theory. As we saw last chapter, Mill discerns two spheres of desirability—*individuality* and *sociality*—based on the hedonic responses of our mind's eye. However, as our mind's eye peruses the sphere of sociality, what we discover is that *certain* actions and objects strike our mind's eye with a particular and peculiar intensity, and it quickly becomes apparent that there is a subset of sociality that we observe as not merely desirable but *obligatory*. Accordingly, the question becomes: what is it that characterizes our experience of the *moral* ought, and how might this experience be at all refined or distilled?

Mill's answer is that we react *morally* to what we believe harms or upholds the general happiness, and that we persist in our belief only insofar as we imagine our reaction to be *impartial*. Thus, to know what morality *truly* entails is to know what opposes or protects "the well-being of all, impartially considered." Hence Philosophical Utilitarianism. Now, on the revisionist reading, this moral value is an axiological premise in search of a moral standard, which necessitates Mill's sanction-based turn. However, on my reading, this moral value is actually a moral *conclusion*: by surveying our distinctively *moral* responses, and by rendering them *impartial*, we arrive at a comprehensive picture of the moral sphere. Impartiality is vital to Mill's analysis, and we will see how the half-Scottish Mill, like his countrymen Smith and Hume, appeals, albeit subtly, to the idea of impartial spectatorship.

From here, it will become clear that the Greatest Happiness Principle is *not* a competing or conflicting moral creed. On the contrary, it is a *practical summary* of what it means to embrace Utility as *the* moral value.

---

7. Mill, *Utilitarianism*, 234.

8. For example, see Jacobson, "Utilitarianism without Consequentialism," 177.

Mill ultimately repurposes the core intuition of Classical Utilitarianism—namely, that morality is all about augmenting or diminishing the general happiness—as an applied synopsis of his own moral doctrine. In short, the Utility Principle *is* the Greatest Happiness Principle, but the Greatest Happiness Principle is nothing more than a declaration of what matters or registers morally for anyone oriented by the general happiness, or "the well-being of all, impartially considered."

My elucidation of Mill's moral theory not only offers what I believe to be an all-embracing exegesis, and not only fuses his value and moral theories together into one seamless whole, but also preserves what is attractive and avoids what is unattractive about both the traditional and revisionist interpretations. Like the traditional reading, Mill's moral theory is all about what the individual is obliged to do or refrain from doing; it avoids the revisionist tendency to frame duty or obligation as an estranged, alienated thing that society just has its *own* interest in exacting from the individual. And like the revisionist reading, Mill's moral theory draws a principled boundary between the moral and nonmoral spheres; it avoids the traditional burden of having to derive or deduce a nonmoral sphere from a general duty or obligation to promote, or maximize, the general happiness.

The story below ends with Mill's theory of justice, which will prepare the way for his social and political philosophy. But the story begins with the following question: What is the first principle of morality? What grounds or justifies our use of moral language?

The First Principle of Morality

As a Utilitarian, Mill regards the general happiness (or Utility) as the foundation of morality. Many scholars exhibit an old tendency to elide the distinction between Mill's endorsement of the Utilitarian moral axiology and what we might call the Benthamite moral directive, which enjoins us to promote, or maximize, the general happiness. This was a standard feature of the literature up to the mid-twentieth century and is still often taken for granted.[9] While this traditional reading can be pardoned, especially given Bentham's habit of eliding this distinction himself, the foundation and the obligations of morality are discrete inquiries for Mill. Naturally, these topics are close cousins, and thus some overlap can be expected between the sections that follow. Nonetheless, my first task is to

9. For instance, see Crisp, *Mill on Utilitarianism*, 97.

expound Mill's reasons for declaring Utility to be the basis of our moral existence.

THE UTILITY PRINCIPLE

Bentham's moral doctrine revolves around the Utility Principle: "By the principle of utility is meant that principle which approves or disapproves of every action whatsoever, according to the tendency which it appears to have to augment or diminish the happiness of the part whose interest is in question: or, what is the same thing in other words, to promote or to oppose that happiness." The morality of any action is measured by its tendency to expand or contract the happiness of whatever part of "the community" the action affects, that is, to expand or contract the general happiness.[10] Bentham advances the Utility Principle as a rational alternative to what he deems to be the, at best, unmeaning and, at worst, oppressive moral criteria espoused by the prevailing ethicists of the day: "Such are the phrases 'law of nature,' 'right reason,' 'natural rights,' 'moral sense.' All these Mr. Bentham regarded as mere covers for dogmatism; excuses for setting up one's own *ipse dixit* as a rule to bind other people."[11] To judge an action moral or immoral by any standard other than the Utility Principle is, for Bentham, to make an empty (often sentimental) claim that typically serves as nothing more than "a cloke, and pretence, and aliment, to despotism."[12]

The Utility Principle is not a moral directive: it does not define, at least not directly, what we are bound to do or refrain from doing. Rather, the Utility Principle is a moral criterion: it defines what makes an action moral or immoral and thus how to justify our moral judgments properly, and, further, how to critique effectively what are reckoned by Bentham to be the fictitious (generally noxious) doctrines of other moralists. To say an action is morally obliged or proscribed is to beg the question "*Why?*" What the Utility Principle says, then, is that the answer—to be admissible, let alone valid or persuasive—must evaluate the action in terms of its effects, positive or negative, on the general happiness: "A man may be said to be a partizan of the principle of utility, when the approbation or disapprobation he annexes to any action, or to any measure, is determined by and proportioned to the tendency which he conceives it to have to augment or

10. Bentham, *Principles of Morals and Legislation*, 1–2, *W* 1.
11. Mill, "Remarks on Bentham's Philosophy," 5, *CW* 10.
12. Bentham, *Principles of Morals and Legislation*, 8 (note to §14).

to diminish the happiness of the community."[13] Nothing but Utility is morally significant; appeals to natural law, or to the moral sense, or to the dictates of reason, or to human rights, are, ultimately, "simple nonsense."[14]

Mill's moral theory has a similar orbit: "The creed which accepts as the foundation of morals, Utility, or the Greatest Happiness Principle, holds that actions are right in proportion as they tend to promote happiness, wrong as they tend to produce the reverse of happiness." Mill's principle is not a moral directive either. Mill's "creed," namely, the Greatest Happiness Principle—the "creed which accepts" Utility "as the foundation of morals"—is not a mandate that supplants all extant "moral laws." Rather, it is the "source from which they derive their authority," and the "test of right and wrong." Utility is "the origin and ground of moral obligation," and the Utility Principle (Mill, like Bentham, uses "utility" and "greatest happiness" interchangeably) is its corresponding criterion—the moral standard. What "actual duties of morality" are to be deduced from this "creed" is another question entirely.[15]

The traditional retort would be to insist that Mill's principle *does* involve an implicit directive aspect. After all, if an action's morality is determined by its tendency to affect the general happiness, then, in theory, we should be able to gauge the moral quality of *any* potential option. The greater the tendency, good or bad, the greater the moral reason to act or forbear accordingly. Hence we have Francis Hutcheson, a Utilitarian forefather, who, in "comparing the moral Qualitys of Actions," concludes "that Action is best, which procures the greatest Happiness for the greatest Numbers; and that, worst, which, in like manner, occasions Misery."[16] Those familiar with Bentham will recognize Hutcheson's language: "the greatest happiness of the greatest number"[17] is Bentham's preferred slogan for describing the proper metric for moral appraisal *and action*. However, to say that an action is right or wrong insofar as it goes for or against Utility is *not* to say that *whatever* goes for or against Utility is right or wrong, nor that *every* action even *has* a Utilitarian tendency; likewise, to say that an action technically has Utilitarian *value* is not to dub it *obligatory*. These are all separate claims, and they are kept separate by Mill.

13. Ibid., 2.

14. Bentham, *Anarchical Fallacies*, 501, W 2.

15. Mill, *Utilitarianism*, 205–207, 210, 257.

16. Hutcheson, *Inquiry into the Original of Our Ideas of Beauty and Virtue*, 125.

17. This phrase appears repeatedly throughout Bentham's corpus. For instance, see Bentham, *Principles of Judicial Procedure*, 8–151 passim, W 2.

MILL'S "CONSIDERATIONS"

Bentham's defense of the Utility Principle, while scattered and unfocused, comes down to the idea that Utility is an integral part of our moral thinking, and that all other moral standards are, at bottom, either meaningless or implicitly Utilitarian: "The principle of utility, or as he afterwards called it 'the greatest-happiness principle,' stands no otherwise demonstrated in his writings, than by an enumeration of the phrases of different description which have been commonly employed to denote the rule of life, and the rejection of them all, as having no intelligible meaning, further than as they may involve a tacit reference to considerations of utility."[18] The morals allegedly derived from intuition, for instance, have factual content and moral weight only insofar as they indirectly, that is, accidentally, refer to what the general happiness calls for. However, barring that association, such morals will, under scrutiny, reveal themselves to be nothing more than arbitrary rules made to satisfy the feelings or interests of the one, few, or many.

Mill's account of the Utility Principle is far richer. As Mill warns at the outset of *Utilitarianism*, "Questions of ultimate ends are not amenable to direct proof." Just like happiness with respect to the good, the general happiness cannot *prove* itself to be the (sole) moral object "in the ordinary and popular meaning of the term." Namely, it cannot be established via formal logic. As a first principle, it must, in the last instance, be admitted "without proof." However, the "rational faculty" need not thereby attest to an arbitrary belief: "Considerations may be presented capable of determining the intellect either to give or withhold its assent to the doctrine; and this is equivalent to proof." The better part of Mill's essay is concerned with detailing such considerations by entering into "the philosophical grounds which can be given for assenting to the utilitarian standard." The question is "considered as one of philosophical theory," where the objective is to engage in rational persuasion without the advantage of fixed, antecedent premises from which to deduce conclusions.[19]

What, then, are Mill's considerations? Well, they are several. In chapter 1 of *Utilitarianism*, Mill argues that all other attempts to ground morality seem invariably to lose their footing and (while stumbling, and if pressed) reveal themselves to be relying (implicitly, and often unwittingly) on an underlying notion of the general happiness. Indeed, the

18. Mill, "Remarks on Bentham's Philosophy," 5.
19. Mill, *Utilitarianism*, 207–208.

Intuitionists will lay down any number of a priori moral rules, but appear lost when asked to provide either the "one fundamental principle or law" that grounds these rules, or "the rule of deciding between the various principles when they conflict," both of which, for Mill, suggest the need for an appeal to a supreme telos—*Utility*. Moreover, Mill observes, first, that the Utility Principle "has had a large share in forming the moral doctrines even of those who most scornfully reject its authority"; second, that there is no "school of thought which refuses to admit that the influence of actions on happiness is a most material and even predominant consideration in many of the details of morals"; and third, that "to all those *a priori* moralists who deem it necessary to argue at all, utilitarian arguments are indispensable."[20] This last point can be grasped by looking at any moral rule and asking *"Why?"* Mill thinks that some contingent *good* must be at stake for a moral claim to be intelligible.

In chapter 2, Mill parries various objections to the Utility Principle. In so doing, he demonstrates its capacity to broaden, deepen, and clarify our moral intuitions, thereby demonstrating its credibility to an otherwise skeptical audience. For example, how does the Utility Principle explain our reluctance to steal, lie, or kill, even when these unholy acts would appear to promote the general happiness? And, before that, how can we even reliably determine *which* actions go for or against the general happiness? In his typical style, Mill argues that certain moral rules—like those outlawing theft, deceit, and murder—are, first, so essential to social well-being that they take on a kind of "transcendant expediency," which almost always trumps the expediency of the moment; and second, so all-encompassing as to do *all* the work of guiding our behavior: the time needed "for calculating and weighing the effects of any line of conduct on the general happiness" has been "the whole past duration of the human species"; since time immemorial, societies "have been learning by experience the tendencies of actions," and it is on this age-old experience that "all the prudence, as well as all the morality of life, is dependent." Thus, Mill's "creed" not only offers the proper moral gravitas and desired practical certainty, but also puts us into intimate contact with the whole moral development of the human race. The "Nautical Almanack" of Utility is the work of all ages; and while it equips us, as moral "sailors," to "go out upon the sea of life with [our] minds made up on the common questions of right and wrong," it also has been, and continues to be, subject to "indefinite improvement."[21]

20. Ibid., 206–207.
21. Ibid., 223–225.

In chapter 3, Mill contends that the Utility Principle is an irreducibly natural, nonartificial (albeit acquired) characteristic of our social-moral psychology. To a cultivated individual, an action's tendency to affect the general happiness is "a thing naturally and necessarily to be attended to, like any of the physical conditions of our existence." The implication here is that, unlike every other moral standard, the Utility Principle does not, or will not, "yield by degrees to the dissolving force of analysis."[22] Other moral dogmas collapse under scrutiny and reveal themselves to be fake or implanted. But not Utility.

And in chapter 5, Mill argues that "general utility"[23] lies at the heart of all our enduring moral judgments, including their limitations, and most evidently with respect to resolving disputes between them. Henry Sidgwick develops this point in *The Methods of Ethics*, where he argues that the Utility Principle provides us with the most all-inclusive and intuitively satisfying account of our most widely shared, commonsense moral norms: "It may be shown, I think, that the Utilitarian estimate of consequences not only supports broadly the current moral rules, but also sustains their generally received limitations and qualifications"; and it "may be shown further, that it not only supports the generally received view of the relative importance of different duties, but is also naturally called in as arbiter, where rules commonly regarded as coordinate come into conflict."[24] Fittingly, Sidgwick cites Mill's words: "Social utility alone can decide the preference" between "conflicting principles of justice."[25]

I skipped chapter 4 because it contains Mill's most famous (or infamous) defense of the Utility Principle, his so-called "proof." It reads as follows:

> The only proof capable of being given that an object is visible, is that people actually see it. The only proof that a sound is audible, is that people hear it: and so of the other sources of our experience. In like manner, I apprehend, the sole evidence it is possible to produce that anything is desirable, is that people do actually desire it. If the end which the utilitarian doctrine proposes to itself were not, in theory and in practice, acknowledged to be an end, nothing could ever convince any person that it was so. No reason can be given why the general

22. Ibid., 230, 232.
23. Ibid., 250.
24. Sidgwick, *Methods of Ethics*, 425–426.
25. Mill, *Utilitarianism*, 254. Justice is a species of morality for Mill. We will return to this later.

happiness is desirable, except that each person, so far as he believes it to be attainable, desires his own happiness. This, however, being a fact, we have not only all the proof which the case admits of, but all which it is possible to require, that happiness is a good: that each person's happiness is a good to that person, and the general happiness, therefore, a good to the aggregate of all persons.[26]

This passage has been subject to brutal, relentless criticism. In fact, this passage almost singlehandedly ruined Mill's reputation as a careful, serious thinker. Traditionally, Mill is charged with two philosophical crimes: first, that he infers what is desirable, or *worthy* of desire, from what is empirically desired, which looks to be a blatant "is-ought" fallacy; and second, that he infers what is desirable to the aggregate of all individuals from what is desirable to each individual, which stumbles over several logical fallacies, including the fallacies of composition, division, and irrelevancy.[27]

There are two responses. First, the literature has made a mountain out of a molehill: this passage is just *not* that important to Mill; it reads like a half-baked aside, and it neither exhausts nor even begins to comprehend Mill's defense of the Utility Principle. Indeed, upon being encouraged by his editor to clarify his meaning (lest he be misunderstood in the very ways he has been misunderstood), Mill acknowledged the need for greater clarity, but then politely declined anyway, citing his busy schedule, which barely hid his basic lack of interest in refining his analysis.[28] And second, there is a perfectly reasonable and straightforward way to interpret Mill's "proof" once we drop the false notion that Mill is attempting an *actual* proof. Countless scholars have tried to reconstruct the formal steps of Mill's "proof," struggling to rescue him from his own absurdity.[29] But this is just tilting at windmills: Mill's "proof" is *not* a proof; formal logic is precisely what his "proof" is *not* meant to succeed at.[30]

To begin, the notion that Mill falls into an "is-ought" fallacy is flatly mistaken. As I argued last chapter, Mill is saying that desire is the only

26. Ibid., 234.

27. See Seth, "Alleged Fallacies in Mill's 'Utilitarianism,'" 469–485.

28. See Mill, "To Theodor Gomperz," 1391, *CW* 16.

29. For instance, see West, "Mill's Proof of the Principle of Utility," 174–183; and Brink, *Mill's Progressive Principles*, 118–125.

30. Scholars insist on taking the word "proof" literally: Mill "warned us prior to the 'proof' that we really can't prove fundamental claims about what is desirable as an end. On the other hand, he clearly gives it a try" (Fumerton, "Mill's Epistemology," 205). But *no*, he does *not*.

evidence we have for what is desirable. What he then argues is that desires "prove" desirability insofar as certain objects or ideals are desired *because* they are desirable. The "ought" is not derived from an "is"; rather, the "is" *is* an "ought." The mind's eye of the well-developed person sees the higher pleasures as not merely attractive but also desirable in the same way that our eyes perceive the tangible, concrete facts of nature. Mill's empiricism is large, but steady.

The steeper climb, though, has been to explain Mill's transition from individual to aggregate desirability, and what significance this would have for the individual even if it were plausible. But, first, recall that, for Mill, there is no possible *proof* when it comes to the foundation of morality. Chapter 4 is titled "Of What Sort of Proof the Principle of Utility Is Susceptible"—that is, not a proof at all, but something that may at least look or feel more like a proof than the potentially persuasive, but still merely pregnant, observations above. And, in a letter, Mill speaks for himself as follows: "When I said that the general happiness is a good to the aggregate of all persons I did not mean that every human being's happiness is a good to every other human being; though I think, in a good state of society & education it would be so. I merely meant in this particular sentence to argue that since A's happiness is a good, B's a good, C's a good, &c., the sum of all these goods must be a good."[31] With this clarification, Mill's "proof" becomes something of a truism. His argument, I think, is as simple as this: happiness is all that matters (all that is good) to each person; thus, happiness is all that matters to all persons taken together; therefore, *when reasoning morally* (that is, when duly minding what matters to persons in general), the only thing to consider is how we might affect the general happiness. Indeed, the critical transition to chapter 4 from the oft-ignored chapter 3 tells the same story: as Mill argues in chapter 3, our natural (*genuine*) moral feelings are associated with the general good; and so, if happiness is our *only* good, as Mill claims in chapter 4, then, ipso facto, our natural sense of morality is bound up with the general happiness alone. Watertight or not, the key point is that Mill's argument is far from illogical and can be *framed* in formal steps—hence the title of chapter 4.

It might be tempting to dismiss Mill's considerations in favor of Utility as flimsy or insufficient. However, there are two replies: one brief excuse and one lengthy addendum. First, Mill is not defending a new idea here but reinforcing a general line of thought that had already been

31. Mill, "To Henry Jones," 1414, *CW* 16.

advanced and developed in various directions by numerous thinkers, from Hutcheson to Hume to Helvétius. *Utilitarianism* is, at core, a popular commentary on the ongoing conflict between the Utilitarians and their critics; it is not meant to be a painstaking treatise. But, second, Mill's corpus offers another, deeper defense of the Utility Principle, one that mirrors his analysis of the higher pleasures. As I argued last chapter, Mill derives the higher pleasures from the attractions of the mind's eye: we take pleasure in the thought of certain ends for supra-hedonic reasons. I called this his hedonic value-sense theory. Similarly, Mill derives his moral criterion from the attractions or, more often, the repulsions of the mind's eye: we take pleasure or pain in the thought of certain ends for distinctively *moral* reasons. This is his hedonic *moral*-sense theory. For Mill, our moral duties are a distinct, and the most basic, subset of the higher pleasures of sociality: we recognize *some* other-regarding ends not only as desirable but also, and more pressingly, as obligatory.

Utilitarian Feelings

Some scholars have argued that the Utility Principle, as presented in *Utilitarianism*, is not *really* Mill's moral criterion. These revisionist scholars focus on the fifth chapter of *Utilitarianism*, where Mill allegedly develops a *sanction-based* moral standard. For these scholars, Mill's final view is that actions are obliged or proscribed only insofar as punishment, whether internal (e.g., guilt) or external (e.g., a tax), would be warranted pro tanto for a failure to comply.[32] In essence, they depict Mill's moral standard as a modified version of Bentham's theory of sanctions: "each individual ought to perform" or "abstain from" whatever tends to be "beneficial" or "pernicious" to "the community"; but "it is not every such act that the legislator ought to compel him to perform" or "abstain from."[33] For Bentham, punishment is justified to enforce *some* obligations. But, for the "Sanction" Mill, justified punishment actually *defines* right and wrong: to be immoral *is* to warrant punishment. Where there is no justified punishment there is no morality, just a nonmoral sphere of activity.

This interpretation is attractive given its promise to unite the moral theory of *Utilitarianism* to the liberal theory of *On Liberty*: if *only* punishable offenses are immoral, then *only* illiberal actions, as defined by the

---

32. For instance, see Lyons, *Rights, Welfare, and Mill's Moral Theory*, 47–65; and Brown, "Mill's Moral Theory," 19–34. For an overview of the argument, see Eggleston, "Mill's Moral Standard," 369–370; and Brink, *Mill's Progressive Principles*, 98–103.

33. Bentham, *Principles of Morals and Legislation*, 144.

Harm Principle, run afoul of Mill's moral theory. However, it is also unattractive in that it "appears to provide the *wrong sort of reason* for thinking an action wrong." As David Brink writes,

> Sanction utilitarianism . . . makes the wrongness of an act depend upon the appropriateness of sanctioning it. But this inverts what many would regard as the usual dependency between wrongness and sanction. Many think that sanctions are appropriate for wrong acts because they are wrong. This requires grounding their wrongness in some independent account; it is not the suitability for sanction that makes an act wrong. Perhaps one ought to sanction wrong acts, but it doesn't seem that they are wrong because one ought to sanction them.[34]

However, whether attractive or not, the basic problem with this interpretation is that it simply misconstrues Mill. Indeed, in the relevant passages from chapter 5 of *Utilitarianism*, Mill is *not* expressing a distinct moral standard but examining our moral sentiments *in defense of* the Utility Principle. The overarching theme of that chapter is the relationship between Utilitarianism and the concept and value of *justice*. An allegation often made against Utilitarians was (and is) that they pay too little attention to the felt absolutism of morality, especially as it pertains to what we justly owe to one another. If our morals are beholden to the general happiness, then we might infer that *all* morals are merely provisional—theft, deceit, or murder is immoral *unless* it best serves the general happiness to steal, lie, or kill. This apparent call to expediency rubs many people the wrong way, for there is a strong tendency to experience our profoundest morals as fixed, immutable principles. In response, Mill wants to show that *his* Utilitarian "creed" not only allows for but, in fact, *demands* just this sort of moral sensibility and resolve. I will address Mill's efforts later on; first, I need to develop his contention that our felt morality is nothing if not a confirmation of the Utility Principle.

At the heart of Mill's defense of the Utility Principle is a hedonic moral-sense theory. Mill accounts for our moral ideas and beliefs by appealing to the distinctive feelings or sentiments that certain actions inspire or provoke. Naturally, Mill's hedonic moral-sense theory is at odds with moral rationalism: reason itself is at a loss to generate moral ideas and beliefs; what is needed (as well) is a nonrational, sensitive moral faculty. Also verboten is any appeal to moral intuitionism: Mill's empirical attitude opposes all claims to instinctual, innate, non-inferential insight into the

34. Brink, *Mill's Progressive Principles*, 106–107.

moral realm—such claims are not only epistemologically vapid but also practically dangerous. And yet, to be a hedonic moral-sense theorist—i.e., to be a moral-sense theorist, but of a strictly non-intuitional, sentimental bent—is not yet to be a Utilitarian. In this section, I retrace Mill's progression from our hedonic sense of morality to the Utility Principle and then proceed to draw the link between his moral analysis and his hedonic value-sense theory from the previous chapter.

MILL'S MORAL SENSE

In his work *An Inquiry into the Original of Our Ideas of Beauty and Virtue*, Francis Hutcheson depicts what he calls a "moral sense," which captures the main thrust of Mill's position: "We are not to imagine, that this moral sense, more than the other senses, supposes any innate ideas, knowledge, or practical proposition: we mean by it only a determination of our minds to receive amiable or disagreeable ideas of actions, when they occur to our observation, antecedent to any opinions of advantage or loss to redound to ourselves from them."[35] The argument that follows is that Mill develops and defends what becomes the Utility Principle on similar grounds; namely, on the testimony of the mind's eye, which, in this case, refers to our moral faculty, or our sentimental "sense" of morality.

This comparison to Hutcheson might furrow some brows, for Mill heaps criticism on those he labels "moral sense" theorists. However, the typical meaning Mill attaches to this label does not apply to the moral sense à la Hutcheson. In fact, as we will see, the moral sense à la Hutcheson is an idea that Mill not only gloms onto but also explicitly refers to as a moral sense. Rather, whenever Mill is critiquing the "moral sense" theorists, he is just talking about the Intuitionists. When on the attack, Mill equates the "theory of the moral sense" to the theory "of moral instincts—or of eternal and immutable morality—or of intuitive principles of morality."[36] Indeed, like Hutcheson, Mill wants to disentangle the *true* moral sense from the misbegotten doctrine of intuitive, inborn, inscrutable moral knowledge.

Neither should we be dissuaded by Mill's observation that the moral standard and the moral sentiments form discrete realms of inquiry: "It is one question what rule we *ought* to obey, and why; another question how our feelings of approbation and disapprobation *actually* originate. The former is the fundamental question of practical morals; the latter is a

---

35. Hutcheson, *Inquiry into the Original of Our Ideas of Beauty and Virtue*, 100.
36. Mill, "Sedgwick's Discourse," 51, *CW* 10.

problem in mental philosophy." To say that they are discrete questions is *not* to say that they cannot, or ought not, be joined together: "David Hume seems to have combined the recognition of utility as the standard or test of morality, with the belief of a moral sense, independent of association."[37] Mill makes a similar connection, remarking in a letter that his forthcoming *Utilitarianism*—which, of course, is chiefly concerned with elucidating and defending the Utility Principle—presents "a theory of our moral feelings."[38] As we saw last section, Mill considers the question of the moral criterion from a variety of angles; but he consistently returns to the moral sentiments as the most perceptive, empirical lens through which to analyze the nature of morality. We have already seen Mill derive desirability from our desirous feelings; now, Mill seeks to derive morality from our moral feelings.

And neither should we be concerned about Mill's distinction between the moral and the sensitive faculties: "Our moral faculty, according to all those of its interpreters who are entitled to the name of thinkers, supplies us only with the general principles of moral judgments; it is a branch of our reason, not of our sensitive faculty; and must be looked to for the abstract doctrines of morality, not for perception of it in the concrete." Again, the contrast drawn here is not meant to deny the moral faculty a sensitivity to moral experience. Instead, it is meant to deny us "recourse to the popular theory of a natural faculty, a sense or instinct, informing us of right and wrong." The mind's eye makes observations to which are adjoined mental feelings. However, rather than fashioning these feelings as "*à priori* principles," the thinking moralist should engage in a searching moral scrutiny. Rationality demands that we discern "the root of all morality," which will prompt us to oppose some sentiments as *falsely* moral, and to promote other sentiments as *truly* moral, even if they are not yet widely shared.[39]

MILL'S MORAL SENTIMENTALISM

Mill begins his sentimentalist account of the Utilitarian "creed" with what he takes to be a truism: "It is a fact in human nature, that we have moral judgments and moral feelings." All moral theorists agree that we engage in moral evaluation: "We judge certain actions and dispositions right, others

37. Mill, "Blakey's History of Moral Science," 26–27, *CW* 10.
38. Mill, "To William George Ward," 650, *CW* 15.
39. Mill, *Utilitarianism*, 206.

wrong." And they all agree that what we apprehend as moral or immoral has a pleasant or painful effect on our conscience: "We have also feelings of displeasure—feelings of dislike and aversion to the latter," which "do not exactly resemble any other of our feelings of pain or pleasure." What moral theorists disagree about, though, is the *source* of our "moral judgments and moral feelings." Namely, it is an undeniable fact that we make moral judgments to which are attached moral sentiments: "Such are the phenomena. Concerning their reality there is no dispute."[40] However, what are we to make of these phenomena? What do they tell us about the nature of morality?

Mill divides all salient replies into two schools of thought. Some account for our moral experience by relying on intuitive, a priori insights into the nature of *the right*. For these moralists, the "distinction between right and wrong is an ultimate and inexplicable fact," such that "the pleasures and pains, the desires and aversions, consequent upon this perception, are all ultimate facts in our nature; as much so as the pleasures and pains, or the desires and aversions, of which sweet or bitter tastes, pleasing or grating sounds, are the object." Mill calls this "the theory of the moral sense." Conversely, others account for our moral experience a posteriori in terms of *the good*. For these moralists, the "distinction between moral and immoral acts is not a peculiar and inscrutable property in the acts themselves," but "flows from the ordinary properties of those actions," namely, "the influence of those actions, and of the dispositions from which they emanate, upon human happiness." This is called "the theory of Utility."[41] The partisans of the moral sense maintain that our moral duties "are evident *a priori*, requiring nothing to command assent, except that the meaning of the terms be understood,"[42] whereas Mill and his fellow Utilitarians contend that our moral judgments and corresponding feelings must be (and *can be*) related back to the general happiness.

But this begs the question: *why* Utility? Again, we begin with Mill's empiricism: as with our knowledge of desirability, our knowledge of morality must be gained via experience or observation; it must be verified by evidence gathered by "our intellects and our bodily senses."[43] We have seen what our desires can tell us about the nature of the good life. Now, what can our morals tell us about the nature of the righteous life? Mill contends that morality arises for us at the point where our sentiments of

40. Mill, "Sedgwick's Discourse," 50–51.
41. Ibid., 51.
42. Mill, *Utilitarianism*, 206.
43. Mill, "Sedgwick's Discourse," 51.

"*ought* and *should*" (which pertain, all things equal, to all desirable ends) "grow into *must.*" Specifically, while our "social feelings" denote the intrinsic value of doing good for, or well by, others, our distinctively "*moral* feelings" introduce the necessity of satisfying a certain *range* of these ends.[44] Henceforth, Mill's moral theory is an attempt to explain when and why the feeling of sociality transforms into the "feeling of duty or obligation." Why are "only some, not all" "beneficial acts" regarded by the mind's eye "as duties," as things we are "bound to do"?[45]

Well, first, what differentiates the feeling of *must* from the feeling of *ought* or *should*? According to Mill, the former is defined by a particularly intense "strength," "gravity," or "pungency,"[46] so much more intense, in fact, than other, less forceful feelings "that the difference in degree" becomes "a real difference in kind," and "assumes that character of absoluteness" that characterizes morality.[47] When self-directed, our moral sentiments cause us to experience such pain in the thought of a prospective action that we "recoil from the very thought of committing the act."[48] Or, having done the act out of weakness or temptation, our moral feeling morphs into that of a "condemning conscience."[49] When other-directed, our moral sentiments exhort us to mete out penalties: "No case can be pointed out in which we consider anything as a duty, and any act or omission as immoral or wrong, without regarding the person who commits the wrong and violates the duty as a fit object of punishment." And even when we decline to inflict punishment on a wrongdoer for reasons of either compassion or expediency, our moral judgment still makes us "feel indignant with him, that is, it would give us pleasure that he should suffer for his misconduct."[50] Thus, the special intensity of the feeling, made manifest by the retributive impulse, is, for Mill, what distinguishes social morality from mere sociality, along with our everyday sense of mere prudence or usefulness:

> We do not call anything wrong, unless we mean to imply that a person ought to be punished in some way or other for doing it; if not by law, by the opinion of his fellow creatures; if not by opinion, by the reproaches of his own conscience. This seems the real turning point of the distinction between morality and simple expediency. It is a part of the notion

44. Mill, *Utilitarianism*, 230–231, 251.
45. Mill, "James Mill's *Analysis of the Phenomena of the Human Mind,*" 241, *CW* 31.
46. Ibid.
47. Mill, *Utilitarianism*, 251.
48. Mill, "Remarks on Bentham's Philosophy," 12. Mill writes, "recoils."
49. Mill, "To William George Ward," 650.
50. Mill, "James Mill's *Analysis of the Phenomena of the Human Mind,*" 241–242.

of Duty in every one of its forms, that a person may rightfully be compelled to fulfil it. Duty is a thing which may be *exacted* from a person, as one exacts a debt. Unless we think that it might be exacted from him, we do not call it his duty. Reasons of prudence, or the interest of other people, may militate against actually exacting it; but the person himself, it is clearly understood, would not be entitled to complain. There are other things, on the contrary, which we wish that people should do, which we like or admire them for doing, perhaps dislike or despise them for not doing, but yet admit that they are not bound to do; it is not a case of moral obligation; we do not blame them, that is, we do not think that they are proper objects of punishment.[51]

The question then becomes: which actions do these felt evaluations map onto? Mill argues that our moral feelings—if, indeed, they *are* moral feelings, and not the arbitrary elevation of our "partialities, passions, and prejudices"[52]—are typified by the sense that a class of action is *harmful*, either in principle or in practice, to the community; they are captured by "the natural feeling of retaliation or vengeance, rendered by intellect and sympathy applicable to those injuries, that is, to those hurts, which wound us through, or in common with, society at large."[53] Our moral sentiments are "grounded" on the general interest: "I feel conscious that if I violate certain laws, other people must necessarily or naturally desire that I should be punished for the violation. I also feel that I should desire them to be punished if they violated the same law towards me."[54] The distinctively *moral* feeling that an individual should be punished can be traced to an "enlarged sympathy" for our "community of interest," or to what Mill calls an "intelligent self-interest," that is, to the "instinct" of "self-defence," "widened so as to include all persons."[55] Morality is *defensive*: we feel moral censure for behavior that seems *injurious* to the general interest, and we feel moral praise for behavior that seems to *preserve* the general interest *from* injury. To be moral is "to abstain from whatever is manifestly pernicious to society," which includes inactions that neglect "the urgency of [a] need."[56] In sum, our moral feelings are, to borrow a phrase, Hippocratic: *do no harm*.

51. Mill, *Utilitarianism*, 246.
52. Mill, "Bentham," 107.
53. Mill, *Utilitarianism*, 249. Mill is referring here to justice as a subset of morality.
54. Mill, "To William George Ward," 649–650.
55. Mill, *Utilitarianism*, 248, 250. See also Tocqueville, *Democracy in America*, vol. 2, §2, chap. 8.
56. Mill, *Utilitarianism*, 220.

This connection between our truly *moral* feelings and the general interest can be exposed by asking others to justify their moral judgments. Again, to claim that we are morally obliged to do or refrain from doing one thing or another is to beg the question *"Why?"* Any answer, then, that makes an intelligible case for the blameworthiness of an action will ultimately appeal to the general interest. As an example, Mill picks the highest-hanging fruit: "All [Kant] shows is that the *consequences*" of violating the categorical imperative "would be such as no one would choose to incur." Mill's point holds even when the general interest is the farthest thing from our mind: "a person whose resentment is really a moral feeling, that is, who considers whether an act is blameable before he allows himself to resent it—such a person, though he may not say expressly to himself that he is standing up for the interest of society, certainly does feel that he is asserting a rule which is for the benefit of others as well as his own." Whenever we have "suffered pain," we are likely to resent the pain, often "indiscriminately"; we might even seek revenge; but we experience our antipathy as a *moral* antipathy (as a feeling that the offender has crossed an objectively forbidden boundary) only insofar as we think the pain inflicted breaks "a rule which all rational beings might adopt *with benefit to their collective interests.*"[57] Our moral sentiments can be, and often are, self-referential expressions of what the general interest calls for.

Now, those with a healthy moral intuition might be unsettled or skeptical at this point, for it might appear that Mill is reducing the entirety of our moral experience to the customs or conventions that make society jive and thrive. And indeed, as the foregoing analysis suggests, this Humean strain is an important aspect of Mill's thinking. However, as the foregoing analysis *also* indicates, Mill discerns a critical moral correspondence between what self-regard advises and what empathy entreats. At the deepest level, what the mind's eye sees as moral is a reciprocity between persons: "In the golden rule of Jesus of Nazareth, we read the complete spirit of the ethics of utility. To do as one would be done by, and to love one's neighbour as oneself, constitute the ideal perfection of utilitarian morality."[58] And what this basic degree of sociality demands is a virtuous regard for the interests that each shares with others, that is, a virtuous regard for the general interest. Thus, even despots, whose particular interests may often conflict

---

57. Ibid., 207, 249. Mill is referring above to Kant's categorical imperative, translated by Mill as, "So act, that the rule on which thou actest would admit of being adopted as a law by all rational beings" (ibid., 207).

58. Ibid., 218.

with the public good, still have a moral reason to refrain from societal harm and, as Mill will argue, perhaps even to relinquish their power.

But, now, those with a strong Utilitarian sensibility might be worried that this analysis, with its talk of the mind's eye "seeing" things, imputes to Mill an unwelcome "moral sense" understanding of morality. And yet, again, Mill does not reject the idea that we have a moral sense. Rather, he simply denies, first, that our moral sense is inscrutable: its insights can be explained in terms of Utility. Second, that our moral sense is innate: "The doctrine of Locke, that we have no *innate* moral sense, [was] perverted into the doctrine that we have no moral sense at all."[59] Indeed, Mill argues that our "sense" of morality, while not inborn, is fully natural and naturally acquired: "Like [our] other acquired capacities," the "moral faculty, if not a part of our nature, is a natural outgrowth from it; capable, like them, in a certain small degree, of springing up spontaneously; and susceptible of being brought by cultivation to a high degree of development."[60] And third, that our moral sense is infallible: for even "the most senseless and pernicious feelings can as easily be raised to the utmost intensity by inculcation, as hemlock and thistles could be reared to luxuriant growth by sowing them instead of wheat."[61] This saddles Mill with the task of defending Utilitarianism by demonstrating how *only* those moral sentiments that are linked to the general interest are able to survive examination. And what would be the alternative anyway? Either a flat sentimentalism, where we give "no reason for the sentiment, but set up the sentiment as its own reason";[62] or, what is undoubtedly far worse, the glorification of our partialities, passions, or prejudices.

All Mill does next is replace "interest" with "happiness." Ultimately, we are interested in happiness alone. This brings us back to the fourth chapter of *Utilitarianism*, where Mill declares that we desire nothing but happiness. Many scholars, reading Mill as a hedonist or the like, regard this claim as quite dubious. However, as I argued last chapter, Mill's conception of happiness departs from Bentham's hedonism by focusing not on pleasure as such, but on a life lived partly for the sake of pleasure, but primarily for the sake of the higher, supra-hedonic pleasures. Happily, Mill's moral theory bears all the markings of this dramatic shift: he evaluates actions not by their hedonic effects per se, but by their relationship to the

59. Mill, "Coleridge," 144, *CW* 10.
60. Mill, *Utilitarianism*, 230.
61. Mill, "Whewell on Moral Philosophy," 179, *CW* 10.
62. Mill, *Autobiography*, 67, *CW* 1.

interests that undergird the Aristotelian ends of "life" and "the good life,"[63] that is, for Mill, "the general and obvious interests of society" and "the permanent interests of man as a progressive being."[64] Thus, in chapter 4, all Mill is really saying is that all that we desire are attractive ends—attractive for either the pleasure they promise or the supra-hedonic quality they project. The reason Mill feels the need to assert what could seem like a truism is that the anti-Utilitarian moralists had stubbornly maintained that certain ideals (like virtue) can, ought, and must be disinterestedly pursued, without concern on the individual's part for what serves their own interests. Of course, Mill wholeheartedly agrees; and yet, as we saw last chapter, he believes that this kind of disinterested interest in virtue depends on the mind's eye taking pleasure in the ideal of virtuous activity. Virtue for its own sake is desired only by those who recognize its intrinsic value—by those who appreciate that virtue is integral to happiness.

After all that, let us return to the Utility Principle, which, again, says that "actions are right in proportion as they tend to promote happiness, wrong as they tend to produce the reverse of happiness." What should be more apparent by now is that Mill is *summarizing*, as the conclusion to an inductive argument, what makes *morally salient* actions either good or bad; he is not promulgating a moral law that stamps all actions whatever. Indeed, the very language of the Utility Principle invites a similar analysis.

The Utility Principle contains two key terms. One is "tend." In saying that an action has a *tendency*, Mill's basic idea is that while all actions have innumerable effects that are contingent, or "accidental," other effects are their "natural result, according to the known laws of the universe." By and large, these natural consequences are catalogued in "the accumulated wisdom of all former ages, embodied in traditional aphorisms," upon which "the whole course of human life is founded." In a healthy society, we learn as children "in what manner [our] actions may affect the interests of other persons."[65] Occasionally, a prospective action will have natural, or "traceable," implications that do not appear to be accounted for in our normal, historical experience, or that may even marshal against our default assumptions. This will make our moral discernment more complex. But, regardless, the point is that when we are talking about morality we are talking about the tendencies of actions, that is, the general repercussions that elicit the approbation or disapprobation of others: "in proportion as

63. Aristotle, *Politics*, I.2.
64. Mill, *On Liberty*, 221, 224.
65. Mill, "Sedgwick's Discourse," 59, 63, 66.

mankind are aware of the tendencies of actions to produce happiness or misery, they will like and commend the first, abhor and reprobate the second."[66] The other key term is "in proportion." The weightier the tendency, the greater the corresponding moral praise or blame for acting or forbearing accordingly.

Together, these terms allow us to read the Utility Principle as a simple abstract of the story above: a preponderance of actions neither favor nor oppose the general happiness to any appreciable extent; but there exist *some* actions (and inactions) the tendencies of which *are* notably tied to the general happiness one way or the other. The failure to act in accordance with what the general happiness requires, or strongly recommends, naturally triggers our retaliatory impulse: "when moralized by the social feeling, it only acts in the directions conformable to the general good."[67] To vindicate a moral judgment in light of the Utility Principle is to delineate how an individual's activity (or inactivity) is naturally opposed to the commonweal. To uncover what this entails for Mill in the way of concrete morals, we first have to study his concept of moral impartiality.

MILL'S ART OF LIFE

When we combine the last chapter's account of the higher pleasures with this chapter's account of morality, we find ourselves mapping out the "departments" of what Mill refers to as "the Art of Life," which is developed in *A System of Logic* and elsewhere, and which can be concisely summarized as follows:

> Mill's supreme principle of teleology or practical reason is [Utility].
> [Utility] evaluates the desirability of objects of desire and evaluates
> *rules of practice* based on the desirability or value of their objects.
> [Utility] is the foundation for each of morality, prudence, [sympathy,]
> and aesthetics and it evaluates these, and other, rules of practice solely
> in terms of the resultant happiness for all sentient beings.[68]

And as we have seen, the "desirability or value" of these objects is derived from Mill's hedonic value- and moral-sense theories. Just as the bodily

66. Mill, "Whewell on Moral Philosophy," 181, 184.

67. Mill, *Utilitarianism*, 249.

68. Fletcher, "Mill's Art of Life," 303. I substituted "Utility" for Fletcher's "principle of utility." As I intimated in the chapter introduction, we immediately fall into confusion by eliding the distinction between Utility as the "supreme principle of teleology" and the Utility Principle as the standard of morality.

senses take in the naturalistic properties of the physical, material world, the mind's eye perceives the normative features of what is valuable or moral in the way of goods, actions, motives, and characters. When these objects come before the mind's eye, they tend to spark reactions upon which certain feelings or sentiments supervene. And on these grounds, we are prompted to formulate propositions that "enjoin or recommend" various actions and rules of action. An artistic proposition does not refer to what "*is*, or *will be*," that is, in "the course of nature" (which is the mark of a *scientific* proposition), but instead pertains to what "*ought or should be.*"[69]

The key detail, though, is that these reactions or judgments, and their corresponding feelings or sentiments, can be distinguished by type: "Every human action has three aspects: its *moral* aspect, or that of its *right* and *wrong*; its *æsthetic* aspect, or that of its *beauty*; its *sympathetic* aspect, or that of its *loveableness*. The first addresses itself to our reason and conscience; the second to our imagination; the third to our human fellow-feeling. According to the first, we approve or disapprove; according to the second, we admire or despise; according to the third, we love, pity, or dislike."[70] In *A System of Logic*, Mill lists "Morality, Prudence or Policy, and Æsthetics; the Right, the Expedient, and the Beautiful or Noble, in human conduct and works";[71] and in *Utilitarianism*, Mill "marks off" morality from the "provinces" of "Expediency and Worthiness."[72] Here, Mill omits the "*sympathetic*" (which otherwise pervades his corpus) and notes "the Expedient," which plays a subsidiary role in his thought; for what is prudent or politic depends on the circumstances.

Fundamental to Mill's break with Bentham is that Mill thinks we are able to make objective and intelligible "ought" statements that have nothing to do with morality. For Bentham, an "ought" statement is meaningful only if it refers to what tends for or against the general happiness: "Of an action that is conformable to the principle of utility, one may always say either that it is one that ought to be done, or at least that it is not one that ought not to be done. . . . When thus interpreted, the words *ought*, and *right* and *wrong*, and others of that stamp, have a meaning: when otherwise, they have none."[73] Thus, Bentham regards all nonmoral uses of "ought" as fictions, rooted in mere partiality, passion, or prejudice. But,

69. Mill, *System of Logic*, 943, 948–949, *CW* 8.
70. Mill, "Bentham," 112.
71. Mill, *System of Logic*, 949.
72. Mill, *Utilitarianism*, 246–247.
73. Bentham, *Principles of Morals and Legislation*, 2.

for Mill, Bentham's view is one-sided. While we must not flout the *"moral"* in favor of the *"œsthetic"* or the *"sympathetic"* (as Romantics are ever wont to do), we also should not fall into Bentham's error—indeed, the error of "moralists in general"—of ignoring the latter two in favor of the former: "This is pre-eminently the case with Bentham: he both wrote and felt as if the moral standard ought not only to be paramount (which it ought), but to be alone; as if it ought to be the sole master of all our actions, and even of all our sentiments; as if either to admire or like, or despise or dislike a person for any action which neither does good nor harm, or which does not do a good or a harm proportioned to the sentiment entertained, were an injustice and a prejudice." While morality is, as Mill says, "paramount," meaning that it has first priority, he refuses Bentham's blinkered attempt to "sink" all of life into morality.[74]

Much has been written on whether we ought to interpret Mill as a cognitivist or instead as a noncognitivist, and much of this scholarship has focused on the passages surrounding and concerning his Art of Life. Briefly, cognitivism is the metaethical view that ethical sentences (like "ought" statements) are *truth-apt*: they are propositions about the world that are either *true* or *false* as a matter of objective fact. To a cognitivist, a sentence like "Murder is wrong" is as truth-apt as a sentence like "Snow is white" or "Cake is healthy," in that *all* such sentences are thought to represent either *valid* or *invalid* descriptions of reality. Noncognitivists deny this; they argue that ethical sentences are *not* truth-apt. When a non-cognitivist hears someone say "Murder is wrong," it is not regarded as a proposition about the world; instead, the sentence is, in effect, translated to mean, for example, "I hate murder! Murder, boo!" (*emotivism*) or "Do not murder! Stop murdering!" (*prescriptivism*).[75]

The cognitivist/noncognitivist debate is a book unto itself, and I cannot dive into its waters at present. Rather, my only concern here is to bold and underline what I have been implicitly arguing throughout; namely, that Mill is a cognitivist. Mill's artistic propositions are generated by his hedonic value- and moral-sense theories, by which the mind's eye identifies *truly* valuable qualities and *truly* moral properties, and by which we thus develop *truth-apt* beliefs and judgments about what we should/must do or refrain from doing. Again, the *evidence* of our desires and morals is meant to *substantiate* Mill's propositions apropos the good and the right;

74. Mill, "Bentham," 113.

75. See Ayer, *Language, Truth, and Logic*, 105–109; and Carnap, *Philosophy and Logical Syntax*, 22–26.

and indeed, it is one of Mill's particular points of emphasis to challenge Bentham's noncognitivism with respect to nonmoral "ought" statements.

In fact, Mill's attitude toward Bentham appears to be that he never outgrew the sophomoric sensibility that asks *why* incessantly; that he never really recognized or appreciated the possibility that truth might often be a function not of rationality and correspondence to the material, but of imagination and responsiveness to the meaningful. As Mill wrote to Carlyle, referring to the limitations of logic in ascertaining the whole truth: "I believe in spectacles, but I think eyes necessary too."[76] Naturally, the imaginative apprehension of meaning cannot promise the certainty of dispassionate, logical investigation; but, nonetheless, the former involves a profound faith without which we definitely cannot live well, and without which we sometimes cannot live at all—a lesson learned by Mill at age twenty.

Now, a challenging inquiry arises here: What is the source or foundation of these values or morals? What justification do we have for assuming a correlation between what we subjectively *experience* and what is objectively *true*? However, Mill is just not exercised by such questions, and here is why. Suppose an emissary from "objective" reality arrives to inform us as to the "true" nature of values or morals: on what basis should we *believe* anything this envoi says? Their testimony will either *succeed* or *fail* in striking a chord with our humanity. But if the latter, then why pay attention? Because the messenger is omniscient and omnibenevolent? God, for all intents and purposes? But how can we distinguish between omnibenevolence and omni*malevolence* except via our human faculties? As Mill indicates in his commentary on Robert Blakey's theological voluntarism, our subjective appraisal of the good and the right is *precisely* what would allow us to differentiate God from the Devil:

> The scriptures, as Mr. Blakey himself says elsewhere, do not enter into speculative questions; they tell us *what* to do, not *why*. But do they not say perpetually, God is good, God is just, God is righteous, God is holy? And are we to understand by these affirmations nothing at all, but the identical and unmeaning proposition God is himself, or a proposition which has so little to do with morality as this, God is powerful? Has God in short no moral attributes? no attributes but those which the devil is conceived to possess in a smaller degree? and no title to our obedience but such as the devil would have, if there were a devil, and the universe were without God? ... Mr. Blakey insists much upon the

76. Mill, "To Thomas Carlyle," 347, *CW* 12.

sublimity of the scriptures, and the perfection of scripture morality; considerations which tell strongly against his own doctrine; for if we are capable of recognising excellence in the commands of the Omnipotent, they must possess excellence independently of his command.[77]

Needless to say, Mill's response to Blakey does not ultimately satisfy the deep desire for *proof*—the demand for *absolute* knowledge. The certainty one gets from mathematics, and the provisional certainty one gets from the scientific method, is not to be found in the study of human values or morals; Mill is a man of immanence and Aristotelian observation, not a man of transcendence and Platonic heavens.[78] Nonetheless, the point is that *objective* truth cannot be divorced from our *subjective* understanding: "All trust in a Revelation presupposes a conviction that God's attributes are the same, in all but degree, with the best human attributes."[79]

And yet, the acceptance of Mill as a cognitivist has been derailed and long delayed by what Mill himself says regarding the status of artistic assertions. For instance, consider the following passage from *A System of Logic*:

> Now, the imperative mood is the characteristic of art, as distinguished from science. Whatever speaks in rules, or precepts, not in assertions respecting matters of fact, is art: and ethics, or morality, is properly a portion of the art corresponding to the sciences of human nature and society. . . . Propositions of science assert a matter of fact: an existence, a coexistence, a succession, or a resemblance. The propositions [of art] do not assert that anything is, but enjoin or recommend that something should be. They are a class by themselves. A proposition of which the predicate is expressed, by the words *ought* or *should be*, is generically different from one which is expressed by *is*, or *will be*.[80]

One could easily take these excerpts to be saying that artistic statements are not about what *is* (not about the world or objective reality), and are thus not truth-apt in the way that scientific statements are. Indeed, these passages, and similar ones, have encouraged many scholars to interpret Mill as a noncognitivist of the prescriptivist variety: "On a plain reading of this text, Mill is endorsing metaethical noncognitivism, the view that moral utterances are not apt for truth. More specifically, his view appears

77. Mill, "Blakey's History of Moral Science," 27–28.
78. See Aristotle, *Nicomachean Ethics*, I.3, I.6.
79. Mill, *Examination of William Hamilton's Philosophy*, 102, *CW* 9.
80. Mill, *System of Logic*, 943, 949.

to be a version of *prescriptivism*."[81] And this reading has been generalized to include all of Mill's ethical statements: an utterance like "Happiness is the supreme good" is translated to mean "Seek happiness."[82]

However, the problem for this rendering of Mill is that the plain reading of the relevant texts actually cuts the other way. To be sure, artistic utterances *are* "in the imperative mood, or in periphrases equivalent to it." And the most factual thing these imperatives express is a particular kind of sentiment: "It is true that, in the largest sense of the words, even these propositions assert something as a matter of fact. The fact affirmed in them is, that the conduct recommended excites in the speaker's mind the feeling of approbation." So far, so noncognitivist: what we have here is a sentiment-based prescription. But what Mill *then* argues is that we can and must *justify* our sentiments: "For the purposes of practice, everyone must be required to justify his approbation: and for this there is need of general premises, determining what are the proper objects of approbation, and what the proper order of precedence among those objects." From here, Mill names the "departments" of "the Art of Life," and adds that "its principles are those which must determine whether the special aim of any particular art is worthy and desirable, and what is its place in the scale of desirable things."[83] The *logic* of practice, as Mill calls it, treats artistic utterances as mere prescriptions; but the *value* of practice is determined by its relationship to what is worthy or desirable.

This analysis is plainly a cognitivist one; perhaps imperatives *themselves* are not scientific propositions, but their justifications *are*. When I declare "You ought not to lie" or "Stop lying" or even "Truth should have out," Mill would admit that I am simply conveying the approbation I have for veracity or the disapprobation I have for deceit. And yet, I can still *justify* my sentiment by offering a scientific proposition in accordance with "Morality" or "the Right" (e.g., "Lying is harmful"); or in accordance with "Æsthetics" or "the Beautiful or Noble" (e.g., "Lying is debased"); or in accordance with "Prudence or Policy" or "the Expedient" (e.g., "Lying is foolish"). And the cogency, or vacuity, of these propositions would depend on the relevant evidence, just like any other scientific claim: do well-developed persons, enduringly across time and place, understand these claims to be, if not absolutely valid, then at least intelligible or reasonable statements about the world?

81. Zuk, "Mill's Metaethical Non-cognitivism," 271–272.
82. Ryan, *Philosophy of John Stuart Mill*, 190.
83. Mill, *System of Logic*, 943, 949.

Now, an interlocutor *could* reply by taking a more inclusive view of Mill's conception of Art; that is, for the sake of argument, maybe the "periphrases" of the imperative mood are intended by Mill to include *any* ethical utterance *whatever*, whether declarative or justificatory.[84] But, if so, we could retort in kind by noting that Mill's conception of Science is rather narrow and does not cover *every* claim one could make about the world. In *A System of Logic*, Mill frequently appears to be referring to what "*is*, or *will be*," in a strictly concrete, physical sense: "A scientific observer or reasoner, merely as such, is not an adviser for practice. His part is only to show that certain consequences follow from certain causes, and that to obtain certain ends, certain means are the most effectual. Whether the ends themselves are such as ought to be pursued, and if so, in what cases and to how great a length, it is no part of his business as a cultivator of science to decide, and science alone will never qualify him for the decision." The very notion that one could be *more* or *less* qualified to make "ought" statements points to an objective sphere of Art beyond the province of Science, the latter of which contains "matters of fact" that are purely material, sensory.[85]

But, alas, therein lies the rub: what *other* "matters of fact" *are there*? Those devoted to the idea that Mill's empiricism is synonymous with naturalism, or that his naturalism is synonymous with materialism, will scarcely appreciate the fact that Mill's empirical sense is quite capacious enough to embrace our normative experiences. From beauty to dignity to nobility, Mill's writings are filled with references to intangible, abstract qualities or properties that are acknowledged to be *really* real independent of our subjective experience, although accessible only *through* our subjective experience. Interestingly, much of what we get from those scholars representing Mill as a noncognitivist is a struggle to explain away what look to be cognitivist moments in his work; they do so having already posited Mill's noncognitivism (often in a state of exegetical unease) either just as a presupposition or out of the perceived need to solve certain problems, such as his alleged naturalistic fallacy.[86]

That said, let us return to the question at hand: What are we obliged to do or refrain from doing? What concrete laws or duties can we derive from the Utility Principle? In the next section, I engage the well-known

84. See Zuk, "Mill's Metaethical Non-cognitivism," 274; and Fletcher, "Mill's Art of Life," 298.

85. Mill, *System of Logic*, 943–944, 950.

86. See Macleod, "Was Mill a Noncognitivist?," 207–209. See also Zuk, "Mill's Metaethical Non-cognitivism," 274–280.

Benthamite dictum that we are duty bound to maximize the general happiness. I think Bentham's own support for, or fidelity to, this dictate is questionable. At times, he seems to want to focus on the morality of legislators and to spare or ignore the individual actor altogether. Indeed, as Mill remarks, "It is fortunate for the world that Bentham's taste lay rather in the direction of jurisprudential than of properly ethical inquiry. Nothing expressly of the latter kind has been published under his name, except the *Deontology*—a book scarcely ever in our experience alluded to by any admirer of Bentham without deep regret that it ever saw the light."[87] For some, Bentham's musings on "private ethics" have added to these doubts.[88] Nonetheless, there is plenty in Bentham's works to suggest that he meant to apply his legislative dogma to individuals as well. And regardless, the maximizing brand of Utilitarianism is tied to Bentham's name and came to typify the Utilitarian outlook in his wake. Thus, with the Utility Principle in tow, the question becomes: Does Mill embrace Benthamism? And, if not, what, then, does Mill imagine moral action to comprise?

Mill contra Benthamism

Having posited the Utility Principle, the Benthamite line takes an extra, supposedly "natural," step from what merely explains or justifies our moral judgments to what becomes the only valid reason for any and all of our actions "under all circumstances."[89] To Bentham, "the greatest happiness of all those whose interest is in question" is "the only right and proper and universally desirable *end* of human action: of human action in every situation";[90] to Sidgwick, "the conduct which, under any circumstances, is objectively right, is that which will produce the greatest amount of happiness on the whole";[91] and to Moore, our duty "can only be defined as that action" which "will cause more good to exist in the Universe than any possible alternative."[92] To act morally is to do that which best advances the happiness of all persons within our sphere of influence.[93]

Given my analysis thus far, it should be immediately apparent that Mill does not (*cannot*) ascribe to this Benthamite ethic. According to Mill,

87. Mill, "Bentham," 98.
88. See Lyons, *In the Interest of the Governed*, 29–34, 50–81.
89. Sidgwick, *Methods of Ethics*, 424–425.
90. Bentham, *Fragment on Government*, 271 (Note *l*), *W* 1.
91. Sidgwick, *Methods of Ethics*, 411.
92. Moore, *Principia Ethica*, §89.
93. See Sen and Williams, "Introduction," 3ff.

morality is only one sphere of life, and it encircles only those (in)actions that have an evident, intrinsic association with the general happiness, such that they naturally engage our moral sentiments. Nonetheless, it is important to exclude the possibility that there are *two* Mills: one of the story above, one of the Benthamite variety. And besides, drawing this distinction between Mill and Bentham will be a good opportunity to review what we have already discussed from another angle, and will also serve as a fitting preface to Mill's ideal of moral impartiality.

BENTHAMISM IN PRACTICE

From its inception, the Benthamite stance has been plagued by a variety of practical criticisms. They are so familiar by now that they scarcely bear repeating. As Mill remarks, it is argued that Utilitarianism is too demanding and too calculating; that it is wholly unfeasible; and that it yields too much to expediency. Consider the wearied Benthamite soul who must "always act from the inducement of promoting the general interests of society"; whose spirit is thus rendered "cold and unsympathizing" from an all-consuming attention to "the dry and hard consideration of the consequences of actions"; whose mind is forever baffled and bent by the impossible task of "calculating and weighing the effects of any line of conduct on the general happiness"; and whose activity bows to "the expedient" and thus lays waste to "social well-being"—for a world in which individuals can, in theory, steal, lie, or kill for the sake of the greatest good is toxic to social virtue and cooperation, let alone peace of mind.[94] These concerns have survived in various forms down to the present day.

However, whatever Bentham may have said to incite these concerns, such criticisms are just fundamentally off base. The Benthamite principle says we are obliged "to minister to general happiness";[95] but what *practices* we ought to follow in order to satisfy this obligation is a separate question entirely. If directly probing the effects of each of our actions is contrary to the general happiness, as the objections above would imply, then this is *not* the right practice to employ. And instead, if adhering to a definite set of rules or norms is what best serves the general happiness, albeit indirectly, then *this* is the right practice to employ; indeed, we would be morally obliged to reject the former and adopt the latter. As Bentham avers, "When a man attempts to combat the principle of utility, it

94. Mill, *Utilitarianism*, 219–220, 223–224.
95. Bentham, *Fragment on Government*, 268, note *h*.

is with reasons drawn, without his being aware of it, from that very principle itself."[96] To claim that Benthamism is to be opposed for being, say,
"dangerous" is to suggest that "it is not consonant to utility, to consult utility," for danger is clearly a disutility, and must thus be duly accounted for.
If an individual blindly adopts a "dangerous" practice—one that spreads
fear and grief via the example or threat of theft, deceit, or murder—then
they are not a very good Utilitarian. In fact, Bentham's system of morals is
built on the assumption that before moral decision making even reaches
the individual level, Utilitarian legislators will have already decided on a
preliminary range of actions and forbearances that ought to be required
and enforced by law.

This is partly what Mill is doing in the latter portion of the second
chapter of *Utilitarianism*: showing how each of the criticisms above
relies on what is, in short, a faulty practice. While here Mill is mostly just
defending Utility as "the first principle of morals," the Utility Principle
naturally forces us to assess the effects of our actions on the general happiness, which prompts Mill to uphold this consideration as practicable. As
we saw, Mill assures us that we need not weigh the effects of each of our
actions afresh, but should rely on the past experience of the human race;
and that when making decisions, most of us need not concern ourselves
with the interest or happiness of the entire society, but only "the interest
or happiness of some few persons."[97] In *On Liberty*, Mill argues that individuals ought to be safeguarded in their individual pursuits. How can such
self-regarding activity be squared with a Utilitarian ethic? Well, for one,
it passes practical muster. As Mill wrote to Carlyle, the general happiness
"can in no other way be forwarded but by the means you speak of, namely
by each taking for his exclusive aim the development of what is best in
himself."[98] Properly cultivating one's self is, according to Mill, what best
serves the most selfless end. In effect, Benthamism is immune from practical objections: if a practical critique holds water then it ought to be poured
into the deliberation of the Utilitarian actor.

Now, a more genuine incongruity in Bentham's moral theory exists
between his commitment to an altruistic morality and his recognition of
psychological egoism. If individuals are bound to be predominantly self-
interested, then we would seem to have the ultimate practical hurdle to
Benthamism: how can we oblige individuals to promote the happiness

96. Bentham, *Principles of Morals and Legislation*, 2.
97. Mill, *Utilitarianism*, 220.
98. Mill, "To Thomas Carlyle," 206–207, *CW* 12.

of the whole when they are necessarily driven chiefly by the happiness of their own part? As the saying goes, *ought* implies *can*. And yet, perhaps this is why Bentham is concerned almost exclusively with laws and institutions: "It has been shown that the happiness of the individuals, of whom a community is composed, that is, their pleasures and their security, is the end and the sole end which the legislator ought to have in view: the sole standard, in conformity to which each individual ought, as far as depends upon the legislator, to be *made* to fashion his behaviour."[99] Thus, Bentham's task is to determine which political arrangements are most conducive to "the greatest happiness of the greatest number." Since the "actual end of action on the part of every individual" is "his greatest happiness," the role of the legislator—as commissioned by the Platonic legislator, Bentham—is to induce the individual to adhere to the "proper end of action," namely, the general happiness, which, in some moods, Bentham regards as our "*real* greatest happiness,"[100] by which he means "that the conduct most conducive to general happiness *always* coincides with that which conduces most to the happiness of the agent"[101]—if only we were enlightened enough to notice!

But, practicality aside, we turn to the Benthamite principle: the obligation always to act so as to produce "the greatest happiness of the greatest number." As Mill notes, Bentham "does not appear to have entered very deeply into the metaphysical grounds" of this doctrine. Instead, Bentham jumps straight to defining what it means to promote the general happiness. And again, while individuals are also supposed to be on the hook, Bentham is absorbed with applying this moral injunction to government; his works are devoted to outlining what it would mean for the Ship of State to adopt "the greatest happiness of the greatest number" as its North Star. Now, when applied to "legislation," Mill thinks that Benthamism is well suited to producing "true and valuable results." However, the question is whether or not Mill adopts the *ethic* of Benthamism: Does Mill, like Bentham, recognize "the production" of "the greatest possible happiness" as "the only fit purpose of all human thought and action"?[102] Are we, as individuals, duty bound to maximize the general happiness?

99. Bentham, *Principles of Morals and Legislation*, 14.
100. Bentham, *Memoirs of Jeremy Bentham*, 560, *W* 10, my emphasis.
101. Frankena, "Sidgwick and the History of Ethical Dualism," 190.
102. Mill, "Remarks on Bentham's Philosophy," 5, 7.

BENTHAMISM IN PRINCIPLE

The answer, I think, is most definitely *no*. Mill just does not speak this way, at least not with any candor or consistency. On the contrary, Mill tends to suggest that our moral duties, when and where they arise, have a special, bounded kind of significance. Returning to the last section, they map onto what can be expected from a socialized person; namely, to avoid whatever is "generally injurious" and to promote the good of others up to but not exceeding what a basic "regard for the public interest," or "regard for the universal happiness," demands.[103] Mill's moral sphere encircles those actions that are characterized by their vital importance to the good of the whole and its parts. In relation to society at large, "acts and forbearances constitute duty" when they are "so necessary to the general well-being, that people must be held to [them] compulsorily."[104] And in relation to the individual, we have those "moral rules which forbid mankind to hurt one another," which by their nature are "more vital to human well-being than any maxims, however important, which only point out the best mode of managing some department of human affairs." On Mill's view, to be perfectly moral is to be "unable to conceive the possibility of happiness to [ourselves], consistently with conduct *opposed* to the general good," and to exhibit "a direct impulse to promote the general good" as "*one of* [our] habitual motives of action." Mill's moral code is fully satisfied by placing ourselves "*in harmony* with the interest of the whole," that is, with the flourishing of individuals and the health and progress of the society that sustains and nurtures their growth.[105]

One telling piece of evidence for this reading is that Mill's theory makes room for supererogation: actions that go "above and beyond" the call of duty; an altruism "which is not obligatory, but meritorious."[106] Benthamism has no room for supererogation, for if an action enhances the general happiness then it is obligatory, even if it ought not to be enforced: "Every act which promises to be beneficial upon the whole to the community (himself included), each individual ought to perform of himself: but it is not every such act that the legislator ought to compel him to perform."[107] We are obliged, for Bentham, to do as much good for others as we possibly can, and if this entails focusing on ourselves sometimes,

---

103. Mill, *Utilitarianism*, 218, 220.
104. Mill, "Thornton on Labor and Its Claims," 651, *CW* 5.
105. Mill, *Utilitarianism*, 218, 255, my emphases.
106. Mill, *Auguste Comte and Positivism*, 337, *CW* 10.
107. Bentham, *Principles of Morals and Legislation*, 144.

then so be it; but the difference is that Mill clearly envisions a perfectly ordered social world where moral obligation is active and relevant only in certain pockets and spheres of life.

Indeed, given its long-accepted status, the evidence for Mill's Benthamism is surprisingly scant. We already discussed the Greatest Happiness Principle. Likewise, Mill makes frequent, and far more common, reference to values like the general happiness and the general interest. However, in accordance with the Utility Principle, these values are put forward as moral justifications, not as objects for maximization. And by preferring to moralize in terms of the *general* happiness, rather than the *greatest* happiness, Mill gives the impression that his interest lies not in maximization, but in a plainer notion of social flourishing.[108]

And even when Mill appears to make a maximizing appeal, the strongest, or most natural, reading suggests a different reality. For instance, having dubbed happiness "the end of human action," Mill declares that "the standard of morality," namely, the Utility Principle, allows us to derive "the rules and precepts for human conduct, by the observance of which [happiness] might be, to the greatest extent possible, secured to all mankind."[109] Now, we can certainly *try* to interpret this in a Benthamite sense. But what Mill appears to be arguing is that certain "rules and precepts" must be generally observed if true happiness is to be a reality, or "secured" to "the greatest extent possible," to all persons on an impartial basis.[110] And even if this *does* bespeak a maximizing ethic, to whom or what is it meant to apply: to individuals as moral actors, or to society as a moral organization?

One rejoinder writes itself: perhaps Mill *does* embrace a maximizing ethic, but simply has a strict, limited understanding of what matrix of practical obligations will best serve "the greatest happiness of the greatest number." Mill appears at various points to imply something of this kind, like in his letter to Carlyle, which I referenced above, and in his commentary on Comte, where he asks rhetorically, "May it not be the fact that mankind, who after all are made up of single human beings, obtain a greater sum of happiness when each pursues his own, under the rules and conditions required by the good of the rest, than when each makes the good of the rest his only object, and allows himself no personal pleasures not indispensable to the preservation of his faculties?"[111] Indeed, in *A System of Logic*, Mill echoes his letter to Carlyle by designating the

108. See Martin, "Mill's Rule Utilitarianism in Context," 34–35.
109. Mill, *Utilitarianism*, 214.
110. See Brown, "Mill's Moral Theory," 10–15.
111. Mill, *Auguste Comte and Positivism*, 337.

general happiness as the be all and end all of his practical philosophy: "My conviction [is] that the general principle to which all rules of practice ought to conform, and the test by which they should be tried, is that of conduciveness to the happiness of mankind, or rather, of all sentient beings: in other words, that the promotion of happiness is the ultimate principle of Teleology."[112] Certainly, these remarks *could* be interpreted to support the idea that a Benthamite directive resides at the center of Mill's moral theory.

However, this would be a mistake. Again, Utility, for Mill, is "the ultimate principle of Teleology." And what Mill is saying is that "all rules of practice"—that is, all *general* rules of practice—properly rise or fall in proportion to their "conduciveness to the happiness of mankind." Some rules are *moral*, and thus fall under the Utility Principle. But other rules are *non*moral, and thus exist not because they are obligatory, but because they have endured as good general practices; these rules are "customs," which ought to have "presumptive" weight for the individual.[113] Indeed, Mill prefaces his remarks above by raising the question of "the foundations of morality." He steps back to note that happiness "is the justification, and ought to be the controller, of all ends," adds that it "is not itself the sole end," and then returns to the moral sphere for an example: "There are many virtuous actions, and even virtuous modes of action," by "which happiness in the particular instance is sacrificed, more pain being produced than pleasure. But conduct of which this can be truly asserted, admits of justification only because it can be shown that on the whole more happiness will exist in the world, if feelings are cultivated which will make people, in certain cases, regardless of happiness." Far from appealing to a maximizing ethic, Mill is simply reaffirming that "the specific pursuit either of [our] own happiness or of that of others" must "give way" to moral duties (and the corresponding, hoped-for "cultivation of an ideal nobleness of will and conduct") "in any case of conflict."[114] Whatever these moral duties *are*, it is with *them* that morality begins and ends.

In truth, what I have just outlined gives the most defensible sense to the assertion that Mill's moral theory advances a maximizing ethic. Mill believes that the general happiness would be best served by establishing, first, a moral sphere, filled with rights and duties, and, second, a nonmoral sphere, filled with liberties, discretion, and free play. Thus, indubitably, we

112. Mill, *System of Logic*, 951.
113. Mill, *On Liberty*, 262.
114. Mill, *System of Logic*, 952.

can soundly argue that the moral and nonmoral spheres alike are justified insofar as they maximize the general happiness. However, this justification has to do with the reasons grounding the basic edifice of the good society; to the order a Platonic legislator would create out of chaos. This justification says nothing about what *actual* (living, breathing) persons are obliged to do or refrain from doing. Indeed, it is Utility that *generates* this inquiry: What rules make up the moral sphere? What actions would be imbued with moral significance by an "enlarged sympathy" or "enlightened self-interest," that is, by an impartial regard for the community? Mill is concerned, as he thinks anyone ought to be, with enhancing the general happiness. But the general happiness is not "the only fit purpose of all human thought and action." Rather, it is the foundation upon which the spheres of human life are to be erected.

For instance, we might ask: how can self-regarding activity be justified? For a Benthamite, the story would go something like this: we are morally obliged to maximize the general happiness; but, as it happens, it is often optimal, in practice, to pursue our own desires or interests as ends unto themselves; that is, we often do what is maximally valuable for the whole by focusing on our own part. The story for Mill, though, is quite different: all individuals have an inherent interest in self-regarding activity; thus, a self-regarding sphere is in the general interest as it pertains to individuals—*full stop*. A founding legislator has reason to introduce it; an impartial citizen has reason to desire and demand it. The moral sphere, in turn, emerges as follows: having identified the general interest of individuality, the mind's eye will gaze with moral pain at actions that transgress the reciprocal pursuit of individuality (hence Mill's liberalism). Also, beyond the general interest of individuals, the mind's eye will feel moral repugnance at whatever tends to contravene the general interest of society at large. Thus, we will, at times, be duty bound to set aside our individuality in service to the community or the body politic. As we will see, Mill consistently links our civic duty to what is needed to protect or reinforce our political or social freedom (hence his civic republicanism). Moreover, Mill regularly defends the idea of civic service—especially in its democratic, participatory guise—as integral to the good life (hence his civic humanism).

All of this accords with last chapter as well. Again, for Mill, we have the higher pleasures of both individuality and sociality—the "individual & social"[115] aspects of happiness. This dichotomy then *raises* the moral

---

115. Mill, "To Harriet Taylor," 9, *CW* 14.

question: what sort of balance should or *must* we observe between these kindred but contending objects? Mill diagnoses most social ills in terms of an imbalance between individuality and sociality. In *On Liberty*, for example, Mill declares, "There has been a time when the element of spontaneity and individuality was in excess, and the social principle had a hard struggle with it"; but "society has now fairly got the better of individuality; and the danger which threatens human nature is not the excess, but the deficiency, of personal impulses and preferences."[116] The negotiation Mill thus mediates between individuality and sociality—i.e., his moral theory— should *not* be read as a total surrender to sociality, with allowances for individuality only insofar as it (indirectly) serves its counterpart. On the contrary, his moral theory is an extension of his theory of happiness: certain balancing acts between the one, few, and many are so tightly bound up with the general happiness that their performance or nonperformance is experienced by socially conscious (or self-interestedly enlightened) persons with a particularly *moral* kind of pleasure or pain.

However, the definitive argument against the notion that Mill adopts a maximizing ethic—along with the clearest understanding of his moral theory—can be realized only by developing his concept of moral impartiality. Both Bentham and Mill hold that morality entails impartiality, and that the Utility Principle is intended to decree whatever moral impartiality demands. Benthamism jumps from here to every action serving "the greatest happiness of the greatest number." Mill, though, takes a different path. In what follows, we drill to the core of Mill's moral theory as revealed in his invocation of the golden rule: "To do as one would be done by, and to love one's neighbour as oneself, constitute the ideal perfection of utilitarian morality." The question becomes: What does it actually mean to embrace the *general* rather than a *particular* happiness? How do we know that our "moral" feelings are not just the glorification of our partialities, passions, or prejudices?

Morality as Impartiality

Bentham's Utilitarians were known as the Philosophical Radicals. They were radical (by the standards of the time) partly because they proposed an egalitarian view of law and policy. Accused of espousing a "dangerous" morality, Bentham retorted, "dangerous it unquestionably is, to every government which has for its *actual* end or object, the greatest happiness of

116. Mill, *On Liberty*, 264.

a certain *one*, with or without the addition of some comparatively small number of others, whom it is matter of pleasure or accommodation to him to admit, each of them, to a share in the concern, on the footing of so many junior partners."[117] Under the Utilitarian banner, *all* individuals—patricians and plebeians alike—were to have their happiness counted and weighed impartially in determining "the greatest happiness of the greatest number." For Bentham and his progeny, this was the *only* morally acceptable rule for the governance of society. As Mill says, "Bentham's dictum, 'everybody to count for one, nobody for more than one,' might be written under the principle of utility as an explanatory commentary."[118]

According to Mill, impartiality is embedded in the Utility Principle itself. To accept the general happiness as the moral standard is to accept impartiality as the arbiter of the general happiness: "It is involved in the very meaning of Utility, or the Greatest-Happiness Principle. That principle is a mere form of words without rational signification, unless one person's happiness, supposed equal in degree (with the proper allowance made for kind), is counted for exactly as much as another's."[119] Mill is correct: to give preference a priori to the happiness of the one, few, or many is to prioritize a particular good over the general good. We might even say that morality, as a concept, by definition, is no respecter of persons: to explain or justify an individual action or institutional policy on *moral* grounds is to offer *reasons* that any implicated person ought to be able to accept from an impartial standpoint, that is, apart from their partialities, passions, or prejudices.[120] But what does it mean to think or act impartially? How exactly is the good Utilitarian to carry the dictum *everybody to count for one, nobody for more than one* into practice?

MORALIZING THE MORAL SENTIMENTS

Bentham gives a complex and (true to form) technical answer to this question. He constructs a "felicific" or "hedonic" calculus that is supposed to determine the relative morality or immorality of any action by measuring

117. Bentham, *Principles of Morals and Legislation*, 2, note †.

118. Mill, *Utilitarianism*, 257.

119. Ibid., 257.

120. This does not mean Mill thinks all preferential treatment is immoral; it just means that such preferences must be impartial: "A person would be more likely to be blamed than applauded for giving his family or friends no superiority in good offices over strangers, when he could do so without violating any other duty; and no one thinks it unjust to seek one person in preference to another as a friend, connexion, or companion" (ibid., 243).

the general value or disvalue of all its resultant pleasures or pains according to their "intensity," "duration," "certainty," "propinquity," "fecundity," "purity," and "extent." This calculus gives rise to a number of theoretical and practical puzzles; but the crucial idea is that we are meant to measure the total amount of pleasure or pain that all affected individuals, weighed equally, will enjoy or suffer as a result of any action we might take: "Take the *balance*; which, if on the side of *pleasure*, will give the general *good tendency* of the act, with respect to the total number or community of individuals concerned; if on the side of pain, the general *evil tendency*, with respect to the same community."[121]

By contrast, Mill gives a simple but (true to form) nuanced answer to this question. The beating heart of Mill's moral theory can be found in this concise, arresting line from *Utilitarianism*: "As between his own happiness and that of others, utilitarianism requires him to be as strictly impartial as a disinterested and benevolent spectator."[122] This maxim condenses and distills Mill's thinking from above. Morality arises out of our moral experience; out of those actions that inspire a special kind of approbation or disapprobation. And yet, in saying this, Mill is referring *only* to those feelings that would be shared by a "strictly *impartial*" observer; *only* to those judgments that would be seconded by "a *disinterested* and *benevolent* spectator." If our moral feelings would not be shared by an impartial observer then they are ipso facto reducible to some partiality; and if our moral feelings are reducible to some partiality then they are ipso facto nonmoral. Indeed, as Mill often suggests, the *non*morality of partiality is implicitly admitted by all those whose partialities lead them to acquire or defend special powers or privileges. Every pragmatic moral apologist for a despotic regime seeks to defend the regime with (cynical) reasons that anyone "should" accept from an impartial standpoint: the medieval monarch claims a divine right; the antebellum slaver claims a superior race; the Victorian patriarch claims a superior sex.[123] And yet all that this goes to show is that impartiality is "an emanation from the first principle of morals,"[124] which, as Mill holds, underlies everyone's moral reasoning to the extent that they endeavor, or simply feign, to reason morally.

---

121. Bentham, *Principles of Morals and Legislation*, 16. For Bentham, this is an ideal metric: it should always "be kept in view," even if it is not, or cannot be, "strictly pursued previously to every moral judgment" (ibid.).

122. Mill, *Utilitarianism*, 218.

123. See Mill, *Subjection of Women*, 261–282, *CW* 21.

124. Mill, *Utilitarianism*, 257.

One thing to notice is that the impartial observer plays the same role in Mill's moral theory that the competent judge plays in his value theory. Indeed, the argument for both is exactly the same: what is truly valuable is derived from our value sentiments, and what is truly moral is derived from our moral sentiments; but, in both cases, Mill is speaking *only* to the sentiments of those who are well developed or properly oriented with respect to what is valuable or moral. The impartial observer is said to be "disinterested and benevolent," whereas the competent judge could be called disinterested yet desirous—that is, both are disinterestedly interested in their respective ethical realms.

SMITH AND HUME

Based on Mill's language, the figures that jump straight to mind are the "impartial spectator" from Adam Smith's *The Theory of Moral Sentiments* and the "judicious spectator" from David Hume's *A Treatise of Human Nature*. Smith and Hume—dear friends and luminaries of the Scottish Enlightenment—both developed their own sentimentalist accounts of morality, each of which has been profoundly influential. And both of their theories recognized the natural, good sense of evaluating our moral sentiments from an abstract, third-party perspective. As Smith explains, in order to "survey our own sentiments and motives," we "remove ourselves, as it were, from our own natural station, and endeavour to view them as at a certain distance from us."[125] And as Hume describes, in order to "prevent those continual *contradictions*" in sentiment that arise from "the distance or contiguity of the objects" and the "peculiar position" we each have "with regard to others," we do well to "fix on some *steady* and *general* points of view."[126] As with Mill, the idea for both Smith and Hume is to experience objects of moral appraisal from a sympathetic but neutral standpoint.

According to Smith, we confer moral approval on behavior insofar as a "fair and impartial spectator" would sympathize with the passions or motives that characterize the behavior: "If, upon placing ourselves in his situation, we thoroughly enter into all the passions and motives which influenced it, we approve of it, by sympathy with the approbation of this supposed equitable judge. If otherwise, we enter into his disapprobation, and condemn it." Hence, we arrive at genuinely moral judgments by dividing ourselves "into two persons"—first, the "spectator, whose sentiments

125. Smith, *Theory of Moral Sentiments*, 133.
126. Hume, *Treatise of Human Nature*, 632.

with regard to my own conduct I endeavor to enter into"; and second, the "person whom I properly call myself."[127] And according to Hume, we "correct" our sentiments of praise or blame by adopting the viewpoint of our fellows as a whole: "every particular person's pleasure and interest being different, 'tis impossible men cou'd ever agree in their sentiments and judgments, unless they chose some common point of view, from which they might survey their object, and which might cause it to appear the same to all of them."[128] Personal sentiments (our feelings of self-love) are one thing; but to express a *moral* sentiment is to expect others to "concur." Therefore, we must "depart from [our] private and particular situation," and must "move some universal principle of the human frame, and touch a string, to which all mankind have an accord and symphony."[129]

In short, Smith and Hume, like Mill, believe that we take our moral cues from sentimental experience, and that these sentiments are classed as *moral* sentiments only insofar as they emerge from an impartial perspective. However, one of the major differences between Smith and Hume concerns *what* exactly our moral sentiments are approving or disapproving *of*. For Hume, our feelings of praise and blame are associated with the *utility* of the "quality or character" evinced by action: "Qualities acquire our approbation, because of their tendency to the good of mankind. This presumption must become a certainty, when we find that most of those qualities, which we *naturally* approve of, have actually that tendency, and render a man a proper member of society: While the qualities, which we *naturally* disapprove of, have a contrary tendency, and render any intercourse with the person dangerous or disagreeable."[130] For Smith, though, while our moral sentiments are certainly "enhanced and enlivened by the perception" of "utility or hurtfulness," utility is secondary to *propriety*: "it will be found, upon examination, that the usefulness of any disposition of mind is seldom the first ground of our approbation; and that the sentiment of approbation always involves in it a sense of propriety quite distinct from the perception of utility."[131] On the Ockhamian principle that "we ought not to multiply causes without necessity," Hume's judicious spectator sympathizes with the interests of humanity alone: "'Tis therefore from the influence of characters and qualities, upon those who have

127. Smith, *Theory of Moral Sentiments*, 133, 136.
128. Hume, *Treatise of Human Nature*, 633, 641.
129. Hume, *Enquiry Concerning the Principles of Morals*, 75.
130. Hume, *Treatise of Human Nature*, 626, 629.
131. Smith, *Theory of Moral Sentiments*, 219–220.

intercourse with any person, that we blame or praise him."[132] However, in the first and principal instance, Smith's impartial spectator sympathizes (or not) with the "original passions" of the individual: "If, upon bringing the case home to our own breast, we find that the sentiments which it gives occasion to, coincide and tally with our own, we necessarily approve of them as proportioned and suitable to their objects; if otherwise, we necessarily disapprove of them, as extravagant or out of proportion."[133] Hume reflects on our "extensive concern for society,"[134] whereas Smith captures our empathetic "fellow-feeling."[135]

Though he was not nearly as focused or detailed in his sentimentalism as either Smith or Hume, we can justly declare that Mill's practical philosophy embraces *both* of their visions and places them on relatively *equal* footing. While Mill concurs with Smith that we naturally sympathize with passions or motives that give meet food to our "human fellow-feeling," he nevertheless deviates from Smith on the precise nature of morality *proper*, where his sensibility aligns more with Hume. Mill differentiates between our distinctively *moral* and our other sympathetic reactions. What is moral, for Mill, *is* a matter of feeling, but for a noble rectitude with respect to the general interest, not for otherwise loveable passions or motives. Recall the previous section: the "*moral*" vision of the mind's eye triggers special, intense feelings of approval or disapproval, whereas its "*sympathetic*" vision sparks feelings of "love, pity, or dislike," which inspire a *non*moral kind of (dis)approbation. Our behavior can be moral even when it fails to garner a more natural sympathy, and vice versa.

Mill looks to the Roman Republic for an example. As students of ancient history will know, the consul Lucius Junius Brutus put his own sons to death for conspiring to bring Tarquin the Proud back to the throne and restore the Roman Kingdom: "The action of Brutus in sentencing his sons was *right*, because it was executing a law essential to the freedom of his country"; but "there was nothing *loveable* in it; it affords either no presumption in regard to loveable qualities, or a presumption of their deficiency. If one of the sons had engaged in the conspiracy from affection for the other, his action would have been loveable, though neither moral nor admirable."[136] In short, Mill would give *cold* approbation to Brutus and *warm* disapprobation to Brutus's condemned son. For while the former

132. Hume, *Treatise of Human Nature*, 629, 633.
133. Smith, *Theory of Moral Sentiments*, 21, 24.
134. Hume, *Treatise of Human Nature*, 630.
135. Smith, *Theory of Moral Sentiments*, Part I, passim.
136. Mill, "Bentham," 112–113.

was loath to show pity (as immortalized in Jacques-Louis David's depiction of the event), and while the latter was, in Mill's imagined rendering, devoted to his brother, they still acted in a manner that was compelled and prohibited, respectively, by the general interest of freedom. What Smith dubs morality, Mill would regard as the passions or motives of sociality. Mill says that our *moral* esteem is inspired by *moral* virtue, while still holding that there are also "other beauties of character which go towards making a human being loveable or admirable."[137]

Now, to be clear, Smith does not disagree with Mill's appraisal—far from it:

> Brutus ought naturally to have felt much more for the death of his own sons than for all that probably Rome could have suffered from the want of so great an example. But he viewed them, not with the eyes of a father, but with those of a Roman citizen. He entered so thoroughly into the sentiments of this last character, that he paid no regard to that tie by which he himself was connected with them; and to a Roman citizen, the sons even of Brutus seemed contemptible when put into the balance with the smallest interest of Rome. In these and in all other cases of this kind, our admiration is not so much founded upon the utility as upon the unexpected, and on that account the great, the noble, and exalted propriety of such actions.[138]

However, in his hypothetical version of the incident, what Mill would say is that moral integrity is at stake for both Brutus and his one son, and yet, so, too, is paternal and fraternal love; and that while the latter virtue ought to give way to the former, all that this shows is that there can be a tragic conflict between what sociality implores and what morality compels. Furthermore, what we can see here is that Smith's moral theory involves sentiments that are patently Utilitarian: it is Brutus's selfless dedication to "the interest of Rome" that garners the impartial spectator's praise. Indeed, what Smith *really* objects to in calling utility the font of human sympathy is the supposed implication that we "have no other reason for praising a man than that for which we commend a chest of drawers,"[139] the idea being that it is Brutus's noble passion or motive *itself* that inspires our sympathy, not *merely* the consequences of his patriotic devotion. Mill would agree with Smith, but would also affirm, with Hume, that we *do*, in

137. Mill, *Utilitarianism*, 221.
138. Smith, *Theory of Moral Sentiments*, 223–224.
139. Ibid., 219.

fact, experience distinctively *moral* sentiments under the impression of an action's general tendency, with a possible exception made for those actions which are incidental, in that they do not reflect any "durable principles of the mind, which extend over the whole conduct, and enter into the personal character."[140] While persons of "reflection and speculation"[141] may be the only ones who are *consciously* aware that they react accordingly to such tendencies, there are nonetheless myriad others who do so unconsciously.

This reading makes intelligible what is often regarded as an enigmatic feature of Utilitarianism: the insistence on divorcing *actions* from *motives*. Concerning motives, Mill argues, "These considerations are relevant, not to the estimation of actions, but of persons; and there is nothing in the utilitarian theory inconsistent with the fact that there are other things which interest us in persons besides the rightness and wrongness of their actions."[142] In short, before we enter into the passions or motives, or assess the quality or character, of the moral actor, we are first interested in the tendency of the action itself. And yet, to say that motives are irrelevant to the moral appraisal of action does *not* mean that they are similarly irrelevant to the actor. Indeed, Mill often makes admiring or censuring remarks about the moral nobility or baseness of real or imagined persons. Rather, by bracketing the morality of actions, all Mill is suggesting is that what defines an action (*as an action*) as moral or immoral is nothing more or less than its relationship to the general happiness. The motive or character *behind* the action might be reprehensible, even *morally* reprehensible; but the action *itself* is still moral insofar as it abides by the demands of the Utility Principle. Conversely, immoral actions do not *become* moral just because our motives are ostensibly pure.

In sum, like Smith and Hume, Mill seeks to moralize our moral sentiments by invoking a neutral, third-party perspective. Of course, all this just begs the question: what does it really *mean* to be an impartial or judicious spectator? Mill does not regard us as prisoners of our own minds; we can, through acts of empathetic, imaginative insight, "enter into the mind and circumstances of another."[143] A very Smithian notion.[144] But to

---

140. Hume, *Treatise of Human Nature*, 626.
141. Smith, *Theory of Moral Sentiments*, 224.
142. Mill, *Utilitarianism*, 221.
143. Mill, "Bentham," 92. Mill writes "enters."
144. Smith believed that sympathy worked by way of empathetic insight, whereas Hume had a "contagion" view of sympathy, where we "catch" the feelings of others. Mill is partial to Smith's locutions, but he sometimes uses Hume's language. See Mill, "Remarks on Bentham's Philosophy," 16; and *Utilitarianism*, 232.

adopt an *impartial* outlook, according to Mill, is to enter into "the mind and circumstances" not of the one, or the few, or the many, but of "a disinterested and benevolent spectator," who, in theory, as an abstract arbiter, stands between and above them all. Again, for Mill, this is what we *already* purport to do when we express, say, moral disapproval; that is, we declare that a particular type of action is opposed to the general happiness and, as such, ought to provoke the same kind of disapproval from *any* impartial ("disinterested") and socially minded ("benevolent") onlooker. Anyone who *cares* about society at large and who is able to *transcend* their partialities, passions, or prejudices *is* Mill's impartial observer. Thus, the goal is to figure out what this vantage point *really* is by establishing what such disinterest *really* involves.

MILL'S IMPARTIAL OBSERVER

As a model of moral impartiality, consider Rousseau's "general will."[145] Rousseau divides each individual into two selves: the (private) person and the (public) citizen. As persons, we each have partialities that may or may not coincide with the partialities of others; these private interests define our *particular* will. As citizens, though, we are supposed to set aside our prejudices and to make laws in accordance with the public interest, or the general will. A citizen deliberates in terms of *reasons*, that is, in terms of considerations that will or should appeal to anyone dedicated to the good of the whole, which, of course, includes the good of its parts. Mill's impartial observer is, in spirit, quite similar to Rousseau's citizen. Indeed, as Mill says, if the "partialities" represented in a legislative body happened to be deadlocked fifty-fifty, then it would require "an enlightened and disinterested minority" from one side or the other to determine which side "was in the right."[146] Similarly, for any dispute involving the one, few, or many, the side "in the right" is the one that prevails on the strength not of their numbers, but of their "strictly impartial" reasons, the kind of considerations that would appeal to "a disinterested and benevolent spectator."

However, the difficulty is that the more idealized an impartial stance becomes, the less capable we are of actually adopting, or even imagining, such a perspective. How, for Mill, can we actually *achieve* an impartial outlook? Must we ascend to a supreme (and perhaps fanciful) kind

145. Rousseau, *Social Contract*, bk. I, chap. VII.
146. Mill, "To Thomas Bayley Potter," 1014, *CW* 16.

of wisdom, like the sort ascribed to Rousseau's legislator?[147] Not at all. I think we can make the speculative but highly judicious claim that Mill is operating with the following notion of impartiality. Mill's impartial observer gauges our behavior from a position of *self-invested neutrality*; that is, she adopts the interests not of the one *or* the few *or* the many, but of the one *and* the few *and* the many, making her equally invested, and thus disinterestedly interested, in the good of all parties concerned.[148] And I think Mill's healthy innovation here is to avoid conceptualizing the impartial observer as a discrete, third-party arbiter. That is, whereas a figure like Smith's adjudicator is no one in particular, Mill's impartial observer is everyone at once; indeed, his moral arbiter would be best realized by a deliberative body of empathetic persons representing all interests with equal wisdom, sway, and energy.[149]

Let me be clear: *nowhere* does Mill lay this out explicitly. But, again, Mill is notorious for his ambiguity about all sorts of things. To give a concrete reading of Mill's moral theory is inevitably to read between the lines at certain points, or to make explicit what Mill leaves largely implicit. Countless scholars have made the "substantive and controversial inference" that Mill's concept of moral impartiality implies or entails a maximizing, "classical utilitarianism."[150] And yet, what coheres far better with Mill's actual moral theory is what I have described above: impartiality moralizes our moral sentiments by inducing each agent to observe all actions with a sense of disinterested interest. From this perspective, certain actions will appear generally harmful or needful and thus cause a *truly* moral feeling of disapproval or approval—hence the Utility Principle, which is, in short, the summary conclusion of Mill's "theory of our moral feelings."

So, what actions or forbearances would Mill's impartial observer declare to be morally required? Of course, precluded are any moral claims that are flatly based on our partialities, passions, or prejudices. But Mill's method *also* allows us to amend any good-faith moral claims that while arising from an "enlarged sympathy," identify only *one* aspect of the public good while neglecting *others*. For instance, Mill often corrects those well-meaning partisans who tend to sympathize with the interests of *either* the individual *or* society at large, rather than the interests of *both* at once.

147. Rousseau, *Social Contract*, bk. II, chap. VII.

148. Thanks to Philip Pettit for suggesting the phrase "self-invested neutrality." Also, the impartial observer is a "she" in keeping with Lady Justice.

149. Hence Mill on representative government.

150. Brink, *Mill's Progressive Principles*, 124, note 3.

These persons fail to adopt an impartial view of the general happiness, and thus fail (at least in principle) to adopt "a morality grounded on large and wise views of the good of the whole, neither sacrificing the individual to the aggregate nor the aggregate to the individual."[151] Our feelings, as they relate to the good of either the individual or society at large, cannot be properly *moral* unless they embody the sentiments of a sympathetic but neutral intermediary: an enlightened arbiter who justly resents "a hurt to society, though not otherwise a hurt to themselves," and who nobly endures "a hurt to themselves, however painful, unless it be of the kind which society has a common interests with them in the repression of."[152] For Bentham, good moral judgment requires nothing more than accurate calculation: "Sum up all the values of all the *pleasures* on one side, and those of all the pains on the other."[153] In theory, Bentham's calculus would be best computed by a morality machine. But, for Mill, good moral judgment is less about accurate calculation and more about having well-developed imaginative capacities; his impartial observer arrives at objectively *moral* judgments by comparing *all* particular interests as objects of *self*-interest.

We could do worse than to compare Mill's impartial stance to Rawls's "original position."[154] Suppose a group of "free and rational persons concerned to further their own interests" has been entrusted to define the scope and content of the moral relationship between the individual and society at large. And suppose these lawgivers—while they "know the general facts about human society," from "political affairs and the principles of economic theory" to "the basis of social organization and the laws of human psychology"—are denied any knowledge related to who and what they are as individual persons: "no one knows his place in society, his class position or social status, nor does anyone know his fortune in the distribution of natural assets and abilities, his intelligence, strength, and the like."[155] Thus, faced with the prospect of being the one *and* the few *and* the many, the question, for Mill, becomes: What duties would they assign to the one *or* the few *or* the many? Would they allow for any exceptions to these rulings? And what modes of enforcement would they select?

Now, I certainly do not mean to imply that Mill is a proto-Rawlsian. On the contrary, whereas Rawls's original position seeks to affect personal

151. Mill, "Utility of Religion," 421, *CW* 10.
152. Mill, *Utilitarianism*, 249.
153. Bentham, *Principles of Morals and Legislation*, 16.
154. See Rawls, *Theory of Justice*, 10–19, 102–167.
155. Ibid., 11, 119.

ignorance, Mill's impartial stance looks to achieve interpersonal knowledge; whereas Rawls's account of justice is ahistorical and a priori, Mill's account of morality is rooted in historical, empirical circumstances; and whereas Rawls's approach is supposedly neutral with respect to the good, Mill's outlook embraces the *summum bonum* of happiness as flourishing. Whether Mill's differences with Rawls on these and other points are to his credit or not, whether Rawls's approach is even possible or not, and whether or not Mill could be subsumed under the Rawlsian banner regardless, is another several books.[156] Rather, my only point here is that the Rawlsian ethic of imagining that you *could* be *anyone* is quite congenial to Mill; his impartial observer sympathizes with each and every party in society as if she *were* each and every party.

At this point, the whole of our discussion so far in this chapter can just slide into this catchall concept of impartiality. Mill's impartial observer is the perfect moral oracle. His spectator is not only focused *solely* on the general happiness but also, and uniquely, *immune* from the partialities, passions, or prejudices that tend to skew the sentiments of the one, few, and many. The many can have a moral reaction to the one, but it takes an impartial observer to confirm or deny their evaluation; to decide whether or not, all things considered, the individual on trial is working for, against, or simply adjacent to the community. As we will see, this is especially important where actions have warring effects; where, say, a certain activity is in the interest of all persons in the larger, general sense, but where any *instance* of this activity might oblige society at large to bear a particular cost. It would be easy, here, for the many to accuse the one of harming the community; and it would take an impartial mind to reply that, actually, the individual is cracking an egg to make an omelet upon which *all* persons are intended or welcome to feast. In essence, to know what the Utility Principle enjoins is to know what actions register as morally relevant for an impartial observer.

However, as perfect as the *idea* of an impartial observer may be, Mill is the first to acknowledge that *we* are not (*cannot* be) perfect. Mill constantly reminds us that we are inherently limited, fallible creatures, eternally prone to partiality, passion, and prejudice. How, then, can we arrive at impartial moral judgments? The reply is that Mill's program for impartiality—as for everything else—is deliberative and iterative: we need to converse about our moral appraisals; to discourse and debate in good faith; to bring to bear our experiences and insights; and we need to have

156. See Turner, "Mill and Modern Liberalism," 576–579.

these exchanges time and again, often over the course of days, decades, or centuries. Indeed, this brings us back to the "Nautical Almanack" of Utility: every generation, while giving implicit weight to the counsel of the past, is bound to reexamine their inherited morals; to edit their Utilitarian Almanac where necessary; and to add fresh, ever alterable entries to it where new issues arise. We *approximate* impartiality, as individuals, by trying to generate moral judgments from a position of self-invested neutrality; and we *best* approximate *true* impartiality by throwing our potentially disparate evaluations into dialogic tension. This is basically what Mill does throughout his writings: he considers all contending points of view, and then adjudicates the dispute as best he can from a disinterestedly interested standpoint. As we will see, this modus operandi is on full display in *On Liberty*.

One concern that might surface here is that Mill's moral theory thus fails to provide absolutely clear moral answers. We might be tempted to critique any moral theory, but perhaps Mill's Utilitarianism in particular, for being opaque or obscure in its moral requirements or recommendations. However, I think such a lack of clarity is actually a virtue of Mill's moral theory, and of any wise moral theory in general. The world is complex and chaotic, and it is the mark of moral maturity, I believe, not to reduce moral judgment to mere formulas. A viable moral theory need not offer definite answers, but should instead provide clear guidance as to what it truly *means* to engage in moral discernment; and that is precisely what Mill's impartial observer is meant to do. And again, in keeping with this theme, Mill's moral theory upholds the reasoning and wisdom of the ages, which is doubtless imperfect or incomplete, and which may even involve internal tensions or conflicts, but which, as an "Almanack," contains our enduring solutions to the perennial moral problems.

In sum, Mill's moral theory is an attempt to discern what moral judgments and feelings would issue from an impartial regard for the general happiness. And what we have begun to illustrate is that, unlike Bentham, Mill imbues only a limited set of interests with moral significance and leaves the remainder of life to the discretion of the individual. For an impartial observer, the good of others will have "a large and prominent"[157] but by no means totalizing role in directing or legitimating our conduct. From here, we can ask: what does our "enlarged sympathy," or "widened" "instinct" of "self-defense," *impartially rendered*, deem immoral? To answer that, we should first consider the structure of Mill's moral sphere.

---

157. Mill, *Utilitarianism*, 218.

With this inquiry, we finally arrive where many scholars embark on their study of Mill's moral theory: the supposed conflict between *Act* and *Rule* Utilitarianism.

Morality contra Expediency

Mill recognizes two potential approaches to decision making in morally salient situations: first, "Expediency"; and second, "Principle" or "the Right." The latter—that is, acting according to right principle—is what it means to take morality seriously; conversely, the former—that is, doing what is "expedient for some immediate object, some temporary purpose, but which violates a rule whose observance is expedient in a much higher degree"—is just a myopic, "hurtful" abdication of moral responsibility.[158] According to Mill, morality just *is* a rule-governed activity: given a moral choice, to assert that we have made *the* right decision is to suggest that all individuals, in any analogous situation, are obliged, presumptively, to do the same—that they must abide by our implicit rule of action.

However, before asking what these rules *are*, we first ought to determine how moral rules manifest themselves, and also how an impartial matrix of moral rules ought to be organized or constituted. How does Mill account for the emergence of moral rules? Does he believe there can be exceptions to or conflicts between moral rules, and how does he intend for such exceptions or conflicts to be defined or resolved?

MORAL RULES AND THEIR LIMITS

As we have discussed, morality emerges out of sociality insofar as the general happiness appears to be generally dependent on certain kinds of behavior. While theft, deceit, or murder is already undesirable for purely aesthetic reasons, having to do with its baseness or ignobility, it is also, and most significantly, verboten for moral reasons, being the type of action which is anathema to social flourishing: "In the case of abstinences indeed—of things which people forbear to do, from moral considerations, though the consequences in the particular case might be beneficial—it would be unworthy of an intelligent agent not to be consciously aware that the action is of a class which, if practised generally, would be generally injurious, and that this is the ground of the obligation to abstain from it."[159] Moral

158. Ibid., 223.
159. Ibid., 220.

rules, then, are properly seen as commands and prohibitions that take root and grow in light of the Utility Principle: "Thou shalt not steal, lie, or kill" is inked on the first page of the Utilitarian Almanac.

And again, apart from such "abstinences," certain *positive* duties may arise—situational efforts upon which the general happiness similarly dangles: "There are cases in which martyrdom is a useless self-sacrifice," but there are "other cases in which the importance of it to the good of mankind is so great as to make it a positive duty, like the act of a soldier who gives his life in the performance of what is assigned to him. There are cases again where without being so necessary as to be, on the utilitarian ground, an absolute duty, it is yet so useful as to constitute an act of virtue, which then ought to receive the praise & honours of heroism." As Mill remarks, it is difficult if not impossible to discern any sharp or stable rules for such positive duties, appearing as they do in such "varying circumstances."[160] Nonetheless, as we have seen, Mill appears confident in associating the sphere of individual duty with an abstract, positive "regard for" the general happiness.

Mill often portrays moral rules as dicta that prevent us from "making exceptions" for ourselves, with the proper metric being the impact our activity *would* have on the general happiness *if* it were accepted as a universal norm. For example, as Mill avers, "one soldier's running away will not lose the battle; accordingly it is not that consideration which keeps each solider in his rank: it is the disgrace which naturally and inevitably attends on conduct by any one individual, which if pursued by a majority, everybody can see would be fatal."[161] This moral reaction springs from, or is confirmed by, the uniquely *moral* pain that an impartial observer takes in excess egoism. Indeed, in a Kantian sense, Mill would have us respect moral rules in the name of "conscience, duty, rectitude."[162] However, unlike Kant, Mill does so in a Utilitarian vein: Kant bans whatever violates the categorical imperative, and, in spirit, so does Mill; but whereas Kant sees this violation as a breach of duty *full stop*, Mill understands this violation as any action that, *as a rule*, selfishly flouts the general happiness. In short, we act morally, for Mill, insofar as our behavior is "capable of being brought under a rule to which it would be for the general benefit that all should conform."[163]

160. Mill, "To Henry S. Brandreth," 1234, *CW* 16.
161. Mill, *Principles of Political Economy*, 371, *CW* 2.
162. Mill, "Whewell on Moral Philosophy," 172.
163. Mill, "To John Venn," 1881, *CW* 17.

However, this summary begs the question: Can a moral rule be legitimately violated insofar as what looks to be expedient for the general happiness *in a specific situation* "clearly" belies the edict's general efficacy? Are moral rules absolute, or do they countenance the possibility of extenuating circumstances? At first, one might say that Mill is of two minds about this. On one hand, he argues that there are weighty, impartial reasons to follow moral rules irrespective of any countervailing logic—justifications which ground our reflexive, sentimental antipathy toward excuse making for rule breaking. But, on the other hand, he confesses that there are conditions, having to do with extreme or otherwise unusual dilemmas, under which any reasonable person should do what is normally forbidden—occurrences that would garner the instinctive sympathy of an impartial onlooker.

To begin, Mill has *three* thick, impartial reasons for wedding us to moral rules, circumstances be damned. First, Mill argues that the general happiness is too mighty an enigma to be engaged without guiding directives: "Those who adopt utility as a standard can seldom apply it truly except through secondary principles." To fancy that any particular action "clearly" goes for or against the general happiness is a mark of mere hubris: "We think utility, or happiness, much too complex and indefinite an end to be sought except through the medium of various secondary ends."[164] The issue here is one of sheer practicality, for the "simple fact is, human interests are so complicated, and the effects of any incident whatever so multifarious, that if it touches mankind at all, its influence on them is, in the great majority of cases, both good and bad."[165] Events unfold in multitudinous, inscrutable ways, and thus the effects of our actions, both now and later, are deeply nebulous. Thus, the only rational way forward is to stick to the Utilitarian Almanac for guidance. As Mill penned in a letter, "I agree with you that the right way of testing actions by their consequences, is to test them by the natural consequences of the particular action, and not by those which would follow if everyone did the same. But, for the most part, the consideration of what would happen if everyone did the same, is the only means we have of discovering the tendency of the act in the particular case." Indeed, Mill thinks "Kant's maxim," purely as a fact-finding tool, is the optimal way to gauge an action's general consequences.[166] And besides, we almost always find ourselves in situations "where time or means do not exist for analyzing the actual circumstances

164. Mill, "Bentham," 110–111. I removed Mill's "the" after "through."
165. Mill, "Nature," 387, *CW* 10.
166. Mill, "To John Venn," 1881.

of the case, or where we cannot trust our judgment in estimating them."[167] Life is not an ethics seminar.

Second, Mill argues that we ought to obey moral rules, even when they appear to be suboptimal, so as to develop or preserve our virtuous aversion to injurious activities: "It would often be expedient, for the purpose" of "attaining some object immediately useful to ourselves or others, to tell a lie. But inasmuch as the cultivation in ourselves of a sensitive feeling on the subject of veracity is one of the most useful, and the enfeeblement of that feeling one of the most harmful, things to which our conduct can be instrumental," we "feel that the violation, for a present advantage, of a rule of such transcendant expediency, is not expedient."[168] Similarly, Mill reproaches Bentham for overlooking the fact that a superficially expedient action can contribute to the cultivation of an inexpedient vice: Bentham typifies "a tone of thinking, according to which any kind of action or any habit, which in its own specific consequences cannot be proved" to be "productive of unhappiness to the agent himself or to others, is supposedly to be fully justified." He neglects to consider "whether the act or habit in question" may not "form part of a *character* essentially pernicious, or at least essentially deficient in some quality eminently conducive to the 'greatest happiness.' "[169] To allow ourselves to steal, lie, or kill—even for solid situational reasons—is to make ourselves more comfortable with, or conformable to, these actions, and thus to make it more likely that we will continue to steal, lie, or kill for increasingly specious or self-serving reasons. Those of you who beheld Walter White's character arc on *Breaking Bad* will know what Mill is talking about.

And finally, Mill argues that moral rules are integral to the reliability of human behavior: "In the conduct of human beings towards one another, it is necessary that general rules should be observed, in order that people may know what they have to expect."[170] Moral rules—absolute, set-in-stone principles—are what forestall uncertainty and enable us to live freely without being unduly perturbed by the threat of arbitrary injuries or thwarted expectations:

> Take, for example, the case of murder. There are many persons to kill whom would be to remove men who are a cause of no good to any human being, of cruel physical and moral suffering to several, and whose whole

167. Mill, *System of Logic*, 946.

168. Mill, *Utilitarianism*, 223.

169. Mill, "Remarks on Bentham's Philosophy," 8.

170. Mill, *On Liberty*, 277.

influence tends to increase the mass of unhappiness and vice. Were such a man to be assassinated, the balance of traceable consequences would be greatly in favour of the act. The counter-consideration, on the principle of utility, is, that unless persons were punished for killing, and taught not to kill; that if it were thought allowable for anyone to put to death at pleasure any human being whom he believes that the world would be well rid of, nobody's life would be safe.[171]

In a word, moral rules offer *security*, or "the feeling of security, or certainty; which is impaired, not only by every known actual violation of good rules, but by the belief that such violations ever occur."[172] Security, for Mill, is the "most vital" of all our social needs: "security no human being can possibly do without; on it we depend for all our immunity from evil, and for the whole value of all and every good, beyond the passing moment; since nothing but the gratification of the instant could be of any worth to us, if we could be deprived of everything the next instant by whoever was momentarily stronger than ourselves."[173] Thus, the awareness of being surrounded by prejudiced, fallible, self-seeking creatures, any of whom might be weighing the option of theft, deceit, or murder, is contrary to the commonweal. And even under the illusion of safety, the absence of shared, unconditional rules of conduct would leave a moral vacuum, to be inevitably filled by "perpetual quarrelling."[174]

In short, whenever we transgress a moral rule, and thus violate the Utilitarian Almanac, our actions are at risk of being ignorant and thus arbitrary unto injurious; unethical and thus weakening unto corrupting; and antisocial and thus destabilizing unto distressing. Epistemically speaking, we have "the impossibility of doing without" these "subordinate principles."[175] Ethically speaking, we have the fact that all acts "suppose certain dispositions, and habits of mind and heart," which "must be fruitful in *other* consequences, besides those particular acts."[176] And socially speaking, we have the weightiest reason of all: "Rules are necessary, because mankind would have no security for any of the things which they value, for anything which gives them pleasure or shields them from pain, unless they could rely on one another for doing, and in particular for

171. Mill, "Whewell on Moral Philosophy," 181–182.
172. Mill, "To John Venn," 1881–1882.
173. Mill, *Utilitarianism*, 251.
174. Mill, "To George Grote," 762, *CW* 15.
175. Mill, *Utilitarianism*, 225.
176. Mill, "Remarks on Bentham's Philosophy," 7.

abstaining from, certain acts."[177] Consequently, Mill believes we ought to adhere to the rules of the Utilitarian Almanac *as if* they were absolute, a priori moral laws, even when expediency whispers contrariwise. There are impartial edicts outlawing actions like theft, deceit, and murder, and they demand full compliance.

And yet, simultaneously, Mill allows for exceptions to moral rules: "It is not the fault of any creed, but of the complicated nature of human affairs, that rules of conduct cannot be so framed as to require no exceptions, and that hardly any kind of action can safely be laid down as either always obligatory or always condemnable. There is no ethical creed which does not temper the rigidity of its laws, by giving a certain latitude, under the moral responsibility of the agent, for accommodation to peculiarities of circumstances."[178] Mill even *enjoins* us to diverge from rules in severe, unique, or otherwise mitigating circumstances, lest we behave like a "mere pedant" or "slave of [our] formulas," and thus exhibit the absurdity of "the old-fashioned German tacticians who were vanquished by Napoleon, or the physician who preferred that his patients should die by rule rather than recover contrary to it."[179] Here and elsewhere, Mill looks to be defending anything *but* static rule following.

However, Mill smoothly resolves any apparent tension between these seemingly divergent positions by maintaining that any exception to a moral rule "*should be itself* a general rule; so that, being of definite extent, and not leaving the expediencies to the partial judgment of the agent in the individual case, it may not shake the stability of the wider rule in the cases to which the reason of the exception does not extend."[180] To wit, a moral exception should emerge only where the stakes are so high, or where the conditions are so atypical, that an impartial observer would actually chastise us for *not* contravening the moral rule normally in force: "Thus, to save a life, it may not only be allowable, but a duty, to steal, or take by force, the necessary food or medicine, or to kidnap, and compel to officiate, the only qualified medical practitioner. In such cases, as we do not call anything justice which is not a virtue, we usually say, not that justice must give way to some other moral principle, but that what is just in ordinary cases is, by reason of that other principle, not just in the particular case."[181] Moral rules are *never* rightly disobeyed; on the contrary, it is

177. Mill, "Whewell on Moral Philosophy," 192.
178. Mill, *Utilitarianism*, 225.
179. Mill, *System of Logic*, 944.
180. Mill, "Whewell on Moral Philosophy," 183, my emphasis.
181. Mill, *Utilitarianism*, 259.

just that there are times when a "proviso" moral rule ought to be applied rather than a "principal" moral rule. Indeed, Mill's matrix of moral rules is like a tree, with a tough, substantial trunk representing the core precepts of Utilitarianism, and with various branches representing its exceptions, or offshoots. What it means for this tree to flourish is, like anything else, properly subject to ongoing deliberation.

Last chapter, Mill advanced two coequal spheres of desirability: *individuality* and *sociality*. On Mill's view, the key problem with most moral doctrines—even those theories that shed light on the higher pleasures—is that they tend to devalue the ends of one sphere or the other; they are partial and thus less than perfectly moral. In some cases, the moralist will just focus on one sphere and merely neglect the other: the "Greek ideal of self-development" synthesizes the worthy but one-sided ideals of "Pagan self-assertion" and "Christian self-denial." However, in other cases, the moralist will exalt one sphere while also denigrating the other. While Mill joins Carlyle in admiring those individuals who "rise above mediocrity" and initiate "all wise or noble things," he regards Carlyle's portrait of history as disturbingly self-aggrandizing: "I am not countenancing the sort of 'hero-worship' which applauds the strong man of genius for forcibly seizing on the government of the world and making it do his bidding in spite of itself," which, besides often being a veritable hell for the dispossessed, is "corrupting to the strong man himself."[182] The dogged pursuit of individuality starves and even scars "the social part of [our] nature."[183] Conversely, while Mill echoes Comte's devotion to an "enlarged altruism," he rebukes Comte's Religion of Humanity for being excessively self-abnegating. As Mill says, Comte "thinks it the grand duty of life not only to strengthen the social affections by constant habit and by referring all our actions to them, but, as far as possible, to deaden the personal passions and propensities by desuetude."[184] The dogged pursuit of sociality leaves our individual nature "pinched and hidebound," "cramped and dwarfed."[185] What Mill sees here are two minds consumed by the half-truths with which they are respectively enamored. Carlyle is prone to "insane rhapsodies" in praise of "power,"[186] whereas Comte subjugates the entirety of life to society: "Comte is a morality-intoxicated man."[187]

182. Mill, *On Liberty*, 266, 269. Carlyle wrote *On Heroes, Hero-Worship, and the Heroic in History*.

183. Ibid., 266.

184. Mill, *Auguste Comte and Positivism*, 335.

185. Mill, *On Liberty*, 265.

186. Mill, *Autobiography*, 168.

187. Mill, *Auguste Comte and Positivism*, 336.

With healthy moderation, Mill seeks to ascertain the impartial mean between these extremes. Mill would urge us to indulge our "egoistic propensities," but "short of excess," and would bind our will to the good of others, but only within reason: "It is not good that persons should be bound" to do "everything that they would deserve praise for doing. There is a standard of altruism to which all should be required to come up, and a degree beyond which it is not obligatory, but meritorious."[188] But where does Mill draw these lines: What would an impartial observer, oriented by the general happiness, regard as blameworthy? From a position of self-invested neutrality, what rules would we regard as morally binding, knowing that we, too, will be required to abide by the same principles?

As we will see, *On Liberty* proposes a definite answer; but we should take note that Mill will not be conjuring a moral order from scratch à la Bentham. On the contrary, Mill is quite sensitive to the profundity of inherited moral wisdom, as he naturally would be given his understanding that moral truth *cannot* be deduced logically, but must instead be cultivated deliberatively. Indeed, to some extent, *On Liberty* is meant to be a clarifying, purifying inquiry into what is already largely "recognised," albeit murkily or distortedly, "by the current opinions."[189] That said, Mill is of course intensely searching when it comes to the moral failings of society and its prospects for improvement and advancement. Certainly, Mill is a progressive; he examines the social landscape through his critical Utilitarian lens in a continuous effort to identify points of moral privation or perversity, where he believes society ought to pursue either better mores or better laws. Nonetheless, Mill also endeavors to be something of a Coleridgian conservator of whatever a more careless progressivism would be inclined to ignore or discard. Even in "the ruins of exploded error," Mill would see to it "that no scattered particles of important truth are buried and lost."[190]

ACT VERSUS RULE UTILITARIANISM

In contemporary moral theory, there is a well-worn distinction between *Act* and *Rule* Utilitarianism. Act Utilitarianism holds that the moral quality of an action is determined by its direct impact on the general happiness, whereas Rule Utilitarianism holds that the moral quality of an action is determined by its obedience to certain rules upon which the general happiness generally depends: "Whereas act utilitarianism judges each

188. Ibid., 337, 339.
189. Mill, *On Liberty*, 227.
190. Mill, *Essays on Some Unsettled Questions of Political Economy*, 264, *CW* 4.

act simply in terms of its effects on happiness, rule utilitarianism judges each act in terms of its compliance with a system of rules that is, in turn, selected on the basis of its effects on happiness."[191] As Richard Brandt, one of the most influential Rule Utilitarian theorists, explains, an Act Utilitarian says "that an *act* is right, or wrong, depending directly on the utility (or expectable utility) of *its* consequences," whereas a Rule Utilitarian places moral evaluation at one remove:

> First, this view affirms that a morality, or moral code, for a society is most desirable . . . if and only if there is no other moral code, the acceptance of which . . . would have greater expectable utility, when we count the cost of getting the code accepted and kept so, as well as its total effects. Now this second theory goes on to hold that the moral rightness of an individual act is fixed by—or even defined as—whether it is permitted or required by the most desirable (not necessarily the actual) moral code for that society.[192]

Consider any morally salient action, such as lying. For an Act Utilitarian, a lie is either right or wrong depending on how it affects the general happiness *as an act*, or "in the particular case." An Act Utilitarian can consult rules against lying, but only as rules of thumb, as guidelines, which become irrelevant and immoral to follow whenever honesty (or dishonesty) would "plainly" be suboptimal (or optimal) for the general happiness—perhaps whenever it appears "expedient, for the purpose" of "attaining some object immediately useful to ourselves or others, to tell a lie." However, for a Rule Utilitarian, a lie is either right or wrong depending on its relationship to the general happiness *as a rule*, or "if practised generally."[193] A Rule Utilitarian judges a lie not as a discrete action, but as an action type, or as a "certain kind of action, as for example, theft, or lying," which would, "if commonly practised, occasion certain evil consequences to society."[194] In short, Act Utilitarianism puts the particular before the general, and vice versa for Rule Utilitarianism.

Now, in practice, these modes of evaluation can intersect. For instance, Bentham is typically classed as an Act Utilitarian, and for good reason: his felicific calculus is supposed to apply to "every action whatsoever." However, as we have seen, this does not mean that Bentham gives quarter to the kind of iniquity—theft, deceit, murder—that Benthamism is often

---

191. Eggleston, "Mill's Moral Standard," 365.
192. Brandt, "Utilitarianism and Moral Rights," 4.
193. Mill, *Utilitarianism*, 220, 223.
194. Mill, "Remarks on Bentham's Philosophy," 7.

accused of making room for. According to Bentham, good moral analysis entails accounting not only for "the primary" but also for "the second-ary" consequences of actions.[195] Most importantly, we ought to weigh the impact that upsetting certain social norms would likely have on pub-lic serenity: "It is necessary to consider, that man is not like the brutes, limited to the present time, either in enjoyment or suffering, but that he is susceptible of pleasure and pain by anticipation, and that it is not enough to guard him against an actual loss, but also to guarantee to him, as much as possible, his possessions against future losses. The idea of his security must be prolonged to him throughout the whole vista that his imagina-tion can measure."[196] Bentham, foreshadowing Mill's thesis, regards the general disutility of the mere *possibility* of theft, deceit, or murder as a decisive point against such allowances. Indeed, as Mill says, it is precisely the foulest of crimes that fare the worst for Bentham: "A moralist on Ben-tham's principles may get as far as this, that he ought not to slay, burn, or steal."[197] Conversely, a Rule Utilitarian might accommodate the moral rea-soning of an Act Utilitarian by introducing more specific rules to account for more specific situations.

Countless gallons of ink have been spilled attempting to determine whether Mill is either an Act or a Rule Utilitarian. Traditionally, Mill was interpreted as an Act Utilitarian; then, in 1953, J. O. Urmson delivered his seminal Rule Utilitarian reading, which triggered an ongoing squabble.[198] However, this conflict just obscures and confuses, far more than it clarifies, our understanding of Mill's moral theory. In the decades since Urmson's reading, several scholars have cogently rejected the tedious propensity to force Mill into an Act versus Rule either/or, and have instead argued that Mill is neither/both: "It is impossible to impose a unified act theory or a unified rule theory on Mill."[199] Some scholars, like Fred Berger, have even ended up reaffirming the story above: Mill believes that "in practi-cal moral reasoning, the determination of what should be done should be made by relatively strict adherence to moral rules, except in exceptional cases, where the right action must be determined by appeal to the conse-quences of the act (including any rule-related tendencies *it* may have)."[200] And yet, even these relatively capacious readings bend toward needless

195. Bentham, *Principles of Morals and Legislation*, 74.
196. Bentham, *Principles of the Civil Code*, 308, W1.
197. Mill, "Bentham," 98.
198. See Urmson, "Interpretation of the Moral Philosophy of J. S. Mill," 33–39.
199. West, *Introduction to Mill's Utilitarian Ethics*, 77.
200. Berger, *Happiness, Justice, and Freedom*, 115.

complexity and interpretive muddle by analyzing Mill's moral theory in Act versus Rule terms.

We can see this straightaway by reviewing Mill's moral theory. The general happiness (Utility) is the societal *telos*, which grounds and governs *all* general rules and practices. And the Utility Principle (or the Greatest Happiness Principle, that is, the "creed" which recognizes Utility as the societal *telos*) is the moral standard, which judges individual actions according to their Utilitarian tendency. So far, so Benthamite. However, Bentham then posits a maximizing ethic and thus sinks all of life into morality, or maybe sinks all of life into morality and thus posits a maximizing ethic. Either way, Bentham thinks that *every* action has a decidedly moral tendency, as determined by felicific calculation. By contrast, by tracing the sentimental emergence of morality from sociality, Mill argues that only *some* actions have even a *seemingly* moral tendency, and that even fewer of these actions have a *truly* moral tendency, as discerned by impartial deliberation. Morality arises—the social *ought* becomes a moral *must*—because *some* (in)actions are, *in general*, or *as a rule*, integral to an impartial regard for the general happiness; hence the first pages of the Utilitarian Almanac. Mill then advances his three considerations explaining why we ought not to contravene these moral principles for light or transient reasons. Critically, these arguments are *not* evidence that Mill endorses either Act or Rule Utilitarianism, as most scholars have postulated. Rather, they are arguments as to why we normally ought to adhere, context notwithstanding, to the edicts of the Utilitarian Almanac; the moral rules themselves are *already presupposed* by these considerations.

Again, the Utility Principle is *not* a moral directive; it is a moral criterion, which tells us what matters or registers morally—the answer, according to Mill, being action tendencies which have an appreciable tie to the general happiness. Naturally, *general* action tendencies might appear, at times, to conflict with *particular* action tendencies. In such cases, Mill's approach is to adjudicate impartially between the general and the particular, granting full scope to their competing moral claims. For instance, to declare that one ought not to steal, lie, or kill *except when xyz* is to beg the question: what rule of action is being tacitly proposed, and would an impartial observer affirm such an exception to the moral rule barring theft, deceit, or murder? There is no avoiding rules in *moral* thinking. Conceivably, the particular could be as general as *except when expediency seems to dictate otherwise*; but unless society is willing to make *that* general of a concession to the particular, the expedient actor would be subjugating morality to their individual will.

To have beliefs about the Utility Principle is to have "beliefs as to the effects of some actions on [the general] happiness," and the "beliefs which have thus come down *are* the rules of morality for the multitude."[201] Indeed, to appeal directly to the Utility Principle *is* to consider whether a specific action would be compelled or prohibited, impartially, in the form of a moral rule, or to adjudicate impartially between clashing moral rules:

> If evil will arise in any specific case from our telling truth, we are forbidden by a law of morality from doing that evil: we are forbidden by another law of morality from telling falsehood. Here then are two laws of morality in conflict, and we cannot satisfy both of them. What is to be done but to resort to the primary test of all right and wrong, and to make a specific calculation of the good or evil consequences, as fully and impartially as we can? The evil of departing from a well-known and salutary rule is indeed one momentous item on that side of the account; but to treat it as equal to infinity, and as necessarily superseding the measurement of any finite quantities of evil on the opposite side, appears to us to be the most fatal of all mistakes in ethical theory.[202]

A relatively young Mill coauthored these lines with George Grote, the eminent classical historian and Philosophical Radical. Despite the Benthamite lingo, this passage underscores a key Millian theme: that morality is all about rules, or "laws," which typically arise for the purpose of inhibiting some "evil"; and that moral judgment often involves resolving conflicts between rules by impartially weighing their "conflicting utilities," which means "marking out the region within which one or the other [rule] preponderates." While the general happiness is "the ultimate destination," rules are "landmarks and direction-posts."[203] And yet, if *general* directions fail, given a radical or rare circumstance, then *particular* directions naturally ought to be followed—provided, of course, that the *same* directions should be followed by *any* traveler, assuming a similar point and condition of embarkation; that is, provided that these special directions *articulate a rule*, at least implicitly.

Thus, the basic problem with the Act versus Rule debate, as it relates to Mill, is the dichotomy it assumes between acts and rules. According to Mill's moral theory, general rules are naturally and necessarily *refined*, and thus limited, by particular acts, and particular acts are naturally and

201. Mill, *Utilitarianism*, 224, my emphasis.
202. Grote and Mill, "Taylor's Statesman," 639–640, *CW* 19. Written under the alias "Φ."
203. Mill, *Utilitarianism*, 223–224.

necessarily *defined*, and thus limited, as general rules. Having already stipulated the Act versus Rule framework, David Brink writes, "Though Mill does not treat secondary principles as mere rules of thumb in utilitarian calculation, he does not think that they should be followed uncritically or independently of their consequences. He thinks that they should be set aside in favor of direct appeal to the principle of utility when following them would be clearly suboptimal or when there is a conflict among secondary principles."[204] While Mill may largely concur with Brink in practice, the critical point is that there is *no such thing* as setting principle aside under the Utility Principle; indeed, what the Utility Principle defines is the standard by which moral principles arise and persist.

The Utility Principle does not describe *what* we must do; it explains *why* we must do what we must do, and thus provides the essential terms in which moral deliberation is properly framed. For example, why is deceit *generally* immoral? Simply, because deceit "does more than any one thing that can be named to keep back civilization, virtue, everything on which human happiness on the largest scale depends."[205] However, why might *this* or *that* deception be lawful or even requisite? Simply, because of the "peculiar nature of the case." Maybe "the rule against deceiving" ought to be "suspended" when we are menaced by "enemies in the field" or "malefactors in private life."[206] If so, then a narrower *but no less general* rule would pertain to this particular action tendency. Namely, whereas one principle would declare *presumptively, deceive not*, another principle would say *deceive any "murderer at the door."* The Utility Principle accounts for *both* directly and alike.

Understanding how the Utility Principle operates is vital to understanding how Mill is led, almost inexorably, to grant *absolute* protection to certain liberal rights. If Mill were merely a Rule Utilitarian, working under a Benthamite ethic, then whenever his matrix of moral rules arguably failed to produce optimal results, the rational temptation would promptly surface to resort to an Act Utilitarian calculus, which could have either liberal or illiberal consequences depending on the circumstances.

However, what Mill develops under *his* Utility Principle is something else altogether. In his essay *On Liberty*, Mill maintains that certain liberal rights—especially the rights to intellectual and ethical liberty—are *essential* to individual and social flourishing. Being bound to the happiness

204. Brink, *Mill's Progressive Principles*, 94.
205. Mill, *Utilitarianism*, 223.
206. Mill, "Whewell on Moral Philosophy," 182.

of *both* the one *and* the many, moral rights prohibiting interference with these liberties naturally justify themselves in Utilitarian court. And yet, Mill's even *deeper* move is to argue that there exist *zero* legitimate exceptions to these liberties. Those parties who would interfere with intellectual or ethical liberty have two options under the Utility Principle: either they must formulate their implicit rule of interference (which Mill thinks an impartial observer would *always* rebuff), or they must confess to acting not by rule, but by mere *will*—which is, indeed, what Mill believes *every* interference with intellectual or ethical liberty to be in the final analysis: an exercise of naked will, that is, of arbitrary power.

Justice Redefined

Before embarking on Mill's social and political philosophy, we must first scale the short ladder connecting his theory of happiness and morality to his theory of liberty and freedom; namely, the concept of *justice*. As Mill notes, the "idea of Justice" is one of "the strongest obstacles" to the acceptance of Utilitarianism. Critics of Utilitarianism contend that by equating morality to expediency, Utilitarianism ignores the fact that we have a higher moral "instinct" (that of justice) that ought to take precedence over any merely utilitarian concerns.[207] One of my main themes in this chapter has been a rebuttal of the assumption that Utility *is* Expediency. Mill attacks this notion outright: "the Expedient" is the *opposite* of—is, in fact, *hostile* to—the Utilitarian "Principle." And whatever his principles, Bentham does not *practice* Expediency either. Indeed, as we have seen, his felicific calculus gives outsized weight to "expectation utilities,"[208] where the heaviest weight goes to assuring people of certain social norms—such as those bound up with the "idea of Justice."

However, this introduces the central puzzle of the fifth chapter of *Utilitarianism*: If the Utility Principle is a *comprehensive* first principle, and if what it comprehends are the secondary principles of *morality*, then why does the language of justice even *exist?* Why do we speak in terms of justice if, indeed, the language of utility already covers the waterfront? Again, Mill's critics would eagerly reply, "Because the Utility Principle is *not* a comprehensive first principle; there are *other* secondary moral principles that fall *outside* the bounds of Utility and *within* the domain of Justice." Mill names the usual suspects: liberty; property; legality; desert; honesty;

207. Mill, *Utilitarianism*, 240.
208. Kelly, *Utilitarianism and Distributive Justice*, 84.

impartiality; and equality. All of these dicta are said to be matters of Justice, *not* Utility: we are obliged to respect liberty or property; to give others their due; to engage in honest dealing; and to treat others fairly or equally, not *only* because it respects the general happiness, but *chiefly* because it would be *unjust* to do otherwise.[209]

Of course, we are well acquainted by now with Mill's response: *all* these secondary principles *are* matters of Utility, and necessarily so. Indeed, they arise historically and entrench themselves socially in direct proportion to their Utilitarian import; they cannot be explained or defended without appealing to the general happiness; and when these rules come into conflict, their true telos, Utility, steps in as arbiter. And most importantly, our moral sentiments are mixed with Utility alone. But if "the origin and progressive growth of the idea of justice" can be brought under Utilitarianism, then we are still left wondering: What use, then, if any, do we have for the concept of justice? Can Mill "distinguish" the obligation of justice "from moral obligation in general," and thus fold justice into Utilitarianism?[210]

PERFECT DUTIES

In reply, Mill distinguishes between two types of moral duty arising under Utilitarianism: "duties of perfect obligation are those duties in virtue of which a correlative *right* resides in some person or persons; duties of imperfect obligation are those moral obligations which do not give birth to any right." A perfect duty bestows a claim-right—a "moral right"—on others, giving them the authority to exact the performance of said duty, and possibly to penalize its nonperformance by either law or opinion. Basically, Mill thinks the category of perfect duty is what we refer to, at least implicitly, whenever we appeal to justice: "the distinction exactly coincides with that which exists between justice and the other obligations of morality," namely, "a claim on the part of one or more individuals, like that which the law gives when it confers a proprietary or other legal right."[211] Justice, then, has conceptual weight and integrity in Mill's Utilitarian scheme; it denotes the *judicial* variety of moral obligation.

But which moral rules fall under justice? Which duties are perfect duties? Mill answers that a moral rule creates a claim-right, and is thus a rule of justice, or a perfect duty, if our obedience to the rule concerns "assignable persons." So, take an *imperfect* duty, like "charity or beneficence."

209. See Dworkin, *Justice for Hedgehogs*, chap. 15.
210. Mill, *Utilitarianism*, 241–244, 246.
211. Ibid., 247.

While we might be duty bound to be charitable or beneficent, no one has "a moral right to our generosity," for there are no "assignable persons" who would necessarily become the beneficiaries of our liberality—no one *in particular* is tied to our (failed) performance of this duty. However, there are myriad cases where moral violations *do* involve definite persons: "Whether the injustice consists in depriving a person of a possession, or in breaking faith with him, or in treating him worse than he deserves, or worse than other people who have no greater claims, in each case the supposition implies two things—a wrong done, and some assignable person who is wronged." Our duties to others establish "moral rights" if they could reproach us based on their relationship to us—we have specifically failed *them*. Thus, according to Mill, we behave justly so long as we do not violate "the rights—that is, the legitimate and authorized expectations—of anyone else."[212]

One addendum and one clarification. First, Mill here overlooks what he elsewhere emphasizes: that we have *social* duties that are tied to *societal* claim-rights; that we can frustrate the "legitimate and authorized expectations" not only of individuals, but also of the community, and can thus wrong the assignable members of society at large. Society has a moral right to certain "labours and sacrifices," which it can compel if necessary: "These conditions society is justified in enforcing at all costs to those who endeavour to withhold fulfilment."[213] And second, we might want to insist that there *are* various "assignable persons" connected to our imperfect duties. Just as we owe "labours and sacrifices" to the *community*, we might want to say that we owe "charity or beneficence" to the *impoverished* or *dispossessed*. True, but confused. An imperfect duty arises where "the particular occasions of performing it are left to our choice"; where we are bound to do one thing or another, "but not towards any definite person, nor at any prescribed time."[214] For instance, when we are obliged to be charitable, there are unlikely to be any "assignable persons" who could claim that our failure to show *them* charity, and *now*, is a violation of our duty, for we could likely fulfill our obligation to be charitable without *them* being the beneficiaries, or the beneficiaries *at this time*. That said, what is normally classed as an imperfect duty can, on occasion, become a perfect duty if "the urgency of [a] need" makes it so that a failure to act worthily in that instance is impartially interpreted as a direct harm by omission.

212. Ibid., 220, 247.
213. Mill, *On Liberty*, 276.
214. Mill, *Utilitarianism*, 247.

IMPERFECT DUTIES

And yet, upon further review, we might be tempted to say that Mill not only includes justice in morality but actually *reduces* morality to justice. In the fifth chapter of *Utilitarianism*, Mill undertakes to define what makes our moral sentiments distinctive and then to distinguish justice from the rest of morality. But, as we saw with respect to Mill's defense of the Utility Principle, our moral sentiments map onto the sphere of harm; and, as we just saw above, Mill thinks the concept of justice maps onto the sphere of perfect duty. However, if violating a perfect duty *is* what constitutes harm—indeed, injustice is *precisely* what would incur the moral ire of an impartial onlooker—then morality and justice are coextensive. This begs the question: in what sense can or does Mill *actually* regard imperfect duties as *moral* duties? This problem is sharpened by the fact that Mill often appears to *dissociate* imperfect duties from morality. Indeed, while Mill rejects the tendency of moralists like Bentham (but more so like Comte) to treat all liberality as a perfect duty and thus to "merge all morality into justice,"[215] he arguably merges all morality into justice the *opposite* way by framing all liberality in terms of sociality—in terms of a social "ought" rather than a moral "must." In his commentary on Comte, Mill once again defines the general ethic that pervades his moral thought:

> As a rule of conduct, to be enforced by moral sanctions, we think no more should be attempted than to prevent people from doing harm to others, or omitting to do such good as they have undertaken. Demanding no more than this, society, in any tolerable circumstances, obtains much more; for the natural activity of human nature, shut out from all noxious directions, will expand itself in useful ones. This is our conception of the moral rule prescribed by the religion of Humanity. But above this standard there is an unlimited range of moral worth, up to the most exalted heroism, which should be fostered by every positive encouragement, though not converted into an obligation.[216]

This passage—very typical of Mill—suggests that an impartial observer would be gripped by moral feelings *only* at the sight of just or unjust activity. Charity, beneficence, generosity: all such matters would inspire positive sentiments, but for the "positive worthiness" of the activity, not

215. Ibid., 248.
216. Mill, *Auguste Comte and Positivism*, 339. If Mill *were* operating with a maximizing ethic then this "moral worth" *would* be obligatory but just *inexpedient* to enforce.

for its moral necessity. And, to press Mill's language, surely these altruisms are oxymoronic when juxtaposed to "necessity." Liberality is *not* liberality unless it is received with social gratitude rather than moral approval. Mill even suggests that liberality is associated with a "milder feeling," not a moral feeling, "which attaches to the mere idea of promoting human pleasure or convenience."[217] Again, to act immorally is to violate a moral rule, and thus to incur just punishment, whether internal or external: "The proper office of those sanctions is to enforce upon everyone, the conduct necessary to give all other persons their fair chance: conduct which chiefly consists in not doing them harm, and not impeding them in anything which without harming others does good to themselves. To this must of course be added, that when we either expressly or tacitly undertake to do more, we are bound to keep our promise."[218] While a miserly bent should provoke painful sentiments, it is not positively *harmful*. Thus, the idea of an imperfect duty does not appear to gel with Mill's moral doctrine.

Naturally, maybe it *should*; maybe Mill gets this wrong. Maybe an impartial onlooker *would* experience moral sentiments at a showing or dearth of charity, beneficence, or generosity. Maybe the line between morality and liberality would be drawn at something like self-abnegation: "We must be altruistic up to but excluding the point at which we would begin to diminish our individual station or damage our individual aims or goals." This would satisfy one of Mill's apparent reasons for confining morality to justice: "the notion of a happiness for all, procured by the self-sacrifice of each, if the abnegation is really felt to be a sacrifice, is a contradiction."[219] But if a contribution is *not* a real sacrifice, then perhaps an impartial onlooker *would* gaze upon miserliness with moral disapproval. Think Scrooge.

Then again, Mill *does* come close to making such an argument. In the second chapter of *Utilitarianism*, Mill says that moral "abstinences" map onto what "would be generally injurious" if "practised generally," but that moral "virtue" maps onto the "multiplication of happiness," which *is* binding within reason. In short, we are obliged, or "called on," to at least "attend to" the good of others. And this duty is more or less extensive depending on our situation: it extends to "private utility," or "some few persons," for most people, but enlarges to "public utility" for that "one in a thousand" who "has it in his power" to be "a public benefactor."[220] And indeed, while Mill's

217. Mill, *Utilitarianism*, 259.
218. Mill, *Auguste Comte and Positivism*, 338.
219. Ibid., 337–338.
220. Mill, *Utilitarianism*, 220.

attention is devoted almost exclusively to the delineation and defense of perfect duties, it would be hard to imagine Mill not affirming the moral significance of a basic degree of liberality. He does not countenance the Benthamite duty to maximize the general happiness—a view that strains morality and distorts liberality. But it would be peculiar for him to deny the duty to take the good we *could* do for others into consideration.

That said, we might wonder why Mill tends to disregard our imperfect duties: why, when discussing morality, does he almost always speak solely to issues of justice? The most likely answer, I think, is that imperfect duties do not generate moral rights and thus do not generate many pressing moral problems: where there is no moral right there is no inherent potential for conflict; and where there is no inherent potential for conflict there is nothing much to concern a thinker of Mill's persuasion—the matter is one of conscience and thus a lower priority for a social, political philosopher. With any luck, the Scrooges of the world will find castigation enough in their own souls (or be visited by spirits), and we can always remonstrate with them. Furthermore, as we will see, society is permitted to extract from us a certain amount of what would, if spontaneously given, be regarded as liberality—for example, taxes. Therefore, in a functioning society, the moral faculty of the citizen will seldom be riled by the sight of miserliness; for miserliness, while not punished as such, will be countered indirectly by society's attempt to meet social needs via cost sharing. Cost sharing represents a perfect duty: to fail to bear your share of costs (free-riding) is to be unjust to your fellow citizens.

JUSTICE REVISITED

In sum, Mill's moral sphere is the most fundamental, most essential subset of sociality; and it is wisest to surmise its containing (all) justice and (basic) liberality. However, Mill also disaggregates justice further. While distinguishing justice from expediency, Mill writes, "Justice is a name for certain classes of moral rules, which concern the essentials of human well-being more nearly, and are therefore of more absolute obligation, than any other rules for the guidance of life; and the notion which we have found to be of the essence of the idea of justice, that of a right residing in an individual, implies and testifies to this more binding obligation." In other words, while the concept of justice covers the entire sphere of perfect duties, Mill thinks we *also* employ the language of justice in an even *more* special way to refer to perfect duties of *particular* import. Specifically, Mill says that the "most marked cases of injustice" are first and foremost "acts of wrongful aggression, or wrongful exercise of power over someone; the next are those which consist in wrongfully withholding from him something which is his due; in both cases, inflicting on him a positive hurt, either in the form of direct suffering, or of the privation of some good which he had reasonable ground" for "counting upon."[221]

Now, in these passages, it sounds at first as if these "marked cases of injustice" involve harm, whereas other, secondary injustices involve different, lesser offenses. If so, this would be another difficulty: for then Mill's sentimentalist account of morality would apply not to *all* injustices, but only to "marked" injustices. However, Mill is careful to correct any such impression. *All* injustices are associated with harm: "Good for good is also one of the dictates of justice; and this, though its social utility is evident, and though it carries with it a natural human feeling, has not at first sight that obvious connexion with hurt or injury, which, existing in the most elementary cases of just and unjust, is the source of the characteristic intensity of the sentiment. But the connexion, though less obvious, is not less real."[222] Our moral feelings are most reflexive and forceful in especially weighty instances of injustice, where the harm is most obvious and significant. These are what we might call the "central" cases of injustice; but they are surrounded by various "peripheral" cases.

On that note, we have covered the expanse of Mill's moral doctrine and can now shift gears to his social and political theory. In the next chapter we encounter the crux of Mill's liberal theory: the Harm Principle. My contention is that to act "harmfully," for Mill, is to violate a perfect duty and thus a moral right. Indeed, *On Liberty* is a painstakingly moral text. As I elaborate, Mill's argument for the inviolability of intellectual and ethical liberty and his analysis of legal or social interference are purely moral deductions; the whole of *On Liberty* is a reflection of the Utility Principle, that is, the moral sense and feeling of an impartial observer. Thus, my interpretation not only unifies the moving parts of *On Liberty* but also brings Mill's liberal theory into perfect harmony with his moral theory. Mill's liberal theory is, at core, an application of his theory of justice.

221. Ibid., 256.
222. Ibid., 255–256.

CHAPTER THREE

Liberal Justice

MILL ON SOCIAL HARM AND
INDIVIDUAL LIBERTY

To suppress free speech is a double wrong. It violates the rights of the hearer as well as those of the speaker.

—FREDERICK DOUGLASS

Jesus answered him, "If I have spoken wrongly, testify to the wrong; but if I have spoken rightly, why do you strike me?"

—JOHN 18:23

IN THIS CHAPTER, we turn our attention to Mill's social philosophy and his seminal liberal treatise *On Liberty*. Having discussed Mill's theory of happiness and morality, the question becomes: What implication does Mill's philosophy have for society in its relationship to the individual? What does it mean for a community of individuals to be well ordered with respect to the good and the right?

The study of Mill's liberal theory revolves around the issue of when and why it is that Mill thinks society ought to interfere with the individual. In general, there have been two conflicting schools of thought on this question. The traditional view says that Mill authorizes society to interfere only insofar as the individual is *harming* others. The spirit of this view is captured by the age-old line, "your right to swing your arm leaves off where my right not to have my nose struck begins."[1] However, the later, revisionist

---

1. Similar quotations have been attributed widely, but a brief search reveals that this line originally comes from an oration delivered by John B. Finch in Iowa City, Iowa, in 1882.

view says that Mill carves out a *circle of liberty*: certain basic rights belong exclusively to the individual (irrespective of any resultant harm), whereas society is authorized to interfere prudentially in whatever is not thereby protected (whether the individual is acting harmfully or not).[2]

In short, the traditional reading treats the sphere of individual liberty as an open question, extending over the entire plane of social life: *wherever* there is harm, society may, in theory, interfere; everywhere *else*, society must relent. While the individual will thus enjoy a blanket protection from society, the blanket is likely to be full of holes; that is, the individual is unlikely to enjoy any *absolute* liberty—for cannot *any* liberty be rightly interpreted, at times, to involve harmful consequences? By contrast, the revisionist reading treats the sphere of individual liberty as a closed question, demarcating separate zones for the individual and society. While this zoning limits the expanse of individual liberty, it conversely guarantees as absolute the basic liberties accorded to the individual.

The key passage in this debate is from chapter 1 of *On Liberty*, where Mill states his principle of liberty, which is known colloquially as the Harm Principle. Accordingly, for traditional scholars, the most vital question in expounding Mill's liberal theory is: what does Mill mean by "harm"? As we will see, interpreters have faced perennial difficulties in addressing this inquiry, which has been, in part, what motivates the revisionist claim that there are irresolvable problems with the so-called Harm Principle, and that the *real* principle of liberty—or doctrine of liberty—can be reconstructed by reconsidering how Mill *actually* argues throughout *On Liberty* and elsewhere. Typically, on this view, Mill's "harm" principle is reduced to an anti-paternalism principle, and his defense of individual liberty is justified by recognizing certain liberal rights as constitutive of human flourishing.

My overarching thesis in this chapter is that the revisionist view is largely correct *in practice*, but for traditional *reasons*. Indeed, what I develop below is a reading of Mill's liberal theory that splits the difference between the traditional and revisionist interpretations. In essence, the Harm Principle *is* the central, pivotal, decisive principle in *On Liberty*; but, properly understood, it does indeed provide guaranteed, absolute protection to a core set of basic liberties, and presumptive security to individual liberty in general.

The key to understanding Mill's liberal theory is to see how it emanates directly from his moral theory. As we saw last chapter, Mill's Utilitarianism,

---

2. For instance, see Jacobson, "Mill on Liberty, Speech, and the Free Society," 276–304.

which culminates in his theory of justice, can be described as the rule-based judgment of an impartial observer. What we get in *On Liberty*, then, is a working out of what this entails for society vis-à-vis the individual. In short, individual liberty is *the* moral rule of society, whereas harm is the *one* exception to this rule. And the question becomes: when does harm arise, and under what circumstances does it become expedient or judicious for society to sanction harm?

The central argument of *On Liberty* is Mill's defense of intellectual and ethical liberty; namely, the individual right to develop and express *any* belief or conception of the truth, and *any* desire or conception of the good. According to Mill, this right is *absolute*: it is *never* harmful, and interference with it is *always* harmful. This claim is one of the main rationales for the revisionist reading; for, on the traditional reading, it is difficult to comprehend how either freedom of speech or self-development could *always* be harmless. And yet, Mill methodically considers and counters the most salient reasons we might have for contending that these rights involve potential harm, or for proposing reasons for social interference—that is, exceptions to individual liberty—*other* than harm. Indeed, as we will see, Mill's defense of intellectual and ethical liberty exemplifies his moral theory at its very richest and rarest.

We will conclude this chapter by looking at two "hard" cases for Mill: *incivility* and *immaturity*. But, to begin, we pick up where we left Mill off last chapter, and consider what makes individual liberty the "first" rule of justice.

Liberty and Interference

Mill's social and political theory is centered on two values: *liberty* and *freedom*. Millian liberty is what Isaiah Berlin—Mill's twentieth-century torchbearer—dubs *non-interference*: "I am normally said to be free to the degree to which no man or body of men interferes with my activity. Political liberty in this sense is simply the area within which a man can act unobstructed by others."[3] When Mill uses terms like *personal freedom* or *individual liberty*, he is typically referring to freedom à la Berlin; to liberty in its "original sense," that is, "freedom from restraint."[4] By contrast, Millian freedom is what Philip Pettit calls *non-domination*. Domination

3. Berlin, "Two Concepts of Liberty," 169.
4. Mill, "Edinburgh Review," 292, *CW* 1.

"is exemplified by the relationship of master to slave or master to servant."[5] To be dominated is to be subject to arbitrary power; to be at the mercy of a *dominus*, one who can interfere with you at will across a certain range of interests. Non-domination, then, is the freedom of a *liber*, or free person, that is, an equal among equals or master among masters, one who is subject only to those interferences that are either congruent with or constitutive of freedom. When Mill uses terms like *political freedom* or *individual independence*, he is typically referring to freedom à la Pettit; to liberty in the sense of "Civil, or Social Liberty."[6]

I will have more to say on this distinction next chapter. In this section, though, I outline Mill's general theory of *liberty*. Mill is part of a long train of liberal theorists who uphold the individual's interest in, or right to, "a certain minimum area of personal freedom."[7] Thus, the question becomes: Why does Mill value liberty? And what does the value of liberty mean for morality? Mill eschews the rights-based liberalism of thinkers like Locke, who see liberty as a natural right and thus valuable a priori: "Men being, as has been said, by Nature, all free, equal and independent, no one can be put out of this Estate, and subjected to the Political Power of another, without his own *Consent*."[8] As a Utilitarian, Mill has no use for any such "abstract right."[9] Individual liberty, like anything else, is significant for Mill only insofar as it conduces to the happiness of the individual or society.

The General Value of Liberty

Bentham's hedonism gives two general reasons to value liberty. First, to be unrestricted in our activity is itself pleasant, and to be restricted in our activity is itself painful: "every restraint imposed upon liberty is liable to be followed by a natural feeling of pain, more or less great, independent of an infinite variety of inconveniences and sufferings which may result from the particular mode of this restraint." Whatever the context, there is "always one reason against every coercive law, and one reason which, were there no other, would be sufficient by itself: it is, that such a law is restrictive of liberty."[10] And second, we need liberty in order to choose and chase our pleasures. Now, this reason is weakened if *more* pleasure

---

5. Pettit, *Republicanism*, 22.
6. Mill, *On Liberty*, 217, *CW* 18.
7. Berlin, "Two Concepts of Liberty," 171.
8. Locke, *Second Treatise of Government*, §95.
9. Mill, *On Liberty*, 224.
10. Bentham, *Principles of the Civil Code*, 301, *W* 1.

can be obtained with relatively *less* liberty—perhaps under the dominion of a wise, benevolent despot. And yet, it can be argued that individuals are, in general, the most reliable, efficient judges of what goods or activities are most agreeable to them. As Henry Sidgwick says, we normally have a "more intimate knowledge of [our] own desires and needs"[11] than do others. So, all things equal: more liberty, more pleasure; more restraint, more pain.

As a supra-*hedonist*, Mill gives every indication that he agrees: "all restraint, *quâ* restraint, is an evil." Liberty is a prerequisite to everything we do—to the pursuit of happiness in all its various forms. Moreover, the power to interfere always risks abuse or tyranny, and interference is generally imprudent or inefficient anyway: "the strongest of all the arguments against the interference of the public with purely personal conduct, is that when it does interfere, the odds are that it interferes wrongly, and in the wrong place." Conversely, there is "no one so fit to conduct any business, or to determine how or by whom it shall be conducted, as those who are personally interested in it."[12] Thus, Mill thinks the individual ought to be given free rein unless there is a moral reason to the contrary: "It is held that there should be no restraint not required by the general good."[13] And indeed, if nothing else, the "presumption" "in favor" of liberty can be admitted as a purely juridical principle: "in practical matters, the burthen of proof is supposed to be with those who are against liberty; who contend for any restriction or prohibition, either any limitation of the general freedom of human action, or any disqualification or disparity of privilege affecting one person or kind of persons, as compared with others."[14] Liberty is valuable a priori on Utilitarian grounds: we all acknowledge our interest in interference being at least explained or defended.

In addition, as a *supra*-hedonist, Mill has a "higher" reason to value liberty having to do with human flourishing: "To be prevented from doing what one is inclined to, or from acting according to one's own judgment of what is desirable, is not only always irksome, but always tends, pro tanto, to starve the development of some portion of the bodily or mental faculties, either sensitive or active; and unless the conscience of the individual goes freely with the legal restraint, it partakes, either in a great or in a small degree, of the degradation of slavery."[15] In this way, Mill undercuts the notion that "true" happiness could ever be realized under the auspices of

11. Sidgwick, *Methods of Ethics*, 401.
12. Mill, *On Liberty*, 283, 293, 305.
13. Mill, *Subjection of Women*, 262, *CW* 21.
14. Ibid., 262.
15. Mill, *Principles of Political Economy*, 938, *CW* 3.

a wise, benevolent despot. For, in general, adherence to such an "immense tutelary power"[16] implies passivity and thus the inactivity of the higher faculties: "Instruction is only one of the desiderata of mental improvement; another, almost as indispensable, is a vigorous exercise of the active energies; labour, contrivance, judgment, self-control: and the natural stimulus to these is the difficulties of life."[17] Naturally, much of what we do on a daily basis does not involve vigorous, active energy, or self-development, to any significant extent. But Mill's intuition is that the interferences most likely to trouble us are rarely, if ever, trotted out for such trivialities. Rather, what motivates *On Liberty* is the tendency for the powers that be to interfere with entire frames of mind and spheres and forms of life.

Finally, as Mill conveys throughout *On Liberty*, the general value of liberty is also psychological: individuals will pursue "true" happiness—will frequently and spontaneously exercise their higher faculties in accordance with the higher pleasures—only where the tides of persecution, ostracism, and stigmatization have receded. Only where liberty reigns as a shared ideal will the higher faculties vibrate energetically; only in an "atmosphere of freedom" will individuals feel empowered and emboldened to think and act for and as themselves. To determine for and as ourselves what we believe to be true or desirable, or to decide for and as ourselves which goods or activities to pursue, is to risk swimming against one current or another. And unless we feel at liberty to do so, we are more likely than not to descend into a sort of mental "pacification," where we do not *exercise* our higher faculties so much as *operate* them in deference or obedience to some reigning dogma or custom. Those few who enjoy the status or power to weather attacks—those "whose bread is already secured, and who desire no favours from men in power, or from bodies of men, or from the public"—may find some happiness even in illiberal climes; but most people are vulnerable.[18]

Thus, based on last chapter, we might say that *liberty* is the moral rule at the heart of *On Liberty*—Mill's "first" rule of justice. But if liberty is a moral rule then the question becomes: does it brook any exceptions? Here we encounter Mill's "principle of liberty,"[19] what is typically called the Harm Principle. As I contend, the Harm Principle holds, simply, that liberty can be restricted pro tanto only to thwart or remedy injustice. Indeed, as we will see, while Mill opposes any and all "morals" legislation based

16. Tocqueville, *Democracy in America*, vol. 2, §4, chap. 6.
17. Mill, *Principles of Political Economy*, 943.
18. Mill, *On Liberty*, 241–242.
19. See ibid., 290, 301, 305.

on mere partiality, passion, or prejudice, he champions the sociopolitical enforcement of morality as impartiality. Mill's practical philosophy is (*his*) Utilitarianism all the way down.

Enforcing Justice

Bentham's ethic of interference is an application of his moral theory: Utility is all that matters morally; to be moral is to be impartial; and to be impartial is to follow the Act Utilitarian dictates of the felicific calculus. Thus, legislators ought to interfere with individual liberty only to promote the general happiness; they have a presumptive reason to require any act "which promises to be beneficial upon the whole to the community," and to prohibit any act "which promises to be pernicious upon the whole to the community." However, Bentham adds that "it is not every such act that the legislator ought to compel him to perform" or "abstain from." The legislator should intervene only when intervention would be optimal in light of the felicific calculus. Indeed, according to Bentham, interference should, under most conditions, be more uncommon than not, considering that most interferences are either "groundless," "inefficacious," "unprofitable," or "needless."[20] Bentham's exposition of these terms is extensive; but the crucial point is that interference, while often suboptimal, is on the table for Bentham whenever the law could be used to compel optimal activity instead of relying on the discretion of the individual—so, in theory, *always*.

Mill follows suit, but entirely on his own terms: Utility is all that matters morally; to be moral is to be impartial; but to be impartial is to adhere to the rule-based directives of an impartial observer—hence Mill's ethic of interference, whereby society has a presumptive reason to interfere with individual liberty, whether by law or opinion, only in order to thwart or remedy injustice. Mill, too, notes that "good reasons" often exist, having to do with "the special expediencies of the case," to refrain from enforcing justice: "either because it is a kind of case in which he is on the whole likely to act better, when left to his own discretion," or "because the attempt to exercise control would produce other evils, greater than those which it would prevent."[21] However, the critical point is that interference, while often inexpedient, is on the table for Mill whenever the one, few, or many violates a claim-right—so, in theory and practice, *sometimes*, its incidence depending on the general state of moral virtue.

---

20. Bentham, *Principles of Morals and Legislation*, 144, *W* 1.
21. Mill, *On Liberty*, 225.

Of course, those familiar with Mill will object: "Mill's ethic of interference is found in *On Liberty* in the Harm Principle." And quite right; but what I will argue below is that the Harm Principle, properly understood, tells the story above precisely. The Harm Principle is simply Mill's Justice Principle. This brings me close to certain scholars who see Mill as having a sanction-based moral theory.[22] But, unlike these readings, I think there is still great interpretive import to the traditional, Benthamesque reading of the Harm Principle, which maintains that "harm" is whatever has "pernicious," or adverse, consequences.

THE HARM PRINCIPLE

On Liberty is Mill's seminal essay on "Civil, or Social Liberty: the nature and limits of the power which can be legitimately exercised by society over the individual." This topic sits at the center of Mill's liberal theory and liberal theory in general. What kind of relationship ought to prevail between "individual independence" and "social control"? What sort of "limit," if any, should be placed on legal or social coercion? Where does "legitimate interference" end and "tyranny" or "despotism" begin? What rule, "on broad grounds of principle," ought to determine "the rights of the individual against society"?[23] Just as the Mill of *Utilitarianism* looks to discern the principle grounding all morality—that is, the Utility Principle—the Mill of *On Liberty* looks to establish the principle grounding all liberty. The result is one of the most revered and reviled passages in the history of political thought.

At the heart of *On Liberty* lies what Mill calls "the principle of liberty," but what is commonly known as the Harm Principle:

> The object of this Essay is to assert one very simple principle, as entitled to govern absolutely the dealings of society with the individual in the way of compulsion and control, whether the means used be physical force in the form of legal penalties, or the moral coercion of public opinion. That principle is, that the sole end for which mankind are warranted, individually or collectively, in interfering with the liberty of action of any of their number, is self-protection. That the only purpose for which power can be rightfully exercised over any member of a civilized community, against his will, is to prevent harm to others. His own good, either physical or moral, is not a sufficient warrant. He cannot rightfully be compelled to do or forbear because it will be better for him

22. For instance, see Brown, "Mill's Moral Theory," 17.
23. Mill, *On Liberty*, 217, 220, 222.

to do so, because it will make him happier, because, in the opinions of others, to do so would be wise, or even right. These are good reasons for remonstrating with him, or reasoning with him, or persuading him, or entreating him, but not for compelling him, or visiting him with any evil in case he do otherwise. To justify that, the conduct from which it is desired to deter him, must be calculated to produce evil to someone else. The only part of the conduct of any one, for which he is amenable to society, is that which concerns others. In the part which merely concerns himself, his independence is, of right, absolute. Over himself, over his own body and mind, the individual is sovereign.[24]

The influence of this passage on liberalism cannot be overstated. The Harm Principle paints *the* classic picture of *the* modern liberal society, one in which individuals are at liberty to think, say, or do whatever *unless* they harm others. Thus, in effect, the Harm Principle rules out all paternalism: verboten is any interference aimed at the good of the individual. Interference can promote or preserve the well-being of the individual incidentally, but that cannot be the basic reason for the interference. Also banned is any interference based on mere "dislikings,"[25] that is, on mere disfavor or disgust. Interference can gratify our partialities, passions, or prejudices incidentally; but, again, that cannot be the basic reason for the interference. Interference is legitimate only insofar as it is required to thwart or remedy harm. And yet, this prompts the perennial question: what, for Mill, *constitutes* harm?

The difficulty in answering this question is that Mill never defines harm directly and appears to be using the concept in various ways. Nonetheless, myriad scholars have labored to pin down what Mill ironically dubs a "very simple principle." Most readings, while diverse, can be grouped under one of two broad headings. Some scholars argue that Mill is operating with an *ordinary* concept of harm; that he is speaking in a common, colloquial manner. For these scholars, the Harm Principle applies to things like "bad consequences,"[26] "perceptible damage,"[27] or "negative impacts."[28] Other scholars argue that Mill is operating with a *special* concept of harm; that he is speaking in a more bounded, idiosyncratic fashion. For these scholars, the Harm Principle refers to injuries to "primary or essential

24. Ibid., 223–224.
25. Ibid., 222.
26. Turner, " 'Harm' and Mill's Harm Principle," 301.
27. Riley, *Mill on Liberty*, 99.
28. Hansson, "Mill's Circle(s) of Liberty," 738.

interests,"[29] "fundamental interests,"[30] or "interests in which [we] have rights."[31] In what follows, I do not resolve so much as dissolve this debate by showing how both of these readings have an essential role to play in *On Liberty* and arrive anyway at the same practical point.

This debate between the ordinary and the special readings straddles a parallel dispute over what Mill means by "self-regarding,"[32] a term he employs several times as a pithy label for the variety of activity that is protected under the Harm Principle. For the better part of a century after the publication of *On Liberty*, Mill's critics took his concept of harm (*other-regarding*) to mean any (in)action that merely *affects* others: "The crucial point in this criticism is the supposition that Mill's principle depends for its vitality on there being some actions, including some important ones, which are free from social consequences, i.e., that they affect no one but the agent himself."[33] Since this standard would seem to apply to very little (in)activity indeed, a more refined interpretation was wanting, and was supplied by J. C. Rees, whose seminal essay argues that Mill's concept of harm is best understood as applying not to what affects others *full stop*, but to what affects the *interests* of others.[34] And yet, this reading still begs the question, because what Mill is focusing his attention on is "such actions as are *prejudicial* to the interests of others."[35] In short, the attempt to define "self-regarding" *directly* is circular, for the fact is that the concept of self-regarding (in)activity is, for Mill, a corollary to the Harm Principle: our (in)activity is "self-regarding" insofar as it is harmless.

Briefly, I should also note an enduring but ultimately false conundrum. As Mill proclaims, the Harm Principle is to "govern absolutely." But how can a Utilitarian make such a declaration? Indeed, how can *any* principle apropos "compulsion and control" be absolute *other* than the Utility Principle? This is one of those perennial problems that has caused endless debate and consternation, where we see scholars attempting to "have their genuine liberalism and eat their utilitarianism too"[36] by inventing every variety of conflicting solution.[37] However, as I suggested above, and as we will see below, the Harm Principle is not an independent liberal axiom

29. Gray, *Mill on Liberty*, 51.

30. Dyzenhaus, "John Stuart Mill and the Harm of Pornography," 546.

31. Brink, *Mill's Progressive Principles*, 174.

32. See Mill, *On Liberty*, 226, 277–279, 281–283, 285, 295–296.

33. Rees, "Re-reading of Mill on Liberty," 115–116.

34. Ibid., 118ff.

35. Mill, *On Liberty*, 292, my emphasis.

36. Weinstein, "Interpreting Mill," 45.

37. See Turner, "Absolutism Problem in *On Liberty*," 322–336.

that in any way competes with the Utility Principle; quite the contrary, the former is an emanation of the latter.

THE ORDINARY READING

To defenders of the ordinary reading, the Harm Principle gives immunity only to what is free from adverse effects. And there is plenty of evidence for this view. For instance, Mill declares that the Harm Principle protects "all that portion of a person's life and conduct which affects only himself," but permits interference with whatever "affects others," constitutes "a social act," or poses a "risk of damage."[38] And in *Principles of Political Economy*, Mill contends that society has no business with what is "personal only, involving no consequences, none at least of a painful or injurious kind, to other people."[39] If "injurious" has a special meaning here, then Mill is not making it clear. Rather, Mill appears to be making the barest distinction between consequences that are either salutary or easily ignored and consequences that are simply *negative*. The special reading aside, there is undoubtedly a solid rationale for the enduring claim that Mill is utilizing an ordinary and thus "expansive"[40] concept of harm.

The traditional issue facing this interpretation is the worry that Mill cannot safeguard liberty with such a weak or thin standard. Virtually *all* activity (*and* inactivity) *can* and often *does* have at least *some* adverse effects. How, then, can the Harm Principle reliably guard the individual against legal or social interference? This dilemma led a century of Mill's detractors to deride *On Liberty* as an unabashed example of liberal atomism.[41] The thought was that Mill *must* be taking the individual to be an island, whose (in)activity is generally consequence free. Yet Mill explicitly rejects liberal atomism: "No person is an entirely isolated being." And accordingly, he deems it "monstrous" to welcome coercive control over *whatever* has adverse effects, for "there is no violation of liberty which it would not justify."[42] But how, then, can Mill defend a wide circle of liberty on the ordinary reading of the Harm Principle? Does it not lead inexorably to this "monstrous" conclusion?

---

38. Mill, *On Liberty*, 225, 282, 296.

39. Mill, *Principles of Political Economy*, 938.

40. Turner, "'Harm' and Mill's Harm Principle," 300–326 passim.

41. For the classic critique on this line, see Stephen, *Liberty, Equality, Fraternity*, 1–32. For a historical overview of this critique, see Rees, "Re-reading of Mill on Liberty," 115–118.

42. Mill, *On Liberty*, 280, 288.

Not at all. The Harm Principle defines what is subject to *potential* interference, nothing more. Society must still meet the ensuing challenge of actually *justifying* interference. Thus, while the ordinary reading opens nearly anything to interference, this does not give society carte blanche. Any proposed interference must still pass Utilitarian muster; that is, it must reflect an optimal "balancing of reasons"[43] or "balance of considerations."[44] From this vantage point, if we saddle Mill with a "direct" Act Utilitarian stance, then, yes, a preponderance of individual (in)activity will be forever at the mercy of society. And indeed, this saddling has led some scholars to infer that Utility cannot *really* be at the heart of *On Liberty*, and that Mill *must* be appealing to a separate standard, like "human dignity."[45] However, if we instead interpret Mill as an "indirect" Act Utilitarian or, better yet, as a Rule Utilitarian, then we can generate any number of reasons for observing rules of thumb or moral rules that strongly favor certain liberal rights. And, of course, Mill offers many such reasons throughout his writings. So, in other words, we might say that the ordinary reading protects as much individual liberty as moral impartiality would see fit to secure.

But this solution raises another problem; namely, it makes the Harm Principle look pointless. On the ordinary reading, the Harm Principle seems to encircle only a vanishing sphere of pristine (in)activity, whereas the Utility Principle looks to be doing *all* the work of drawing the lines between the individual and society. Indeed, by the logic above, Mill could just omit the Harm Principle and rely directly on the Utility Principle. This conclusion is obviously troubling to those scholars who believe that Mill's liberalism has, or ought to have, normative priority; that his defense of liberty is not, or should not be, dependent on his Utilitarianism. Regardless, the difficulty for us remains: if basically *all* (in)activity is, in theory, open to interference—and, so, if any case for interference ultimately rests on its Utilitarian merits—then why not jettison the Harm Principle and just proceed with the Utility Principle?

The typical reply is that the Harm Principle makes the small but key contribution of *expressly* forbidding all reasons for interference *other* than harm. The Harm Principle "implies that when the only argument for interference is the person's own good, then there is no valid [Utilitarian] argument for such interference."[46] In other words, the Harm Principle

43. Hansson, "Mill's Circle(s) of Liberty," 747.
44. Turner, "'Harm' and Mill's Harm Principle," 309.
45. Kateb, "Reading of *On Liberty*," 28.
46. Hansson, "Mill's Circle(s) of Liberty," 738.

outlaws paternalism; and again, it also bans interferences that are meant to satisfy a mere partiality, passion, or prejudice. Whether it forbids even *more* reasons for interference, like offense or anguish, is debatable.[47] What this reply suggests, though, wittingly or not, is that the Harm Principle simply *is* the Utility Principle in an applied, sociopolitical form. On the ordinary reading, Mill is making the Utilitarian claim that the only legitimate reason for interference is *disutility*—or what in social or political discourse we might call *harm*. Thus, while the Harm Principle is most definitely *not* pointless (for Mill does not formulate the Utility Principle as such elsewhere in *On Liberty*), one nonetheless finds that it just parrots his Utilitarianism.

However, I think the Harm Principle is also playing another, deeper role on the ordinary reading, one that is not as well appreciated. In truth, there *is* an area of life that, *in itself,* is *necessarily* free from adverse effects: *inward liberty.* Inward liberty is associated with "the inward domain of consciousness," and comprises "liberty of conscience," "liberty of thought and feeling," "freedom of opinion and sentiment," and "liberty of taste."[48] The critical thing to observe is that *none* of these inward liberties, *in themselves,* can have *any* outward consequences. Simply, you cannot affect anything merely by thinking or feeling or desiring something. Outward consequences issue only from (in)activity, which has a contingent relationship to your inward existence. Thus, the ordinary reading involves a thicker standard than is usually recognized. Interference is confined not to disutility alone, but, more precisely, to the disutility *of (in)activity* alone. The "ordinary" Harm Principle bars society from invading the inner sanctuary of your mind, heart, and soul. Violating inward liberty is a nonstarter for Mill *whatever* the excuse, paternalistic or otherwise.[49]

But what justifies the "ordinary" Harm Principle? On what basis does Mill restrict interference to disutility alone and also preclude all interference with inward liberty? The first part—which forbids all reasons for interference *other* than harm—is just the Utility Principle in sociopolitical garb: all that matters morally is the general happiness, and thus the only legitimate reason for interference is the Utilitarian tendency of (in)activity. The second part—which, in essence, declares there to be *no* Utilitarian case for *ever* interfering with inward liberty—is the central argument of

47. See Turner, "'Harm' and Mill's Harm Principle," 310–311.

48. Mill, *On Liberty,* 225–226. Mill writes, "tastes."

49. That is, the protection of inward liberty is not just the obverse of anti-paternalism. Society might want to control your inward life for reasons having nothing to do with you or your good.

the second and third chapters of *On Liberty*. As I expound below, Mill contends that the liberty to develop (and also to express) *any* belief or conception of the truth (chapter 2), and the liberty to develop (and also to express) *any* desire or conception of the good (chapter 3) are each in the impartial interest of *both* the individual *and* society at large; that they are thus moral rules, and doubly weighty; and that there are *zero* impartial exceptions to them—at least not in "peacetime." In sum, Mill's defense of the "ordinary" Harm Principle is, first, his previous account of the Utility Principle, and, second, his subsequent account of intellectual and ethical liberty.

As Mill penned in a letter while completing *On Liberty*, "the Liberty it treats of is moral and intellectual rather than political."[50] Now, we should not be misled: while *On Liberty* basically shelves political freedom proper (a subject Mill fixes on elsewhere), his essay clearly tackles the issue of social freedom.[51] Nonetheless, Mill's comment is illuminating. From one vantage point, what the Harm Principle is doing is elevating inward liberty— the essence of "l'autonomie de l'individu," or individual autonomy—and proclaiming it to be sacrosanct. As soon as the inward turns outward, the (in)active individual is subject to the demands of "l'intérêt general," or the general interest, which triggers Mill's moral theory.[52] Thus, the "ordinary" Harm Principle, fully unfolded, makes the profound claim that to have an impartial regard for the general happiness is to regard the exercise of inward liberty as inviolable: "Over himself, over his own body and mind, the individual is sovereign."

THE SPECIAL READING

To defenders of the special reading, the Harm Principle is far more generous in its protections. The fact that (in)activity has adverse effects is not enough to label it harmful; it is harmful only if it vitiates vital interests or violates moral rights. And, as before, there is plenty of evidence for this view. For example, while harmless acts must be let alone, Mill writes, "Acts injurious to others require a totally different treatment. Encroachment on their rights; infliction on them of any loss or damage not justified by his own rights; falsehood or duplicity in dealing with him; unfair or ungenerous use of advantages over them; even selfish abstinence from defending

50. Mill, "To Theodor Gomperz," 539, *CW* 15.
51. See Mill, "To Pasquale Villari," 534, *CW* 15.
52. Mill, "To Emile Acollas," 1832, *CW* 17.

them against injury—these are fit objects of moral reprobation, and, in grave cases, of moral retribution and punishment." Mill looks to be *equating* "injurious" to rights violations or other grave wrongs. Indeed, echoing his theory of justice, Mill says that even to be "*subject*" to "moral reprobation" (the lighter sanction for harm) an action must "involve a breach of duty to others."[53] Hence, there is also a solid rationale for the latter-day "consensus" that Mill is utilizing a special and thus "restrictive" concept of harm.[54]

One of the alleged issues facing the special reading is the fact that Mill plainly allows for interference with what appear to be relatively trivial (in)activities. Many proponents of the "special" Harm Principle argue that interference is admissible only where "vital interests are endangered,"[55] chiefly the interests of freedom and security. But this is plainly false; Mill approves of interferences where no vital interests are at stake. For instance, he avers that certain "violation[s] of good manners," in particular, "offences against decency," can "rightfully be prohibited."[56] Furthermore, the special reading faces the problem of being rather counterintuitive. Under the special reading, Mill is assuming a highly idiosyncratic, moralized notion of harm, under which it is *false* to think about adverse effects *as harms* as long as the offending party is acting within its rights. Can the special reading account for Mill's full range of interferences? And what about the peculiarity of this concept of harm?

The special reading can embrace all of Mill's interferences as long as it is framed as an extension of his theory of justice—so, as involving not vital interests only, but *anything* to which we have a moral right, whether peripheral or central. Hence, if it is resolved that public decency is morally significant, then we cannot act indecently without flouting our duty to the "assignable"[57] members of society at large. Reading the "special" Harm Principle as Mill's Justice Principle also allows for an intuitive account of the special concept of harm. On the special reading, Mill is just using a "public law" notion of harm: harm in the sense of a crime or tort. The interests (minor or major) covered by the "special" Harm Principle "depend for their existence on social recognition and are closely connected with prevailing standards about the sort of behaviour a man can

53. Mill, *On Liberty*, 279, my emphasis.
54. Turner, "'Harm' and Mill's Harm Principle," 300.
55. Gray, *Mill on Liberty*, 52.
56. Mill, *On Liberty*, 295–296.
57. Mill, *Utilitarianism*, 247, *CW* 10.

legitimately expect from others."[58] Where there is "no right to complain"[59] there is no harm, which is an acquired but natural outlook; it is how we think, or, for Mill, how we *ought* to think, as social, political animals.

One might even say that *On Liberty* is written for and from the perspective of the impartial observer. The "special" Harm Principle reflects the moral consciousness that Mill lays out in his moral theory: "a person whose resentment is really a moral feeling, that is, who considers whether an act is blameable before he allows himself to resent it—such a person, though he may not say expressly to himself that he is standing up for the interest of society, certainly does feel that he is asserting a rule which is for the benefit of others as well as for his own."[60] From a self-invested but neutral standpoint, the upright citizen will see harm only in the infraction of a moral rule; only in the defiance of a disinterestedly interested standard of behavior. The injuries, pains, or damages that an individual can suffer at the hands of the one, few, or many are not harmful (in this special sense) unless they are "blameable." Morally virtuous persons will never detect harm in morally innocent (in)activity, for they will always sympathize with the impartial interests being protected as objects of self-interest. A noble soul will perceive harm only in iniquity.

And indeed, the closer one looks at *On Liberty* the more one is struck by the cogency of the special reading: "In the conduct of human beings towards one another, it is necessary that general rules should for the most part be observed, in order that people may know what they have to expect; but in each person's own concerns, his individual spontaneity is entitled to free exercise."[61] In this allusion to the Harm Principle, Mill draws a line between behavior that "concerns" only the individual and behavior that is regulated by the "general rules" of society. Thus, when Mill uses a term like "concerns" in a seemingly ordinary manner, perhaps he is *really* referring to what "concerns" the one, few, or many in their capacity as rights-bearing parties. Maybe the "*extra*ordinary" Harm Principle speaks to what "affects" us not as egocentric persons, who are wont to resent *any* adverse effects, but as conscientious citizens, who are disinclined to recognize any presumptive reason for interference unless the malefactor is clearly flouting the common good.

Even more transparently, Mill analyzes the Harm Principle as follows. Self-regarding faults should elicit measured displeasure: "He may be to

58. Rees, "Re-reading of Mill on Liberty," 119.
59. Mill, *On Liberty*, 278.
60. Mill, *Utilitarianism*, 249.
61. Mill, *On Liberty*, 277.

us an object of pity, perhaps of dislike, but not of anger or resentment; we shall not treat him as an enemy of society." But other-regarding *harms* should incite *moral* displeasure: "It is far otherwise if he has infringed the rules necessary for the protection of his fellow creatures, individually or collectively. The evil consequences of his acts do not then fall on himself, but on others." A self-regarding fault is a "defect of prudence or of personal dignity," whereas an other-regarding harm is "an offence against the rights of others." The smoking gun is that Mill adjoins "evil consequences" to rule infringements, which implies that the ordinary reading's focus on adverse effects is valid yet confused: Mill is talking about *general* effects (i.e., adverse *tendencies*) in the spirit of the Utility Principle. Conduct is "taken out of the self-regarding class," and is "amenable to moral disapprobation in the proper sense of the term," only when it violates "a distinct and assignable obligation to any other person or persons."[62]

That said, there are moments in *On Liberty* that throw this whole line of interpretation into question: "The acts of an individual may be hurtful to others, or wanting in due consideration for their welfare, without going the length of violating any of their constituted rights." Now, maybe "*constituted*" means something akin to *central* (think "statutory") rights, as opposed to *peripheral* (think "customary") rights, which would be a clue as to why Mill insists that society is "justified in enforcing" them "at all costs." And yet, in the same passage, Mill appears to define our "constituted rights" as "certain interests, which, either by express legal provision or by tacit understanding, ought to be considered as rights," which looks to cover the gamut of central *and* peripheral rights. Also, there is Mill's notion that *all* trade is "a social act," and thus "comes within the jurisdiction of society," simply because it "affects the interests of other persons."[63] In short, while the special reading provides an astute, incisive analysis of *On Liberty*, the ordinary reading cannot be dismissed.[64]

But well that it cannot. There is a palpable desire in *On Liberty* to give meaning not just to self-regarding conduct, but to "*purely* self-regarding" conduct; conduct that not only respects rights but also exists *conceptually* within the province of individuality. The *two times* Mill uses the phrase "purely self-regarding" in *On Liberty*, he is referring to drunkenness: "No person ought to be punished simply for being drunk; but a soldier or a policeman should be punished for being drunk on duty."[65] This is

62. Ibid., 279–281.

63. Ibid., 276, 293.

64. For further analysis, see Turner, "'Harm' and Mill's Harm Principle," 305–309.

65. Mill, *On Liberty*, 282, 295.

telling. Like having a thought or feeling, being drunk is an *inward* experience, only contingently related to outward (in)activity. Drunkenness *itself* affects nothing but the brain and body, just like thinking or feeling *itself* affects nothing but the mind, heart, or soul. So, despite the acuity of the special reading, the ordinary reading has a profound role to play: to accentuate Mill's commitment to inward liberty.

INTERFERING IMPARTIALLY

More important, though, than what exactly Mill *means* by harm is how Mill actually *reasons* in *On Liberty*. However we read him, the reality is that Mill negotiates the relationship between society and the individual in accordance with his moral theory. The ordinary and special readings look forward and backward, respectively, to the Utility Principle. The ordinary reading sits at the base of Mill's moral theory: what we have here are raw moral feelings, as yet untreated by the moral filter of impartiality. Conversely, the special reading stands atop the peak of Mill's moral theory: what we have here are moral rights, derived from the moral discernment of the impartial observer. The Harm Principle gives society at large—that is, the "assignable" one, few, or many—whatever jurisdiction would be granted over the individual by an impartial regard for the general happiness. Whatever "harm" is, the upshot is that the individual is answerable for unjust (in)activity alone.

Mill begins the fourth chapter of *On Liberty* by restating the essay's core question: "What, then, is the rightful limit to the sovereignty of the individual over himself? Where does the authority of society begin? How much of human life should be assigned to individuality, and how much to society?" And Mill answers, "Each will receive its proper share, if each has that which *more* particularly concerns it. To individuality should belong the part of life in which it is *chiefly* the individual that is interested; to society, the part which *chiefly* interests society."[66] Harm, shmarm—this reply cuts right to the chase. The object of *On Liberty* is to divide the world between the individual and society in a balanced, reasonable manner. Indeed, the implicit idea is to adopt the viewpoint of an impartial observer. While an (in)activity can concern *both* the individual *and* society at large, the (in)activity "chiefly" concerns *either* the individual *or* society at large depending on what a sympathizing spectator, identifying with both parties, would judge to be the weightier interest.

66. Ibid., 276, my emphases.

In short, to enforce justice, the community ought to observe "large and wise views of the good of the whole, neither sacrificing the individual to the aggregate nor the aggregate to the individual, but giving to duty on one hand and to freedom and spontaneity on the other their proper province."[67] To be "large and wise" is to be "disinterested and benevolent."[68] For example, individual well-being falls within the province of the individual not because individual well-being is of *no* interest to the aggregate, but because the individual "is the person *most* interested in his own well-being: the interest which any other person, except in cases of strong personal attachment, can have in it, is *trifling*, compared with that which he himself has; the interest which society has in him individually (except as to his conduct to others) is *fractional*, and altogether indirect."[69] "Most," "trifling," and "fractional" are comparative terms. From a position of self-invested neutrality, Mill believes the individual's lopsided interest in being free from paternalism will be manifest.

For Bentham, the question of interference is settled by impartial calculation: would legislation of one kind or another in this or that case be more or less likely to promote the general happiness? But, for Mill, the question of interference is decided by impartial *deliberation*: does political or social interference of one kind or another in this or that case hold water from a disinterestedly interested standpoint? This inquiry does not lend itself to calculation, for the weight of the interests at stake cannot be reduced to a single, measurable value, like overall pleasure. Rather, the interests at stake are to be compared on the basis of their relative importance to individual and social flourishing. Thus, whereas the ordinary reading says that *nothing* justifies curbing inward liberty, the special reading says that the flourishing of society permits interference *only* to enforce justice. These readings together provide a holistic, complementary appraisal of the position Mill actually defends in *On Liberty*, regardless of what he may have precisely meant by the concept of harm.

IMPARTIAL INTERFERENCES

Most if not all of the interferences that Mill sanctions throughout his corpus (not just in *On Liberty*) can be naturally and reasonably deduced from the Harm Principle. That is, the vast majority of the interferences Mill

67. Mill, "Utility of Religion," 421, *CW* 10.
68. Mill, *Utilitarianism*, 218.
69. Mill, *On Liberty*, 277.

endorses can be naturally and plausibly deduced from his moral theory, specifically his theory of justice. In both *On Liberty* and elsewhere, Mill reserves the force of law or opinion for situations where the offending party is violating an impartial moral rule, specifically a perfect duty or claim-right.

Take lying—a quintessential injustice. In *Utilitarianism*, Mill says that deceit works against "the principal support of all present social well-being," namely, "the trustworthiness of human assertion," and thus justly incurs the opprobrium of public opinion. Veracity is an indubitable moral rule, albeit one that admits of certain impartial exceptions: "Yet that even this rule, sacred as it is, admits of possible exceptions, is acknowledged by all moralists; the chief of which is when the withholding of some fact (as information from a malefactor, or of bad news from a person dangerously ill) would preserve someone (especially a person other than oneself) from great and unmerited evil, and when the withholding can only be effected by denial." Now, in order to preserve our general "reliance on veracity," the "limits" of such a caveat should be generally "defined."[70] Nevertheless, under certain atypical conditions, Mill thinks an impartial observer might allow or even oblige us to speak falsely in good conscience. Similarly, in *On Liberty*, Mill writes, "When a person, either by express promise or by conduct, has encouraged another to rely upon his continuing to act in a certain way—to build expectations and calculations, and stake any part of his plan of life upon that supposition—a new series of moral obligations arises on his part towards that person, which may possibly be overruled, but cannot be ignored."[71] The ability to depend on one another, and to have confidence in our mutual devotion to fair play, is crucial to Mill. Indeed, to ignore these perfect duties, or claim-rights, is to warrant pro tanto, at minimum, the censure of society.

Likewise, Mill endorses interference pro tanto in the interest of interpersonal security;[72] compossible liberty;[73] and unbiased, fair dealing.[74] But, again, these moral rules are subject to exceptions. Apropos interpersonal security: "To save a life, it may not only be allowable, but a duty, to steal, or take by force, the necessary food or medicine, or to kidnap, and compel to officiate, the only qualified medical practitioner."[75] An impartial observer would weaken our sense of security just enough to enable us to

70. Mill, *Utilitarianism*, 223.
71. Mill, *On Liberty*, 300.
72. Mill, *Utilitarianism*, 251.
73. Mill, *On Liberty*, 226.
74. Mill, *Utilitarianism*, 243.
75. Ibid., 259.

react, within reason, to extreme contingencies. Apropos compossible liberty: "If either a public officer or anyone else saw a person attempting to cross a bridge which had been ascertained to be unsafe, and there were no time to warn him of his danger, they might seize him and turn him back, without any real infringement of his liberty; for liberty consists in doing what one desires, and he does not desire to fall into the river."[76] From an impartial standpoint, the traveler would desire a world where everyone is urged and inclined to protect one another from imminent and unseen dangers. And apropos unbiased dealings: "A person would be more likely to be blamed than applauded for giving his family or friends no superiority in good offices over strangers, when he could do so without violating any other duty; and no one thinks it unjust to seek one person in preference to another as a friend, connexion, or companion."[77] Neither does Mill deem it unjust to discriminate against persons who exhibit a repellent character: "A person who shows rashness, obstinacy, self-conceit—who cannot live within moderate means—who cannot restrain himself from hurtful indulgences—who pursues animal pleasures at the expense of those of feeling and intellect—must expect to be lowered in the opinion of others. . . . We are not bound" to "seek his society; we have a right to avoid it."[78] Thus, Mill thinks that the preferential order resulting from our organic, reciprocal social relations is kosher from an impartial perspective.

Again, one of the refreshing things about Mill's ethics is that *none* of this is based on a priori deduction or felicific calculation. Rather, everything Mill argues proceeds from a deliberative appeal to what we have discerned about justice historically, and to what we ought to take into greater consideration going forward. We can disagree with *all* the verdicts Mill advances above, and we can do so by the light of his own principles. Moreover, Mill's doctrine allows us to paint fine lines with a broad brush. For instance, Mill remarks that a "person may cause evil to others not only by his actions but by his *inaction*, and in either case he is justly accountable to them for the injury."[79] But, indeed: *when*? The answer is that there is no grand, definite answer; *it depends*, which would be frustrating if it were not for the fact that we as a society, and as individuals, have some idea as to what kinds of inactions we impartially regard as unjust and thus punishable.

However, there is one major interpretive issue that arises here. Many scholars have argued that Mill often strays beyond the Harm Principle by introducing various *positive* interferences, that is, interventions intended

76. Mill, *On Liberty*, 294.
77. Mill, *Utilitarianism*, 243.
78. Mill, *On Liberty*, 278.
79. Ibid., 225, my emphasis.

not to thwart or remedy harm, but to *promote* the general interest. The Harm Principle has often been understood to describe something like the "night-watchman state," where state power is limited "to affording protection against force and fraud." And yet, for Mill, the legitimate use of state power is "considerably more multifarious"[80] than this rendering of the Harm Principle would allow: "There are also many positive acts for the benefit of others, which [we] may rightfully be compelled to perform."[81] Court testimony;[82] national defense;[83] trade regulation;[84] labor regulation;[85] the provision, via taxation, of public goods and social welfare;[86] compulsory education[87]—Mill is no libertarian. But can these interventions be brought under the Harm Principle?

On the special reading, effortlessly. Again, the Harm Principle says that "the only purpose for which power can be rightfully exercised over any member of a civilized community, against his will, is to prevent harm to others." But, now, the key phrase is *"against his will."* If a law or norm is in the general interest (or if it has passed through the just processes by which we collectively decide what is in the general interest), then there are two possibilities: either the individual *willingly* abides by the law or norm, in which case the power exercised is congruent with the Harm Principle, or the individual contravenes the law or norm, in which case the individual *is* guilty of harm—the injustice of violating the moral rule against free-riding; or of neglecting to satisfy the rightful claims of our dependents; or of failing to provide our "fair share"[88] of labor or resources. Society has a claim on us to satisfy those laws or norms that are determined to be in the general interest—which is not to say that these laws or norms cannot be *challenged*; but we still have a prima facie obligation to obey them.[89]

But what about the ordinary reading? The trouble here is that the flouting of laws or norms can often be said to be free from perceptible, adverse consequences: "even if individuals do have a right to public goods, there's a question of whether individual restrictions on liberty involved in the state provision of those goods can be justified as preventing harm, inasmuch as individual contributions typically have a negligible effect on

80. Mill, *Principles of Political Economy*, 800.
81. Mill, *On Liberty*, 224–225.
82. See Ibid., 225.
83. See Ibid., 225, 276.
84. See Ibid., 293.
85. See Mill, *Principles of Political Economy*, 956–957.
86. See Ibid., 800–807, 960.
87. See Mill, *On Liberty*, 301–302.
88. Ibid., 225.
89. For a similar point, see Ten, *Mill on Liberty*, 59–61.

the provision of the good."[90] However, the ordinary reading need not focus *only* on (in)activity that has *actualized* consequences: I can be faulted on the ordinary reading for dropping a banana peel on the ground even if no one actually slips and falls on it. Similarly, I can be faulted for obstructing the provision of a public good even if the public good is provided in full despite my obstruction. The degree of risk is irrelevant: I am acting *adversely* by creating a potential, however remote, for harm. An (in)activity is "calculated to produce evil" based on its *general* tendency. Recall Mill's letter from last chapter: "the consideration of what would happen if everyone did the same" is "the only means we have of discovering the tendency of the act in the particular case."[91] Nonetheless, there can be no doubt that, at least optically speaking, the ordinary reading sits rather awkwardly next to Mill's positive interferences. But, again, the ordinary reading is playing only a limited (albeit profound) role in *On Liberty*; and thus, it is not surprising that the more we examine Mill's interferences, the more we must rely on the special reading.

There are also various points where Mill opts to *regulate* activity without *really* interfering with it. Consider Mill's take on the sale of items often used for criminal purposes: "The seller might, for example, be required to enter in a register the exact time of the transaction, the name and address of the buyer, the precise quality and quantity sold; to ask the purpose for which it was wanted, and record the answer he received." In this way, Mill squares the circle between liberty and security: "Such regulations would in general be no material impediment to obtaining the article, but a very considerable one to making an improper use of it without detection." Likewise, Mill squares the circle between liberty and "the public weal" by allowing for hedonistic doings—e.g., "drunkenness," "idleness," "fornication," "gambling"—but requiring them to be conducted "with a certain degree of secrecy and mystery, so that nobody knows anything about them but those who seek them."[92] (Victorian prudery?)

INWARD-OUTWARD LIBERTY

That said, there is a sense in which Mill's theory of interference is of secondary importance to his theory of *non*-interference. Chapters 2 and 3 of *On Liberty* are mainly concerned with defending our moral right to

---

90. Brink, *Mill's Progressive Principles*, 185.
91. Mill, "To John Venn," 1881, *CW* 17.
92. Mill, *On Liberty*, 295–297.

intellectual and ethical liberty—the right to develop and express our own beliefs and desires; the right to carry the fruits of our inward liberty into the marketplace of ideas or the public square. For Mill, these rights are absolute, inviolable moral rules; they admit of no exceptions; indeed, their exercise is *never* unjust, and interference with them is *always* unjust. Naturally, this does *not* mean that speech or action itself is not subject to impartial regulation. Rather, it just means that the *ideas* or *ideals* underlying speech or action cannot themselves be targeted.

Intellectual and ethical liberty are, in essence, inward liberty turned outward, a transition that Mill regards as only natural: "The liberty of expressing and publishing opinions may seem to fall under a different principle, since it belongs to that part of the conduct of an individual which concerns other people; but, being almost of as much importance as the liberty of thought itself, and resting in great part on the same reasons, is practically inseparable from it." (The *not*-different principle Mill is referring to is the "ordinary" Harm Principle.) Likewise, mere liberty of taste becomes "liberty of tastes and pursuits; of framing the plan of our life to suit our own character; of doing as we like, subject to such consequences as may follow."[93] Liberty of thought is affixed to liberty of speech and discussion, and liberty of feeling is affixed to liberty of action and pursuit.

This inward-outward association is implicit in Mill's theory of happiness: thoughts and feelings that remain inward are like unstaged plays; their fulfillment, that is, the gratification we derive from them, is realized only in their free and open expression. But Mill's stated thesis—having to do with liberty of speech and action "resting" on "the same reasons" as liberty of thought and feeling—harks back to his theory of individual and social well-being. According to Mill, what best serves the general happiness—what allows both the individual and society at large both to progress and to conserve their progress—is liberty of thought *and* speech, and liberty of feeling *and* action.

Intellectual Liberty

In chapter 2 of *On Liberty*, Mill argues that we have an inviolable moral right to liberty of thought, speech, and discussion. Mill has the richly deserved reputation of being a free speech absolutist: "If all mankind minus one, were of one opinion, and only one person were of the contrary opinion, mankind would be no more justified in silencing that one person,

93. Ibid., 225–226.

than he, if he had the power, would be justified in silencing mankind."[94] But why does he advance, and how does he manage to defend, such a radical, sweeping principle? Mill's argument, in essence, is that there is *never* a rhyme or reason, from an impartial vantage point, to restrict or repress intellectual liberty; that it is *always* unjust for individuals to be anything less than perfectly free in their individual and social deliberations.

This does *not* mean—as many readers have assumed—that Mill objects to all speech regulations prima facie. Mill readily entertains the need for interfering with certain speakers in certain contexts. His corn-dealer example is particularly well known and oft cited: "Opinions lose their immunity, when the circumstances in which they are expressed are such as to constitute their expression a positive instigation to some mischievous act. An opinion that corn-dealers are starvers of the poor" may "justly incur punishment when delivered orally to an excited mob assembled before the house of a corn-dealer, or when handed about among the same mob in the form of a placard."[95] Rather, by objecting to speech regulation, Mill means that the *content* of our speech must be sacrosanct: this view on corn-dealers is being restricted because its utterance then/there creates an imminent threat of violence, *not* because of the view itself. Intellectual liberty covers the fruits of our inward liberty: *what* we believe and *why*. Regardless of when/where speech should have free rein, Mill's contention is that there are *no* legitimate reasons for policing the *substance* of speech at/in those times/places. While the marketplace of ideas can be subject to impartial regulations, Mill holds that it must preserve a laissez-faire policy as to which ideas are bought or sold.

The absolutist strain of Mill's position is captured by Justice Thurgood Marshall's reading of the First Amendment to the U.S. Constitution: "above all else, the First Amendment means that government has no power to restrict expression because of its message, its ideas, its subject matter, or its content."[96] But, as Chief Justice Charles Evans Hughes notes, this does *not* mean that the law cannot restrict the "time, place, and manner"[97] of expression. The First Amendment bars almost all "content-specific" regulations, while permitting any number of "content-neutral" regulations.[98] Neither the First Amendment nor chapter 2 of *On Liberty* grants you the right to trumpet your opinions via megaphone on

94. Ibid., 229.
95. Ibid., 260.
96. *Police Department of the City of Chicago v. Mosley*, 408 U.S. 92, 95 (1972).
97. *Cox v. New Hampshire*, 312 U.S. 569 (1941).
98. *Ward v. Rock against Racism*, 491 U.S. 781 (1989).

a residential street at 3 AM. You could be reciting the First Amendment itself—people are trying to sleep.

It is worth emphasizing this point, for Mill has been frequently hounded for supposedly imagining speech to be always and everywhere *innocuous*; indeed, he has been criticized or outright dismissed as a disciple of the "*sticks-and-stones* theory, after the nursery rhyme that concludes 'but words will never harm me.'"[99] In response, some of Mill's defenders have sowed even *more* confusion by arguing that Mill actually recognizes the potential harmfulness of *all* speech-acts, and that while his defense of free speech therefore does not (cannot) have anything to do with the Harm Principle, he nonetheless supports free speech on the same grounds as free trade, that is, pragmatically:

> As the principle of individual liberty is not involved in the doctrine of Free Trade, so neither is it in most of the questions which arise respecting the limits of that doctrine; as for example, what amount of public control is admissible for the prevention of fraud by adulteration; how far sanitary precautions, or arrangements to protect workpeople employed in dangerous occupations, should be enforced on employers. Such questions involve considerations of liberty, only in so far as leaving people to themselves is always better, *cæteris paribus*, than controlling them: but that they may be legitimately controlled for these ends, is in principle undeniable.[100]

Simply replace "Trade" with "Speech"—that is the "pragmatic interpretation."[101] However, both the prosecution and the defense are getting their respective cases wrong here. For starters, there is no reason to believe that Mill endorses the sticks-and-stones theory; on the contrary, as Mill intimates near the end of chapter 2 of *On Liberty*, speech-acts that are armed with "weapons" like "invective, sarcasm, [and] personality" ought to be subject, if not to interference, then to disavowal.[102] And yet, this does not mean that Mill's entire doctrine of free speech must thereby revert to a pragmatic reckoning. Rather, the principled thesis of chapter 2 of *On Liberty* is that no matter what regulations are placed on speech-acts, they must always be content-neutral, never content-specific—indeed, the free-trade protocols listed above have nothing to do (directly) with what sellers can sell or buyers can buy.

99. Jacobson, "Mill on Freedom of Speech," 443.
100. Mill, *On Liberty*, 293.
101. See Jacobson, "Mill on Freedom of Speech," 441–446.
102. Mill, *On Liberty*, 258–259. We will return to this point later.

THE MORAL RIGHT TO INTELLECTUAL LIBERTY

Let us begin with some context. One of Mill's central themes is that we are each marked by a particular cast of mind and character; by a particular slew of preconceptions and predispositions; and by a particular range of life experiences. Taken as individuals, Mill thinks we are limited in our thinking and feeling; prone to certain outlooks and attitudes; and oblivious to the totality of the human condition in all its breadth, depth, color, and complexity. Indeed, consider the native state of the intellect:

> What has been the opinion of mankind, has been the opinion of persons of all tempers and dispositions, of all partialities and prepossessions, of all varieties in position, in education, in opportunities of observation and inquiry. No one inquirer is all this; every inquirer is either young or old, rich or poor, sickly or healthy, married or unmarried, meditative or active, a poet or a logician, an ancient or a modern, a man or a woman; and if a thinking person, has, in addition, the accidental peculiarities of his individual modes of thought. Every circumstance which gives a character to the life of a human being, carries with it its peculiar biases; its peculiar facilities for perceiving some things, and for missing or forgetting others.[103]

When it comes to our beliefs, there is always a perspective, or "side," to which we feel "most inclination." This is how Mill explains the general tendency of individuals to light upon only "one-sided" "half-truths," truths that are "exaggerated, distorted, and disjoined from the truths by which they ought to be accompanied and limited."[104] For Mill, such half-truths define the history of ideas and, indeed, of the world. Human history is partly driven by intellectual cycles, in which half-truths counter and supplant one another to the beat of a pendulum. Intellectual culture advances only insofar as these cycles become less pronounced over time, with each oscillation becoming "less extreme in its opposition," and denying "less of what is true in the doctrine it wars against, than had been the case in any previous philosophic reaction."[105] As long as they are "enforced and defended with equal talent and energy," half-truths can keep each other within "the limits of reason and sanity."[106]

---

103. Mill, "Bentham," 90–91, *CW* 10.
104. Mill, *On Liberty*, 245, 252–254.
105. Mill, "Coleridge," 125, *CW* 10.
106. Mill, *On Liberty*, 253–254.

Given this native state of the intellect, Mill thinks we can develop intellectually only by embracing a liberal frame of mind; only by engaging in dialectic or discourse with *other* minds, especially those which appear to be discordant with our own. Other minds, insofar as they contain truths of their own, make us ever wiser: "nine times out of ten," what we "fancied to be sheer error, had perhaps as much of truth in it as our own contrary opinion; that what we ascribed to a mental defect, really arose from some good quality, not excessive in itself, but unaccompanied by some other which ought to have qualified and corrected it, and which, again, in our own mind, stands as much in need of correction from the former, over which, in its turn, it unduly predominates."[107] As Mill says, "The hardiest assertor" of "the freedom of private judgment" is "the very person who most needs to fortify the weak side of his own intellect, by study of the opinions of mankind in all ages and nations, and of the speculations of philosophers of the modes of thought most opposite to his own. It is there that he will find the experiences denied to himself—the remainder of the truth of which he sees but half—the truths, of which the errors he detects are commonly but the exaggerations."[108] For Mill, our intellectual well-being is wholly dependent on our willingness to converse with "persons of every variety of opinion" and consider "every character of mind."[109]

Alone, the individual may derive a certain degree of gratification from intellectual activity. However, in a healthy society, the opportunity for intellectual fulfillment is enlarged exponentially. How much joyful activity—how many untold higher pleasures—would be lost on a budding intellect if it were not for a life replete with canonical authors, enriching tutors, and eager interlocutors? How much in the way of argument, insight, or wisdom—whether political, literary, economic, scientific, or spiritual—would our intellectual faculties be denied if left to their own devices? So much for happiness as aggregation. But what Mill begins to argue above is that dialogue is also the font of intellectual flourishing. The more the intellect engages other minds in curious and humble good faith—that is, the more the intellect is expanded, deepened, enriched, challenged, and enlivened, or, in short, liberalized—the more virtuous or excellent the intellect will become. Intellectual vices or deficiencies—like prejudice, illogic, and insularity—will give way to reason, logic, and openness. The intellect will develop toward a general wisdom: the capacity and

---

107. Mill, "Smart's Outline of Sematology," 426, *CW* 23.
108. Mill, "Bentham," 91.
109. Mill, *On Liberty*, 232.

proclivity to assume fallibility or ignorance; to explore a subject or inquiry from all angles; to think critically; to see and feel deeply; to empathize broadly; to balance or combine competing values or interests; to compare ideals to reality; to convert principles into practice. And with growing wisdom, the activity of the intellectual faculties will become ever more engrossing, edifying, and ennobling.

To illustrate by contrast, take Bentham, who, for Mill, is a prime example of what happens when the intellect is walled off from other minds. Bentham's navel-gazing mentality—that is, his total lack of intentionality in expanding his intellectual horizons—made his thinking narrow and shallow: Bentham's "determination to create a philosophy wholly out of the materials furnished by his own mind" was "his first disqualification as a philosopher. His second, was the incompleteness of his own mind as a representative of universal human nature. In many of the most natural and strongest feelings of human nature he had no sympathy," and "the faculty by which one mind understands a mind different from itself, and throws itself into the feelings of that other mind, was denied him by his deficiency of Imagination." In fact, there is a sense in which Bentham could be seen, at least to some extent, as subject to the sway of prejudice and thus intellectually unfree. We might say that Bentham the philosopher was autarchic but not fully autonomous, in that he could reason through his views but had "never been made alive to the unseen influences which were acting on himself."[110] This is surely harsh toward Bentham, but it is in keeping with Mill. Indeed, it has even been speculated that Mill's mental breakdown was in no small part caused by his being suddenly struck by what he considered to be "the low intellectual quality of Bentham's thought and writing."[111]

This is certainly not to suggest that our intellectual tendencies are at all regrettable. On the contrary, we ought to mine our intellectual caverns for all their riches, for that is not only our particular vocation but also how progress is made more generally: "For our own part, we have a large tolerance of one-eyed men, provided their one eye is a penetrating one: if they saw more, they probably would not see so keenly, nor so eagerly pursue one course of inquiry."[112] Mill encourages the individual to travel back and forth between private rumination and public discussion: we ought to consult with ourselves; to bring our insights or ideas before others;

---

110. Mill, "Bentham," 91–92. See also Baum, "J. S. Mill on Freedom and Power," 200–203.

111. Milligram, "Mill's Epiphanies," 14.

112. Mill, "Bentham," 94.

and to carry their conversation back to the domain of our inward sanctuary before emerging once again. In this way, we will be able to develop our own intellect while also moderating and supplementing its peculiar excesses and deficiencies.

With this as background, Mill's argument for the moral right to intellectual liberty commences thusly: "The peculiar evil of silencing the expression of an opinion is, that it is robbing the human race; posterity as well as the existing generation; those who dissent from the opinion, still more than those who hold it. If the opinion is right, they are deprived of the opportunity of exchanging error for truth: if wrong, they lose, what is almost as great a benefit, the clearer perception and livelier impression of truth, produced by its collision with error." Society needs the marketplace of ideas to market any and all ideas so that intellectual culture can not only progress further but also conserve what progress it has already made. Fresh truths cannot be discovered or disseminated without intellectual liberty, and society cannot preserve a "vivid conception" of or "living belief" in its extant wisdom in the absence of vigorous collisions with competing outlooks. Of course, society's interest in free expression also covers its practical interest in obtaining complete and correct empirical facts, without which society cannot diagnose problems accurately or prescribe solutions effectively. And intellectual liberty loses none of its importance even if we think we have *all* the relevant facts: "Very few facts are able to tell their own story, without comments to bring out their meaning."[113] Thus, intellectual liberty is vitally important to society at large.

And to bolster Mill's thesis, we might add that he is being, if anything, overly sanguine about the intellectual health of society. His argument above tacitly assumes that the "opinion" in question is grasped and appreciated by everyone—its avowed opponents as well as its ardent supporters—for what it really and truly is. Consider a vanilla example of Mill's contention at work: a theist ought not to censor or silence an atheist; for however confident the former may be in their belief, they could always be wholly or partially wrong; and regardless, theism has been nothing if not continually refined and invigorated by its historical contest with atheism. But notice: no explicit thought is given to the possibility that the theist is actually *lacking* in the requisite comprehension of *what* the atheist *actually* believes and *why*. Instead, there is an assumption of mutual clarity and regard.

Naturally, Mill would agree that partisans and factions are wont to sully and twist disfavored persons and opinions, often "as a badge of hatred,

113. Mill, *On Liberty*, 229, 231, 247.

a relic of persecution."[114] However, in presenting chapter 2 of *On Liberty*, it is crucial to stress this point: much if not most of the time, our would-be censors do not have the fullest or even foggiest understanding of—or concern for or openness to—what is being thought, felt, or suggested. Even worse, they often exhibit a reflexive, hostile antipathy toward what they presume to be its nefarious, absurd, or disingenuous content; and they often cynically malign persons and ideas they might actually know to be benign. Needless to say, there has never been any shortage of nefarious, absurd, and disingenuous opinions; however, the trouble is that, very frequently, there is zero interest shown in separating the wheat from the chaff, and, indeed, no apparent recognition that there *is* wheat in need of harvesting. This obstacle to rational, sympathetic dialogue has grown exponentially in our age of hyperpolarization and political echo chambers, which have encased an ever-expanding legion of hearts and minds within warring ideological shells and tossed gasoline on the fire of our innate proclivity toward tribalism.

Hence, before even considering how the ever-buzzing gadfly of intellectual liberty serves the general interest by expanding and conserving our reservoir of truth, we already have an independent reason to be deeply suspicious of any rationale for curbing or violating intellectual liberty. Indeed, in the *first* instance, the best argument for intellectual liberty is not that the opinion in question might be true, or that it benefits the truth even if false, but that we cannot be at all confident that our would-be censors even know or understand what the opinion really is or care what its merits actually are. This observation is apparent in much of what Mill argues throughout *On Liberty*: "Orthodox Christians who are tempted to think that those who stoned to death the first martyrs must have been worse men than they themselves are, ought to remember that one of those persecutors was Saint Paul."[115]

But, getting back to his thesis, Mill's contention *also* applies to individuals. First, the individual cannot truly develop or exercise the intellectual virtues or excellences—the individual cannot progress—without having access to an open marketplace of ideas:

> In the case of any person whose judgment is really deserving of confidence, how has it become so? Because he has kept his mind open to criticism of his opinions and conduct. Because it has been his practice to listen to all that could be said against him; to profit by as much of it

114. Ibid., 240.
115. Ibid., 236.

as was just, and expound to himself, and upon occasion to others, the
fallacy of what was fallacious. Because he has felt, that the only way in
which a human being can make some approach to knowing the whole
of a subject, is by hearing what can be said about it by persons of every
variety of opinion, and studying all modes in which it can be looked at
by every character of mind. No wise man ever acquired his wisdom in
any mode but this; nor is it in the nature of human intellect to become
wise in any other manner.[116]

Mill singles out Cicero, whose writings very likely influenced Mill on this
point, as a sterling example of this ethos.[117] What is more, unless intellectual liberty is protected and fostered, individuals will be unable to conserve whatever truth or wisdom they have already acquired: "However
unwillingly a person who has a strong opinion may admit the possibility
that his opinion may be false, he ought to be moved by the consideration
that however true it may be, if it is not fully, frequently, and fearlessly discussed, it will be held as a dead dogma, not a living truth." Wisdom is not
just obtained but also sustained and continually refreshed only by those
individuals who are adapted to defending their beliefs. Whenever a belief
is spared the challenging encounters that go along with intellectual liberty,
there is "a progressive tendency to forget all of the belief except the formu-
laries, or to give it a dull and torpid assent" until "it almost ceases to connect itself with the inner life of the human being." Free thought and deliberation are crucial to the *perpetual* "cultivation of the understanding."[118]
Therefore, intellectual liberty is vitally important to individuals as well.

Now, recall last chapter. If intellectual liberty was in the interest of the
one but *not* the many, or vice versa, then an impartial mind would have to
determine which interest takes precedence, and thus which interest *truly*
reflects the *general* interest. However, what Mill argues above is that intellectual liberty is in the interest of *both* the one *and* the many. Hence, what
we have here is a *consensus* moral rule: do not interfere with liberty of
thought, speech, or discussion. A violation of intellectual liberty is a universal injustice. But also recall that all moral rules are subject to potential
exceptions. Certain special or extenuating circumstances can exist where a
"principal" moral rule is temporarily superseded by a "proviso" moral rule:
"In such cases, as we do not call anything justice which is not a virtue, we
usually say, not that justice must give way to some other moral principle,

116. Ibid., 232.
117. Ibid., 245.
118. Ibid., 243–244, 248.

but that what is just in ordinary cases is, by reason of that other principle, not just in the particular case."[119]

However, the *really* striking thing about Mill's thesis is that the moral right to intellectual liberty is said to exist "absolute and unqualified."[120] According to Mill, there are *no* legitimate exceptions to this principle; an impartial observer would search for caveats to intellectual liberty and find *none*. This is the deepest argument of chapter 2 of *On Liberty*. Mill does not want us to see the right to intellectual liberty as just another moral rule, something generally but not always binding. Rather, he wants us to see the right to intellectual liberty as an *inviolable* standard of sociopolitical morality. Thus, Mill spends the better part of the chapter confronting and combatting various exceptions to this moral right.

THE INVIOLABILITY OF INTELLECTUAL LIBERTY

Mill first tackles the notion that an exception can be made for what are declared to be false beliefs; that neither the one nor the many have any interest in falsehoods. Well, actually, as we saw above, Mill thinks they *do*. But before Mill makes that argument, he first rejects the *falsity proviso* outright: "To refuse a hearing to an opinion, because they are sure that it is false, is to assume that *their* certainty is the same thing as *absolute* certainty. All silencing of discussion is an assumption of infallibility. Its condemnation may be allowed to rest on this common argument, not the worse for being common." The core of the falsity proviso is rotten: none are infallible, and thus none can claim the epistemic authority to identify and suppress false beliefs. Importantly, this does *not* mean that individuals cannot be very learned or ignorant or wise or foolish—Mill is certainly no skeptic, and he believes intellectual authority should naturally flow in a liberal society to those who acquire the (contestable and often contentious) reputation of being one of "the teachers of mankind."[121] Rather, this just means that an impartial observer would not *concede* this power to the powers that be, or to whomever the dominant faction or factions have avowed to be the most learned or wise: "There are no determinable and universal marks by which wisdom is to be known. To whom will you give the power of determining what men are the most enlightened?"[122]

119. Mill, *Utilitarianism*, 259.
120. Mill, *On Liberty*, 226.
121. Ibid., 229, 247, 251.
122. Mill, "Free Discussion," 10–11, *CW* 22.

Mill's judgment is bolstered by the fact that human beings, while often aware in theory of their own fallibility, are typically loath to act accordingly: "for while everyone well knows himself to be fallible, few think it necessary to take any precautions against their own fallibility, or admit the supposition that any opinion, of which they feel very certain, may be one of the examples of the error to which they acknowledge themselves to be liable." Naturally, the situation is worst with those "who are accustomed to unlimited deference," like "princes." But even those "who sometimes hear their opinions disputed, and are not wholly unused to be set right when they are wrong, place the same unbounded reliance on such of their opinions as are shared by all who surround them, or to whom they habitually defer."[123] Thus, an impartial mind ought to reject the falsity proviso not only on its own terms, but also in recognition of the fact that even the best-intentioned minds are usually prejudiced or distorted by their particular bubble or echo chamber, and so cannot be trusted to apply this exception judiciously.

Mill then turns to a more *refined* version of the falsity proviso: what if this exception for falsehoods was made *only* where the interfering party had done all it could to counteract its innate fallibility? As an interlocutor might contend,

> It is the duty of governments, and of individuals, to form the truest opinions they can; to form them carefully, and never impose them upon others unless they are quite sure of being right. But when they are sure (such reasoners may say), it is not conscientiousness but cowardice to shrink from acting on their opinions, and allow doctrines which they honestly think dangerous to the welfare of mankind, either in this life or in another, to be scattered abroad without restraint, because other people, in less enlightened times, have persecuted opinions now believed to be true. Let us take care, it may be said, not to make the same mistake: but governments and nations have made mistakes in other things, which are not denied to be fit subjects for the exercise of authority: they have laid on bad taxes, made unjust wars. Ought we therefore to lay on no taxes, and, under whatever provocation, make no wars? Men, and governments, must act to the best of their ability. There is no such thing as absolute certainty, but there is assurance sufficient for the purposes of human life. We may, and must, assume our opinion to be true for the guidance of our own conduct: and it is

123. Mill, *On Liberty*, 229–230.

assuming no more when we forbid bad men to pervert society by the propagation of opinions which we regard as false and pernicious.[124]

This explanation sounds reasonable: if most of what we do is done without practical certainty, then why should suppressing "bad" opinions be any different? But, again, the premise is self-defeating. The only way to form a "conscientious conviction" is to treat intellectual liberty as sacred: "Complete liberty of contradicting and disproving our opinion, is the very condition which justifies us in assuming its truth for the purpose of action; and on no other terms can a being with human faculties have any rational assurance of being right." Unless "the lists are kept open," we cannot hope to approach that "amount of certainty attainable by a fallible being."[125] Naturally, most actions and inactions are based on fallible beliefs, and every parliamentary debate must at some point call the question; but whereas the decision to act or not cannot *not* be made, there is no inexorable *need* to restrict intellectual liberty—in fact, quite the reverse, considering that our decisions cannot be optimally conscientious without drawing freely from the wellspring of thought, speech, and discussion.

Of course, the spirit of the passage above is that certain truths are *so* well-established, or, to us, *so* obvious or critical, that it would be absurd to go to any lengths to protect a contrary view. But, for Mill, this is just an assumption of infallibility on stilts: "Strange that they should imagine that they are not assuming infallibility, when they acknowledge that there should be free discussion on all subjects which can possibly be *doubtful,* but think that some particular principle or doctrine should be forbidden to be questioned because it is so *certain,* that is, because *they are certain* that it is certain." What can decide whether or not a subject, principle, or doctrine is doubtful other than its being doubted? And what rational confidence can anyone have in an answer that cannot be questioned? Even if something as undeniable as "the Newtonian philosophy were not permitted to be questioned, mankind could not feel as complete assurance of its truth as they do now."[126] And as a German-born Swiss patent clerk would demonstrate a half century later, Mill was even more right than he knew. Thus, an impartial mind would also dismiss this artificial refinement of the falsity proviso.

124. Ibid., 230–231.
125. Ibid., 231, 232.
126. Ibid., 232, 233.

Putting the falsity proviso aside, perhaps an impartial mind would make an exception for the expediency of opinions: "There are, it is alleged, certain beliefs, so useful, not to say indispensable to well-being, that it is as much the duty of governments to upholds those beliefs, as to protect any other of the interests of society. In a case of such necessity," "something less than infallibility may, it is maintained, warrant, and even bind, governments, to act on their own opinion, confirmed by the general opinion of mankind." Conversely, there are opinions that are decried for their inexpediency; they are said to promote "pernicious consequences," and are thus said to be circulated only by "bad men" who seek to "weaken" our "salutary beliefs." In short, the *expediency proviso* "makes the justification of restraints on discussion not a question of the truth of doctrines, but of their usefulness." An opinion, whether false or true, can be seen as beneficial or detrimental, which can be taken as a pretext for interference. How could there be anything unjust "in restraining bad men"?[127]

However, the expediency proviso fares no better than its predecessor: "Those who thus satisfy themselves, do not perceive that the assumption of infallibility is merely shifted from one point to another. The usefulness of an opinion is itself a matter of opinion: as disputable, as open to discussion, and requiring as much, as the opinion itself." And again, this judgment is buttressed by the fact that society has a "dreadful" record in evaluating the expediency of opinions, there being many "instances memorable in history, when the arm of the law has been employed to root out the best men and the noblest doctrines; with deplorable success as to the men, though some of the doctrines have survived to be (as if in mockery) invoked, in defence of similar conduct towards those who disagree with *them*." Indeed, Mill thinks an impartial observer could refuse the expediency proviso on the strength of just two names: Socrates and Christ—and in the name of the early Christians, who were persecuted by Marcus Aurelius, ironically himself, according to Mill, a Christian ethicist "in all but the dogmatic sense of the word."[128] Hence, the expediency proviso does nothing more than grant authority to an arbitrary power: "It is obvious, that there is no certain and universal rule for determining whether an opinion is useful or pernicious; and that if any person be authorized to decide, unfettered by such a rule, that person is a despot."[129]

127. Ibid., 233–234.
128. Ibid., 233, 235–236.
129. Mill, "Law of Libel and Liberty of the Press," 6, *CW* 21.

But, again, Mill then turns to a more *refined* version of the expediency proviso: "that persecution is an ordeal through which truth ought to pass, and always passes successfully, legal penalties being, in the end, powerless against truth, though sometimes beneficially effective against mischievous error." The thesis is that in suppressing intellectual liberty, society cannot *ultimately* harm true or salutary opinions, but may very well expunge false or harmful ones, in which case we can have our cake and eat it too. Persecution is an intellectual filtering mechanism. As we might expect, Mill regards this as utter nonsense: "The dictum that truth always triumphs over persecution, is one of the pleasant falsehoods which men repeat after one another till they pass into commonplaces, but which all experience refutes. History teems with instances of truth put down by persecution. If not suppressed forever, it may be thrown back for centuries." Truth only *appears* to endure persecution, for it tends to be rediscovered time and again by successive generations until "one of its reappearances falls on a time when from favourable circumstances it escapes persecution until it has made such head as to withstand all subsequent attempts to suppress it." Thus, an impartial observer would not be moved by the supposed progressivism of repression; it is nothing more than "a piece of idle sentimentality that truth, merely as truth, has any inherent power denied to error."[130]

And finally, even if we were to *concede* the cogency of the falsity and expediency provisos, Mill argues that false or noxious opinions are nonetheless invaluable *precisely* for the challenge or threat they pose to true or salutary beliefs. Falsehoods afford us the vital opportunity to reacquaint ourselves with "the grounds of our opinion," and to deepen and solidify our conception of the truth: "When we turn to subjects infinitely more complicated [than mathematics], to morals, religion, politics, social relations, and the business of life, three-fourths of the arguments for every disputed opinion consist in dispelling the appearances which favour some opinion different from it. . . . He who knows only his own side of the case, knows little of that." Every purportedly false opinion provides yet another opportunity to assess and refresh the validity and significance of our own beliefs. And it is not enough just to know what these opposing opinions are: "He must be able to hear them from persons who actually believe them; who defend them in earnest, and do their very utmost for them." Key to the cultivation of the intellect is not only knowing but also being made "to

130. Mill, *On Liberty*, 237–239.

feel the whole force of the difficulty which the true view of the subject has to encounter and dispose of," which can be done only by engaging "those who think differently."[131] This is the obverse to Mill's response to the falsity proviso: you cannot have any genuine knowledge of or confidence in either *their* falsehoods or *your* truths unless intellectual liberty is allowed free rein.

Likewise, contending with allegedly wrong or pernicious opinions is critical to preventing our valued beliefs from becoming ossified or enfeebled: "There are many reasons, doubtless, why doctrines which are the badge of a sect retain more of their vitality than those common to all recognised sects," but "one reason certainly is, that the peculiar doctrines are more questioned, and have to be oftener defended against open gainsayers. Both teachers and learners go to sleep at their post, as soon as there is no enemy in the field." Beliefs, when relieved or preserved from struggle or conflict, morph from matters of "controversy" into mere ornaments of conventional wisdom, which deprives them of everything that made them "deeply impressed on the mind." Such beliefs, no longer "grounded on conviction," lose their meaning and vigor, and are thus "apt to give way before the slightest semblance of an argument." Now, while it is only natural for certain beliefs to win general acceptance, Mill believes it is incumbent on society to find a "substitute" for controversy, like the "Socratic dialectics"—a curious suggestion for society in general, but a well-taken prescription for things like universities. But, in short, the false or noxious fruits of intellectual liberty should be seen as a boon to anyone who has "any regard for either the certainty or the vitality of our convictions," that is, for both the "clear apprehension and deep feeling of [our] truths."[132]

Intellectual liberty is a consensus moral rule to which an impartial mind would grant no exceptions. Indeed, if nothing else, the inviolability of intellectual liberty can be referred to Mill's observation that to allow for caveats to intellectual liberty is to imperil, and thus to chill, the intellectual activity of *anyone* who might otherwise disagree with the dogmas of the prevailing faction: "But it is not the minds of heretics that are deteriorated most, by the ban placed on all inquiry which does not end in the orthodox conclusions. The greatest harm done is to those who are not heretics, and whose whole mental development is cramped, and their reason cowed,

131. Ibid., 244–245.
132. Ibid., 244, 249–252.

by the fear of heresy."[133] Even if we ignore all the analysis above, it is still the case, drawing on Mill's Utility Principle, that *any* exception to a moral rule is hopelessly corrupt unless it is itself a tightly defined moral rule. But, marked by nothing but ambiguity, the falsity and expediency provisos are just *begging* to be abused in a cynical effort to suppress dissent. Thus, curbing intellectual liberty is *always* unjust, for it *always* contravenes a standing moral right, appeals to truth or expediency notwithstanding.

There is a sense, though, in which Mill's argument for the sanctity of intellectual liberty has hitherto been something of an aside. Thus far, Mill has been considering cases where an opinion is declared to be false and/or noxious and thus a legitimate target for suppression, and where the response has been something like, "Given our innate fallibility, not to mention our tendency toward prejudice, no impartial observer would allow for these exceptions; and given the susceptibility doctrines have for losing their vitality, no one possessed of enlightened self-interest would choose to quash even the most baneful views." But notice: all of this assumes that we are dealing with cases where the light of truth is on one side, and where the darkness of toxic untruth is on the other side. However, according to Mill, this does not accurately describe the vast majority of intellectual conflicts:

> We have hitherto considered only two possibilities: that the received opinion may be false, and some other opinion, consequently, true; or that, the received opinion being true, a conflict with the opposite error is essential to a clear apprehension and deep feeling of its truth. But there is a commoner case than either of these; when the conflicting doctrines, instead of being one true and the other false, share the truth between them; and the nonconforming opinion is needed to supply the remainder of the truth, of which the received doctrine embodies only a part. Popular opinions, on subjects not palpable to sense, are often true, but seldom or never the whole truth. They are a part of the truth; sometimes a greater, sometimes a smaller part, but exaggerated, distorted, and disjoined from the truths by which they ought to be accompanied and limited. Heretical opinions, on the other hand, are generally some of these suppressed and neglected truths, bursting the bonds which kept them down, and either seeking reconciliation with the truth contained in the common opinion, or fronting it as enemies, and setting themselves up, with similar exclusiveness, as the whole truth. The latter case is hitherto the most frequent, as, in the human

133. Ibid., 242.

mind, one-sidedness has always been the rule, and many-sidedness the exception. Hence, even in revolutions of opinion, one part of the truth usually sets while another rises.[134]

Intellectual quarrels, especially enduring ones, are normally clashes not between truth and falsehood, but between half-truths, where the whole truth is to be found in a higher balance, or even a higher synthesis, between valid but one-sided creeds. And so, insofar as individuals are fallible, limited creatures, society at large cannot approximate "the" truth without the corrective influence of intellectual liberty: "Unless opinions favourable to democracy and to aristocracy, to property and to equality, to co-operation and to competition, to luxury and to abstinence, to sociality and individuality, to liberty and discipline, and all the other standing antagonisms of practical life, are expressed with equal freedom, and enforced and defended with equal talent and energy, there is no chance of both elements obtaining their due; one scale is sure to go up, and the other down." Indeed, everything else aside, the most pressing reason to reject the provisos above is that these caveats would entrust the powers that be not only to eschew partisanship in favor of moderation, but also to identify the peculiar cases where an alleged "error" is not even "blended" with a "portion of truth."[135]

Ethical Liberty

As with speech, Mill holds that actions should be subject to certain restrictions: "Acts, of whatever kind, which, without justifiable cause, do harm to others, may be, and in the more important cases absolutely require to be, controlled by the unfavourable sentiments, and, when needful, by the active interference of mankind." But, as with intellectual liberty, Mill thinks the ethical *content* of our actions ought to be inviolable: "But if he refrains from molesting others in what concerns them, and merely acts according to his own inclination and judgment in things which concern himself, the same reasons which show that opinion should be free, prove also that he should be allowed, without molestation, to carry his opinions into practice at his own cost."[136] Ethical liberty covers the fruits of our inward liberty: *what* we desire and *why*. Regardless of when/where action should have free rein, Mill argues that there are *no* legitimate reasons for policing the *substance* of action at/ in those times/places. While the public sphere can be subject to impartial

134. Ibid., 252.
135. Ibid., 252–253.
136. Ibid., 260.

regulations, Mill holds that it must preserve a laissez-faire policy as to which ideals, pursuits, or lifestyles can be publicized.

ETHICAL LIBERTY: AN ABSOLUTE MORAL RIGHT

Having defended the absolutism of intellectual liberty in chapter 2 of *On Liberty*, Mill turns his gaze to ethical liberty in chapter 3. And the basic argument is exactly the same:

> That mankind are not infallible; that their truths, for the most part, are only half-truths; that unity of opinion, unless resulting from the fullest and freest comparison of opposite opinions, is not desirable, and diversity not an evil, but a good, until mankind are much more capable than at present of recognising all sides of the truth, are principles applicable to men's modes of action, not less than to their opinions. As it is useful that while mankind are imperfect there should be different opinions, so is it that there should be different experiments of living; that free scope should be given to varieties of character, short of injury to others; and that the worth of different modes of life should be proved practically, when anyone thinks fit to try them. It is desirable, in short, that in things which do not primarily concern others, individuality should assert itself.[137]

As with intellectual liberty, Mill's thesis is that to interfere with ethical liberty is to commit a universal injustice: ethical liberty is a moral right with *zero* exceptions. Without ethical liberty, the individual cannot select and enjoy their own higher pleasures, let alone develop any kind of practical virtue or excellence: "The human faculties of perception, judgment, discriminative feeling, mental activity, and even moral preference, are exercised only in making a choice. . . . Such are the differences among human beings in their sources of pleasure, their susceptibilities of pain, and the operation on them of different physical and moral agencies, that unless there is a corresponding diversity in their modes of life, they neither obtain their fair share of happiness, nor grow up to the mental, moral, and aesthetic stature of which their nature is capable." And likewise, society at large needs ethical liberty in order both to unearth new practices and to preserve the vitality of old practices. On one hand, there is society's interest in "new and original" modes of action: "There is always need of persons not only to discover new truths, and point out when what were

137. Ibid., 260–261.

once truths are true no longer, but also to commence new practices, and set the example of more enlightened conduct, and better taste and sense in human life." And on the other hand, without ethical liberty, society becomes "a stagnant pool," making it practically impossible not only to unearth new modes of action, but also to "keep the life in those which already existed."[138]

To wit, Mill's cautionary tale regarding dead dogmas applies to our ideals and values no less than to our ideas and truths: "There is only too great a tendency in the best beliefs and practices to degenerate into the mechanical; and unless there were a succession of persons whose ever-recurring originality prevents the grounds of those beliefs and practices from becoming merely traditional, such dead matter would not resist the smallest shock from anything really alive, and there would be no reason why civilization should not die out, as in the Byzantine Empire." Here and elsewhere, Mill espouses a kind of progressive conservatism that is perhaps best encapsulated by Bob Dylan: "He not busy being born is busy dying."[139] Moreover, ethical liberty enables us, as members of society, to "partake" of other characters, which makes our lives all the more "rich, diversified, and animating."[140] Of course, to "partake" of them does not mean to become *like* them; it just means that the fruits of *their* individuality can become sources of enjoyment and self-cultivation for *us*—how many untold charms, insights, and memories would countless millions ascribe to Dylan's music and lyrics? Indeed, in Mill's literary essays, we find him charting his poetic development, even though he admits that he himself never actually became a poet.[141] And yet, Mill relished the poetic efforts of others and thereby managed to cultivate his aesthetic sensibility, sentimental nature, and imaginative capacity far beyond what he could have managed independently. In short, our communion with other individuals—those with their own natural vocations, and with their own aesthetic, ethical, and spiritual sensibilities—is an inimitable means of "furnishing more abundant aliment to high thoughts and elevating feelings."[142]

Thus, once again, an impartial observer would not have to adjudicate between the interests of the individual and the interests of society at large,

138. Ibid., 262, 267, 270.
139. Bob Dylan, "It's Alright, Ma (I'm Only Bleeding)," track 10 on *Bringing It All Back Home* (New York: Columbia Records, 1965).
140. Mill, *On Liberty*, 266–267.
141. Mill, *Autobiography*, 19, *CW* 1.
142. Mill, *On Liberty*, 266.

for *both* parties have a general interest in there being a moral right to the most extensive possible sphere of ethical liberty consistent with justice. And the point-counterpoint regarding potential exceptions would play out exactly the same way here: to say that a particular conception of the good, or a certain mode of action, is either *false* or *inexpedient* is, in the first place, an opinion; and, as such, its validity is as fallible, disputable, and ambiguous as opinions *about* opinions.

INDIVIDUAL ORIGINALITY

However, there is a challenge facing Mill in chapter 3 of *On Liberty* that he does not encounter as such in chapter 2:

> In maintaining this principle, the greatest difficulty to be encountered does not lie in the appreciation of means towards an acknowledged end, but in the indifference of persons in general to the end itself. If it were felt that the free development of individuality is one of the leading essentials of well-being; that it is not only a co-ordinate element with all that is designated by the terms civilization, instruction, education, culture, but is itself a necessary part and condition of all those things; there would be no danger that liberty should be undervalued, and the adjustment of the boundaries between it and social control would present no extraordinary difficulty. But the evil is, that individual spontaneity is hardly recognised by the common modes of thinking, as having any intrinsic worth, or deserving any regard on its own account. The majority, being satisfied with the ways of mankind as they now are (for it is they who make them what they are), cannot comprehend why those ways should not be good enough for everybody; and what is more, spontaneity forms no part of the ideal of the majority of moral and social reformers, but is rather looked on with jealousy, as a troublesome and perhaps rebellious obstruction to the general acceptance of what these reformers, in their own judgment, think would be best for mankind.[143]

In short, in chapter 3, Mill is confronted with the obverse to the falsity proviso, what we might call the *validity proviso*: Individuals *may* come to act or live well by the light of their own reason or feeling, but why bother with uncertainty, especially when the "certainty" already available is evidently desirable? Why not just encourage (and, if need be, enforce) conformity to

143. Ibid., 261.

widely accepted, time-tested modes of action and forms of life? Mill's basic reply (above) is his moral defense of ethical liberty. But Mill extends his analysis via his theory of individual originality, which deepens and refines his theory of happiness.

By focusing too exclusively on chapter 3 of *On Liberty*, some scholars have gone too far in associating Mill's conception of happiness with an unbridled individualism. There is a caricature of Mill as an enemy of social custom, whose principal desire is for "experiments in living,"[144] and who wants above all else to liberate the would-be genius from the stultifying irons of conformity. This depiction is, at best, a slanted half-truth. The whole truth is that Mill's critique of *mere* conformity is the Individualist yin to his Aristotelian yang. A happy life is a life engaged in virtuous or excellent activity—the activity of the higher faculties in accordance with the higher pleasures. And what Mill argues in *On Liberty* is that by *merely* conforming to customary modes of thought or feeling, the higher faculties will not only remain inactive but also repress the active nature of the individual. Mere conformity is mindless passivity; indeed, the "despotism of custom"[145] imposes a kind of dull hedonism.[146]

For Mill, the activity of the higher faculties entails *originality*—not novelty per se, but *self-origination*: anyone who "gets at his convictions by his own faculties" is "an original thinker."[147] As Mill argues in *On Liberty*, the activity of the higher faculties must issue from the individual's own mind or will—they cannot be *other*-developed, they must be *self*-developed: "The mental and moral, like the muscular powers, are improved only by being used." Thus, mere conformity—acquiescence to thoughts or feelings which we have not authorized—is antithetical to human flourishing: "If the grounds of an opinion are not conclusive to the person's own reason, his reason cannot be strengthened, but is likely weakened, by his adopting it: and if the inducements to an act are not such as are consentaneous to his own feelings and character," it is "so much done towards rendering his feelings and character inert and torpid, instead of active and energetic." Chapter 2 of *On Liberty* focuses on the activity of our intellectual faculties in accordance with truth or wisdom: the cultivation of the "intellect," "judgment," and "understanding" is brought about only by "bold, vigorous, independent train[s] of thought." And chapter 3 focuses on the activity

144. Ibid., 261, 267, 281, 306.

145. Ibid., 272, 273.

146. Mere conformity, like mere pleasure, implies or entails a passive state of being or feeling.

147. Mill, "On Genius," 332, *CW* 1.

of our practical faculties in accordance with the higher pleasures in toto: "He who lets the world, or his own portion of it, choose his plan of life for him, has no need of any faculty than the one of ape-like imitation. He who chooses his plan of life for himself, employs all his faculties. He must use observation to see, reasoning and judgment to foresee, activity to gather materials for decision, discrimination to decide, and when he has decided, firmness and self-control to hold to his deliberate decision." Rather than being truly virtuous or excellent, we are just "automatons in human form" to the extent that our higher faculties are being turned like gears by arbitrary influences.[148]

Furthermore, given our dissimilar "character[s] of mind" and "varieties of character," Mill thinks that the good life for each individual is not only rooted in originality but also marked by *individuality*: "Human nature is not a machine to be built after a model, and set to do the work prescribed for it, but a tree, which requires to grow and develop on all sides, according to the tendency of the inward forces which make it a living thing."[149] The growth of each tree is a unique variation on its essential, tree-like properties. Likewise, the telos of each individual is a unique expression of our shared human nature and good:

> Human beings are not like sheep; and even sheep are not undistinguishably alike. A man cannot get a coat or a pair of boots to fit him, unless they are either made to his measure, or he has a whole warehouseful to choose from: and is it easier to fit him with a life than with a coat, or are human beings more like one another in their whole physical and spiritual conformation than in the shape of their feet? If it were only that people have diversities of taste, that is reason enough for not attempting to shape them all after one model. But different persons also require different conditions for their spiritual development; and can no more exist healthily in the same moral, than all the variety of plants can in the same physical, atmosphere and climate. The same things which are helps to one person towards the cultivation of his higher nature, are hindrances to another. The same mode of life is a healthy excitement to one, keeping all his faculties of action and enjoyment in their best order, while to another it is a distracting burthen, which suspends or crushes all internal life.[150]

148. Mill, *On Liberty*, 242, 244, 262–263.
149. Ibid., 232, 261, 263.
150. Ibid., 270.

Given their individuality, different persons will be driven to devote their lives to different goods or activities. Some will pursue the arts, while others will pursue the sciences; some will pursue a public life, while others will pursue a private vocation. (Indeed, some trees are maples, while others are oaks or redwoods.) Also, our individuality will drive us in a multiplicity of directions even with respect to the *same* goods or activities. All the great philosophers have their own intellects, interests, and insights. All the great heroes go on their own journeys or adventures. All the great painters commit their own style or vision to the canvas. Ty Cobb did not bat like Cap Anson, Marlon Brando did not act like Laurence Olivier, and Gene Kelly did not dance like Fred Astaire. (Indeed, every oak among oaks has an idiosyncratic branch pattern.) Hence, full individuality is the apex of happiness: "It is not by wearing down into uniformity all that is individual in themselves, but by cultivating it and calling it forth, within the limits imposed by the rights and interests of others, that human beings become a noble and beautiful object of contemplation."[151] Indeed, even if the higher faculties *could* be other-directed, the activity that befits a given individual is much too complex and indeterminate to be fixed a priori. To develop our personal *variety* of embodied virtue or excellence, we need to go our own way.

In this call to individual originality, we encounter Mill's most anxious remarks on the dangers of society to human flourishing. At one level, *On Liberty* is an extended lament on the fate of the individual in modern society. Like Tocqueville, Mill is fearful that the democratic age has toppled the tyrannical few above us only to replace them with the tyrannical many around us; that is, "the tyranny of the majority" is the new apprehension. And one of Mill's core tenets is that tyranny is not just a political threat but also—and in the democratic age, chiefly—a cultural threat. Political tyranny is bad enough; but, if anything, Mill is even more concerned about the sway of society itself: "Society can and does execute its own mandates: and if it issues wrong mandates instead of right, or any mandates at all in things with which it ought not to meddle, it practises a social tyranny more formidable than many kinds of political oppression, since, though not usually upheld by such extreme penalties, it leaves fewer means of escape, penetrating much more deeply into the details of life, and enslaving the soul itself." The "tyranny of the magistrate" is typically more severe but usually less permeating and suffocating than the "tyranny of the prevailing opinion and feeling." A democratic society in which "the spirit of

151. Ibid., 266.

liberty" is lacking will resemble a reverse panopticon, with the individual at the center of the social prison, encircled by the monitoring masses.[152]

One might say that Mill's core objective in *On Liberty* is to promote through argument, but even more so through rhetoric, the cultural and moral ethos of liberalism, which Mill regards as vital to the protection of the individual from the peculiar, nascent danger posed by a democratic society. Under the censuring eye, and at the censoring mercy, of the demos—and without recourse to "any substantive power in society, which, itself opposed to the ascendancy of numbers, is interested in taking under its protection opinions and tendencies at variance with those of the public," that is, an aristocracy—the individual will be overwhelmingly given to "bend the knee to custom," and thus to adopt an unoriginal intellectual and ethical posture. Furthermore, in a flattening, mass society, homogenizing forces—technological, educational, commercial—are bound to be ascendant: "The circumstances which surround different classes and individuals, and shape their characters, are daily becoming more assimilated." Therefore, barring a Millian transformation in public sentiment, the most immediate "fix" to the democratic paradox—i.e., more equality, less liberty—is "the mere example of nonconformity."[153] Mill has sometimes been mocked as replacing "bourgeoise nonsense" with "bohemian nonsense" in his call for experiments in living.[154] However, given the nature of the problem Mill was trying to solve, such an experiment is best interpreted as a simple refusal to capitulate to the ideas or ideals of an increasingly stifling society; that is, to "experiment" is to think or act for ourselves, which will *appear* like eccentricity in a culture of mere conformity.

And, to clarify, Mill does not oppose custom itself, nor does he mean to suggest that we should blithely discard norms or traditions. In fact, norms and traditions are usually the best starting point for deliberation: "No one who does not thoroughly know the modes of action which common experience has sanctioned, is capable of judging of the circumstances which require a departure from those ordinary modes of action."[155] As we saw last chapter, every moral actor should be well schooled in the edicts of the Utilitarian Almanac—and a similar thing can be said for each individual: "It would be absurd to pretend that people ought to live as if nothing whatever had been known in the world before they came into it; as if experience had as yet done nothing towards showing that one mode of experience, or

152. Ibid., 219, 220, 272.
153. Ibid., 269, 274–275.
154. Anschutz, *Philosophy of J. S. Mill*, 25.
155. Mill, *Considerations on Representative Government*, 425, *CW* 19.

of conduct, is preferable to another. Nobody denies that people should be so taught and trained in youth, as to know and benefit by the ascertained results of human experience." Extant practices should be understood as "presumptive evidence" of what is desirable, and should thus "have a claim to [our] deference." So, in sum, all Mill means to say is that, as individuals, we ought to be governed by the activity of our higher faculties, which might lead the many to embrace custom, but which might lead the few to take a different tack if their "character" proves "uncustomary."[156]

Nor is there anything patronizing in Mill's suggestion that "the many" might prefer established norms or traditions. Customs, when they are valuable, embody enduring, time-honored ways of exercising the higher faculties in accordance with the higher pleasures. For most, such customs can be reasonably or even perfectly suited to their purposes. For example, many teachers will be able to realize their full, often quite prodigious, potential as educators by employing tried and true pedagogical tools. And indeed, there need be nothing in custom itself to prevent a teacher's unique personality, methods, and intelligence from shining through. That said, there will naturally be a few teachers who, due to their peculiar sensibilities, will be better able to serve their students by employing an uncustomary pedagogy. However, what is uncustomary here is not necessarily "superior" to what is customary—John Keating was not a "better" teacher than William Hundert, at least not "obviously."[157] In fact, Mill's hope is that uncustomary practices, if proved worthy, will be "converted into customs." Mill advocates and celebrates the avant-garde in reaction to what he sees as a dearth of unconventionality: "Eccentricity has always abounded when and where strength of character has abounded; and the amount of eccentricity in a society has generally been proportional to the amount of genius, mental vigour, and moral courage which it contained. That so few now dare to be eccentric, marks the chief danger of the time."[158] And yet, conventionality can exude just as much "genius," "vigour," and "courage" as unconventionality: "Whosoever, to the extent of his opportunity, gets at his convictions by his own faculties" is a "*genius*; nor matters it though he should never chance to find out anything which somebody had not found out before him. There may be no hidden truths left for him to find, or he may accidentally miss them; but if he have courage and opportunity he

156. Mill, *On Liberty*, 262.

157. Keating (Robin Williams) and Hundert (Kevin Kline) are the focal teachers from the films *Dead Poets Society* and *The Emperor's Club*. Keating is eccentric and enchanting, while Hundert is old-school but altogether effective and inspirational.

158. Mill, *On Liberty*, 269.

can find hidden truths; for he has found all those which he knows, many of which were as hidden to *him* as those which are still unknown."[159] The orthodox genius of William Hundert is manifest in the lasting devotion of nearly all his former students. Mill's gentle nod to novelty is that new ideas and practices (the catalysts of progress and vitality) are more likely to emerge where "genius," "vigour," and "courage" abound; novelty is one key *symptom*, not the *summation*, of social flourishing.

Incivility and Immaturity

As I have indicated throughout this chapter, the central strain of argument in *On Liberty* is fairly straightforward. The fifth chapter of *Utilitarianism* elucidates Mill's theory of justice. And in *On Liberty*, Mill applies this theory to the value of liberty as non-interference. This application is condensed as Mill's "principle of liberty," or the Harm Principle. In the second and third chapters of *On Liberty*, Mill argues that intellectual and ethical liberty, respectively, are absolute, sacrosanct moral rights; that justice brooks no exception to the injustice of their limitation or suppression. Conversely, Mill notes a variety of cases where justice *does* warrant interference pro tanto. The validity of Mill's proposed interferences is beside the point—indeed, Mill would certainly welcome debate concerning his analysis. Rather, the crucial thing to recognize here is the sublime simplicity of Mill's outlook: it is just to violate the first rule of justice only to thwart or remedy injustice. Nonetheless, there is an additional pair of complicating concerns that demand our attention.

LIBERAL CIVILITY

One critique that is often raised is that Mill has a rather rosy, naïve view of what discourse or dialogue, and certainly of what political speech or discussion, actually looks like in practice. To wit, Mill is often accused of refusing to appreciate the performative, bigoted, sophistical, hateful, demagogic things that people often do with their language; he is regularly identified as the chief exponent of "the utopian assumption" that "conversation works by exchange of reasons: one party offers its reasons, which are then countered by the reasons of an opponent, until the truth ultimately emerges."[160] And indeed, the view of the "realist"—that is, that

159. Mill, "On Genius," 332.
160. Stanley, *How Fascism Works*, 67.

dialogue often operates by totally different means—requires no further confirmation than a brief survey of the quality of conversation presently taking place between the wingnuts and moonbats that currently abound wherever and whenever you are reading this book. And it often gets worse from there, with the moderate, capacious center getting hollowed out by despair, apathy, and fatigue; and with echo-chamber tribalism on such a tear that the very idea of civil discourse swells the soul with Romantic longing. What relevance can the Mill of chapter 2 of *On Liberty* have in such a cuckoo world?

However, unlike the rosy, naïve Mill depicted above, Mill was well aware of how unreasonable, vitriolic, and enflaming discourse can be. Indeed, what Mill offers in chapter 2 of *On Liberty* is not an idealistic *expectation* but rather a moralistic *demonstration*. Mill is describing not how discourse *is*, but how it *ought* to be; and how we, as individuals, have a moral obligation—indeed, a perfect duty to whomever we are discoursing with—to promote this state of affairs in our own lives. In other words, Mill is not depicting an empirical reality but instead portraying "the real morality of public discussion." And Mill regards this is as an eminently practical doctrine. Suppose you "conscientiously strive" toward this ideal: either your interlocutors will go tit for tat, such that *your* civility draws out *their* civility; or they will respond to you with incivility regardless, in which case they come off looking like exactly what they are, namely, persons steeped in "malignity, bigotry, or intolerance."[161] Intellectually speaking, a reasonable person cannot lose at discussion—they can lose only the argument, in which case, being reasonable, they win anyway.

And yet, without limiting intellectual liberty, one might argue that society ought to *enforce* a degree of civility in freedom of discussion. Here we have "the doctrine, that *calm* and *fair* discussion should be permitted, but that ridicule and invective ought to be chastised."[162] People often argue that "the free expression of all opinions should be permitted, on condition that the manner be temperate, and do not pass the bounds of fair discussion." Unfair discussion takes several forms: "The gravest of them is, to argue sophistically, to suppress facts or arguments, to misstate the elements of the case, or misrepresent the opposite opinion." And there is also the problem of "intemperate discussion, namely invective, sarcasm, personality, and the like," along with the tendency "to stigmatize those who hold [a] contrary opinion as bad and immoral men." In short, the

---

161. Mill, *On Liberty*, 259.
162. Mill, "Law of Libel and Liberty of the Press," 15.

object of incivility is to score a false or cheap victory by evading rather than engaging in honest intellectual dialogue. Naturally, this definition is not meant to apply to things like needling, irony, satire, or caricature— and, as we might predict, the question of where to draw these lines is one of Mill's worries: "Much might be said on the impossibility of fixing where these supposed bounds are to be placed."[163] And yet, Mill quickly brushes past this concern to address incivility on its own terms.

The hypothetical content-neutral argument for interfering with incivility can be compared to the destination-neutral case for instituting and enforcing traffic laws. To motorists, society declares, "Drive wherever you are driving, but, while traveling, obey the speed limits and traffic lights." Similarly, to speakers, society might declare, "Say whatever you believe, but, while expressing yourself, observe certain rules of the dialogic road." Dialogic traffic laws are implicitly present in almost every human interaction, and there are contexts today in which they are largely absent where they are sorely needed (like social media). In principle, Mill is sympathetic to enforcing rhetorical rules of the road in order to compel a certain civility: "Undoubtedly the manner of asserting an opinion, even though it be a true one, may be very objectionable, and may justly incur severe censure."[164] If what you are expressing in fact *depends* on incivility for its potency, then you are a Sophist—and, as a devotee of Socrates, Mill has no inclination to view such expressions as substantive.

Nonetheless, the problem is that such rules would be nigh impossible to impose judiciously. Unfairness is a natural and ubiquitous aspect of discussion, and is not even always intentional as such: "all this, even to the most aggravated degree, is so continually done in perfect good faith, by persons who are not considered, and in many other respects may not deserve to be considered, ignorant or incompetent, that it is rarely possible on adequate grounds conscientiously to stamp the misrepresentation as morally culpable; and still less could law presume to interfere with this kind of controversial misconduct."[165] Rather than holding each and every person, on pain of social censure, to an impossibly lofty standard of enlightened deliberation, it would be much wiser and healthier to put it upon colleagues, friends, and associates to register and correct instances of unfairness when and as they arise, and to exhort their colleagues, friends, and associates to improve or amend their mode of discussion. In short, we

163. Mill, *On Liberty*, 258–259.
164. Ibid., 258.
165. Ibid., 258.

might aver that we have a moral duty to engage in fair discussion, but that it is generally inexpedient to punish alleged violations of this duty, and that such violations should instead be understood and addressed as occasions for prudential advice and moral counsel.

Moreover, it strains credulity to imagine such rules being enforced equitably. This is even more apparent when it comes to the varieties of intemperance, the "denunciation" of which "would deserve more sympathy if it were ever proposed to interdict them equally to both sides; but it is only desired to restrain the employment of them against the prevailing opinion: against the unprevailing they may not only be used without general disapproval, but will be likely to obtain for him who uses them the praise of honest zeal and righteous indignation." To encourage society to *punish* intemperance is almost certain to boost the power of the prevailing faction. Thus, rather than *denouncing* those who speak intemperately, it is wiser and healthier to rely on the same tools as before. Indeed, regardless of power dynamics, *everyone* has an impulsive tendency to interpret their interlocutors as immoderate or untoward in their speech: "every opponent who pushes them hard, and whom they find it difficult to answer, appears to them, if he shows any strong feeling on the subject, an intemperate opponent."[166] Temperance: a moral duty—but one that is better left to conversation and conscience.[167]

What about this consideration: are we morally bound to extend *friendship* to our interlocutors? No: Mill acknowledges and even embraces the fact that we will often disdain or despise those with whom we disagree. For most people with a pulse, this kind of animosity is often inescapable: "Those who, having opinions which they hold to be immensely important, and the contraries to be prodigiously hurtful, have any deep regard for the general good, will necessarily dislike, as a class and in the abstract, those who think wrong what they think right, and right what they think wrong." Of course, we should never be "insensible to good qualities in an opponent," but civility does not require us to *like* our adversaries. Rather, it just obliges *respect* for them, which is a more realistic, and also a rather ennobling, standard: "I grant that an earnest person, being no more infallible than other men, is liable to dislike people on account of opinions which do not merit dislike; but if he neither himself does them any ill office, nor connives at its being done by others, he is not intolerant: and the

166. Ibid., 258–259.
167. Actually, I believe there should be *plenty* of space for intemperate speech in a hearty, healthy society.

forbearance, which flows from a conscientious sense of the importance to mankind of the equal freedom of all opinions, is the only tolerance which is commendable, or, to the highest moral order of minds, possible."[168] The fracas of public life is not a philosophy seminar, and Mill does not believe that it can or ought to be conducted with demure urbanity. However, we can both engage in and benefit from passionate and rigorous, and frequently enraging, public discourse by observing *jus in bello*.

Furthermore, we ought to be triply concerned about extending civility to those who voice dissenting views, and we might also consider what social censures *could*—given "the circumstances of the individual case"—be justified when intemperance is being used to harass or intimidate those who express unpopular opinions: "In general, opinions contrary to those commonly received can only obtain a hearing by studied moderation of language, and the most cautious avoidance of unnecessary offence, from which they hardly ever deviate even in a slight degree without losing ground: while unmeasured vituperation employed on the side of the prevailing opinion, really does deter people from professing contrary opinions, and from listening to those who profess them."[169] What does an orthodoxy have to fear from an articulate critic other than the truth, or other than that aspect of the truth that the dominant faction is ignoring or suppressing? Of course, to worry that a *definite* falsehood will triumph is to assume infallibility; but, even worse, it is to assume that *not* you but those *around* you are too gullible, stupid, or ignorant to see through chicaneries, lies, and illusions.

And yet, today, the invective, and even outright hostility, directed at speakers regularly appeals to the assumption that listeners will be affronted or disturbed, or that a speaker is merely offensive or disreputable and thus not worthy of a soapbox. Topics like political correctness, free speech, and cancel culture have become hot-button issues over the past several years. Needless to say, Mill would regard our illiberal tribalism with a mixture of horror and resolve. Moreover, in *On Liberty*, he speaks briefly to our present moment. We might call this the *offense proviso*: "There are many who consider as an injury to themselves any conduct which they have a distaste for, and resent it as an outrage to their feelings"; likewise, they are "offended" by any "opinion" that appears to disregard the "feelings of others."[170] Indeed, what about the *emotional* or *psycho-*

168. Mill, *Autobiography*, 51–53.
169. Mill, *On Liberty*, 259.
170. Ibid., 283.

logical "harm" done to listeners by content that they take to be abhorrent, unpleasant, or otherwise beyond the pale?

Mill has two direct responses. First, from a position of self-invested neutrality, there is "no parity between the feeling of a person for his own opinion, and the feeling of another who is offended at his holding it; no more than between the desire of a thief to take a purse, and the desire of the right owner to keep it." This is one of Mill's more explicit allusions in *On Liberty* to impartial weighing: the appeal to "offense" is dwarfed by the interest speakers have in their intellectual liberty, as well as by the interest society at large has in either acquiring new truths or contending with falsehoods. Besides, it is supremely doubtful that guarding individuals against what offends them is actually in their *own* interest.[171]

However, the more critical issue, for Mill, is that the offense proviso is boundlessly restrictive and liable to perpetual abuse. In a phrase, offense exists in the mind of the offended, and is thus an ever-ready excuse for cynical salvoes: "if the test be offence to those whose opinion is attacked, I think experience testifies that this offence is given whenever the attack is telling and powerful."[172] Recall Mill's treatment of rule-bound exceptions: the problem is that the offense proviso cannot be solidly defined or applied. It is impossible to falsify an offense claim, for it is "inherently a subjection reaction."[173] And speakers cannot represent themselves against the charge of being offensive except through the very process of dialogue and discussion that the offense proviso means to suppress. And indeed, the offense proviso can be (and has been) wielded arbitrarily against ideas and doctrines of whatever kind, and is very likely to be trotted out against the deepest and most profound speakers precisely because their ideas and doctrines undercut the dogma of the moment.

In short, whenever faced with a potential moral rule or rule-based exception, Mill asks the question: "How likely is its application to change depending on which creed or interest holds the power?" Better yet: "How reliably are we able to *guess* which faction or orthodoxy is in charge by the nature of the application?" The various moral rules and exceptions that Mill endorses, while certainly up for debate, are not *ripe* for abuse; we do not catch the foul stench of partiality or prejudice *whenever* they are applied. For instance, when Jill rebukes Jack for his dishonesty, we do not immediately think to ask, "What is Jill's ideology?" Nor does the malodor

171. See Lukianoff and Haidt, *Coddling of the American Mind*, esp. pt. I.
172. Mill, *On Liberty*, 258, 283.
173. Waldron, *Harm in Hate Speech*, 107.

of partisanship sting our nostrils *whenever* a politician condemns an act of gratuitous violence; indeed, now imagining such a hypothetical case, we cannot *reliably* predict which party the politician belongs to. However, only a naïve individual would admit an application of the offense proviso without a healthy dose of skepticism. In fact, only a very naïve individual would not endeavor first to *listen* to the speaker speak—that is, to do exactly what the offense proviso would seek to prevent the individual from doing. The individual should listen and ponder; should hold out for the possibility that others think *differently*; and should, if necessary, expose the illogic and iniquity of the speaker for others to see, knowing that odious ideas, when pushed into the shadows, are more likely than not to deepen, warp, and metastasize into something even more malevolent and less manageable. Besides, as experience has shown time and again, nothing is so disarming as the olive branch of friendly good will.

Of course, this case against the offense proviso assumes that the speaker in question is engaging their audience in a reasoned, deliberative manner. But what about naked, overt hate speech: malicious, venomous speech-acts which, at their very mildest, amount to nothing but a verbal snarl or gut-punch? Free speech advocates do themselves no favors by espousing the sticks-and-stones theory, where speech is understood, in contrast to action, to be intrinsically innocuous; nor by imagining that hostile, degrading speech-acts are something that a free society just needs to weather and disavow from a position of strength, as if dealing with hate speech is all about growing a thick skin and keeping a stiff upper lip; as if it does not pollute the social atmosphere for everyone, or does not have substantial, deleterious effects on those persons or peoples targeted with "group libel."[174]

This prompts what we can dub the *hate proviso*, which is related to but importantly distinct from the offense proviso. Whereas the offense proviso states, "I am offended," the hate proviso declares, "That is hateful." Naturally, you can also say, "That is offensive," but the meaning is the same: "That is likely to cause offense," that is, to produce a certain *subjective* reaction. Conversely, to pronounce, "That is hateful," is to make an *objective* assertion; for instance, that the content under consideration *is* an "expression that vilifies or harasses on the basis of the target's race, gender, sexual orientation, or other forms of group membership."[175] Clearly, those who engage in hate speech are "hoping for certain psychological

---

174. See ibid., chap. 3.
175. Brink, "Millian Principles, Freedom of Expression, and Hate Speech," 131.

effects—hoping to cultivate among minority members a traumatic sense of not being trusted, not being respected, not being perceived as worthy of ordinary citizenship, a sense of being always vulnerable to discriminatory and humiliating exclusions and insults." However, "the root of the matter" is how hate speech targets "a person's standing in society." In essence, the "hurt, shock, and anger" that hate speech induces or provokes, while of course deeply significant, is not what *makes* hate speech *hate speech*.[176]

Not only is hate speech objective, and thus more tangible than mere offense, it also appears to defy Mill's opening defense of intellectual liberty. Again, hate speech is partly characterized by its eschewal of reasoned, deliberative expression. The purpose of hate speech is not to offer an argument in support of a proposition, for that would conceal the real feeling and soften the desired blow. Rather, the point of hate speech is to spit in the eye of or flip the bird at whatever persons or peoples have attracted the mindless ire of the hater. Indeed, the object of hate speech is not wisdom, truth, or understanding, but the very opposite: "hate speech evokes visceral, rather than articulate, response; it provokes violence or, more commonly, silences through insult or intimidation," and it also "contributes to a hostile environment that undermines the culture of mutual respect necessary for effective expression and fair consideration of diverse points of view."[177] Worse than an outlook that some might find offensive, hate speech actively scorns and strikes at the sociality upon which any good society is ultimately founded—it is a barking, snapping reversion to something base and animal.

Hate speech: objectively and inherently malignant—so, why not interfere? Now, we can always make arguments about the efficacy of such interference, like "The only salutary or enduring solution to bad speech is more good speech," or "Hate speech compels people to band together and reaffirm their values in opposition to what they find detestable," which faintly echoes Mill's theory concerning the utility of falsehoods. But, however persuasive (or not) we find such arguments to be, the more fundamental issue is how hate speech regulation *itself* is to be regulated: What, for the purpose of legal or social interference, constitutes hate speech? When, specifically, is speech *objectively* hateful?

As always, the vital question—especially when there are other, less invasive means at society's disposal for dealing with iniquitous speech-acts, including exhortation and disavowal, as well as correlated rules

176. Waldron, *Harm in Hate Speech*, 106–107.
177. Brink, "Millian Principles, Freedom of Expression, and Hate Speech," 139, 141.

banning things like harassment and explicit or proximate incitement to violence—is how to formulate the actual rule or law so as to prevent it from being applied too broadly or becoming an all-purpose tool for censorship. For one, an "atmosphere of freedom" cannot survive if the accusation of "hate" can legitimately extend to whatever one reckons a speaker *might* be thinking or feeling, or to how their speech *could* be interpreted, or to what it *really* means—that is, to hold water, the accusation of "hate" must be objective, not subjective or speculative. Neither can a free environment persist if every faux pas becomes a cause célèbre. Making critical, mature allowances for human imperfection generally entails suspending moral judgment for the vast majority of unseemly or insensitive statements.[178]

Furthermore, what could otherwise be construed as hateful language should not, and truly cannot, be classified as such as long as it is properly contextualized. What might justly provoke "hurt, shock, and anger" in one context can be integral to something artistic or humane in another. Consider, for instance, the often brutal, but purposive, language utilized in outstandingly moral literary masterpieces like *Huckleberry Finn* and *To Kill a Mockingbird*. And relatedly, there is plenty that is said and argued, especially in deliberative settings, that may happen to give aid and comfort—often unintentionally, often irrationally—to hateful attitudes: "For instance, it is difficult to see how one could have an open and vigorous discussion of the merits of affirmative action without allowing the expression of views that might reflect and encourage racial stereotyping."[179] Naturally, we should all be invited and nudged to be as responsible as possible in what we say and how we say it; but, alas, to be irresponsible is to be human, not hateful. Indeed, it is rather paradoxical to classify *any* rational analysis or reasoned account as hate speech, for anything presented or framed as *persuasion* is, in effect, an explanation as to why a certain idea or perspective is *not* hateful—just like *truth* is an absolute defense against a defamation suit. Of course, we might imagine that a "suspect" speaker is just giving a cynical rationale for their *true* thoughts or feelings, filled as they *must be* with hate; but, again, we have thereby ditched reality for mere fantasy or conjecture.

So, with that, how should we, as a society, understand hate speech? The answer we get from Mill-minded scholars often goes something like this: hate speech is a stark, direct weaponization of particular insults,

---

178. Of course, this in no way precludes what ought to be encouraged: offering modest, well-intentioned moral appeals to others.

179. Brink, "Millian Principles, Freedom of Expression, and Hate Speech," 139.

terms, or symbols "that have a long, ugly, and sometimes violent history." And we can extend this definition to include any stark, direct expression with even a *short*, ugly history, where an evident parallel can be drawn to past hatred and violence. On this view, critics of, say, affirmative action do not engage in hate speech unless they employ "racial epithets to vilify or wound," or unless they exploit "traditional epithets or symbols of derision to vilify on the basis of group membership."[180]

The question becomes: what *are*—or how *ought* society to categorize—these insults, terms, or symbols? Objectively, hate speech should be something *obvious*, something *blatant*, something that leaves *nothing* to the imagination—something where, if hate speech codes did *not* exist, we would be tempted to introduce them *specifically* for this or that expression or mode of expression. Thus, perhaps we might be tempted to follow the U.S. Supreme Court's hoary obscenity standard: "I know it when I see it."[181] And yet, whereas one person sees a *Peace-Love-Israel* sign and thinks *pro-apartheid*, another person sees a *Boycott-Divest-Sanction* sign and thinks *anti-Semitic*. This is not to give credence to either reaction; this is just to remark that Justice Potter Stewart's criterion would open the factional floodgates.

So, how can we classify something as naked and overt, but still as open-ended, as hate speech? The key, I think, is to ask the right questions: Can a given expression, or mode of expression, be reasonably dissociated from the belief or attitude that a particular group, as a group, is humanly inferior, unworthy of equal regard, or somehow contemptible? That is, can the speaker in question reasonably deny the following equation: "If you say or signal x then you *must* think or feel y," where y is an assertion of inferiority, disregard, or contempt? Alternatively, can we imagine an interlocutor who *disagrees* with the speaker nevertheless acknowledging their good faith and good will, and even respecting their viewpoint? While many controversial, and even confrontational, terms, views, and symbols can answer more or less ably to such questions, we can readily catalog many that do not: you cannot drape a Nazi banner from your window and explain that although the Holocaust was unfathomably evil, you just really admire the Reichsautobahn; of course, you *can*, but no reasonable person will believe you. Indeed, I would venture to propose that *if* society is going to restrict hate speech (and, again, I believe that Mill's theory *may* allow for this *one* content-specific restriction *in theory*) then it ought to be

180. Ibid., 119, 139.
181. *Jacobellis v. Ohio*, 378 U.S. 184 (1964).

as specific as possible about *precisely* which insults, terms, or symbols—which expressions or modes of expression—are convicted by the questions above, or by similar questions. This approach would make our deliberations less slippery and more concrete, hence respecting liberty while also targeting "hate" with a singular force and clarity.

In saying all this, I am aware that what makes the expression of hate speech so truly concerning, and so deeply personal, for so many, is that it is generally utilized to denigrate, harass, or intimidate vulnerable groups in society, whose equal standing in the community was historically delayed and might still be fairly precarious. The question of how hate speech ordinances relate to liberal rights, like free speech, might appear to be beside the point when the more basic issue is what we need to do in order fully and firmly to integrate *all* persons and peoples into the liberal order—*particularly* when it is the abuse *of such liberal rights* that makes this denigration, harassment, or intimidation even *possible*.

In truth, what we ultimately have here is an especially arresting example of a deeper, and very old, dilemma: how do you make liberalism more egalitarian—how do you democratize liberalism—without undermining or damaging liberalism itself? According to Mill, the liberal order is *the* framework for individual and social flourishing; and so, in pursuing liberty and justice for all, it ought to be preserved and conserved in every respect. Mill's Tao of Progress is to do anything and everything we can to promote universal sociality and justice without jeopardizing the integrity or sacrosanctity of the basic liberties. After all, what kind of progress can we expect from a situation where illiberal means are used to pursue liberal ends? Do we not thus exacerbate the very frictions and fractures that made the pursuit necessary to begin with? And what sort of mutual, enduring peace can we expect as a consequence?[182] These are challenging questions, to be sure; regardless, getting clear on when and where things like hate speech restrictions would compromise or contravene things like intellectual liberty is essential to knowing where we stand, whether together or apart.

PATERNALISM FOR THE IMMATURE

In chapter 1 of *On Liberty*, Mill qualifies his *entire* doctrine of liberal justice in what is undoubtedly the most controversial passage in his corpus:

---

182. Indeed, the argument for *liberal* democratization can be compared to the argument made by those like Martin Luther King for *civil* disobedience.

It is, perhaps, hardly necessary to say that [the Harm Principle] is meant to apply only to human beings in the maturity of their faculties. We are not speaking of children, or of young persons below the age which the law may fix as that of manhood or womanhood. Those who are still in a state to require being taken care of by others, must be protected against their own actions as well as against external injury. For the same reason, we may leave out of consideration those backward states of society in which the race itself may be considered as in its nonage. . . . Despotism is a legitimate mode of government in dealing with barbarians, provided the end be their improvement, and the means justified by actually effecting that end. Liberty, as a principle, has no application to any state of things anterior to the time when mankind have become capable of being improved by free and equal discussion. Until then, there is nothing for them but implicit obedience to an Akbar or a Charlemagne, if they are so fortunate as to find one.[183]

Until children or peoples are capable of "being guided to their own improvement by conviction or persuasion," "compulsion" can be legitimately used "as a means to their own good."[184] In other words, Mill supports paternalism for those deemed to be in the immaturity of their faculties, for educating their capacity to govern themselves in a competent and moral manner. Mill has been heavily criticized for this aspect of his thought. While it is not my purpose here to attack or defend this passage, it should be noted that recent scholarship has underscored various subtleties in Mill's views on barbarism and civilization, where Mill comes out looking far less wantonly imperialist—and perhaps even far more liberal and liberal-minded on a global scale—than we might automatically assume.[185]

However, as far as *On Liberty* itself is concerned, the passage above provokes an intriguing question. Mill gives the okay to paternalism for children and barbarians, with the former being found in *both* lower *and* higher states of society, and with the latter being found *only* in *lower* states of society. But what about those childlike or barbaric *adults* who are found in *higher* states of society? Mill has a tendency to talk about societies as if each individual member advances in lockstep with others: "as soon as *mankind* have attained the capacity of being guided to their

183. Mill, *On Liberty*, 224.
184. Ibid., 224.
185. See Marwah, "Complicating Barbarism and Civilization," 345–366; and Tunick, "Tolerant Imperialism," 586–611. Cf. Pitts, "Legislator of the World?," 219–225.

own improvement," interference "is no longer admissible as a means to their own good, and justifiable only for the security of others."[186] But it is perfectly conceivable that only a majority, a plurality, or even a minority of any given society will overcome the "difficulties in the way of sponta-neous progress."[187] There will always be adults who develop tendencies toward ethical incompetence. What, then, is society to do, if anything, if the activity of the individual at hand is plainly characterized by aimless-ness or dissipation?

Consider also: an individual cannot be dubbed "mature" for Mill with-out having achieved a certain level of personal autonomy. Scholars often associate Mill's notion of autonomy with "critical reflection"[188] or "critical evaluation,"[189] a kind of introspective analysis of one's will and desires. Self-criticism of this sort is the hallmark of contemporary liberal theories of personal autonomy, the idea being that to be a free actor is to be "guided by forces which are self-imposed," a condition that can be realized only insofar as we "reflect on [our] emerging values [&c.] in light of reasonable alternatives."[190] Mill has often been read, and justly so, as an early expo-nent of this view. And yet, Mill also argues that such self-criticism will be pointless if we have not first acquired "the habit, and thence the power,"[191] of exercising the "executive" virtues. Virtues like self-discipline and self-control enable us to act intentionally and to parry the forces of lethargy and temptation: "none but a person of confirmed virtue is completely free."[192] This implies the need for the right kind of education, where we are "systematically disciplined in self-mortification," that is, "taught, as in antiquity, to control [our] appetites, to brave dangers, and submit volun-tarily to pain."[193] What, then, is society to do, if anything, if the activity of the individual at hand is plainly characterized by heteronomy?

Mill's apparent reply is rather unsatisfying: "If society lets any consid-erable number of its members grow up mere children, incapable of being acted on by rational consideration of distant motives, society has itself to blame for the consequences." One may very well grant that given its "absolute power over [individuals] during all the early portion of their

186. Mill, *On Liberty*, 224, my emphasis.
187. Ibid., 224.
188. Baum, "J. S. Mill on Freedom and Power," 201.
189. Gray, *Mill on Liberty*, 77.
190. Christman, "Liberalism and Individual Positive Freedom," 345.
191. Mill, "Coleridge," 133.
192. Mill, *System of Logic*, 841, *CW* 8.
193. Mill, *Auguste Comte and Positivism*, 339, *CW* 10.

existence," society has only itself to blame.[194] But does society's past irresponsibility bind it to present irresponsibility? Is society—perhaps even an entirely *new* generation—barred from remedying its historical errors and oversights?

Indeed, in what is an odd turn of events upon reflection, Mill describes the manner in which we can, short of treading on individual liberty, react to those who display a willful contempt for, or ignorance of, the higher pleasures:

> I do not mean that the feelings with which a person is regarded by others, ought not to be in any way affected by his self-regarding qualities or deficiencies. This is neither possible nor desirable. If he is eminent in any of the qualities which conduce to his own good, he is, so far, a proper object of admiration. He is so much the nearer to the ideal perfection of human nature. If he is grossly deficient in those qualities, a sentiment the opposite of admiration will follow. There is a degree of folly, and a degree of what may be called (though the phrase is not unobjectionable) lowness or depravation of taste, which, though it cannot justify doing harm to the person who manifests it, renders him necessarily and properly a subject of distaste, or, in extreme cases, even of contempt: a person could not have the opposite qualities in due strength without entertaining these feelings. Though doing no wrong to any one, a person may so act as to compel us to judge him, and feel to him, as a fool, or as a being of an inferior order.[195]

Mill stops short of declaring such an individual to be immature, which is perplexing, considering that this individual clearly looks to fail the standard for maturity laid down in *Utilitarianism*: "no intelligent human being would consent to be a fool, no instructed person would be an ignoramus be an ignoramus, no person of feeling and conscience would be selfish and base." And when a once-mature person abandons the life of "a human being" in favor of that of "a pig," it is normally because the individual has already been rendered "incapable" of the latter.[196] This description seems to capture in a nutshell the individual who, in *On Liberty*, is either dead or dumb to the attractions of self-development. Also, as I noted before, Mill believes that we ought to be "taught and trained in youth, as to know and benefit by the ascertained results of human experience." Of course, having

194. Mill, *On Liberty*, 282.
195. Ibid., 277–278.
196. Mill, *Utilitarianism*, 212–213.

been thus inculcated, Mill states that we must then be permitted to "interpret experience in [our] own way."[197] But does Mill's anti-paternalism still hold if individuals, in their youths, were *not* instructed or educated in this manner? What remedial options, if any, can or should society consider?

In sum, throughout *On Liberty*, Mill is speaking of a society that, *as a society*, has met a whole host of characterological and psychological prerequisites, but none of which are necessarily met by *all* the individual members of that society. Mill always falls back upon the principle that our interest in protecting the individual's decision to be "a fool" or "a pig" outweighs the intrusion of society at large: "Considerations to aid his judgment, exhortations to strengthen his will, may be offered to him, even obtruded on him, by others; but he himself is the final judge. All errors which he is likely to commit against advice and warning, are far outweighed by the evil of allowing others to constrain him to what they deem his good."[198] The difficulty, though, is that the persons in question are not necessarily acting "*against* advice and warning." On the contrary, they may, in fact, be already immune or insensible to such exhortations. As Mill writes in *Utilitarianism*, "Capacity for the nobler feelings is in most natures a very tender plant, easily killed, not only by hostile influences, but by mere want of sustenance."[199] It is one thing when Cato, with "a philosophical flourish," "throws himself upon the sword."[200] However, it is quite another thing when we witness our neighbor yielding irrationally to vice or despair. What reason does Mill have to forbid society from providing "sustenance," albeit via compulsion, to a moldering soul?

I do not think Mill could truly have (or has) any *principled* objection to such paternalism. However, this does not preclude Mill from rejecting such paternalism for *prudential* reasons. Indeed, there is the possibility that paternalism will *worsen* the predicament: "If there be among those whom it is attempted to coerce into prudence or temperance, any of the material of which vigorous and independent characters are made, they will infallibly rebel against the yoke. No one such person will ever feel that others have a right to control him in his own concerns," and "it easily comes to be considered a mark of spirit and courage to fly in the face of such usurped authority, and do with ostentation the exact opposite of what it enjoins."[201] In short, compulsion risks increasing resistance, whereas

197. Mill, *On Liberty*, 262.
198. Ibid., 277.
199. Mill, *Utilitarianism*, 213.
200. Melville, *Moby-Dick*, chap. 1.
201. Mill, *On Liberty*, 282–283.

with a softer form of paternal care, we can keep trying to move the ball forward while also keeping the game going. Furthermore, by granting society the power to interfere paternalistically, we are thereby granting it the power to interfere "wrongly, and in the wrong place," and are also discounting "the fruit of a thousand years of experience," namely, "that things in which the individual is the person directly interested, never go right but as they are left to his own discretion, and that any regulation of them by authority, except to protect the rights of others, is sure to be mischievous."[202] Indeed, even when society as a whole is deemed to be in its "nonage," Mill thinks it must be "so *fortunate* as to find" "an Akbar or a Charlemagne"—a *noble and wise* paternalistic authority is one in an epoch.

That said, I do not think anything Mill argues, even prudentially, helps us to respond to the plight of a sister watching her brother succumb to opioids—for, after all, he might have a lucid rationale! Alas, I do not think Mill's general theory is built for such circumstances. In such situations, I believe a true Millian must make a dramatic moral exception: there are imaginable cases (however infrequent) where the Harm Principle must be set aside for the sake of preserving the barest potential for human life and well-being; cases of clear "catastrophic moral horror,"[203] where even the most liberal society ought to act against its very nature—like the Roman Republic appointing a dictator.

Then again, there *are* resources in *On Liberty* we can draw upon to defend such a conclusion. In chapter 1, Mill admits that a critical, perpetual danger can render an otherwise excessive system of interference morally acceptable: "The ancient commonwealths thought themselves entitled to practise" the "regulation of every part of private conduct by public authority, on the ground that the State had a deep interest in the whole bodily and mental discipline of every one of its citizens; a mode of thinking which may have been admissible in small republics surrounded by powerful enemies," and "to which even a short interval of relaxed energy and self-command might so easily be fatal." In like manner, might society be given at least *some* leeway to protect us from, and to compel us to fortify ourselves against, those "powerful enemies" that tend to attack our minds and wills, our hearts and souls, whenever our self-devotion to virtue or excellence is "relaxed"? Also, in chapter 5, Mill bars individuals from abdicating their freedom: "By selling himself for a slave, he abdicates his liberty; he foregoes any future use of it beyond that single act.

---

202. Mill, *Subjection of Women*, 273.
203. Nozick, *Anarchy, State, and Utopia*, 30.

He therefore defeats, in his own case, the very purpose which is the justi-fication of allowing him to dispose of himself."[204] This argument is often viewed as inconsistent with the Harm Principle, which would appear not to acknowledge any notion of *self*-harm. And yet, the entirety of *On Liberty* rests on the axiom that liberty is essential to our well-being. Thus, Mill's "meta" point would seem to be that our rightful liberty can be voided if we *fundamentally* impair its utility. On this basis, might society have at least *some* leeway to prevent us from using (or abusing) our liberty in ways that essentially corrupt or diminish our capacity to act in a virtuous or excellent manner?

In theory—key word: *theory*—I think Mill would reply *yea* to both inquiries. The absolutism of inward liberty applies to the activity of our higher faculties, but not necessarily to our passive submission to appetite, impulse, or lethargy. Nonetheless, Mill is extremely wary of conceding any interfering power to society, for it is rarely recovered, is liable to abuse, and will rear its head in an indefinite array of unintended circumstances. Thus, just as it will often be inexpedient to interfere with harmful con-duct, it is generally unwise to treat immaturity with even the most refined equivalent of "whips and scourges."[205] Mill's core idea is that the general happiness will be best served by trying to cure our ethical ills through exhortation and persuasion, as well as through improving education. And his underlying premise seems to be that a society that must depend on its parental guardians to keep it sheltered from vice and ruin has either failed to escape the nursery or has already gone to hell in a handbasket.

Indeed, Mill would likely say that if society cannot keep itself oriented toward virtue or excellence without relying on interference, then it has fallen to the obverse of barbarism: *decadence*. And decadence can be over-come only by some process of barbaric regeneration: "When the Roman empire, containing all the art, science, literature, and industry of the world, was overrun, ravaged, and dismembered by hordes of barbarians, everybody lamented the destruction of civilization, in an event which is now admitted to have been the necessary condition of its renovation."[206] In short, Mill does not have much in the way of practical solutions to offer to a truly profligate or putrefying society. Rather, he is theorizing atop a liberal peak between the twin valleys of preliberal barbarism and postlib-eral decadence. The ideal society of *On Liberty* is something that liberal

---

204. Mill, *On Liberty*, 226, 299.
205. Ibid., 277.
206. Mill, "De Tocqueville on Democracy in America [II]," 191, *CW* 18.

reformers like Mill must work toward promoting or preserving, often over the course of decades or centuries of struggle. It can be too soon for *On Liberty*—but it can also become too late.

What, if anything, though, might keep society perched atop its liberal peak? What is most likely to prevent society from tumbling downhill, whether backward or forward? Mill replies with his theory of freedom and republican justice, to which we now turn.

CHAPTER FOUR

Republican Justice

MILL ON THE NATURE AND
VALUE OF FREEDOM

*Let us suppose, therefore, that the government is entirely at one with
the people, and never thinks of exerting any power of coercion unless in
agreement with what it conceives to be their voice. But I deny the right
of the people to exercise such coercion, either by themselves or by their
government. The power itself is illegitimate.*

—MILL, *ON LIBERTY*

IN THIS CHAPTER, we turn our attention from Mill's liberal social philosophy to his republican political philosophy. The guiding idea in this chapter is that to enjoy the right breadth of individual liberty, or free rein, is not enough for Mill; morally speaking, our liberty must *also* have the depth that comes with true *freedom*. But what does Mill mean by individual freedom? How does it differ from individual liberty, and why is this significant?

For generations, Mill's treatment of liberty and freedom has attracted and inspired a diverse and often conflicting array of political philosophers. More than any other aspect of Mill's practical philosophy, the reception of his theory of liberty and freedom has been typified by Harold Bloom's remark concerning the Bard, which we encountered in the introductory chapter: "You can bring absolutely anything to Shakespeare and the plays will light it up."[1] To wit, political thinkers of all persuasions have routinely found whatever it is that they were looking for in Mill's writings.

1. Bloom, *Shakespeare*, xxii.

And indeed, Mill's political works certainly lend themselves to a variety of conceptual interpretations and practical applications.

Nonetheless, *however* one understands Mill's political philosophy, and *whatever* lessons one takes from it, my overarching thesis in this chapter is that Mill's chief political value is individual freedom, understood as non-domination. Is Mill a classical liberal? A modern liberal? A liberal socialist? Does he favor democracy? Aristocracy? The modest goal of this chapter is not to solve any such puzzles but to frame all such discussions in terms of Mill's predominant political commitment; namely, a zero-tolerance policy for arbitrary power. Any true Millian platform must demonstrate, *first* and *last*, how it promotes and preserves individual freedom.

The key to understanding Mill's republican theory is to see how it emanates directly from his liberal theory. Mill defends intellectual and ethical liberty as absolute, inviolable liberal rights; this establishes a sphere of basic liberties that it is *always* arbitrary to interfere with, and that demands *guaranteed* protection. Incidentally, this is the actual basis for the revisionist reading from last chapter; wittingly or not, these scholars are stressing the core *republican* strains of *On Liberty*, which we will shortly exhume. Furthermore, after examining the various reasons why an impartial observer would proclaim non-domination as a moral rule, we will see Mill reprise his role as devil's advocate and rebut the several excuses an interlocutor could make for denying freedom to this or that individual or group.

In sum, how does Mill's conception of individual freedom differ from his conception of individual liberty? And what importance does this distinction hold for understanding his political vision? The discussion below concludes with a brief meditation on what Mill's political philosophy recommends or entails for the individual in relation to political life and participation. However, risking anachronism, we begin by introducing and framing Mill's political philosophy by way of contemporary political theory.

Freedom as Non-domination

Last chapter, we saw Isaiah Berlin define liberty in terms of non-interference: "If I am prevented by others from doing what I could otherwise do, I am to that degree unfree; and if this area is contracted by other men beyond a certain minimum, I can be described as being coerced, or, it may be, enslaved."[2] On this view, to be perfectly free is to have total

2. Berlin, "Two Concepts of Liberty," 169.

free rein, that is, to enjoy "carte blanche in determining how to act."[3] For Berlin, the purest political liberty belongs to an absolute despot; and even a despot's "subjects" are free insofar as the despot is relatively "liberal-minded" and grants them "a wide area of liberty." As individuals, we may desire or value more than mere liberty; but, to get these things, Berlin maintains that we are forced to trade off and thus surrender our liberty: "To avoid glaring inequality or widespread misery I am ready to sacrifice some, or all, of my freedom: I may do so willingly and freely; but it is freedom that I am giving up for the sake of justice or equality or the love of my fellow men." Liberal societies characteristically restrict the liberty *of* each individual in order to secure a "minimum area of personal freedom" *to* each individual.[4]

Liberty as non-interference is a distinctively modern idea. Before the late eighteenth century, political theorists normally dealt in terms of a different concept of liberty, what Philip Pettit calls freedom as non-domination. To be dominated is to be subject to arbitrary power, a condition "exemplified by the relationship of master to slave." To be unfree on this view is to be under the "sway" of a *dominus*: an overseer that can interfere with you arbitrarily, that is, "at will and with impunity."[5] Non-domination, then, describes "the position of the independent person who has no master or *dominus* in their life."[6] Such an individual enjoys *libertas*, or the status of a *liber*, or free person—again, an equal among equals or master among masters. In this way, liberty is defined as a matter of equal standing: we are perfectly free insofar as we are preserved from being the dependent or inferior in an interference relationship.

Theorists often refer to non-interference and non-domination as the *liberal* and *republican* concepts of freedom. However, I use the term "libertarian" instead of liberal, for liberalism is a broader term that covers certain strands of republicanism as well. I think "libertarian" better specifies the idea of unrestrained individual activity. Also, Berlin himself appears to associate non-interference with the label "libertarian."[7]

The quarrel between the libertarian and republican concepts of freedom is best exhibited by the fact that we can suffer domination without interference, and interference without domination. For instance, consider a master and his slaves. According to liberty as non-interference, slaves

---

3. Pettit, *Just Freedom*, 1.
4. Berlin, "Two Concepts of Liberty," 172, 175–176.
5. Pettit, *Republicanism*, 22, 52.
6. Pettit, *Just Freedom*, 4.
7. See Berlin, "Two Concepts of Liberty," 171, 177.

are unfree only insofar as they face *actual* interference at the hands of their master—for example, Solomon Northup enjoyed more liberty as non-interference under William Ford than under Edwin Epps.[8] But, according to freedom as non-domination, slaves are *slaves*, and are thus unfree *full stop* irrespective of their allotted free rein. A relatively gentle or obliging master can make slavery relatively more tolerable or less miserable for his slaves, but he nonetheless leaves them in a state of subjection to a *dominus*. Antebellum slavers governed their slaves with total discretion. Their behavior notwithstanding, they retained the capricious *power* to act tyrannically whenever it suited their fancy: "What constitutes domination is the fact that in some respect the power-bearer has the capacity to interfere arbitrarily, even if they are never going to do so."[9] Thus, while Northup preferred the outward benevolence of Ford to the outright malevolence of Epps, he was under either similarly unfree.

Conversely, suppose an authority is "forced to track [the] interests and ideas" of society; that is, the authority "can be relied upon to act on a non-factional basis: on a basis that is supported by non-sectional interests and ideas."[10] For example, when a healthy republic creates a law, that law can be expected to reflect "the avowable common interests—and only the avowable common interests—of those who live under the law." Here, we have interference sans domination. If a government is bound to track the general interest then it does not relate to its citizens as a master relates to his slaves; its actions "will not carry any such deprivation of status in its wake."[11] On the contrary, its authority will resemble that of an agent, beholden to and controlled by its principals. Furthermore, those laws that *protect* us from arbitrary power, and that thereby *establish* freedom as non-domination, are not only congruent with but also *constitutive* of liberty: "The laws and norms of your society promote your freedom in the sense of providing the security that it requires. They are not causal means or instruments that bring the ideal of freedom closer; to the extent that they provide the required security, they are means that constitute the very freedom they serve."[12] Unlike the libertarian, who is inclined to say that checks on arbitrary power are justified *limits* on liberty, the republican understands these laws and norms as the institutionalization of liberty *itself*.

8. See Northup's autobiography *Twelve Years a Slave*. There is also an acclaimed 2013 movie adaptation.

9. Pettit, *Republicanism*, 63.

10. Ibid., 65.

11. Pettit, "Keeping Republican Freedom Simple," 345, 350.

12. Pettit, *Just Freedom*, 24.

LIBERTARIAN VERSUS REPUBLICAN

At first glance, one might regard the libertarian-republican distinction as needless. Recall our discussion of *On Liberty*. Mill begins with the value of liberty as non-interference; he then proceeds both to restrict and to fortify the sphere of liberty in accordance with justice. But the concept of freedom as non-domination would lead Mill to the same spot: What is the execution of justice but a nonarbitrary interference? What are individual rights but republican checks? What is the impartial observer but an oracle for tracking the general interest?

However, the libertarian-republican distinction is significant for two main reasons. On one hand, republican freedom is *more* sensitive to power itself than is libertarian freedom. There are "some kinds of autocracy" under which liberty as non-interference can plausibly thrive: "Liberty in this sense is principally concerned with the area of control, not with its source. Just as a democracy may, in fact, deprive the individual citizen of a great many liberties which he might have in some other form of society, so it is perfectly conceivable that a liberal-minded despot would allow his subjects a large measure of personal freedom."[13] Of course, a libertarian can object to domination for *other* reasons—for security, or equality, or democracy, all of which can be said to be essential to protecting the value of individual liberty. But already the dissent is one value removed. And if one believes that non-interference is all one requires to live freely, then an attitude of indifference can easily prevail with respect to domination, provided the power of the *dominus* is exercised benignly, or at least prudently.

But this just motivates the question: Which, if either, better defines liberty: the thinner, libertarian concept, or the thicker, republican concept? While this inquiry can spark all sorts of disagreements, the predominant reason to conceptualize freedom along republican lines is the fact that domination itself involves the interposition of an external will no less than does actual interference: "insofar as I have the resources to interfere without cost in a choice of yours—insofar as I have the power and knowledge required—your ability to make the choice is dependent on my will as to what you should do, and you are in that sense subject to my will."[14] Interference qua interference does not violate individual liberty: a sudden burst of rain can "interfere" with our baseball game, but we are unlikely to maintain that our freedom has been thereby infringed. Indeed, what is

13. Berlin, "Two Concepts of Liberty," 176.
14. Pettit, "Instability of Freedom as Non-interference," 707.

relevant about certain interferences to our state of liberty is the sense of being subject to the will of another—a condition that *always* exists under the thumb of a *dominus* even if he rarely pushes down.

Now, one might argue that different despots will manifest different degrees of domination in accordance with their relative, positive willingness to recognize republican morals or norms. That is, not all arbitrary power is equally despotic in nature; some despots are not only kindly to their subjects but also friendly to formal restraint. As Mill remarks,

> However little probable it may be, we may imagine a despot observing many of the rules and restraints of constitutional government. He might allow such freedom of the press and of discussion as would enable a public opinion to form and express itself on national affairs. He might suffer local interests to be managed, without the interference of authority, by the people themselves. He might even surround himself with a council or councils of government, freely chosen by the whole or some portion of the nation; retaining in his own hands the power of taxation, and the supreme legislative as well as executive authority. Were he to act thus, and so far abdicate as a despot, he would do away with a considerable part of the evils characteristic of despotism.[15]

However, what is the despot going to do when the people reject his policies or rebuff his desires or counsels? If the despot yields for moral, normative reasons—reasons that are recognized by both the despot and the people—then the people are no longer subjects and he is "no longer a despot, but a constitutional king; an organ or first minister of the people." What we have here is an imperfect, unwritten republican constitution. Alternatively, if the despot cracks down then he was never observing republican morals or norms to begin with, just delegating his still capricious power. And if the despot *tries* but *fails* to crack down, having lost his implicit authority, then he will have created an "antagonism," perhaps a "permanent" one, between himself and the people, and it will be only a matter of time before another chapter is added to the historical struggle between the rulers and the ruled.[16]

On the other hand, republican freedom is *less* sensitive to interference itself than is libertarian freedom. If interference is made to track the general interest, then your liberty is not restricted, for you are not subject to an alien will; rather, you are subject to the general will—that is, to *your*

---

15. Mill, *Considerations on Representative Government*, 401–402, *CW* 19.
16. Ibid.

will, not as an atomistic entity but as a member of the body politic. Some interferences are *never* in the general interest and are thus *always* arbitrary. In *On Liberty*, these include any "content-specific" interferences with intellectual or ethical liberty. Other interferences are *always* in the general interest and are thus *never* arbitrary—pro tanto. These include proper interferences for interpersonal security, public goods, and also "equal liberty," by which Mill basically means non-domination: "the liberty [I] stand up for is the equal liberty of all, and not the greatest possible liberty of one, and slavery of all the rest."[17] Needless to say, the interests that affect law and policy are often clashing or diverging: urban interests are not always rural interests; capital interests are not always labor interests; progressive interests are not always conservative interests—incommensurability, moderation, and compromise are, in a healthy political society, the order of the day. Nonetheless, what allows for any resulting configuration of law and policy to be reflective of each person's will *as a citizen* is a well-ordered constitution; for Mill, this means that political bodies must provide for comprehensive proportional representation and be accountable to general contestation.[18]

The libertarian-republican divide thus implies a profound difference in general attitude. The libertarian outlook on interference is starkly individual: liberty is the hallmark of our precivic, presocial existence; our idyllic condition as free individuals is one of total free rein, bound perhaps only by natural law; but every human interference (even the body politic itself) is a limitation on our natural liberty—at best, a necessary sacrifice borne for the sake of our individual or collective interests. Conversely, the republican outlook on interference is decidedly communal: freedom as non-domination is the hallmark of our civic, social existence; we are political beings first and foremost; as such, any interference that respects or affirms our equal standing is congruent with our freedom, even in those instances where our selfish impulses cause us to resent what our civic or social consciousness would have us affirm or accept—everyone loves speed limits until they get pulled over. What we have here, then, is, for the libertarian, a necessary tension between the individual and society, but, for the republican, a potential for harmony between these eternal frenemies.

But, again, this just begs the question: How should we regard interference: as individuals prior to citizens, or as citizens prior to individuals?

---

17. Mill, "Education Bill," 385, *CW* 29.
18. See Mill, "Thoughts on Parliamentary Reform," 322ff., *CW* 19; and "Recent Writers on Reform," 358ff., *CW* 19.

Should we interpret nonarbitrary interferences as acceptable limitations on our individuality, or as affirmative expressions of our sociality? One might argue, drawing on Mill, that sociality is to some extent obligatory, and that liberty ought to be understood accordingly. But that would be not to describe but to moralize freedom ad hoc. Rather, what we are asking here is whether individuals should interpret the relationship between liberty and interference in reference to their individuality, or in reference to their sociality. It is not that one or the other is our "real" or "true" self (at least not in Berlin's sense, which we will address below); it is that one or the other must take precedence when they come into conflict, that is, when we are faced with a particular interference that accords with our sociality but not with our individuality.

For instance, suppose society prevents me from mugging you: has my liberty been thereby restricted? The libertarian, who interprets interference vis-à-vis individuality, would say *yes*: society limits my liberty in this instance for the sake of order, peace, or justice. But the republican, who interprets interference vis-à-vis sociality, would say *no*: thwarting muggers is in the general interest (*my* interest) and thus does not infringe my liberty (my *will*) as a member of the polity, only as a rogue individual. Indeed, for the republican, I would have to be a rather daft mugger to assert that by being stopped, I was somehow being subjected to the will of another, that is, of *particular* persons—for, all things equal, what could I infer about my apprehenders other than the fact that they value the same rule of law which I would find perfectly congenial had *I* been *you*? But the question remains: which "will" ought to take theoretical priority in appraising interference: my particular will or the general will?

The most potent and obvious argument for the libertarian view is one of presumption: we are individuals before we are anything else; society can be introduced, and we can associate ourselves with it, but, at bottom, society is just an artificial collection of individuals, united by necessity and common interests. An analogy can be drawn here to the psychological hedonists from chapter 1. Psychological hedonism posits that pleasure is our only natural desire, and therefore that other objects or ends are desired only insofar as we come to associate them with pleasure. Similarly, libertarianism posits that individuality is our only natural identification, and therefore that other identifications can be ascribed to individuals only insofar as these identifications comport with their individuality—an interference is congruent with liberty only if the individual assents to the interference.

One way to employ this very logic *against* libertarianism, and thus to defend republicanism, is to argue that the interpretive priority of sociality is *itself* sanctioned by individuality. This is the essence of Locke's social contract theory. Given the intolerable inconveniences of precivic, presocial life, the imagined persons in the state of nature will promptly agree to contract into political society. Thus, any interference they subsequently face at the hands of government in accordance with its constitutional mandate has been authorized by them individually: "The *natural liberty* of man is to be free from any superior power on earth, and not to be under the will or legislative authority of man, but to have only the law of nature for his rule. The *liberty of man*, in society, is to be under no other legislative power, but that established, by consent, in the common-wealth; nor under the dominion of any will, or restraint of any law, but what that legislative shall enact, according to the trust put in it."[19] Now, the difficulty for Locke—and the eternal rejoinder of the libertarian—is that consent is a hard (perhaps even fanciful) thing to corroborate for actual individuals, most of whom were thrust into political society at birth.[20] Absent their explicit consent, can we appeal to *tacit* consent? And if not, can we fall back upon *hypothetical* consent?[21]

These are thorny questions. How lucky for us, then, that Mill dismisses social contract theory out of hand: "society is not founded on a contract," and "no good purpose is answered by inventing a contract in order to deduce social obligations from it."[22] Instead, going back to chapter 3 of *Utilitarianism*, Mill would say that the interpretive priority of sociality is "a natural outgrowth" of human nature:

> The social state is at once so natural, so necessary, and so habitual to man, that, except in some unusual circumstances or by an effort of voluntary abstraction, he never conceives himself otherwise than as a member of a body; and this association is riveted more and more, as mankind are further removed from the state of savage independence. Any condition, therefore, which is essential to a state of society, becomes more and more an inseparable part of every person's conception of the state of things which he is born into, and which is the destiny of a human being. . . . Not only does all strengthening of social ties, and all healthy growth of society, give to each individual a stronger personal interest in practically consulting the welfare of others; it also

19. Locke, *Second Treatise of Government*, §22.
20. See Hume, "Of the Original Contract," 465–487.
21. See Pitkin, "Obligation and Consent," 996–999; and Halldenius, "Locke and the Non-arbitrary," 266–273.
22. Mill, *On Liberty*, 276, *CW* 18.

leads him to identify his *feelings* more and more with their good, or at least with an ever greater degree of practical consideration for it. He comes, as though instinctively, to be conscious of himself as a being who *of course* pays regard to others. The good of others becomes to him a thing naturally and necessarily to be attended to, like any of the physical conditions of our existence.[23]

This is not to say that every individual always feels like this. In fact, in an imperfect world, the social feeling in individuals is usually "much inferior in strength to their selfish feelings, and is often wanting altogether." Rather, this is simply to say that for those in whom the social feeling prevails, "it possesses all the characters of a natural feeling." It might be useful here to invoke Mill's competent judge: those who are "equally acquainted with," "equally capable of appreciating and enjoying," and "equally susceptible to" both individuality and sociality identify themselves primarily as "a social being."[24] They may not *act* this way unfailingly—for selfishness is an inborn and indefatigable beast—but they naturally *feel* this way, such that their selfish (that is, immoral) activity will, upon reflection, give them the sense of working against, not for, themselves. What we get here from Mill is a kind of empirical teleology: what we naturally, or truly, are is what we are in our most developed, cultivated state; and our most developed, cultivated state is defined by what individuals who are sensible to various alternatives tend to gravitate toward, if not in practice then in a spirit of admiration for others and wishful yearning for themselves.

Consequently, a nonarbitrary interference just *is* an expression of our will, for it represents what "a social being" would affirm. For a developed, cultivated person, being inhibited from acting on a selfish impulse is like being stopped from falling into a calamity: "If either a public officer or anyone else saw a person attempting to cross a bridge which had been ascertained to be unsafe, and there were no time to warn him of his danger, they might seize him and turn him back, without any real infringement of his liberty; for liberty consists in doing what one desires, and he does not desire to fall into the river." The seized individual has cause for thanks. Of course, in an imperfect world, many individuals will not feel this way more generally and will begrudge interferences willy-nilly. But all that this means for Mill is that they are, to some extent, still childlike or barbaric in outlook. And while Mill shuns paternalism for societies

---

23. Mill, *Utilitarianism*, 230–232, *CW* 10.
24. Ibid., 211, 213, 233.

that are capable of spontaneous human progress, he happily notes that an impartial system of interference can have the incidental effect of improving those persons whose selfish nature still predominates in them: "To be held to rigid rules of justice for the sake of others, developes the feelings and capacities which have the good of others for their object."[25] Of course, this is not to suggest that *any* prosocial interference is compatible with freedom. As we have seen, to be other-regarding is to recognize the intrinsic value of individuality; thus, only interferences that manifest a proper interplay between individuality and sociality (i.e., impartial interferences) will be consistent with freedom for "a social being."

What I argue below, and what my analysis has already begun to suggest, is that Mill is a republican theorist to his core. The hallmark of republican theory is that in a just society, individual citizens are perfectly or completely free: they are not subject to the whims or caprices of a *dominus*, and they endure only those interferences that are congruent with or constitutive of their equal standing as *liberi*. Unlike libertarian theory, which equates perfect or complete liberty either to a lonely state of nature or to a position of absolute power, republican theory equates perfect or complete liberty to a state of sociopolitical equality. But before reading Mill on these lines, we should take a brief detour through Berlin.

BERLIN AND THE LIBERTARIAN TRADITION

In his famed essay "Two Concepts of Liberty," Berlin surveys a conflict in the history of ideas between what he calls *negative* and *positive* liberty. Negative liberty is just liberty as non-interference: freedom from obstacles, coercion, or restraint. Positive liberty, conversely, refers to a notion of self-rule or self-realization, where the *higher* self dominates the *lower* self. The higher self is associated "with reason, with my 'higher nature,' with the self which calculates and aims at what will satisfy in the long run, with my 'real,' or 'ideal,' or 'autonomous' self, or with my self 'at its best,'" whereas the lower self is associated with "irrational impulse, uncontrolled desires, my 'lower' nature, the pursuit of immediate pleasures, my 'empirical' or 'heteronomous' self, swept by every gust of desire and passion, needing to be rigidly disciplined if it is ever to rise to the full height of its 'real' nature."[26] To enjoy positive liberty is to enjoy self-mastery; to be governed by the higher self.

---

25. Mill, *On Liberty*, 266, 294.
26. Berlin, "Two Concepts of Liberty," 179.

As Berlin stresses, the clash between negative and positive liberty is not strictly logical but rather psychological. Historically, those who espouse a monistic vision or theory of what "true" or "real" freedom ought to look like have been less disposed to tolerate those individuals who use their negative liberty for "lower" ends, and have been more inclined to enforce obedience to "higher" objects or ideals, believing that to do so is nothing less than liberation for the individual: "Once I take this view, I am in position to ignore the actual wishes of men or societies, to bully, oppress, torture them in the name, and on the behalf, of their 'real' selves, in the secure knowledge that whatever is the true goal of man (happiness, performance of duty, wisdom, a just society, self-fulfilment) must be identical with his freedom—the free choice of his 'true,' albeit often submerged and inarticulate, self."[27] Berlin detects this tyrannical proclivity in many of positive liberty's architects, including Rousseau and Hegel.[28]

Theorists have responded to Berlin's reading of the positive liberty tradition in various ways. Some have taken exception to his interpretations of particular thinkers; others have attempted to reconstitute the concept of positive liberty in accordance with negative liberty. Typically, this involves the "content-neutral" recognition that a fruitful, authentic engagement with negative liberty implies the possession of certain "executive" virtues, like self-control and self-awareness. Naturally, Mill agrees, and we gauged the potential implications of his agreement at the end of last chapter. But one might be concerned that the interpretive priority Mill assigns to sociality denotes a division between a *higher* and a *lower* self and thus tends toward oppression à la Berlin. However, individuality is not "untrue" or "non-ideal" for Mill; nor is it "lower." Individuality and sociality are coequal elements of happiness. The perception that individuality is somehow debased, or false, or lesser, is the wont of a thinker like Comte, whom Mill repudiates on this front. Mill merely holds that, as social beings, we naturally identify with the proper balance between individuality and sociality, which carries no greater risk of tyranny than any doctrine of sociopolitical morality.

Regardless, one consequence of Berlin's essay was the creation of "the philosophical illusion that, details aside, there are just two ways of understanding liberty: in one, freedom consists in the absence of external obstacles to individual choice; in the other, it involves the presence, and usually the exercise, of the facilities that foster self-mastery and self-fulfilment."[29]

27. Ibid., 180.
28. See Berlin, *Freedom and Its Betrayal*, chaps. 2 and 4.
29. Pettit, *Republicanism*, 18.

As a result, various and diverse thinkers were all mixed into the same batter of "negative" liberty as non-interference: Hobbes, Locke, Smith, Burke, Bentham, Montesquieu, Constant, Tocqueville, Paine, Jefferson—and, of course, Mill.

In recent decades, there has been a concerted effort among scholars to complexify the landscape of sociopolitical freedom, and among republican theorists especially to uncover, and thus "recover," the republican core of certain of Berlin's "negative" luminaries. For instance, the republican content of Locke's political theory, particularly as articulated in *Second Treatise of Civil Government*, has been cogently expounded.[30] However, when it comes to Mill, I believe there is as yet a great deal of work to be done.

A REPUBLICAN READING OF MILL

Since the publication of Berlin's essay, it has been standard practice to characterize Mill as a theorist of liberty as non-interference: Berlin "set the tone of Mill scholarship."[31] By depicting Mill as the archetypal devotee of negative liberty, Berlin established the enduring assumption that Mill affirms an inherent conflict between liberty and interference: "Mill's view" was "the same as Bentham's. *Every* law restricts liberty: 'It converts into offenses acts which would otherwise be permitted and unpunishable.'"[32] This depiction of Mill, while ultimately mistaken, is quite understandable. Many of Mill's works, most notably *On Liberty*, focus on the vital importance of giving individuals as much latitude as possible for the free play of their individuality and the free exercise of their higher faculties. After all, the Harm Principle *looks like* a libertarian manifesto—a principle of radical non-interference.

Moreover, it has always been tempting to lump Mill in with Bentham, who was instrumental in advancing an idea of freedom based solely on the absence of constraint: "In the same proportion as it creates obligations, the law curtails liberty: it converts into offences, acts which would otherwise be permitted and unpunishable."[33] Prompted by his psychological and ethical hedonism, Bentham had no evident desire to look beyond the satisfaction of our hedonic proclivities: if the dominated are granted access to every potential pleasure by their *dominus*—or, better yet, if they

---

30. See Halldenius, "Locke and the Non-arbitrary," 261–266.

31. Urbinati, *Mill on Democracy*, 161. A bibliography can be found in Baum, "J. S. Mill on Freedom and Power," 188.

32. Waldron, "Mill on Liberty and on the Contagious Diseases Act," 31.

33. Bentham, *Principles of the Civil Code*, 301, W 1.

are *helped* to their pleasures by a benevolent *dominus*—then what could be the *intrinsic* problem? And indeed, the libertarian concept of freedom granted Bentham a lower hurdle for sociopolitical reform. Had Bentham admitted an inherent divergence between pleasure and domination then he would have been logically compelled to attempt to flatten the despotisms of the age, like that of husband over wife and master over servant: "These may well have been challenges at which he balked. He could look for universal freedom as noninterference without having to embrace such radicalism, for the wife of a kind husband, or the servant of a kind master, can be free in this thinner sense."[34]

Nonetheless, my contention is that Mill's concept of liberty is best understood in terms of freedom as non-domination. Mill belongs to the older, republican way of thinking about freedom. When other scholars make this claim, their evidence is usually drawn from Mill's later essay, *The Subjection of Women*. Indeed, *On Liberty* and *Subjection* are often seen as representing what might be called the "libertarian" and "republican" Mills.[35] However, I think this characterization is wrong on both counts. *Subjection* does *not* define freedom as non-domination; in fact, it does not really *define* freedom at all. *Subjection* gives us reasons to *value* non-domination, and Mill argues that marital despotism is horribly *immoral*; but as far as what social or political freedom *is*, Mill's feminist treatise is mum. Ironically, it is in *On Liberty*, not *Subjection*, where we find Mill *conceptualizing* freedom as non-domination.

Mill checks every republican box. Across his writings, Mill rejects mere non-interference, or liberty as free rein, in favor of a procivic, pro-social concept of liberty, which he frames as the antithesis of domination. Indeed, Mill avows that institutions are constitutive of freedom insofar as they reduce the risk of domination, whereas institutions are contrary to freedom insofar as they allow for domination. And Mill holds that nonarbitrary interferences are congruent with freedom, and that only arbitrary interferences are incongruent with freedom. Taken together, these observations bring Mill's concept of liberty fully into harmony with the main tenets of the republican notion of freedom.

In *On Liberty*, Mill introduces his concept of liberty as "Civil, or Social Liberty: the nature and limits of the power which can be legitimately exercised by society over the individual."[36] Freedom is defined in terms of

34. Pettit, *Just Freedom*, 15.

35. Cf. Spector, "Four Conceptions of Freedom," 787. But even here the author brushes past *On Liberty* to get to *The Subjection of Women*.

36. Mill, *On Liberty*, 217.

legitimacy, that is, in terms of the individual's relationship to power. If the "nature" and "limits" of society's power exhibit a certain kind of relationship to the individual then the individual enjoys absolute liberty with respect to society. Again, Mill distinguishes this intrinsically civic-social concept of liberty from what he calls liberty in its "original sense," that is, "freedom from restraint," which, like liberty as non-interference, implies that "every law, and every rule of morals, is contrary to liberty," and which equates perfect freedom to being "entirely emancipated from both."[37] With overt contempt, Mill dismisses this atomistic concept of liberty as a form of "savage"[38] or "rude independence,"[39] and advances an alternative view that reconciles "spontaneity and individuality" with "the social principle."[40] Hence, the question becomes: what kind of relationship to power constitutes freedom for the individual?

According to Mill, the individual's relationship to power runs afoul of freedom, and is thus illegitimate, insofar as the individual is dominated: subjected to arbitrary power; placed at the mercy of a despot; enslaved to the will of a master. As Mill indicates in *On Liberty*, there are two forms that domination takes, what we might call the *vertical* and *horizontal* forms of domination.[41] Vertical domination refers to an asymmetrical relationship in which a superior dominates an inferior: for example, the despot over his subjects; the master over his slaves; the Victorian husband over his wife. Horizontal domination refers to a symmetrical relationship, such as democratic equality, out of which an asymmetry nevertheless emerges: for example, the "tyranny of the majority," or the tyranny of "those who succeed in making themselves accepted as the majority." The "flock" lacks freedom insofar as it is (vertically) dominated by the "vultures," and the "community" lacks freedom insofar as it is (horizontally) dominated by "the strongest party therein." Civic or social freedom is perfected, then, to the extent to which the individual retains "complete security" against both types of subjugation.[42]

What makes Mill's concept of freedom as non-domination so difficult to identify is the fact that when Mill mentions liberty, especially in *On Liberty*, he is usually referring not to his deeper concept of freedom, but to liberty of action in the ordinary, practical sense of the phrase. We could point

37. Mill, "Edinburgh Review," 296, *CW* 1.
38. Mill, *Considerations on Representative Government*, 394, 415, 435.
39. Mill, "Bentham," 105, *CW* 10.
40. Mill, *On Liberty*, 264.
41. For a similar distinction, see Pettit, *Just Freedom*, chaps. 4–5.
42. Mill, *On Liberty*, 217–219.

to countless examples in Mill's works of this colloquial way of speaking: "The liberty of the individual must be thus far limited; he must not make himself a nuisance to other people." But whenever Mill considers freedom "in general terms," he draws on the language of non-domination.[43] Indeed, at the conceptual level, Mill is upholding "that liberty against which the system of Slavery is the deepest outrage";[44] defending "that full freedom of choice" which is indicative of "equality of rights on both sides";[45] and rejecting absolute power as "the flattest contradiction of all the principles of free government."[46] At the heart of Mill's political theory lies an either/or between liberty and subjection: "the possession of [a] monopoly by individuals constitutes *not* freedom *but* slavery; it delivers over the public to the mercy of those individuals."[47] The "spirit" of political "freedom" is "precisely the reverse" of political "domination."[48] To be denied "freedom" is to be "brought under the power of a superior."[49] What offends freedom is not interference itself but the despotic form of control from which interference arbitrarily springs: "The power *itself* is illegitimate."[50]

Mill's concept of freedom is further clarified when he turns to examine the essential role that institutions play in establishing freedom. Mill aligns himself with a long history of republican agitation for liberty. As he describes in *On Liberty*, the earliest popular movements attempted to institute freedom by placing "constitutional checks" on power: "By liberty, was meant protection against the tyranny of the political rulers"; the "aim" was "to set limits to the power which the ruler should be suffered to exercise over the community; and *this limitation was what they meant by liberty*."[51] These "limits" were viewed as *constitutive* of freedom; they enabled the people to restrain their superiors, which, in theory, would neutralize this asymmetrical relationship and thus shield the people against arbitrary power.

However, the "lovers of liberty" later altered their strategy. Instead of placing "constitutional checks" on power, they sought to institute freedom by changing the "nature" of power; namely, they advocated for

43. Ibid., 217, 260.
44. Mill, "To John A. Elliot," 1380, *CW* 16.
45. Mill, "To Lord Amberley," 1693, *CW* 17.
46. Mill, "French News," 460, *CW* 23.
47. Mill, "Regulation of the London Water Supply," 434, *CW* 5, my emphases.
48. Mill, *Principles of Political Economy*, 944, *CW* 3.
49. Mill, "Notes on the Newspapers," 216, *CW* 6.
50. Mill, *On Liberty*, 229, my emphasis.
51. Ibid., 217–218, my emphasis.

electoral democracy. The previous equivalence between liberty and "limits" morphed into an equivalence between liberty and "the periodical choice of the ruled." The question of "Liberty" versus "Authority" became: *who* interferes—our "tenants or delegates," or a *dominus*? Perfect liberty reigned for the people as long as every act of interference embodied "the power of the people over themselves," that is, as long as interference always tracked the "interest and will of the nation."[52] In short, the "lovers of liberty" are understood by Mill to have been fighting for the "right which constitutes them members of a free state, and the violation of which, by the sense of all ages and nations, forms the *casus belli* between a people and their government."[53]

And yet, as Mill observes, the principle of establishing liberty via "popular government" has been subverted in practice by two "faults [or] infirmities." First, most democratic institutions do *not* tend to embody "the power of the people over themselves," but instead tend to funnel power to "the most numerous or most active *part* of the people." Indeed, horizontal domination tends to follow hard on the democratic levelling of vertical domination. And second, even if democratic institutions *do* reflect "the power of the people over themselves," the "tyranny of the majority" tends to reach beyond the legislative arena. Society itself can "impose, by other means than civil penalties, its own ideas and practices as rules of conduct on those who dissent from them." As we saw last chapter, Mill notes that the penalties characteristic of "social tyranny," that is, the tyranny of opinion, stigma, and surveillance—the tyranny of the reverse panopticon—are not as draconian as most legal sanctions; but they nonetheless leave "fewer means of escape, penetrating much more deeply into the details of daily life, and enslaving the soul itself." Thus, the need for "limits" on the power of *both* the state *and* society "loses none of its importance" under a democratic regime.[54]

The trouble, though, as Mill sees it, is that "the practical question, where to place the limit—how to make the fitting adjustment between individual independence and social control—is a subject on which nearly everything remains to be done." In most societies, "the rules laid down for general observance" have reflected the "likings and dislikings" of the powerful rather than what is demanded by individual "independence." Hence, Mill arrives at the principal question of *On Liberty*: What range

52. Ibid., 217–219.
53. Mill, "Radical Party and Canada," 417, *CW* 6.
54. Mill, *On Liberty*, 219–220.

of interferences are compatible with freedom as non-domination? What sphere of non-interference would be protected in a perfectly free society? In short, what makes interference either nonarbitrary or arbitrary? When is interference either congruent or incongruent with our status as *liberi*, or free persons? Mill's primary goal in *On Liberty* is to delineate, decry, and delegitimize the various ways an ascendant faction might employ its political or social advantage to interfere with others arbitrarily. When coupled with "free institutions" in the vertical sense, a society that enforces checks against all arbitrary uses of power is a society in which the individual is "completely free."[55]

In other words, the Mill of *On Liberty* asks: if democratic institutions cannot reliably secure non-domination, then what "limits" on power must we adhere to in order to make up the difference? Mill is looking to check interferences that are dependent on or expressive of the de facto arbitrary power of a dominant faction. As Mill suggests, there are two categories of interference. The first category contains interferences that reflect mere partiality, passion, or prejudice, and which thus signify the naked power of the interfering party. These interferences can be reduced to things like "custom," "feelings," "preferences," "taste," "opinions," "envy," "superstitions," "affections," "jealousy," "arrogance," "desires," "self-interest," "sentiments," "aversions," "fears," and "contemptuousness." By contrast, the second category contains interferences that are, in a word, *reasonable,* and which thus track either "the permanent interests of man as a progressive being" or "the general and obvious interests of society." Indeed, the main concern of *On Liberty* is not just *any* liberty but our "rightful liberty," that liberty that embodies freedom as non-domination. And the principal task of *On Liberty* is to distinguish between "illegitimate interference" (which is wrong and thus verboten) and "legitimate interference" (which might simply be "allowable" or "admissible," but might also be "right" or "to be approved of").[56] Legitimate interference respects, whereas illegitimate interference infringes, the principle of freedom as non-domination.

Thus, in true republican fashion, Mill gives a list of basic liberties: liberties that *must* exist "absolute and unqualified" in accordance with the individual's status as a *liber*; liberties that it is *always* arbitrary to interfere with:

> This, then, is the appropriate region of human liberty. It comprises, first, the inward domain of consciousness; demanding liberty of conscience,

55. Ibid., 220–222, 226–227.
56. Ibid., 217–224, 288–289, 298.

in the most comprehensive sense; liberty of thought and feeling; absolute freedom of opinion and sentiment on all subjects, practical or
speculative, scientific, moral, or theological. The liberty of expressing
and publishing opinions may seem to fall under a different principle,
since it belongs to that part of the conduct of an individual which concerns other people; but, being almost of as much importance as the liberty of thought itself, and resting in great part on the same reasons, is
practically inseparable from it. Secondly, the principle requires liberty
of tastes and pursuits; of framing the plan of our life to suit our own
character; of doing as we like, subject to such consequences as may
follow: without impediment from our fellow-creatures, so long as what
we do does not harm them, even though they should think our conduct
foolish, perverse, or wrong. Thirdly, from this liberty of each individual, follows the liberty, within the same limits, of combination among
individuals; freedom to unite, for any purpose not involving harm to
others: the persons combining being supposed to be of full age, and not
forced or deceived.[57]

To interfere with intellectual or ethical liberty is to violate freedom not
because of the interference itself, but because the interference instantiates
the interfering party's arbitrary control—justice and freedom are cotermi-
nous. In fact, Mill makes a clear distinction between a denial of freedom
itself (i.e., where a despot simply *exists*) and interferences that are merely
symptomatic of unfreedom (i.e., when a despot *behaves* despotically).
Mill differentiates "practical oppression" from "a system of despotism."[58]
Despotism is oppressive *in principle* because it violates freedom: "it is
the great error of reformers" in "our time, to nibble at the consequences
of unjust power, instead of redressing the injustice itself."[59] However, a
benevolent despot can be relatively "innocuous."[60] Thus, we are denied
freedom *in practice* only insofar as we are "arbitrarily oppressed," or "systematically plundered," by our *dominus*.[61]

In sum, the amount of free rein required for absolute liberty is coextensive with the sphere of "legitimate liberty."[62] As long as interference
is guaranteed to square with "Civil, or Social Liberty," then the individual

57. Ibid., 225–226.
58. Mill, *Autobiography*, 221, *CW* 1.
59. Mill, *Principles of Political Economy*, 953.
60. Mill, *Autobiography*, 221.
61. Mill, *Principles of Political Economy*, 113, *CW* 2.
62. Mill, *On Liberty*, 284.

can enjoy "perfect freedom."[63] Had Mill conceptualized liberty as non-interference, then our civic or social freedom could never be "perfect," only optimal; we would have to sacrifice some liberty to better secure our share of liberty. But the "spirit of liberty," for Mill, is neither the "barbarian" spirit of "individual freedom of action" nor the "ancient" spirit of "subjection of every individual to the State." Rather, it is the spirit of "individual independence," namely, "freedom of action," "moderated and limited" by our natural sociality.[64] Mill's spirit of liberty, that is, the "love of individual independence," is part and parcel of the "spirit of equality."[65]

The Value of Non-domination

Having unfurled Mill's concept of freedom, we can now ask the most pertinent question: Why is freedom as non-domination valuable? What is so bad about being under a *dominus*? Naturally, better to have a benevolent despot than a malevolent despot: "Even despotism does not produce its worst effects, so long as individuality exists under it."[66] But why bother with checking or balancing arbitrary power in the first place as long as we are currently and foreseeably granted all the free rein we could ask for?

Traditionally, non-domination has been valued for two key reasons. The first, *instrumental*, reason is that domination makes tyranny more likely, whereas non-domination is a security for good government. As we will see, this describes the classic Utilitarian rationale for curtailing despotism. The second, *intrinsic*, reason is that domination is just incompatible with the status of a *liber*, or free person: "an independent source of human activity," an "entity with a will of its own, intending to act in accordance with it (whether it is good or legitimate, or not), and not to be ruled, educated, guided, with however light a hand, as being not quite fully human, and therefore not quite fully free."[67] On this view, freedom is its *own* justification. What I argue below is that, in addition to making the Utilitarian argument, Mill strikes a middle path: he offers ends-based yet noninstrumental reasons for valuing freedom; freedom is not simply a means to but actually a *constitutive* aspect of human happiness.

63. Mill, "Diary," 661, *CW* 27.
64. Mill, "Guizot's Essays and Lectures on History," 274, *CW* 20.
65. Mill, "Claims of Labour," 375, *CW* 4.
66. Mill, *On Liberty*, 266.
67. Berlin, "Two Concepts of Liberty," 202–203.

Naturally, Mill has every reason to balk at domination on libertarian grounds. However, what has yet to be fully teased out is Mill's reasons for valuing non-domination on republican grounds—his reasons for valuing freedom *itself*. In *On Liberty*, Mill writes that, "far from being in any way countenanced by the principle of liberty," domination (in this case, specifically marital despotism) is a "direct infraction of that principle, being a mere rivetting of the chains of one-half of the community, and an emancipation of the other from reciprocity of obligation towards them."[68] Domination is a pure example of civic or social harm, or injustice. It is not just that domination makes injustice in the form of arbitrary interference more *likely* (though it does), but that domination is *itself* an injustice, and an injustice of the worst kind. To an impartial mind, domination itself violates the moral right to freedom, and thus every *dominus* has a perfect duty to abdicate its arbitrary power—which, incidentally, is exactly what Mill did before wedding Harriet Taylor.[69]

In what follows, I survey what I have found to be six distinct, though related, justifications Mill gives for opposing domination itself, any of which an impartial observer might regard as sufficient grounds for dubbing despotism immoral. Again, these are reasons why domination is objectionable on moral grounds separate and apart from the tangible, perceptible interferences that may follow. Freedom *is* non-domination for Mill; but freedom is *valuable* under Mill's Utilitarian theory for the ensuing reasons. Free rein (mere liberty) is not enough. The apogee of the just society is freedom itself.

DOMINATION AS INFANTILIZATION

As we noted last chapter, the activity of the higher faculties entails *originality*—not newness per se, but self-origination. The development of our higher nature is a falsehood (it is not *really* happening) unless *we*, the *self*, are actively "cultivating it and calling it forth." Cultivation sans originality is purely mechanical: a calculator works through problems much faster than most human beings, but it does not *think*; the internet is bursting with information, but only a human being can be *knowledgeable*. Without originality, we are just "automatons in human form," who, though perhaps able to explain our beliefs or actions by rote, merit no more admiration than an impressive machine. This is why originality, for Mill, is the

68. Mill, *On Liberty*, 290.
69. See Mill, "Statement on Marriage," 99, *CW* 21.

wellspring of "the ideal perfection of human nature."[70] Originality is the hallmark of any "cultivated intelligence and will."[71]

What we run into here is the idea of personal autonomy: self-government; self-authorship; self-determination. Interestingly, Mill's concept of personal autonomy is analogous to his concept of civic or social freedom. Mill likens heteronomy to being dominated by "inclination" or "authority."[72] To be an unfree actor is to be under the sway of passion or impulse, whereas to be a free actor is to be one's own master: "A person feels morally free who feels that his habits or his temptations are not his masters, but he theirs: who even in yielding to them knows that he could resist."[73] To be a free thinker is to assume fallibility and to be prepared to enlarge or modify one's beliefs, whereas to be an unfree thinker is to have an intellectual *dominus*: "the creed remains as it were outside the mind, incrusting and petrifying it against all other influences addressed to the higher parts of our nature; manifesting its power by not suffering any fresh and living conviction to get in, but itself doing nothing for the mind or heart, except standing sentinel over them to keep them vacant."[74] And just like basic republican laws and norms are constitutive of freedom, the virtues of self-awareness, self-criticism, and self-discipline are constitutive of autonomy: "none but a person of confirmed virtue is completely free."[75] For Mill, the free soul is a microcosm of the free society.[76]

However, there is a key social aspect to this: our capacity for originality is dependent on good education. Originality, like sociality, is natural but acquired; it must be fostered and nurtured in order to flourish. Originality in action entails things like self-knowledge; deliberation; forming a "plan of life"; "reasoning and judgment"; "discrimination"; "firmness and self-control."[77] And all of this demands a certain kind of self-mastery that only strength-training can inculcate. As Mill muses, "Something has been lost as well as gained by no longer giving to every citizen the training necessary for a soldier."[78] Originality in thought entails similar self-discipline, especially the ability and desire to think critically and capaciously. And as Mill contends, the cultivation of the intellect profits immeasurably from

---

70. Mill, *On Liberty*, 263, 266, 278.
71. Mill, "Inaugural Address Delivered to the University at St. Andrews," 217, *CW* 21.
72. Mill, *On Liberty*, 245.
73. Mill, *System of Logic*, 841, *CW* 8.
74. Mill, *On Liberty*, 248.
75. Mill, *System of Logic*, 841.
76. We might be reminded here of Plato's *Republic*.
77. Mill, *On Liberty*, 262–263.
78. Mill, *Auguste Comte and Positivism*, 339, *CW* 10.

an early course in spontaneity. Much can be imposed on pupils by "cramming their memory with details," but mere cram does not involve *thinking*, or "mental exercise," and thus does not promote or develop any kind of intellectual dynamism.[79] By contrast, Mill praises his father's educative method, especially its emphasis on self-instruction: "He strove to make the understanding not only go along with every step of the teaching but if possible precede it. His custom was, in the case of everything which could be found out by thinking, to make me strive and struggle to find it out for myself, giving me no more help than was positively indispensable." An education of cram makes students "mere parroters of what they have learnt," whereas Mill's education set him on a lifelong course of "independent thought."[80]

Mill's first critique, then, of domination itself is that the *dominus* is incentivized to promote the exact *opposite* type of education; an education geared not toward seeing individuals realize "the maturity of their faculties,"[81] but toward locking them in a prison of perpetual childhood, forever deferential to their parental rulers. We can follow Nadia Urbinati in calling this category of injustice *domination as infantilization*. Urbinati pays particular attention to the mode of despotic control described in *Subjection*:

> Despotism—as described in *The Subjection of Women*—is a form of total and absolute power because it operates on the emotions, not just on actions. The depot, unlike the tyrant, strikes with fear and love simultaneously. Subjects of the tyrant long to rebel; under the despot they become affectionate chattel slaves. In the first case of repression, potential freedom is always latent; in the other, a condition of total surrender and pacification defines "complete abnegation." Tyranny represses action and violates negative liberty. Despotism violates the individual's very determination to act and robs her of self-reliance.

Effective despots manipulate their subjects into transferring "their choice- and decision-making power to their masters, who eventually will be seen as a source of tutelage rather than of coercion."[82] Indeed, the most sinister husband in *Subjection* is not the one who engages in explicit, transparent tyranny like an everyday brute. Rather, the true household terror, for Mill, is the one who utilizes his supremacy to wage a subtle campaign of

79. Mill, "Inaugural Address Delivered to the University at St. Andrews," 217, 218.
80. Mill, *Autobiography*, 34.
81. Mill, *On Liberty*, 224.
82. Urbinati, "Many Heads of the Hydra," 90.

emotional control, social conditioning, and general intimidation. Worst, he desires "to compel women to internalize a self-conception as dependent sexual beings."[83] Naturally, it is not that every husband invents this game, or that every wife falls for it afresh; Mill is describing a culture of marital despotism in which all persons are raised, and to which all couples are expected to conform. One of Mill's goals in *Subjection* is to crack through the dogmatic malaise of what is viewed as "normal" and explain how the subjection of wives to husbands is actually *abnormal*; as Mill avers, it is, in truth, the final and most stubborn legacy of "the law of the strongest."[84]

The central point for our purposes is that this tendency "cannot be reduced to interference with women's natural freedom of choice or direct and crude repression."[85] Marital despotism does not prosper via "libertarian" interference. Instead, it thrives by grooming women for perpetual infancy. Wives become "contented" subjects: "All women are brought up from the very earliest years in the belief that their ideal of character is the very opposite to that of men; not self-will, and government by self-control, but submission, and yielding to the control of others. All the moralities tell them that it is the duty of women, and all the current sentimentalities that it is their nature, to live for others; to make complete abnegation of themselves, and to have no life but in their affections."[86] And what is true of marital despotism is also true of despotism generally. In *On Liberty*, Mill depicts the "despotism of custom," under which individuals obey society as children obey their parents—reflexively and unthinkingly: "I do not mean that they choose what is customary, in preference to what suits their own inclination. It does not occur to them to have any inclination, except for what is customary."[87] And when the government wields total power, the bent is toward "political infancy," which, like marital and social infantilization, turns out to be "more crushing in its effects on the character and capabilities of the nation than tyranny itself."[88] In short, domination is unjust, first, because it inclines toward keeping subjects in the immaturity of their faculties. And even those who mature nonetheless are still encouraged to *appear* like children; namely, to "disguise" themselves in order to avoid the consequences of "intolerance."[89]

83. Morales, "Rational Freedom in John Stuart Mill's Feminism," 49.
84. Mill, *Subjection of Women*, 264–265, *CW* 21.
85. Urbinati, "Many Heads of the Hydra," 90.
86. Mill, *Subjection of Women*, 271–272.
87. Mill, *On Liberty*, 264–265, 272–273.
88. Mill, "Centralisation," 582, *CW* 19.
89. Mill, *On Liberty*, 241.

DOMINATION AS DEMORALIZATION

As Mill laments in *Utilitarianism*, the individual's general desire to engage in higher activity is a precious but delicate thing: "Capacity for the nobler feelings is in most natures a very tender plant, easily killed, not only by hostile influences, but by mere want of sustenance; and in the majority of young persons it speedily dies away if the occupations to which their position in life has devoted them, and the society into which it has thrown them, are not favourable to keeping that higher capacity in exercise." Good activity is natural to us, but it does not come easily; thus, unless we have cultivated a solid impulse toward the good, we tend to slide into lesser, baser forms of activity. Moreover, the key noble feeling is our "sense of dignity,"[90] that is, the "feeling of personal exaltation and degradation which acts independently of other people's opinion, or even in defiance of it."[91] The dignity of being human—of being a higher creature, endowed with a higher nature, naturally oriented toward a higher mode of existence—is, for Mill, what ennobles and first induces us to conduct ourselves in a manner befitting our higher faculties. Without a "sense of dignity," we tend to partake not in the good, but in the "self-regarding faults," which are characterized in their ignobility by a "want of personal dignity and self-respect."[92]

Thus, the question becomes: What sociopolitical arrangements tend to promote or oppose "the nobler feelings"? What "influences" or "occupations" tend to erode our "sense of dignity"? Under what conditions will an otherwise competent individual fail to take pleasure in the thought or idea of higher activity and thus abjure the pursuit of happiness? What accounts for demoralization, a state epitomized by a kind spiritual sloth?

There are several answers to this question. Mill would certainly acknowledge the demoralizing effects of pervasive tyranny, poor education, and grinding poverty. However, for us, the key thing to notice is the emphasis Mill places on the demoralizing effects of sociopolitical inferiority, dependency, subjugation. Domination *itself* robs the dominated of their dignity, their honor, their self-respect. The dominated are cast as lesser persons or mere objects—the antebellum slave is chattel; the loathed minority is a pariah; the Victorian wife is a puppet in a doll's house.[93] What we have here, in the very first instance, are status deprivations that are entwined

90. Mill, *Utilitarianism*, 212–213.
91. Mill, "Bentham," 95–96.
92. Mill, *On Liberty*, 279.
93. See Pettit, *Just Freedom*, xiii–xxiii.

with a sense of powerlessness or base dependency. Domination obliges the dominated "to toady or fawn or kowtow, to bend the knee or doff the cap or tug the forelock, to placate or ingratiate or seek the good graces of one's betters, to live in servitude and servility."[94] Non-domination is vital to the inverse, where individuals can stand with their heads high and shoulders back; where each individual "can look others in the eye without reason for the fear or deference that a power of interference might inspire."[95]

Let us designate this category of injustice *domination as demoralization*. According to Mill, subjection to a *dominus* lowers our "grade of existence," which strikes at our human nobility or dignity, and thus undermines our general attraction to higher activity. For Mill, this demoralizing tendency applies to domination in all its many forms; and crucially, it holds true irrespective of how kindly or cruelly we are treated by the powers that be. Consider the following passage from *Subjection*, where we find Mill concluding a discussion on the general benefits of women's equality:

> The widening of the sphere of action for women would operate for good, by raising their education to the level of that of men, and making the one participate in all improvements made in the other. But independently of this, the mere breaking down of the barrier would of itself have an educational virtue of the highest worth. The mere getting rid of the idea that all the wider subjects of thought and action, all the things which are of general and not solely of private interest, are men's business, from which women are to be warned off—positively interdicted from most of it, coldly tolerated in the little which is allowed them— the mere consciousness a woman would then have of being a human being like any other, entitled to choose her pursuits, urged or invited by the same inducements as anyone else to interest herself in whatever is interesting to human beings, entitled to exert the share of influence on all human concerns which belongs to an individual opinion, whether she attempted actual participation in them or not—this alone would effect an immense expansion of the faculties of women, as well as enlargement of the range of their moral sentiments.[96]

The important thing to highlight in this passage is that Mill isolates domination itself as an obstacle to human flourishing. Indeed, the wife's very "idea" of her state of subjection, of not being "entitled" to govern

94. Martí and Pettit, *Political Philosophy in Public Life*, 148.
95. Pettit, *On the People's Terms*, 84.
96. Mill, *Subjection of Women*, 326–327.

herself—that is, her very "consciousness" of being denied the same status or standing of a "human being like any other"—is *itself* an impediment to an "immense expansion" and "enlargement" of her faculties and sentiments. It is not what her husband might *do* that Mill underscores; it is the fact that, as a second-class citizen, she is powerless under him. The pleasure her mind's eye would otherwise naturally take in the ennobling thought of virtue or excellence is replaced by the pain her mind's eye takes in her undignified circumstances. The lowly degradation of marital despotism profoundly damages her passion or desire for self-cultivation, notwithstanding how her husband treats her.

And as Mill adds, men feel the exact same way about their own situation in life. Despotism is, for most men, the "greatest grievance of all"—and again, this holds true even when the political despot proves to be "unexceptionable," "good," and "skilful," or even when the parental despot is "loved" by and "affectionate" toward their son. Upon exiting the dependency of "boyhood" and entering upon the independency of "manhood," men "feel twice as much alive, twice as much a human being, as before." Prolonged subjugation is directly opposed to the "ennobling influence" of sociopolitical equality. Domination itself divests men of the "sentiment of personal dignity," which would otherwise give "nerve and spring" to "all the faculties." The gratification, and thus the animating vigor, of higher activity depends on men unshackling themselves from what is, after childhood, a degrading state—and it is a wanton sort of ignorance to "imagine that women have none of these feelings."[97]

Domination is also a demoralizing offense against the nobility of self-reliance and self-subsistence. It is an undignified thing to have to consciously credit our liberty to the allowances of another. Mill makes this point several times in *Considerations on Representative Government*:

> Very different is the state of the human faculties where a human being feels himself under no other external restraint than the necessities of nature, or mandates of society which he has his share in imposing, and which it is open to him, if he thinks them wrong, publicly to dissent from, and exert himself actively to get altered. No doubt, under a government partially popular, this freedom may be exercised even by those who are not partakers in the full privileges of citizenship. But it is a great additional stimulus to any one's self-help and self-reliance when he starts from even ground, and has not to feel that his success depends on the impression he can make upon the sentiments and dispositions

97. Ibid., 337–338.

of a body of whom he is not one. It is a great discouragement to an individual, and a still greater one to a class, to be left out of the constitution; to be reduced to plead from outside the door to the arbiters of their destiny, not taken into the consultation within. The maximum of the invigorating effect of freedom upon the character is only obtained, when the person acted on either is, or is looking forward to becoming, a citizen as fully privileged as any other.[98]

Despotism demoralizes us, in the first instance, not from any tyrannical exercise of power, nor even from the denial of any sources of self-cultivation ("this freedom may be exercised even by . . ."), but from the way domination itself makes us *feel*: dependent, discouraged, and suppliant. Conversely, those who are ennobled by being not only allowed but also entitled to engage politically, and who thus start from "even ground," will feel a "great additional stimulus" to their life pursuits. And even those who are not yet permitted to participate politically, but who nonetheless have the dignity of "looking forward" to this moral entitlement, will immediately feel the "invigorating effect of freedom." However, it is a "great discouragement" to our self-development to suffer the humiliation and degradation of having to ingratiate ourselves with the "arbiters of [our] destiny." Any "political arrangement" that takes no cognizance of certain "opinions and wishes," either de jure or de facto, is "revolting" to the "sense of dignity which it is desirable to encourage in every human being." Mill thinks this explains why the "distribution of what may be called social dignity is more unequal in England than in any other civilized country of Europe."[99] The same sentiment is found in *On Liberty*, where the language of bondage and supplication appears with some frequency—for example, the many "bend the knee to custom."[100] And in *Autobiography*, Mill fears the dispiriting effects of a world in which a democratic despot leaves us "all equals, but all slaves."[101]

In sum, Mill holds that domination itself tends to deflate our will to the good. This is not to say that the dominated will find no pleasure in their daily pursuits. Rather, this is just to say that the pursuit of "true" happiness must be *motivated*; and it must be motivated by what Mill, following Bentham, calls a "spring of action."[102] An individual will pursue a particular good only insofar as they retain a passion or desire that propels them

---

98. Mill, *Considerations on Representative Government*, 411.
99. Ibid., 354, 637.
100. Mill, *On Liberty*, 269.
101. Mill, *Autobiography*, 202.
102. See Bentham, *Table of the Springs of Action*, 205, *W* 1.

toward that good when the opportunity arises. The mind's eye must take pleasure in the very thought or idea of a good if that good is to spring the individual into action. But what is true of particular goods is also true of the good in toto—of individual well-being or flourishing. Before we can discern and pursue what our individual good consists in, we must first be animated by the very thought or idea of realizing the good itself; we must not be insensible to, or, worse, scornful of, the possibility of happiness. And what domination itself tends to instill in the dominated is a disheartened or dejected attitude, where the choice of the competent judge— between living like "a human being" or "a pig"—fails to resonate with the dominated party, for he has *already* been forced "to sink into what he feels to be a lower grade of existence."[103] Domination as demoralization shines a light on the "humiliation and misery of dependence."[104]

DOMINATION AS UNCERTAINTY

Perhaps the most obvious concern one can have about domination is the mere fact that the *dominus* is empowered to act tyrannically; oppressive, arbitrary interferences are more likely to befall the ruled insofar as their rulers wield arbitrary power. This was the classic Utilitarian critique of despotism. In "Essay on Government," Mill's father, James, defends representative democracy for no fundamental reason other than its being the optimal feasible way to fortify the people against the egoistic tendencies of human nature, and thereby to promote the general happiness: "Whenever the powers of government are placed in any hands other than those of the community, whether those of one man, of a few, or of several, those principles of human nature which imply that government is at all necessary, imply that these persons will make use of them to defeat the very end for which government exists."[105] This is also the basic reason why a libertarian would support republican checks and balances: as instruments for ensuring an optimal sphere of liberty as non-interference.

For his part, Mill writes unremittingly about the importance of "securities for good government."[106] Republican checks and balances are, at one

103. Mill, *Utilitarianism*, 211–212.
104. Mill, "Claims of Labour," 379.
105. Mill, "Essay on Government," 9–10.
106. This expression and those similar to it appear throughout Mill's writings. For instance, see Mill, "Edinburgh Review," 296, 300; "Radical Party and Canada," 417; "Rationale of Representation," 30, *CW* 18; *Considerations on Representative Government*, 572; "Law of Libel and Liberty of the Press," 24, *CW* 21; and "Pledges," 503, *CW* 23.

level, the means by which would-be despots, both vertical and horizontal, are counteracted, and thus by which the general interest is most likely to be promoted and defended. However, Mill also underscores the way that domination interferes with our happiness prima facie by making us *feel* insecure. Mill pithily summarizes this concern in *Considerations*: "however great an amount of liberty the citizens might practically enjoy, they could never forget that they held it on sufferance, and by a concession which under the existing constitution of the state might at any moment by resumed; that they were legally slaves, though of a prudent, or indulgent, master."[107] Those who are granted liberty by a *dominus* can "never forget" the latent threat of chains.

A similar sentiment is woven throughout *On Liberty*. While discussing majority tyranny, Mill declares, "the mind itself is bowed to the yoke: even in what people do for pleasure, conformity is the first thing thought of"[108]—not just *done*, but *thought*; that is, even when the majority leaves us alone, a cloud hangs over our thoughts, words, and conduct, especially if we are at all inclined toward independence. Thus, there is just no such thing as a "happy" slave for Mill—indeed, it is a contradiction in terms: "no freedom is worth much when held on so precarious a tenure."[109] According to Mill, our tendency to venture onto the pathways of self-development is negatively correlated with our vulnerability to potential obstacles. Recalling my analysis in chapter 2, this is what makes the inviolability of moral rules so significant: "Rules are necessary, because mankind would have no security for any of the things which they value, for anything which gives them pleasure or shields them from pain, unless they could rely on one another for doing, and in particular for abstaining from, certain acts."[110] The feeling of security is the most vital prerequisite to human flourishing, which makes freedom as non-domination Mill's most imperative moral rule.

However, to drill down even further, Mill contends that the feeling of insecurity is less a function of the *probability* of interference (which waxes and wanes depending on how a given despot behaves over time) and more a function of the *uncertainty* of interference (which is necessarily a constant irrespective of how said despot behaves over time). Indeed, what we might be inclined to dub *domination as insecurity* is actually better defined as the injustice of *domination as uncertainty*. With domination comes insecurity and thus "uncertainty," "the associated anxiety

107. Mill, *Considerations on Representative Government*, 402.
108. Mill, *On Liberty*, 265.
109. Mill, *Subjection of Women*, 292.
110. Mill, "Whewell on Moral Philosophy," 192, *CW* 10.

and inability to plan," and "the need to exercise strategy with the powerful, having to defer to them and anticipate their various moves."[111] While the dominated might reasonably predict that their despot *probably* will not interfere arbitrarily with their interests, they cannot truthfully declare that their despot *definitely* will not act despotically. And it is this lack of a *guarantee*—inherent to all forms of domination, vertical and horizontal—that Mill sees as anathema to individual well-being: "Insecurity paralyzes where the means of self-protection are lacking."[112]

Consider the following passage from "Catiline's Conspiracy," where a young Mill introduces a theme that he would echo many times in less ostentatious ways:

> Now a government of law is always preferable to a government of arbitrary will. However oppressive the laws might be, they might at any rate be known. Though the law might take from us nine tenths of the produce of our industry, it would be something to know, that the remaining tenth would be secure. I can hardly imagine any laws so bad, to which I would not rather be subject than to the caprice of a man: whose ever varying will could never for an instant be known—who would punish me today for executing his yesterday's commands,—who would load me today with riches and honours and send me to the scaffold tomorrow. I would rather if I must choose, be habitually overtaxed, than live in constant fear that the whole of my property might be taken from me at a moment's warning by the fiat of a despot. I would rather have every action controlled—every movement chained up by restrictive laws which iniquitous as they might be would not destroy my security, since I should only have to obey them and be safe: than lead a life of incessant anxiety lest by some of my acts I should unwittingly infringe against a will which had never been made known to me, and violate prohibitions which had never existed anywhere but in the royal bosom. Nor is this utter insecurity, this constant sense of alarm, confined to those who are sufficiently conspicuous to attract the notice of the despot, and sufficiently wealthy to excite his cupidity or his jealousy. If the great body of the people is not the prey of the despot, it is the prey of his subordinate instruments: petty tyrants, whom experience has proved to be the worst of tyrants and who are but the more likely to be tyrants because they themselves are slaves.[113]

111. Pettit, *Republicanism*, 89.
112. Mill, *Principles of Political Economy*, 881.
113. Mill, "Catiline's Conspiracy," 346, *CW* 26.

Mill is saying that a smaller but *secure* sphere of non-interference is preferable to a larger but *insecure* sphere of non-interference; and, indeed, that a greater but *certain* amount of illegitimate meddling is preferable to a lesser but *uncertain* amount of illegitimate meddling. For Mill, the most benign *dominus* is actually *worse* than a semi-republican rule of law, for at least the latter promises to delimit and define the quantity and quality of arbitrary interference that the powers that be can perpetrate, whereas the despot, despite all his benevolence, leaves our future prospects forever ambiguous. As Mill says in *Principles of Political Economy*, the uncertain atmosphere of martial despotism can be defined as one of systemic tyranny, regardless of how much practical tyranny a particular wife is confronted with: "When the law makes everything which the wife acquires, the property of the husband, while by compelling her to live with him it forces her to submit to almost any amount of moral and even physical tyranny which he may choose to inflict, there is some ground for regarding every act done by her as done under coercion."[114] Conversely, as Mill notes in his commentary on George Grote, those individuals who live under "the unimpeded authority of law" can nevertheless enjoy that "mental tranquility which is also one of the conditions of high intellectual or imaginative achievement" insofar as their "life and property" are "secure."[115] The will to the good requires the general foundation of certainty against arbitrary reprisals.

Now, one might argue that Mill is exaggerating things—after all, if a despot proves to be consistently benevolent in every particular then what could trouble his subjects other than a mild case of paranoia? But to think thusly is to forget the words of Lord Acton: "Power tends to corrupt, and absolute power corrupts absolutely. Great men are almost always bad men, even when they exercise influence and not' authority: still more when you superadd the tendency or the certainty of corruption by authority. There is no worse heresy than that the office sanctifies the holder of it."[116] Like Acton, Mill believes that (arbitrary) power corrupts, and that the chill of uncertainty neither can nor should dissipate even under a "good" despot.

Of all the convictions Mill held by his last years, this one had been with him the longest. At sixteen, he wrote that "upon the whole there are few exceptions, or rather none at all, to the principle that all men who have power will infallibly abuse it."[117] And eight years before he died, Mill

---

114. Mill, *Principles of Political Economy*, 953.
115. Mill, "Grote's History of Greece," 316, *CW* 11.
116. Dalberg-Acton, *Acton-Creighton Correspondence*, 9.
117. Mill, "Securities for Good Government," 63, *CW* 22.

declared it to be "contrary to all experience of human nature to suppose that [a *dominus*] will not abuse its power."[118] So, to put despotism and benevolence in the same phrase is, for Mill, a nonstarter. And *even if* it were possible for a *dominus*—whether one, few, or many—to behave consistently in what they intend to be a benevolent manner, they would *still* pose a risk of mistakes and blunders. As Mill stresses, we are far from infallible; and benign despots, assured of their faultless course of action, may, in fact, be acting tyrannically. Mill's prized example is the Roman Emperor Marcus Aurelius: "This man, a better Christian in all but the dogmatic sense of the word, than almost any of the ostensibly Christian sovereigns who have since reigned, persecuted Christianity."[119] Thus, the shadow of uncertainty persists, and ought to persist, notwithstanding the despot's apparent proclivities.

DOMINATION AS DIMINUTION

As we have seen, Mill believes that there is and ought to be a maximally wide array of higher activities for the individual to engage in, and that the individual should be entitled and encouraged to exercise their higher faculties in a maximally wide range of human arenas. Individual happiness consists in virtuous or excellent activity; but every worthy object, end, or ideal involves its own particular variety or instantiation of virtue or excellence; and so, the potential for individual happiness will either expand or contract in relation to the breadth and depth of the worthy objects, ends, or ideals available to the individual.

Thus, things get dicey when we are given the opportunity to ransom activity in exchange for convenience. From studying philosophy to navigating the sea to imparting friendship to participating politically, the sphere of human activity is enormously diverse; and as a society, we should take stock of the implications of liberating ourselves from the drudgery of doing things *for ourselves*. Indeed, one of the costs of technology, for Mill, is that we often find it no longer necessary to exert ourselves, which snaps certain branches off the tree of human flourishing: "Supposing it were possible to get houses built, corn grown, battles fought, causes tried, and even churches erected and prayers said, by machinery—by automatons in human form—it would be a considerable loss to exchange for these automatons even the men and women who at present inhabit the more

118. Mill, "To John Boyd Kinnear," 1103, *CW* 16.
119. Mill, *On Liberty*, 236.

civilized parts of the world, and who assuredly are but starved specimens of what nature can and will produce."[120]

One of the key problems with domination, then, is that the higher faculties of the dominated are constricted across whatever range of interests or activities the *dominus* controls. By having a *dominus*, a certain sphere of interest or activity is taken out of the hands of the dominated and delegated to the wit and will of the powers that be. Hence, the dominated are denied the responsibility or opportunity to develop or cultivate themselves accordingly. Despotism—even the most benevolent, ideal despotism imaginable—inexorably narrows the potential for individual happiness. Consider an idyllic political despot:

> What should we then have? One man of superhuman mental activity managing the entire affairs of a mentally passive people. Their passivity is implied in the very idea of absolute power. The nation as a whole, and every individual composing it, are without any potential voice in their own destiny. They exercise no will in respect to their collective interests. All is decided for them by a will not their own, which it is legally a crime for them to disobey. What sort of human beings can be formed under such a regimen? What development can either their thinking or their active faculties attain under it? On matters of pure theory they might perhaps be allowed to speculate, so long as their speculations either did not approach politics, or had not the remotest connexion with its practice. On practical affairs they could at most be only suffered to suggest; and even under the most moderate of despots, none but persons of already admitted or reputed superiority could hope that their suggestions would be known to, much less regarded by, those who had the management of affairs. A person must have a very unusual taste for intellectual exercise in and for itself, who will put himself to the trouble of thought when it is to have no outward effect, or qualify himself for functions which he has no chance of being allowed to exercise. The only sufficient incitement to mental exertion, in any but a few minds in a generation, is the prospect of some practical use to be made of its results.[121]

Despotism is diametrically opposed to the virtues or excellences of citizenship; of self-governance; of political discourse. At best, the politically dominated will develop "a *dilletante* knowledge" of political matters

120. Ibid., 263.
121. Mill, *Considerations on Representative Government*, 400.

and activities, "like that which people have of the mechanical arts who have never handled a tool." The dilettante of all stripes knows what self-cultivation, in theory, would consist in, but never actually self-cultivates in practice—like the would-be batter who peruses Ted Williams's *The Science of Hitting* but never actually steps to the plate. Even worse, when some modes of flourishing are starved in the individual, other modes will take on an exaggerated, unhealthy significance: "the intelligence and sentiments of the whole people are given up to the material interests, and when these are provided for, to the amusement and ornamentation, of private life."[122] And the more that individuals waste themselves on the solitary pleasures of the private sphere, the less capable and willing they will be to fend off the vultures in the public square. For such reasons, Mill leans toward entrusting individuals with the responsibility to attend to whatever vital interests or activities they can manage for themselves, not only as a check against "the great evil of adding unnecessarily" to a central authority, but also "as a means to their own mental education—a mode of strengthening their active faculties, exercising their judgment, and giving them a familiar knowledge of the subjects with which they are thus left to deal."[123]

Domination diminishes the scope of human activity and thus introduces a fourth category of despotic injustice: *domination as diminution*. Naturally, Mill does not bemoan the human tendency to specialize in specific activities. After all, that is one of the marks of individuality fully realized. Nor does he regard all merely theoretical interests as lowly or ignoble. On the contrary, one of the great boons of a flourishing society is that each individual is able to take joy in, and, to some extent, partake in, the activities of others. Mill was, by his own admission, a merely academic lover of poetry, and yet the poetry of Wordsworth, Shelley, and Tennyson added immeasurably to Mill's life and development. Rather, what Mill is contending in his critique of domination as diminution is the diminishing notion that the activities over which the *dominus* reigns supreme are, for lack of a better phrase, none of our business. Where the despots above or around us retain absolute control, entire regions of human inquiry or action will be removed from the province of the dominated, who will tend to respond—particularly if their *dominus* is kindly and competent—by retreating into those domains of thought or activity over which they retain control or sovereignty: "A people among whom there is no habit of spontaneous action for a collective interest—who look habitually to their

122. Ibid., 400–401.
123. Mill, *On Liberty*, 305–306.

government to command or prompt them in all matters of joint concern—who expect to have everything done for them, except what can be made an affair of mere habit and routine—have their faculties only half developed; their education is defective in one of its most important branches."[124]

DOMINATION AS TRIBALIZATION

Recall that the good life comprises both individuality and sociality; happiness is most fully realized in a complementary and mutually reinforcing balance of self-regarding and other-regarding activity. However, as I have noted several times, while Mill thinks that both individuality and sociality are natural, and, in fact, that sociality, once cultivated, is felt to be even more integral to our well-being, only individuality is inborn—that is, while we innately sympathize with ourselves, we are dependent on education and experience to develop and nurture our sympathy for other people. As Mill says in his essay on Plato's *Gorgias*, this education might entail "associating [virtue] with our most impressive conceptions of power and beauty"[125] through the poetic-prose of Socrates or Christ. Or, as Mill says in *Subjection*, this experience might entail observing those with whom we already sympathize, or those whom we admire, and imbibing the unselfish, conscientious ways in which they treat one another: "the family in its best forms" is "a school of sympathy, tenderness, and loving forgetfulness of self."[126] Or, as Mill says in *Utilitarianism*, this cultivation might entail being reared by a system of laws and norms that establishes "in the mind of every individual an indissoluble association between his own happiness and the good of the whole,"[127] a theme that appears, as we have seen, in *On Liberty* as well. But, in short, the point is that sociality requires soil, water, and sunlight—unlike individuality, it is not inherently active.

And this leads Mill to an important move: just as plants are in continual need of soil, water, and sunlight, so, too, are individuals in continual need of an environment in which sociality is actively nurtured and fostered. Again, while our social feelings are natural, and, when blooming, predominant, they are also innately "inferior in strength to [our] selfish feelings."[128] Our individuality will undercut our sociality if our individuality is left totally unchecked, or if our sociality is placed in a hostile

---

124. Mill, *Principles of Political Economy*, 943.

125. Mill, "The Gorgias," 150, *CW* 11.

126. Mill, *Subjection of Women*, 288.

127. Mill, *Utilitarianism*, 218.

128. Ibid., 233.

environment. We are in perpetual danger of forgetting ourselves and allowing our ever-present selfish impulses to encroach ever further on our social sensibilities. Thus, the question becomes: what, if anything, besides a good education and nutritious experiences, is essential to keeping our natural sociality thriving?

One answer stands out for Mill: sociopolitical equality. On the positive side, sociopolitical equality actively encourages individuals to see one another as friends rather than enemies, as partners rather than rivals, as people rather than predators or prey: "The equality of married persons before the law, is not only the sole mode in which that particular relation can be made consistent with justice to both sides, and conducive to the happiness of both, but it is the only means of rendering the daily life of mankind, in any high sense, a school of moral cultivation. Though the truth may not be felt or generally acknowledged for generations to come, the only school of genuine moral sentiment is society between equals." Mill's theory of sociality and justice is a reinforcing cycle: justice is bolstered by sociality, but sociality is also bolstered by justice. Mill believes (as an empirical teleologist) that "sympathetic association," which promotes "society in equality," and vice versa, is "the normal state" of "society." But, to realize this ideal, we must be molded by the law of "reciprocal superiority," where we can lead one another without being compelled or subjugated.[129]

On the negative side, sociopolitical equality prevents our selfish, egoistic impulses from making inroads. Mill believes that where the formal backdrop of sociopolitical equality is absent, the primal, barbaric tendency of individuals to regard one another as challengers for dominance, or as potential predators or prey, will reassert itself. Indeed, the overstepping of individuality is "hardly ever kept under restraint by anything but want of power."[130] Where freedom is lacking, what rushes in to fill the void is the despotic *daemon*. Thus, one of the main issues with domination is that it undercuts the development and subsistence of sociality: "The moralization of the personal enjoyments we deem to consist" in "cultivating the habitual wish to share them with others, and with all others, and scorning to desire anything for oneself which is incapable of being so shared. There is only one passion or inclination which is permanently incompatible with this condition—the love of domination, or superiority, for its own sake; which implies, and is grounded on, the equivalent depression of other people."[131]

---

129. Mill, *Subjection of Women*, 293–294, 335.
130. Mill, *On Liberty*, 227.
131. Mill, *Auguste Comte and Positivism*, 339.

Whenever and wherever individuals have lived outside the strictures of sociopolitical equality, their selfish compulsions and aspirations have been far more likely to gain the upper hand: "What better is to be looked for under the existing form of the institution [of marriage]? We know that the bad propensities of human nature are only kept within bounds when they are allowed no scope for their indulgence."[132]

For instance, Mill observes that marital despotism often induces both men and women to allow their selfish sympathies to overtake their whole being. Consider husbands: "There is nothing which men so easily learn" as "self-worship: all privileged persons, and all privileged classes, have had it." As in all things, there are certainly "honourable exceptions," but "proportionally fewer than in the case of almost any other human infirmity." The only thing that can balance the outsized influence of individuality is "that practical feeling of the equality between human beings." And, being denied equality with their husbands, wives fare no better. They often harbor an intelligible resentment, and often succeed in setting up a "counter-tyranny" for the sake of "self-protection," what Mill calls "the power of the scold, or the shrewish sanction," which makes "victims in their turn chiefly of those husbands who are least inclined to be tyrants."[133] This is the natural result of vertical domination: a reciprocal, self-absorbed antipathy between the ruler and the ruled.

However, the issue is even more pronounced in the case of horizontal domination. Mill often reminds us that societies governed by "mere will" rather than the "arms of reason" are characterized by an antagonistic politics in which prejudiced factions jostle with one another for the opportunity of being "the strongest party therein." Domination, especially when it is up for grabs, results in a Hobbesian state of *society*. Rather than preemptively attacking our adversaries, as we would in Hobbes's state of nature, we instead find ourselves vying for the power to interfere arbitrarily with one another: "These are the elements of a people of place-hunters; in whom the course of politics is mainly determined by place-hunting," where "the contests of political parties are but struggles to decide whether the power of meddling in everything shall belong to one class or another."[134] But if the subordinate faction—whomever it turns out to be—is guaranteed to retain the moral rights of sociopolitical equals, then the interfactional stakes of power are drastically lowered, and thus

---

132. Mill, *Subjection of Women*, 289.
133. Ibid., 289, 293.
134. Mill, *Considerations on Representative Government*, 420, 478.

the natural corruption done to sociality by political conflict is, to that extent, greatly reduced.

We can call this category of injustice *domination as tribalization,* for the key effect of domination here is to separate individuals into warring groups—men and women, Left and Right, and so on. Rather than coalescing through the natural impulse of sociality, the specter of arbitrary power causes individuals to see one another as threats or foes, and thus to build walls and go on the attack or defense. The antithesis of tribalization is anything truly communal, beginning with a healthy family: "The family, justly constituted, would be the real school of the virtues of freedom. It is sure to be a sufficient one of everything else. It will always be a school of obedience for the children, of command for the parents. What is needed is, that it should be a school of sympathy in equality, of living together in love, without power on one side or obedience on the other."[135] Indeed, the despotism of parents over children is only an appearance insofar as the parents are educating their children for liberty rooted in sociality—for a world without despotism.

DOMINATION AS ENERVATION

One of the classic tensions in political theory is between public and private life: their duties, their benefits, their virtues, their dangers. There is a hoary conviction among many scholars that Mill expounds an essential antagonism between the individual and society; between the public and private spheres. As Gertrude Himmelfarb writes, Mill's philosophy asserts "a radical disjunction between the individual and society, indeed, an adversarial relationship, with the individual assigned all the positive, honorific attributes, and society the negative, pejorative ones."[136] As last chapter would suggest, and as I will discuss again shortly, I do not think this reading is correct; in fact, quite the reverse—Mill's ideal is that of a radical *union* between the individual and society, indeed, a cooperative relationship, where the positive, honorific attributes of the individual enhance society, and vice versa, and where the only negative, pejorative attributes are reserved for those societal actors—whether one, few, or many—who upset this harmony via the discordance of injustice.

That said, there can be no doubt that Mill was in love with what Benjamin Constant called the liberty of the Moderns, which consists of

---

135. Mill, *Subjection of Women,* 295.
136. Himmelfarb, "One Very Simple Principle?," 533.

"peaceful enjoyment and private independence."[137] While Mill also lauded the importance and necessity of political participation (as we will see), he focused heavily, especially in *On Liberty*, on establishing proper checks on power in the name of securing a realm of non-interference for the private individual. The private sphere—from socializing, to reading, to cooking, to traveling, to painting—offers boundless charms and joys, all the more so the more that we allow family, friends, and confidantes to mix their private lives with ours. Mill himself is fond of remarking on his quasi-Romantic love of natural scenery and the countryside, and his private letters reveal a rich intellectual and social correspondence. It should be noted that, in Mill's time and in ours, countless people were and are subject to exhausting and degrading labor, such that the notion of a vibrant private life could be regarded as a cruel fantasy. Mill is sensitive to these sorts of issues, and worked to propose practicable reforms for laborers.[138] He thought that leisure time ought to be the province of all persons, not just the upper classes, and he believed labor itself ought to exhibit less mechanical, more active characteristics: "Men may be competent lawyers without general education, but it depends on general education to make them philosophic lawyers—who demand, and are capable of apprehending, principles, instead of merely cramming their memory with details. And so of all other useful pursuits, mechanical included. Education makes a man a more intelligent shoemaker," but "not by teaching him how to make shoes; it does so by the mental exercise it gives, and the habits it impresses."[139] But the key point is that in any minimally good society, there will be much more to life than what Constant called the liberty of the Ancients, which "consisted in an active and constant participation in collective power."[140]

Thus, Mill's final type of despotic injustice speaks to the fact that dominated individuals are more than likely to be unduly distracted from cultivating a rich private life. The dominated always find themselves in one of three tiresome, irksome scenarios: either they are having constantly to invigilate an unpopular despot, like a monarch or emperor, in an effort to predict or sway or preempt its changeable activity; or they are attempting to steer or repel the activity of a popular despot, like an unchecked democracy; or they are able neither to monitor nor to control the despot, and are

---

137. Constant, "Liberty of Ancients Compared with That of Moderns."

138. See King and Yanochik, "John Stuart Mill and the Economic Rationale for Organized Labor," 28–34.

139. Mill, "Inaugural Address Delivered to the University at St. Andrews," 218.

140. Constant, "Liberty of Ancients Compared with That of Moderns."

instead forced to live their ostensibly private lives with eyes in the back of their head, forever in the shadow of arbitrary power.

Of course, there is also a fourth box: the dominated individuals who can neither monitor nor control their *dominus*, but who do not much care or fret one way or the other, and who just go about their private lives with an indifferent shrug. I do not think it takes much imagination to fathom what Mill would say about these individuals—well, in short, only a foolish, banal hedonism could inspire so little concern or be so little worth defending. But, in any event, we might dub this category *domination as enervation*:

> While we are on the subject, we will pause to ask, what considerable improvement of the public mind is to be looked for under governors whom every patriotic citizen, who mingles in public affairs, must not only be perpetually *watching* with both his eyes, but perpetually *holding* with both his hands, to hinder them from seizing on absolute power? It required all the energy of the press and of public discussion applied unremittingly to the subject for six months, to raise such a storm as was sufficient to blow away these fourteen Bastilles; even now it is said, the scheme is only postponed, and the fight must be renewed next year; during all this time spent in repelling encroachments on the ground which has been already gained, no progress is made towards gaining more. While the public mind must be kept by its leaders and instructors perpetually *en garde*, for the purpose of parrying some expected or unexpected thrust at the very vitals of its freedom, it cannot find time or attention for literature or philosophy, or social morals, or education, or the best part of politics—the *improvement* of the spirit and details of its institutions.[141]

Again, Mill is not criticizing or bewailing civic involvement—there is nothing Mill cherishes more. However, Mill does not want public life necessarily to become an all-consuming demand. True to his moderate tendencies, Mill wants us to accrue the advantages of both public and private liberty, without either one reaching diminishing marginal returns or intruding on the benefits of the other: "Mill proposes a motive [for attending to the general interest]: if people alternate public involvement with attention to their private welfare, they will cultivate the full range of their powers. The promise is self-development, the cultivation of a many-sided self."[142]

---

141. Mill, "Quarterly Review of France," 594–595, *CW* 23.
142. Rosenblum, *Another Liberalism*, 130.

Indeed, tying this in with our previous categories, the problem here with domination is that it leaves us either uncertain and demoralized in the private sphere, or consumed and thus self-neglected by the struggle of the public sphere.

FREEDOM AS AN ABSOLUTE RIGHT

In chapter 3, I elucidated Mill's argument for treating intellectual and ethical liberty as moral rights; then, I explained how these moral rights do not admit of any exceptions. Intellectual and ethical liberty are *inviolable* moral rights. In the same way, Mill argues that freedom as non-domination is an inviolable moral right. An impartial observer would not only regard freedom as a moral right but also protect freedom as an *absolute* principle of sociopolitical justice.

In *On Liberty*, Mill goes through and dismisses a series of potential exceptions to the moral rights of intellectual and ethical liberty. Similarly, in various places, especially in the first chapter of *Subjection*, Mill encounters and rebuffs several potential excuses for violating freedom as non-domination. Mill begins with the contention that domination can be justified insofar as it has persisted in some form or another since time immemorial, and that "it can only" have "been preserved to this period of advanced civilization by a well-grounded feeling of its adaptation to human nature."[143] We might call this the *realism excuse*: the idea being that the command-obedience, despot-subject model of authority has endured forever, and has reemerged consistently across time, place, and culture, for no reason other than its being best or most realistically suited to the governance of human affairs. The realist excuse is the outlook characteristic of the eye-rolling authoritarian.

However, Mill traces the origin of domination not to any idea of "what conduce[s] to the benefit of humanity or the good order of society," but to "the law of superior strength." And, having identified its source, Mill argues that domination endures only because of "the great vitality and durability of institutions which place right on the side of might." As Mill says, no society has ever chosen, or would ever choose, a command-obedience model as "the result of deliberation." This is quite the loaded expression. Consider: if the dominated can deliberate well enough *to make* such a momentous decision, then they can deliberate well enough to govern themselves, in which case they are either abdicating their freedom,

---

143. Mill, *Subjection of Women*, 265.

which Mill thinks is a contradiction in terms, or being denied their freedom, which, for Mill, defines much of the long, sad history of human governance. Conversely: if the dominated *cannot* deliberate thusly then they
are either being readied for freedom by a soon-to-abdicate despot, which
is a preposterous thought, or being arrested in their political infancy and
pacified with the toys of pleasure and material progress, which describes
the craftier, cannier authoritarian regimes. Of course, on Mill's view, society will organically obey "the law of the strongest"[144] as long as it is still
working through the earlier stages of development. The decision, then, for
a more advanced society is either to hope for "spontaneous progress"[145] or
to intervene—and we should note Mill's eventual disillusionment with the
latter course of action.[146]

Having dispensed with the realist excuse, Mill turns to a related idea,
namely, that domination can be natural—in this case, for women: "Some
will object, that a comparison cannot fairly be made between the government of the male sex and the forms of unjust power which I have adduced
in illustration of it, since these are arbitrary, and the effect of mere usur-
pation, while it on the contrary is natural." The *naturalism excuse*, which
stretches back to Aristotle, says that "there are different natures among
mankind, free natures, and slave natures."[147] The threat of natural slavery
may seem dated to a society that has dispensed with institutional slavery;
however, the underlying spirit of the idea, which says that some people are
naturally superior and others naturally inferior, is very much present in
contemporary life. Mill saw it in Victorian marriage; and we see it whenever the *logos* of the individual is ignored or belittled on the basis of some
arbitrary factor about their identity or background.

Mill has three basic rejoinders. First, what is deemed "natural" is often
just a relic from a long-abjured practice. Where sociopolitical equality
is dubbed unnatural, Mill replies "that unnatural generally means only
uncustomary." The "subjection of women to men," for instance, is nothing more than a fossilized, latter-day artifact of "the law of the strongest."
Second, what is deemed "natural" is often just a product of *nurture*—of the
way that sociopolitical inferiors are deformed by their superiors and the
trappings of their inferiority. Again, Mill points to Victorian wives: "What
is now called the nature of women is an eminently artificial thing—the
result of forced repression in some directions, unnatural stimulation in

144. Ibid., 264–265.
145. Mill, *On Liberty*, 224.
146. See Bell, "John Stuart Mill on Colonies," 52–56.
147. Mill, *Subjection of Women*, 269.

others"; and "men, with that inability to recognise their own work which distinguishes the unanalytic mind, indolently believe that the tree grows of itself in the way they have made it grow, and that it would die if one half of it were not kept in a vapour bath and the other half in snow."[148] Besides, as we discussed above, the dominated tend to be twisted into docile, manageable subjects; a process that, over time, encourages them to adopt the most convenient persona for their predicament. And third, what is deemed "natural" is often just what is *innate* or *inborn*. That is, even if the dominated seem to lack the capacity for sociopolitical equality, this may only be because they have not had the education and experience necessary to activate and cultivate this capacity. As Mill writes in one of his earliest essays, "Another question, which it does not suit those who make the ignorance of the people a plea for enslaving them to put, is, why are they ignorant? because to this question there can be only one answer, namely, that if they are ignorant, it is precisely because that discussion, which alone can remove ignorance, has been withheld from them."[149] Society has untold benefits to gain from sociopolitical equality and very little to lose: "what is contrary to women's nature to do, they never will be made to do by simply giving their nature free play."[150] In short, the belief that some persons are marked out for subjection or other forms of inequality is bound to be either a baseless conjecture or a self-fulfilling prophecy.

Leaving these disputes behind, Mill then tackles the view that domination can be (tacitly) voluntary or consensual: "But, it will be said, the rule of men over women differs from all these others in not being a rule of force: it is accepted voluntarily; women make no complaint, and are consenting parties to it."[151] This attitude underlies the archaic notion of the "happy" slave; but it also underlies the ever contemporary notion that maltreatment, double standards, and discrimination are fair game as long as the game is played without complaint or controversy. How does Mill deal with what we might dub the *voluntarism excuse*?

For one, the power relations of superiority-inferiority can make it difficult for the have-nots to voice or publicize their criticisms or grievances. Given a door, the have-nots have consistently walked through it: "Ever since there have been women able to make their sentiments known by their writings," an "increasing number of them have recorded protests against their present social condition." Moreover, where complaints or

---

148. Ibid., 270, 276–277.
149. Mill, "Law of Libel and Liberty of the Press," 11.
150. Mill, *Subjection of Women*, 280.
151. Ibid., 270.

controversies *do* arise, they are often framed practically rather than morally: "It is a political law of nature that those who are under any power of ancient origin, never begin by complaining of the power itself, but only of its oppressive exercise."[152] Hence, the reality of general "consent" is often far different from its mere appearance. In addition, what looks like consent is often just the end result of what Urbinati calls "a vicious school of habit formation."[153] Again, this goes back to *domination as infantilization*, where the consent of the afflicted is engineered, not persuaded. And while Mill looks to the subjection of women as his primary example, he would apply all the same observations to other forms of subjugation: "Not a word can be said for despotism in the family which cannot be said for political despotism."[154]

More broadly, though, Mill points to the role that pure inertia plays in sustaining "voluntary" systems of domination; he argues that human beings have an instinctual propensity to associate the way things are with the way they ought to be, or to see the way things are as the way they cannot *not* be. Rather than asking what they "prefer," the individual is prone to ask, "what is suitable to my position? what is usually done by persons of my station and pecuniary circumstances?"[155] Expectations, norms, the path of least resistance: these are powerful, primal influences on the haves and have-nots alike. And the issue is compounded for the dominated (certainly for those who are subject to arbitrary abuse or neglect) by the fact that self-surrender is most likely to be the best or only way to satisfy their most immediate desires. Indeed, a Victorian wife's desire for "consideration" and "all objects of social ambition" can "be sought or obtained by her only through [her husband]."[156] Subjugated individuals tend to "consent" to their predicament for the same reason that competent individuals tend to pursue lower pleasures at the expense of higher pleasures: because it is, or is a means to, "the nearer good."[157] And to stand up for justice is to risk alienation, which is not to say that you ought not to, but rather that no one could truly *expect* you to: "We cleave to our group's values not mainly because of their epistemic merits but because they are guarantors of a social world without which we would feel disoriented and vulnerable."[158]

152. Ibid., 270–271.
153. Urbinati, *Mill on Democracy*, 174.
154. Mill, *Subjection of Women*, 286.
155. Mill, *On Liberty*, 264.
156. Mill, *Subjection of Women*, 272.
157. Mill, *Utilitarianism*, 212.
158. Zakaras, "John Stuart Mill, Individuality, and Participatory Democracy," 205.

The voluntarism excuse is as absurd as deeming the mugger's quip, "Your money or your life," to be a real choice.

In sum, there is *no* valid excuse: freedom as non-domination is an absolute moral right. As we have touched on several times, Mill withholds this right from persons who have yet to reach "the maturity of their faculties"—or so he claims. Mill does not really mean "*despotism*" when he says that despotism "is a legitimate mode of government in dealing with barbarians [and children]." By despotism, or domination, Mill typically means total, unchecked power; but the power of the "despot" in this passage is constrained by the moral requirement that their power be exercised for the "improvement" of the ruled.[159] Parents in *On Liberty* have theoretically enforceable duties to their children. Mill's "despot" in *On Liberty* is not at liberty to act unjustly: "The right to become, and be, an independent person belongs to *all* human beings by virtue of their being human. It is the actual enjoyment that is deferred, not its possession. This is the argument that frames Mill's proposal of *temporary* paternalism."[160] Indeed, in *On Liberty*, Mill is not referring to despotism; rather, he is referring to paternalism.

Moreover, in an equal society, individuals must be guaranteed the equal opportunities that go along with equal rights. For instance, Mill says that a just society must secure to women, as *liberi*, the "free use of their faculties," the "free choice of their employments," and must provide them with "the same field of occupation and the same prizes and encouragements as to other human beings." However, perhaps this does not go far enough—perhaps Mill is too classically and reservedly liberal. For, first, what about the initial disadvantage that women (or any other group) will find themselves at after being dominated for so long? And second, what about the residual impact or influence—despite good-faith attempts at moral exhortation—that "the law of the strongest" might have on the prejudices that the former *dominus* might bear toward the formerly dominated, and vice versa?[161]

The first question points to the problem of the inequality of opportunity that naturally arises whenever some have a head start or others are held back. While Mill could hardly be expected to promote basic equality *and* corrective justice *in tandem*, it would be easy to imagine a reasonable Millian debate being had over such issues as affirmative action

159. Mill, *On Liberty*, 224.
160. Urbinati, *Mill on Democracy*, 177.
161. Mill, *Subjection of Women*, 264–265, 326.

and reparations. Regarding opportunity more broadly, Mill thinks that inequality will naturally and necessarily arise in any free competition for resources, positions, or accolades, which is actually acceptable or even desirable as long as it conduces to the general happiness—an ethic similar in spirit to Rawls's difference principle.[162] However, Mill is also plainly sympathetic to the idea that "all start fair"[163]—to what Rawls dubs *fair* equality of opportunity, where talent and effort alone determine success, and where individuals are not disadvantaged by arbitrary, extraneous factors having to do with their drawing in the lottery of birth.[164]

And the second question points to the partialities, bigotries, or preconceptions that many people arbitrarily harbor on the basis of race, sex, class, religion, and so on, and which can corrupt individuality, sociality, and impartial dealing de facto despite sociopolitical equality de jure. Again, Mill believes that sociopolitical equality, vertical and horizontal, is *itself* the chief and greatest school of moral progress; and, to this end, Mill advocates things like martial equality and worker cooperatives.[165] But, nonetheless, a good Millian debate can and ought to be had over what proequality or antidiscrimination policy ought to look like. For instance, I suspect that Mill would have taken kindly, in theory, to some of the general lines of jurisprudence that have emerged under the Fourteenth Amendment to the U.S. Constitution. However, what is certain is that Mill would reject any policy that undermines the liberal-republican order, either by violating the basic liberties or by introducing an element of arbitrary power.

Political Flourishing

In this final section, I explore the relationship Mill sees between political participation and the general happiness. According to Mill, the most important sphere for interaction between the individual and society is the sphere of politics. Naturally, political liberty—the right to free speech, a free press, association, elections, voting, and so forth—is constitutive of non-domination. But beyond acknowledging the moral *right* to political liberty, Mill also enjoins us to *exercise* our political liberty; an active citizenry is, for Mill, essential to the well-being of both society and the individual. In what follows, Mill argues, first, that political participation

---

162. See Rawls, *Theory of Justice*, 52–65.
163. Mill, *Principles of Political Economy*, 811.
164. See Rawls, *Theory of Justice*, 73–78.
165. See Barker, *Educating Liberty*, 193–195.

is a necessary check on government; and second, that the good life for the individual can be fully realized only in the political arena.

CIVIC REPUBLICANISM

In *Considerations*, Mill offers a bevy of reasons for why the good of both the individual and society can be best served only by having individuals become active political participants. In the first place, neither the rights or liberties of the individual nor the interests of either the individual or society can be optimized without a vibrant democratic polity:

> Its superiority in reference to present well-being rests upon two principles, of as universal truth and applicability as any general propositions which can be laid down respecting human affairs. The first is, that the rights and interests of every or any person are only secure from being disregarded, when the person interested is himself able, and habitually disposed, to stand up for them. The second is, that the general prosperity attains a greater height, and is more widely diffused, in proportion to the amount and variety of the personal energies enlisted in promoting it.[166]

A healthy, participatory democracy not only protects individuals but also promotes the general interest by addressing the plurality of social interests and drawing on the knowledge and experience of every sector of society. So, first, we have what Dennis Thompson labels the "protective"[167] aspect of Mill's participatory appeal: "in the absence of its natural defenders, the interest of the excluded is always in danger of being overlooked; and, when looked at, is seen with very different eyes from those of the persons whom it directly concerns."[168] And second, we have what Nadia Urbinati regards as Mill's solution to the information-gap between rulers and the societies they mean to rule: "Mill's insight was that the complexity of modern society itself demanded free government."[169] An increasingly complex modern society cannot be well-governed without making wall-to-wall, bottom-up fact finding an integral part of the governance model. Thus, widespread participation is indispensable. Mill's political ideal is "the greatest dissemination of power consistent with efficiency; but the greatest possible centralization of information, and diffusion of it from the centre."[170]

166. Mill, *Considerations on Representative Government*, 404.
167. Thompson, *John Stuart Mill and Representative Government*, 13–53.
168. Mill, *Considerations on Representative Government*, 405.
169. Urbinati, "Many Heads of the Hydra," 83.
170. Mill, *Considerations on Representative Government*, 432.

Mill's ideal government is composed of two basic bodies: the one, focused on deliberation, judgment, and contestation—i.e., "talking"—is to be properly democratic; the other, tasked with things like drafting legislation and administering laws—i.e., "doing"—is to be aristocratic, that is, open to specialized knowledge, skill, and competence.[171] The former is a proper "representative assembly," whereas the latter are "specialized legislative commissions charged with formulating the details of legislation and putting their legislative proposals in front of the elected assembly for approval or rejection."[172] The democratic body is a "place where every interest and shade of opinion in the country can have its cause even passionately pleaded, in the face of the government and of all other interests and opinions, can compel them to listen, and either comply, or state clearly why they do not." Thus, one of the principal benefits accorded by a well-constituted democracy is that it fortifies the polity against the despotic tendencies inherent to *any* political regime: "a representative assembly is to watch and control the government: to throw the light of publicity on its acts; to compel a full exposition and justification of all of them which any one considers questionable; to censure them if found condemnable, and, if the men who compose the government abuse their trust," to "expel them from office."[173] Political participation is integral to non-domination. And indeed, the more we abdicate our participatory role, the less capable and more needy we become, which spirals us into a Tocquevillian abyss: "It approaches as nearly as the organic difference between human beings and other animals admits, to the government of sheep by their shepherd, without anything like so strong an interest as the shepherd has in the thriving condition of the flock. The only security against political slavery, is the check maintained over governors, by the diffusion of intelligence, activity, and public spirit among the governed."[174]

But, beyond that, political participation also prevents the "doing" element of any regime from becoming indolent and lethargic:

> It is not, also, to be forgotten, that the absorption of all the principal ability of the country into the governing body is fatal, sooner or later, to the mental activity and progressiveness of the body itself. Banded together as they are—working a system which, like all systems, necessarily proceeds in a great measure by fixed rules—the official body are under the constant temptation of sinking into indolent routine,

171. Ibid., 433. See also Urbinati, *Mill on Democracy*, 42–47.

172. Varouxakis, "Mill on Democracy Revisited," 460.

173. Mill, *Considerations on Representative Government*, 432–433.

174. Mill, *Principles of Political Economy*, 943–944.

or, if they now and then desert that mill-horse round, of rushing into some half-examined crudity which has struck the fancy of some leading member of the corps: and the sole check to these closely allied, though seemingly opposite, tendencies, the only stimulus which can keep the ability of the body itself up to a high standard, is liability to the watchful criticism of equal ability outside the body. It is indispensable, therefore, that the means should exist, independently of the government, of forming such ability, and furnishing it with the opportunities and experience necessary for a correct judgment of great practical affairs.[175]

This is the institutional parallel to the "dead dogma" concern from *On Liberty*. Just as the truth needs to be "fully, frequently, and fearlessly discussed"[176] in order to conserve its vibrancy and meaning, so, too, must political bodies be fully, frequently, and fearlessly prodded by the citizenry in order to keep them intellectually vigorous and practically responsive. Institutions are in perpetual danger of falling victim to "stagnation and routinization."[177] The tendency for any institution, just like any intellect, is to lose its "vital principle"[178] in the absence of forced innovation and dialogic challenge, and thus to "degenerate into a pedantocracy."[179] Unless the citizenry are ready and willing to be critically aware, and critical, of the activity of their institutions, the worst case scenario will naturally be despotism, but the *best* case scenario will be political enervation and bureaucratic pencil pushing.

In short, Mill has expansive practical reasons for framing popular civic participation as significant. The constitution and preservation of a just society is entirely dependent on the individual's public role: "it is evident, that the only government which can fully satisfy all the exigencies of the social state, is one in which the whole people participate; that any participation, even in the smallest public function, is useful; that the participation should everywhere be as great as the general degree of improvement of the community will allow; and that nothing less can be ultimately desirable, than the admission of all to a share in the sovereign power of the state." Without active engagement, the citizenry dooms itself to some mixture of despotism, ineptness, and lassitude. In order to "secure" good government, the people must be "self-*protecting*" and "self-*dependent*."[180]

175. Mill, *On Liberty*, 308.
176. Ibid., 243.
177. Urbinati, "Many Heads of the Hydra," 84.
178. Mill, *Considerations on Representative Government*, 439.
179. Mill, *On Liberty*, 308.
180. Mill, *Considerations on Representative Government*, 404, 412.

CIVIC HUMANISM

But the other side to Mill's summons to popular civic engagement has to do with individual and social flourishing; what Dale Miller, following Thompson, calls the "educative" aspect of Mill's political theory: "the real heart of the case for the importance of widespread civic participation is the claim that it has tremendous educational value; this is both the more distinctive point and the one on which [Mill] places the greatest emphasis."[181] We saw this general point developed above under the heading *domination as diminution*. But the deepest core of Mill's "educative" defense of a vibrant, participatory democracy is the potential exponential enlargement of our social sensibilities and enjoyments:

> Salutary is the moral part of the instruction afforded by the participation of the private citizen, if even rarely, in public functions. He is called upon, while so engaged, to weigh interests not his own; to be guided, in case of conflicting claims, by another rule than his private partialities; to apply, at every turn, principles and maxims which have for their reason of existence the common good: and he usually finds associated with him in the same work minds more familiarized than his own with these ideas and operations, whose study it will be to supply reasons to his understanding, and stimulation to his feeling for the general interest. He is made to feel himself one of the public, and whatever is for their benefit to be for his benefit. Where this school of public spirit does not exist, scarcely any sense is entertained that private persons, in no eminent social situation, owe any duties to society, except to obey the laws and submit to the government. There is no unselfish sentiment of identification with the public. Every thought or feeling, either of interest or of duty, is absorbed in the individual and in the family. The man never thinks of any collective interest, of any objects to be pursued jointly with others, but only in competition with them, and in some measure at their expense. A neighbour, not being an ally or an associate, since he is never engaged in any common undertaking for joint benefit, is therefore only a rival. Thus even private morality suffers, while public is actually extinct.[182]

This passage captures the crux of Mill's outlook: civic engagement is essential to widening and deepening our social feelings and pleasures, and thus vital to enforcing social morality without resorting to force. The individual

181. Miller, "John Stuart Mill's Civic Liberalism," 91.
182. Mill, *Considerations on Representative Government*, 412.

develops a love for society and the common good by being entrusted with others and the public welfare. Political participation makes the individual "feel that besides the interests which separate him from his fellow-citizens, he has interests which connect him with them, that not only the common weal is his weal, but that it partly depends on his exertions." And what is on the other side of the ledger? A Tocquevillian dystopia: "wherever public spirit is not cultivated by an extensive participation of the people in the business of government in detail," the populace is "mean and slavish,"[183] and "the utmost aspirations of the lawgiver" prove unable to "stretch" further than "making the bulk of the community a flock of sheep innocently nibbling the grass side by side."[184] Civic activity is *the* bulwark against the kind of society that produces "small men."[185]

As many scholars have remarked, though, this picture of a "discursive,"[186] public-spirited democracy looks to be at odds with other things Mill has to say about the nature of democratic life. For instance, Mill seems to suggest that civic engagement, especially discussion on contentious issues, can promote factionalism and division rather than understanding and unity: "I acknowledge that the tendency of all opinions to become sectarian is not cured by the freest discussion, but is often heightened and exacerbated thereby; the truth which ought to have been, but was not, seen, being rejected all the more violently because proclaimed by persons regarded as opponents."[187] However, Mill does not think this problem is intrinsic to political life or dialogue; it is a problem relating to particular historical moments. Indeed, when Mill turns to other examples, the story is quite different: "Notwithstanding the defects of the social system and moral ideas of antiquity, the practice of the dicastery and the ecclesia raised the intellectual standard of an average Athenian citizen far beyond anything of which there is yet an example in any other mass of men, ancient or modern."[188] For Mill, the Athenian polity was a veritable model of public-spirited civic engagement.

The question becomes: what accounts for this stark contrast between one democratic society and another? The key detail, for Mill, is that while civic engagement can be a catalyst for sociality, there already needs to be *some* felt basis for sociality before civic interaction can be anything but an

183. Mill, "De Tocqueville on Democracy in America [II]," 169, *CW* 18.
184. Mill, *Considerations on Representative Government*, 412.
185. Mill, *On Liberty*, 310.
186. Zakaras, "John Stuart Mill, Individuality, and Participatory Democracy," 207.
187. Mill, *On Liberty*, 275.
188. Mill, *Considerations on Representative Government*, 411.

engine of discord; there has to be a seed to water; there must be at least a presumption of "fraternal sympathy with one's fellow citizens."[189] Mill's most explicit treatment of the foundations of a flourishing society comes in his essay "Coleridge," where he lays out three indispensable conditions for a healthy political order:

> First: There has existed . . . a system of *education*, beginning with infancy and continued through life, of which . . . one main and incessant ingredient was *restraining discipline*. To train the human being in the habit, and thence the power, of subordinating his personal impulses and aims, to what were considered the ends of society. . . . And whenever and in proportion as the strictness of the restraining discipline was relaxed, the . . . State became disorganized from within; mutual conflict for selfish ends, neutralized the energies which were required to keep up the contest against natural causes of evil; and the nation, after a longer or briefer interval of progressive decline, became either the slave of a despotism, or the prey of a foreign invader. The second condition of permanent political society has been found to be, the existence, in some form or other, of the feeling of allegiance, or loyalty. . . . The third essential condition of stability in political society is . . . a principle of sympathy, not of hostility; of union, not of separation. . . . We mean, that one part of the community do not consider themselves as foreigners with regard to another part; that they set a value on their connexion; feel that they are one people, that their lot is cast together, that evil to any of their fellow-countrymen is evil to themselves; and do not desire selfishly to free themselves from their share of any common inconvenience by severing the connexion. How strong this feeling was in those ancient commonwealths which attained any durable greatness, everyone knows.[190]

So, first, we need "*restraining discipline*"—this is what turns Mill's barbarians into competent citizens. However, the critical issue facing the society of *On Liberty*—and the reason why its discourse is all-too-often factional and hostile—is found in the source of its "feeling of allegiance, or loyalty," which presumably influences its feeling of social "connexion." What Mill is noticing in real-time in *On Liberty* is that factionalism and hostility are basically *baked into* the status quo. Rather than feeling meaningfully allied or loyal to the polity as a whole, the individual in *On Liberty* feels

189. Miller, "John Stuart Mill's Civic Liberalism," 100.
190. Mill, "Coleridge," 133–135, *CW* 10.

exclusively allied or loyal to "his party, his sect, his church, his class of society."[191] While any normal polity will inevitably be divided along such lines, the trouble, as Mill sees it, is that these loyalties are total and tribal. As such, *there is no* actual society, only a series of interest groups that just so happen to be unstably entangled by the inertia of age-old borders and institutions.

In other words, the question, for Mill, is *not*: does deliberation produce harmony or disharmony? It can do both/either. Rather, the question is: are the members of the polity ultimately *friends*, such that they are wont to disagree without being disagreeable, and to conflict without being conflictual? If so, then the Athenian spirit is possible; if not, then the Hobbesian state of society is the final destination. To fix the problem, Mill does not advocate the revivification of throne and altar. Mill thinks the only thing that either can or ought to unify a modern society is a civic religion; a shared ideal. And this is what Mill is doing in his philosophy: advancing the ideal that he hopes will lay the foundation—the "principles of individual freedom and political and social equality."[192]

The specter of factionalism and creeping selfishness is also why Mill advocates republican policies like public voting: "the duty of voting, like any other public duty, should be performed under the eye and criticism of the public; every one of whom has not only an interest in its performance, but a good title to consider himself wronged if it is performed otherwise than honestly and carefully." Mill wants to give society the power to check our "disposition to use a public function for [our] own interest, pleasure, and caprice."[193] According to Mill, publicity fosters social responsibility, which can, incidentally, foster genuine sociality: "Even the bare fact of having to give an account of their conduct, is a powerful inducement to adhere to conduct of which, at least, some decent account can be given." Conversely, the secret ballot allows the individual to "yield himself up" to his "selfish partialities," "free from all sense of shame."[194] While voting is a political right, the vote ought to be considered a public *trust*; a "matter of duty," which binds the individual to exercise it "according to his best and most conscientious opinion of the public good."[195]

But the concern, then, of course, is that the voter will succumb to the powers that be: dominant factions; influential persons; stigmatizing glares.

191. Mill, *On Liberty*, 230.
192. Mill, "Coleridge," 134.
193. Mill, *Considerations on Representative Government*, 489–490.
194. Mill, "Thoughts on Parliamentary Reform," 335.
195. Mill, *Considerations on Representative Government*, 489.

How can public voting serve its moral function, and how can it allow individuals to "express dissent," if it exposes the individual to "hostile pressure?"[196] However, we must remember, again, that Mill is not theorizing to and for all time, but to and for historical moments. According to Mill, the worry over the danger of publicity is salient only if the powers that be are horizontal *dominī* and thus able to hold their power over the unprotected citizen as an ever-present threat: "But in the more advanced states of modern Europe," the "power of coercing voters has declined and is declining; and bad voting is now less to be apprehended from the influences to which the voter is subject at the hands of others, than from the sinister interests and discreditable feelings which belong to himself, either individually or as a member of a class."[197] If a democratic culture—along with its economic reality—is far enough advanced for the factions on the ground to be checked by either good morals or good laws or norms, then publicity is anodyne and salutary. Indeed, whenever the *individual* is genuinely socially empowered to demand an account from the *majority*, the inverse is unlikely to trouble a Millian democrat.

Regardless, the point is that political participation is, in theory, essential to social flourishing. Mill's critique of an apolitical life is thoroughly Tocquevillian: the individual who fails to venture beyond the threshold of their private life, and who thus fails to become an active citizen, is, to put it bluntly, consigned to a life of atomistic self-seeking, which both stunts and scars the pursuit of the good life. Mill even *compels* us to participate in various ways—we mentioned public voting, but there are also others responsibilities, like the duty "to give evidence in a court of justice."[198] But, to clarify, Mill is consistent here in his anti-paternalism, for such demands are not justified by their relationship to the good life. While it is good for us to serve on juries, we are not so obliged just *because* it is good for us. Rather, we are obliged to serve on juries as a perfect duty; as an obligation of justice. While civic engagement in all its forms enhances the well-being of the individual and society, Mill "never calls for requiring individuals to take on any public function which does not make a fairly direct contribution to preventing harm to others; he never rests the case for compulsory participation entirely upon its educational benefits."[199] It is the hallmark of a Millian idea that what best respects or benefits others also seems to best serve ourselves.

196. Zakaras, "John Stuart Mill, Individuality, and Participatory Democracy," 211.

197. Mill, *Considerations on Representative Government*, 491.

198. Mill, *On Liberty*, 225.

199. Miller, "John Stuart Mill's Civic Liberalism," 111.

CHAPTER FIVE

Other "Isms"

MILL AND HIS CRITICS

... wherever the argument, like a wind, tends, thither must we go.

—PLATO, *REPUBLIC*

IN THIS FINAL CHAPTER, we dig a bit deeper into several elements of Mill's practical philosophy by looking at a few salient criticisms of his thought. By no means is this chapter meant to represent an exhaustive survey of all the concerns one might have with all the various aspects of Mill's practical philosophy. On the contrary, this chapter is an opportunity to meditate on several of the central themes laid out in the preceding chapters by placing them in conversation with certain "big" critiques. Thus, what follows below is a critical reflection on some of the key threads we have seen woven throughout the tapestry of Mill's corpus.

Too Libertarian?

Unlike many liberal-minded modern theorists, but much like his beloved ancients, Mill bases his practical philosophy on an account of the good life, and a rather rich, thick account at that. As we have seen, his theory of happiness, or well-being, is generally Aristotelian in flavor, but also includes important Christian and Romantic ingredients; it is all about virtuous or excellent activity, but with an emphasis on reciprocal sympathy and individual self-realization. Moreover, we can debate Mill's hedonistic credentials, or lack thereof, until the cows come home; but there can be no doubt that his vision of the good life is markedly opposed to many of the dispositions or indulgences that are commonly associated with hedonism—in short, any variety of sensuality that either offends, injures, or starves the higher faculties would be anathema to Mill's competent judge.

And yet, unlike those ancient theorists, but much like his fellow moderns, Mill is fundamentally opposed to having his conception of the good life compelled by law or opinion. *Morals*, yes: Mill's system of justice is meant to be administered by the least draconian, least invasive, most expedient means available. But when it comes to *value*, Mill relies entirely upon individual responsibility first and exhortation from others second. Paradoxically, the very vision of the good life upon which Mill's theory of the good society is founded is not supposed to be directly enforced by society. Of course, we have seen why Mill argues thusly: human flourishing is pluralistic; compulsion induces conformity rather than originality; and to entrust the enforcement of value to society is undoubtedly to surrender it to the forever arbitrary and always contestable "likings and dislikings"[1] of the one, few, or many. In sum, we might say that an impartial mind should reject the enforcement of value precisely for the sake of that value which ought not to be enforced.

However, a devil's advocate could deliver a few remarks here. First, Mill is likely overconfident in the potential for "the uncoerced pursuit of the good," and he likely underestimates the extent to which a society committed to his principles will drift toward "the noncoerced pursuit of the bad."[2] In *On Liberty*, Mill imagines a society in which the tendency toward "self-indulgent" activity is an exception rather than an everyday rule: "But we are now speaking of conduct which, while it does no wrong to others, is supposed to do great harm to the agent himself: and I do not see how those who believe this, can think otherwise than that the example, on the whole, must be more salutary than hurtful, since, if it displays the misconduct, it displays also the painful or degrading consequences which, if the conduct is justly censured, must be supposed to be in all or most cases attendant on it." However, the notion that "self-indulgent" activity will be considered significant or noteworthy enough to be "displayed" (like a black mark on a white canvas), or that society will feel compelled to "censure" such activity (short of treating the individual "like an enemy of society"), or that such activity will not have any sort of "pernicious effect" on others (as the example of "doing wrong to others with impunity" apparently does) is sure to sound rather fanciful to anyone living in a Millian society.[3] As the lived

---

1. Mill, *On Liberty*, 222, *CW* 18.
2. Galston, *Liberal Purposes*, 87.
3. Mill, *On Liberty*, 279, 283.

experience of liberalism has arguably revealed, the human tendency is to elide the distinction between morals and values; that is, people tend to believe or assume that whatever is permissible is also thereby unobjection-able. Hence, the individual in a Millian society tends to believe or assume that as long as you are not "harming" anyone else, your activity must lie beyond ethical reproach; at worst, you can be accused of imprudence. In fact, perversely, what do we find in harm-morality culture other than the move to make an injustice out of extending ethics beyond morals—the move to censure as a "judgmental" enemy anyone who offers supra-moral persua-sions or exhortations?

In addition, Mill is likely overconfident in the potential for chang-ing hearts and souls via mere persuasion or exhortation; and he likely underestimates the extent to which many individuals, having never been habituated to the higher pleasures, or having been habituated to the lower pleasures, will remain blind to the light of the good barring active interfer-ence. Indeed, Mill is arguably guilty here of what Aristotle would regard as a category error between intellectual virtue and moral virtue: the for-mer is acquired via instruction or teaching, whereas the latter is acquired via habituation or practice.[4] Then again, in *Utilitarianism*, Mill *does* say that those who devote themselves to "inferior pleasures" or "sensual indulgences" have generally "become incapable" of aspiring to the higher pleasures.[5] But, if so, then of what practical utility does the Mill of *On Lib-erty* expect persuasion or exhortation to be? Also, the implicit notion that interference is opposed to originality is arguably at odds with the Millian belief that association can often be the seedbed of originality: If habitu-ation via association in *early* life can originate a life devoted to higher activity, then why not habituation via interference in *later* life? Assuming (assuming!) it is well-tailored, what is legal or social interference with vice other than remedial association? Alternatively, what if society interferes with only the *sources* of vice and makes them scarce, such that vice *itself* is not penalized but instead just hard to come by? After all, Mill *already* believes that the purveyors and partakers of certain vices ought to be com-pelled to observe "a certain degree of secrecy and mystery."[6]

And finally, Mill's own *moral* logic would seem to imply that he could have no principled objection to interference with dissolute indul-gences. Consider: the enforcement of justice is, for Mill, fundamental to the

4. See Aristotle, *Nicomachean Ethics*, II.1.
5. Mill, *Utilitarianism*, 212–213, *CW* 10.
6. Mill, *On Liberty*, 297.

well-being of both the individual and society; thus, although moral rules are *always* contestable (the Utilitarian Almanac is open to edits or add-ons!), they still ought to be enforced as they currently are. However, for Mill, the avoidance of habitual vice is *also* fundamental to the well-being of both the individual and society: for the individual, vice is the dissolution of happiness itself; and for society, each descent into vice is one more person who is *not* "more" but *less* "valuable to himself" and thus *not* "more" but *less* capable of being "valuable to others." Naturally, as with morals, what *counts* as vice ought to be subject to contestation. And yet, if *morals* should be enforced anyway, given their vital significance, then why not the good as well, or at least abstention from the bad?

Mill cannot say that paternalism is *intrinsically* unjust here, for as he admits in one of his more Socratic moments, the descent into vice is *not* strictly *voluntary*,[7] and thus "the greater good of human freedom" is not *really* at stake. Indeed, as we saw in chapter 3, the dissipated individual can be interpreted as being in the immaturity of their faculties. Moreover, the legal or social conquest of vice need not even be understood as paternalistic; for just as a single lie, while perhaps inconsequential by itself, is, as a rule, antisocial—that is, not merely self-regarding but self-*indulgent* or *selfish*—so, too, is any instance of vice. At least Mill thinks so: "I fully admit that the mischief which a person does to himself may seriously affect, both through their sympathies and their interests, those nearly connected with him, and in a minor degree, society at large." However, instead of turning to the elephant in the room, Mill blames "society" for failing to educate these "grown persons" properly.[8] But why is "society" *as a whole* to blame rather than just the family, the mayor, the school? Why must society allow the failings of these parties to dominate the lives of their neglected charges?

All of these points are meant to provide a context and feel for what is *the* classic conservative critique of Mill: the accusation that he is *too libertarian*; that, by hook or by crook, he sophistically evades the just rationale and general need for legal or social interference with debased or ignoble activity. This is one of the key contentions of Mill's greatest critic, Sir James Fitzjames Stephen, who "believed that society *can* and *should* legislate morality; the failure to do so would lead to intemperance, debauchery, torpor, and anarchy."[9] With a caustic wit and satirical flair,

7. Mill, *Utilitarianism*, 212–213.
8. Mill, *On Liberty*, 281–282.
9. Pullam, "Victorian Case for Ordered Liberty."

Stephen attacked and mocked Mill relentlessly for his impossibly circumspect attitude toward *all* so-called experiments in living:

> How can the State or the public be competent to determine any question whatever if it is not competent to decide that gross vice is a bad thing? I do not think the State ought to stand bandying compliments with pimps. "Without offence to your better judgment, dear sir, and without presuming to set up my opinion against yours, I beg to observe that I am entitled for certain purposes to treat the question whether your views of life are right as one which admits of two opinions. I am far from expressing absolute condemnation of an experiment in living from which I dissent (I am sure that mere dissent will not offend a person of your liberality of sentiment), but still I am compelled to observe that you are not altogether unbiassed by personal considerations in the choice of the course of life which you have adopted (no doubt for reasons which appear to you satisfactory, though they do not convince me). I venture, accordingly, though with the greatest deference, to call upon you not to exercise your profession; at least I am not indisposed to think that I may, upon full consideration, feel myself compelled to do so." My feeling is that if society gets its grip on the collar of such a fellow it should say to him, "You dirty rascal, it may be a question whether you should be suffered to remain in your native filth untouched, or whether my opinion about you should be printed by the lash on your bare back. That question will be determined without the smallest reference to your wishes or feelings; but as to the nature of my opinion about you, there can be no question at all."[10]

If Mill is Socrates here, then Stephen is clearly channeling Aristophanes. And the biting, comic absurdity of this exchange, along with its barbed finale, underscores a perennial conservative argument; namely, that persuasion or exhortation will not cut the mustard (will appear almost *silly* in its impotence) *unless* it is denouncing, shaming, stigmatizing— in short, all the things Mill appears to rebuff. Now, true conservatives will enjoin us to hate the sin but love the sinner; and they will argue that these sanctions ought to be rooted not in ad hominem attacks (we might pardon Stephen for his temper), but in the force and intensity of our ethical criticism. And yet, the concern remains: without the legal or social capacity to *reprimand* individuals, the slope to Sin City will be paved and greased.

10. Stephen, *Liberty, Equality, Fraternity*, 84–85.

Depending on your philosophical, political, or religious bearings, you will find yourself at this point either rolling your eyes, nodding vigorously, or something in between. But, regardless, as an interpretive matter, this is a profound critique; for if Mill is sure of *anything*, it is the fact that there exists a *higher* and a *lower* "manner of existence."[11] Thus, it becomes increasingly unclear as we consider the observations above why Mill's position did not actually gravitate *more* toward Stephen's frame of mind.

Before taking up this challenge directly, it should be said that the specter of hedonistic vice was clearly not on Mill's mind or agenda while writing *On Liberty*. Those unfortunate beings who just so happen to lead dissolute or indolent lives play an almost intrusive role in the essay; they pester Mill like a nuisance to be ignored. Indeed, when Mill talks about experiments in living, he is not thinking about Stephen's "pimp." Mill has in mind the avant-garde, the innovator, the unbound mind, the eccentric soul. He is talking about the Socratic gadfly, the fool for Christ, the Romantic hero. He is saying, "Attention society: do not kill Socrates; do not silence Galileo; do not imprison Oscar Wilde." For every Galileo, there is a Copernicus who speaks only in death; and for every Copernicus, there is an unknown genius who never spoke at all. More generally, Mill is also referring to our distinctive intellects and characters, and how each individual is not only "born either a Platonist or an Aristotelian," or "either a Benthamite or a Coleridgian," but also born inimitably and essentially *an individual*.[12] All this is to say that *nothing* in the observations above undercuts the argument that Mill lays out in *On Liberty* or the rest of his corpus. Rather, it merely adds (or forces) an inquiry that Mill would rather brush aside: should the children-barbarian exception *also* apply to obdurate vice?

In response, the best we can do is to offer a series of counter-considerations. So, first, we might ask: what counts as vice? As we saw in chapter 2, Mill argues that motivation, or internality, is extrinsic to the morality or immorality of an action—theft, deceit, or murder is contrary to the commonweal irrespective of why it was done; thus, while we might have a sympathetic reason for acting unjustly, the injustice of our action is still discernable. However, the same is not true of value or disvalue: internality, and context, is essential to appreciating the desirability or lack thereof of many activities. For instance, I have little doubt that Stephen would be one to grab "pot-smoking hippies" by the scruff of the neck. But

---

11. Mill, *Utilitarianism*, 211.
12. Mill, "Coleridge," 121, *CW* 10.

what about those who smoke pot responsibly for social or recreational purposes? And what about those who smoke pot and then compose *Rubber Soul*? Do we *really* want to forfeit any of the Beatles' albums *just* to keep them sober? Sure, there will exist shiftless potheads, and particular harms may arise from particular uses of pot, as from any one of a thousand sources. But what better way to separate the wheat from the chaff, while also preserving "the greater good of human freedom," than to follow Mill's counsel: target actual harm, not alleged vice.

Furthermore, those activities, desires, or lifestyles that are *truly* opposed to human flourishing are arguably those that are more likely than not to involve general harmful tendencies—meaning that genuine vice tends to generate a legitimate pretext for legal or social interference. For instance, there is a long-standing, rich scholarly debate as to whether or not Millian principles would have us censor or regulate pornography. First, there is the question of whether or not pornography even counts as freedom of speech or expression on Millian grounds. But, with respect to our present inquiry, there is also the question of pornography's general harmful tendencies, including and especially harm to women.[13] Again, the idea here is that our *non*moral disapproval will often be buttressed doubly so by perceptible harms, and thus that by following Mill, we will be able to separate the wheat from the chaff while also being cautious with the exercise of power.

An obvious retort: does this mean that society must *wait* for harms to emerge before taking action? Well, in one sense, *yes*: to give prejudiced, fallible, and corruptible human beings the power to determine what is going to be harmful a priori is to grant them the power to interfere with *anything*—an insupportable result. But, in another sense, *no*: just as society does not have to wait around for rocketing traffic fatalities before instituting traffic laws, society does not have to dillydally before introducing whatever laws or policies the Utilitarian Almanac would propose as being essential to the general good. Of course, the question is: what does, or what should, the Utilitarian Almanac say? And people can disagree about this, which is why we need just procedures for settling these disputes.

In addition, we can always fall back upon the classic Millian observations that, at the individual level, societal interference is prone to be misapplied or ineffectual; to deprive individuals of their self-reliance; to yield unintended and even disastrous consequences; and to be abused by

13. See McGlynn and Ward, "Would John Stuart Mill Have Regulated Pornography?," 500–522; and Dyzenhaus, "John Stuart Mill and the Harm of Pornography," 534–551.

prejudiced, fallible, and corruptible persons or factions. Besides, who *are* these noble, wise guardians of virtue, and what makes us think they will inevitably hold sway? And what makes us think that interference is an all-purpose tool, when the ebb, flow, and flux of human affairs is influenced by forces far too complex to grasp, let alone to combat or harness? What quicker way is there to exhaust a public morality than to couple it with coercion? Why not take stock of the long arc of history and put our faith in the principles of rediscovery and renewal? What better path is there to take for a wise, humble individual than to plant and nurture the seeds of what they dearly hold to be good and virtuous whenever and wherever they can, starting at the personal, local level, and growing from there?

And regardless, the fact is that Mill's edict against disciplining vice is actually quite limited in scope. Remember: if we *accept* or *consent* to interference then Mill has no quarrel. His quarrel is only with "the despotism of custom,"[14] where society produces a kind of irrationality (an inability to give and take reasons) in its dominated subjects; and where society at large publicly stamps or ostracizes a luckless dissenter for stepping out of line. In other words, Stephen's satire is off base: Mill would not object prima facie to free citizens, on terms of equality, pillorying or belittling one another. After all, it was *Mill* who stooped to branding his Conservative Party colleagues "stupid."[15] And he certainly would not object to a sister reprimanding her brother, or to a friend rebuking his friend, or to a rabbi chastising a congregant. In such cases, it is easy to see how verbal castigation could be received, or even *embraced*, as natural to the relationship. Interference, too: when my brother covertly robs my home of sweets to nudge me toward better dieting, I do not chuck *On Liberty* at him; in fact, I chuckle and nod—because he is my brother. Maybe you would be angry in this situation (indeed, he even filches my favorite pastries); but hopefully there are analogous persons in your own life—familial, collegial, civic, congregational—who are implicitly authorized to "give you hell," or worse, for speaking or behaving poorly. *This* is most, if not *all*, of what goes into *truly* promoting virtue or preventing vice, and into persuading or dissuading any sayings or doings that we regard as desirable or undesirable. Once this is *not* happening—that is, once society *at large* would have to intervene—there will typically be deeper, more pressing concerns afoot.

14. Mill, *On Liberty*, 272–273.
15. Mill, "Representation of the People," 85, *CW* 28.

Too Progressive?

Now, ironically, the *other* main conservative critique of Mill is that he is *too progressive*. The general theme of this reading is that Mill was entirely antagonistic to all traditional—especially religious, particularly Christian—beliefs and practices, and that he looked forward to a time when society would shuffle off this dogmatic coil; when society would adopt Comte's Religion of Humanity as its sacred touchstone and become in everything progressive and flawlessly rational. To this end, so the reading goes, Mill wanted elites eventually to indoctrinate the masses in Utilitarianism and uproot all traces of Judeo-Christianity. In short, Mill is said to exemplify a "doctrinaire secularism."[16]

To begin, the evidence for Mill's authoritarian progressivism is scant at best, and the evidence that is typically cited is generally misinterpreted. For instance, in his classic revisionist criticism, Joseph Hamburger argues that despite the scholarly consensus to the contrary, Mill does *not* give absolute protection to self-regarding activity—far from it:

> Yet these interpretations of Mill's position are not compatible with the following statement in chapter four of *On Liberty*: "*A person may suffer very severe penalties at the hands of others, for faults which directly concern only himself*" (278; emphasis added). . . . Mill went on to describe both the kind of conduct that would suffer very severe penalties and the character of those penalties. The objectionable conduct, Mill explained in chapter four, reflected the "lowness or depravation of taste" of "inferior" persons (278). The consequences they faced also were clear: they would become "necessarily and *properly* a subject of distaste, or, in extreme cases, even of contempt" (278; emphasis added). Distaste and contempt are instruments of control, and the persons exposed to them would find their liberty threatened and reduced.[17]

For starters, Hamburger is a tad overeager in his interpretation of Mill's meaning: the "inferior" persons mentioned are "inferior" not for any want of secular rationalism, but rather for exhibiting that "degree of folly" that makes for "a fool"—the same "fool" who, in *Utilitarianism*, is insensible to the higher pleasures. Indeed, in the lines cited, Mill is really just making a commonsensical point: individuals can exhibit qualities that "compel" either "admiration" or "the opposite of admiration." And more importantly,

---

16. Gregg, "John Stuart Mill's Intolerant Faith."

17. Hamburger, *John Stuart Mill on Liberty and Control*, 8. Pages correspond to *CW* 18.

the "severe penalties" that Mill alludes to are *not* "instruments of control," but "the natural, and, as it were, the spontaneous consequences of the faults themselves." Far from being a coercive weapon, what Mill has in mind is the inexorable price that every recess field ball hog or hot dog will ineludibly pay; namely, the loss of affection, attention, or association that naturally flows from an inability or unwillingness to conduct oneself in a properly socialized manner: "A person who shows rashness, obstinacy, self-conceit—who cannot live within moderate means—who cannot restrain himself from hurtful indulgences—who pursues animal pleasures at the expense of those of feeling and intellect—must expect to be lowered in the opinion of others, and to have a less share of their favourable sentiments." Self-regarding activity is still perfectly safe: the one boy is free to be a ball hog, but the other boys are free to get another ball and leave him to shoot hoops alone; he will have "no right to complain."[18]

To digress for a moment, one genuine concern here for a Millian is the fact that some individuals may be faced with these "spontaneous consequences" not as a natural reaction to any social faults or obvious foolishness of theirs, but simply as a result of being unconventional, eccentric, or unsatisfactory in a social environment where people are freely exercising their *own* basic liberties, in particular to associate with others *or not*:

> An individual can contribute to informal social pressure on others merely by making quotidian decisions about her own life—exercising her own freedom of speech or association. Decisions to associate in some social circles, innocuous in themselves, can communicate judgment of those excluded. Societal patterns of socialization can effectively isolate and marginalize some in reliable ways. Such a prospect may function as effectively as the threat of intentional sanction to exact conformity. Reliable patterns in who is recognized and esteemed (and who is left out of such recognition) can similarly function as a strong social pressure. Such patterns do not need to be maliciously or even intentionally created in order to function in this manner. Associational choices, expression of dislike, or patterns of approbation that reward conformity can create cultures in which people internalize social norms.[19]

According to Mill, our sociality is more than just our sympathy and altruism *for* others; it is also our basic need to be approved of and included *by* others. Individuals, by and large, are desperately attached to being well

18. Mill, *On Liberty*, 278.
19. Threet, "Mill's Social Pressure Puzzle," 548.

thought of and admired by their fellows: "Through all departments of human affairs, regard for the sentiments of our fellow-creatures is in one shape or other, in nearly all characters, the pervading motive."[20] In short, making oneself attractive to one's community of interest is, for most, a tremendously powerful drive. Therefore, perhaps the contrast between social interference (like stigma) and informal social pressure—whereby individuals are, say, "marginalized and isolated due to patterns of socialization"—is a distinction without a difference. This triggers what Dan Threet labels the *social pressure puzzle*: "The project of limiting the authority of society over the individual seems to require constraints in the very domain in which we are concerned to liberate individuals."[21]

Yet, barring an unfeasible (and insane) form of despotic control, nothing is going to change the fact that people always "like in crowds."[22] What Mill is attempting to change, via moral exhortation, is the suffocating, stultifying culture of social oppression—of majority tyranny—in which even most "reasonably independent" persons "feel it necessary to hide their opinions and conform." Losing friends or companions as a product of our individuality is nothing to minimize or undervalue; but it is another thing entirely for these fair-weather friends to turn around and actively participate in stigmatizing, harassing, or ostracizing us. And besides, the social cost imposed by freedom of association is not *final*: while individuals can be disliked or spurned in a Millian society "for their unusual sex lives, gender presentations, religious convictions, unpopular opinions, dissent from norms of propriety, and other choices," these individuals will be far more likely to find other like-minded persons, who, given the reduced threat of actual social interference, will be far more likely to express themselves in kind; and consequently, these individuals, unified and concentrated, might be able to reach back into the general community from a position of greater strength.[23]

Returning to Hamburger, he also perceives in Mill an authoritarian desire "to promote a consensus of enlarged duties, and with this consensus, stifle debate." However, Mill's drive for moral consensus on issues like "gender inequality" is intended to be the product of the exact kind of arguments and testimony that characterizes any good, liberal politics: "Mill believes that society could 'advance' to moral agreements about important matters, but the new consensus does not mean that it cannot

20. Mill, "Utility of Religion," 411, *CW* 10.
21. Threet, "Mill's Social Pressure Puzzle," 549, 558.
22. Mill, *On Liberty*, 265.
23. Threet, "Mill's Social Pressure Puzzle," 561, 558.

be disputed."[24] To be sure, Mill had his points of view, and plenty of them; and perhaps he would have "liked" others to be Utilitarians of his persuasion. But this describes *any* political philosopher with respect to *any* of their basic beliefs; and this certainly does not mean that Mill was ready to exert authoritarian coercion or control to promote his beliefs or agenda. Quite the contrary, apropos his own practical philosophy: "Mill's chief concern is to guard against indoctrination."[25]

The most popular argument for Hamburger, though, centers on Mill's apparent devotion to Comte's Religion of Humanity, and Mill's alleged desire to uproot Judeo-Christianity and install Comte's humanocentric spirituality in its place. As Maurice Cowling writes,

> [Mill] may be accused of more than a touch of something resembling [Comte's] moral totalitarianism. His emphasis on social cohesion and moral consensus at all periods of his life was of the greatest consequence; whilst commitment to elevate character and make moral reasoning self-critical leaves less room for variegated human development than some writers have imagined. . . . Mill's doctrine was liberal: but his liberalism was neither comprehensive nor libertarian: it attempted dogmatically to erode the assumptions on which competing doctrines were based. One competing doctrine was Christianity: in Mill's hands, Liberalism was not compatible with it.[26]

Certainly, Mill was, at core, a secular humanist: he believed in progressing toward a society that combined the best of Enlightenment rationality with the best of humanity's sentimental, aesthetic, imaginative wisdom; and he believed that in a good, liberal order, a good, "liberal education"[27] should be the lot and right of all. And while Mill was in certain ways admiring of Comte's Religion of Humanity, he was profoundly critical of it as well. Indeed, Mill dubbed it "liberticide"[28] and thus took pains to develop his *own* version of it, in which an impartial balance is struck between individuality and sociality. While acknowledging that Mill allows for nonaltruistic motives, Cowling reads Mill's call for total impartiality as an enforceable law to the effect that all actions must be geared toward maximizing the aggregate happiness.[29] But this is wrong: total impartiality means that we

24. Tercheck, "Limits of Mill's Tolerance," 584.
25. Finlay, "Mill on Education and Schooling," 510.
26. Cowling, *Mill and Liberalism*, xlviii–il.
27. Mill, "Inaugural Address Delivered to the University of St. Andrews," passim, *CW* 21.
28. Mill, "To Harriet Mill," 294, *CW* 14.
29. See Cowling, *Mill and Liberalism*, 37–39.

must abide by the Utilitarian Almanac, which means that we must obey those moral rules that prohibit injustice. Mill's Utilitarian creed smacks of no more "totalitarianism" than does Locke's Law of Nature. Most of Mill's moral rules will be age-old edicts à la Hume; and any new entries or alterations to the Almanac will have to be codified via argument and persuasion.

But, second, Mill is not opposed or hostile to Christianity; rather, he is opposed or hostile to *dogmatism*, and to dogmatism *of all kinds*. In "Civilization," we find Mill advocating the liberalization of the university system:

> Are these the places of education which are to send forth minds capable of maintaining a victorious struggle with the debilitating influences of the age, and strengthening the weaker side of Civilization by the support of a higher Cultivation? This, however, is what we require from these institutions; or, in their default, from others which should take their place. And the very first step towards their reform should be to unsectarianize them wholly—not by the paltry measure of allowing Dissenters to come and be taught orthodox sectarianism, but by putting an end to sectarian teaching altogether. The principle itself of dogmatic religion, dogmatic morality, dogmatic philosophy, is what requires to be rooted out; not any particular manifestation of that principle.[30]

Dogmatism, for Mill, is the tendency to induce *irrational* belief, that is, to produce religious, moral, or philosophical souls who are incapable of *deliberating* about what they believe: "Teaching should not be in the spirit of dogmatism, but in that of enquiry. The pupil should not be addressed as if his religion had been chosen for him, but as one who will have to choose it for himself."[31] Did Mill see a conflict between his philosophy and *dogmatic* Christianity? Most definitely. Does this mean that Mill wanted to combat Christianity *itself* or see it expunged from the world? Nothing could be further from the truth, as is beautifully documented in Timothy Larsen's biography of Mill, a mediation on the myriad ways in which Mill's not-so-secular life was, in fact, saturated with Christianity and theism: in his most devoted friendships; in his closest family ties; in his personal habits; in many of his most cherished, impactful readings; and, indeed, in his own mature beliefs.[32] Mill was wont to spout off snide remarks about

30. Mill, "Civilization," 143–144, *CW* 18.
31. Mill, "Inaugural Address Delivered to the University of St. Andrews," 249–250.
32. Larsen, *John Stuart Mill*, passim.

religion; he imagined Christianity might naturally fade away; and he was keen to critique Christian theology, as he often did in dialogue with his best friend and "staunch Churchman,"[33] John Sterling. But it would be taking liberties to say that Mill was looking to *hasten* Christianity's demise, or that he would not shed tears at its passing.

Mill's general attitude is that of a secular thinker (*not* "irreligious," just "not religious") who is perfectly willing to have religious beliefs and practices flourish separately from, but alongside, the institutions of the liberal order. For example, public education "must be education for all" and thus "purely secular,"[34] and private education must be subject to "systems of inspection and examination that promote quality."[35] But, beyond that, Mill believes that "different religious denominations should be left to organize [their] teaching as they please" on the "voluntary principle."[36] In education, as in everything else, Mill's attitude was one of moderation: we must provide a good, "liberal education" to everyone, but we must also prevent the state from wielding centralized, despotic power. As Alan Ryan says, "Some continental countries forbade private citizens to set up schools; Mill was emphatic that this was liberticide. The state's role was to make parents do their duty, and to exercise a supervisory role to ensure that schools and teachers are of an adequate quality."[37]

What little explicit guidance *On Liberty* provides bolsters this gentler narrative. Mill cites religious liberty as the first and (as of then) *only* case of liberal justice "in which the higher ground has been taken on principle and maintained with consistency, by any but an individual here and there." Moreover, given his remarks on the "tyranny" of crusading against religious communities, we might assume that Mill would be generally disinclined to interfere with private religious practices. And while Mill defends compulsory education, he also advocates keeping schooling at the most local level possible for the sake of that "diversity in opinions and modes of conduct"—including, presumably, various religious "sects"—that only "diversity of education" can produce.[38] True, this evidence for Mill's religious tolerance is rather thin—just like the evidence for his intolerance. Mill did not *ignore* religious liberty, but we might conclude that he just

33. Ibid., 58.
34. Mill, "Secular Education," *CW* 28, 4.
35. Finlay, "Mill on Education and Schooling," 511.
36. Mill, "To Sir Charles Wentworth Dilke," 1732, *CW* 17.
37. Ryan, "J. S. Mill on Education," 662.
38. Mill, *On Liberty*, 302.

"wasn't greatly interested in religious freedom."[39] In short, he saw religion like any other philosophy, creed, doctrine, ethos, or sentiment: it is protected by justice insofar as its followers are willing to extend the same justice to others.

One conservative charge that could stick is that Mill amplified an unhealthy zeal for reform or innovation that was certain eventually to rid itself of *his* immersion in and respect for the past. For instance, Mill is a political secularist; but he *also* believes that "the Constitution and Church of England, and the religious opinions and political maxims professed by their supporters, are not mere frauds, nor sheer nonsense—[they] have not been got up originally, and all along maintained, for the sole purpose of picking people's pockets; without aiming at, or being found conducive to, any honest end during the whole process."[40] In a Coleridgian spirit, Mill thinks that progress is not truly progressive if it is not marked, or even slowed or limited, by an awareness of and appreciation for the vital *meaning* of old things. Similarly, Mill is a Romantic individualist; but he *also* wants society to pass down its precious wisdom and customs. According to Patrick Deneen, Mill thinks that to "follow custom was to be fundamentally unreflective and mentally stagnant." Now, what Mill *actually* thinks is that to "follow custom" *unreflectively* and *stagnantly* is "to be fundamentally unreflective and mentally stagnant." However, what Deneen is *really* targeting is the ways in which society "has been transformed along Millian lines," and a conservative reader might indeed fault Mill for expecting the world that *On Liberty* birthed to be as nuanced as its author.[41]

Too Conservative?

And yet, to others, any lack of progressive zeal for marshaling the power of law or opinion against certain (illiberal?) elements of society should actually be regarded as an oversight or shortcoming. To take Millian liberalism seriously, one might say, is to allow legal or social interference, at least in principle, with whatever undermines individual originality. For the sake of clarity, let us narrow our discussion down to an all-purpose test case: what possible reason could there be for society to give parents the prerogative to cramp, kink, or color the free development of children by raising them to believe certain truths and value certain goods? True, as Mill argues,

39. George, "John Stuart Mill and John Henry Newman on Liberty and Conscience," 42.
40. Mill, "Coleridge," 146.
41. Deneen, *Why Liberalism Failed*, 145–146.

children ought to be governed paternalistically; but this power need only extend to readying them for lives as good Millian liberals. Should parental paternalism *also* involve the (arbitrary?) power to transmit special beliefs or values to children, especially insofar as these beliefs or values may not even cohere perfectly with the precepts of Millian liberalism? Why should children be formed for *anything* other than a life spent exercising the "power of self-formation"?[42]

After all, Mill is adamant about how he thinks parents ought to instruct their children about the less definite, more contestable topics, like religion:

> I do not think that there should be any *authoritative* teaching at all on such subjects. I think parents ought to point out to their children when the children begin to question them, or to make observations of their own, the various opinions on such subjects, & what the parents themselves think the most powerful reasons for & against. Then, if the parents show a strong feeling of the importance of truth, & also of the difficulty of attaining it, it seems to me that young people's minds will be sufficiently prepared to regard popular opinion or the opinions of those about them with respectful tolerance, & may be safely left to form definite conclusions in the course of mature life.[43]

Open, probing, unsure, reflective; but eventually, albeit cautiously, settled and confident—an inquiring Socrates in every cradle and a judicious Plato in every carriage: *that* is Mill's model of the well-developed soul. Why, then, should society abide or tolerate the absorption by children of particular doctrines, traditions, or religions? Why not commission society to replace any purportedly undesirable, illiberal influences with desirable, liberal influences? If the "uncultivated cannot be competent judges of cultivation," and if those "who most need to be made wiser and better, usually desire it least," then why ought society to stomach those parents who are deemed to be uncultivated or unwise?[44]

The first, and most important, thing to note is that, for Mill, what we might dub our parental inheritance (or, thinking more broadly, our communal inheritance) is not strictly incompatible with individual originality. Again, the key word in the passage above is *"authoritative."* When it comes to our inheritance, the only *sworn* enemy of individual originality is the parental-communal effort to induce unthinking, dogmatic,

---

42. Mill, *System of Logic*, 842, *CW* 8.
43. Mill, "To Charles Friend," 1469, *CW* 16.
44. Mill, *Principles of Political Economy*, 947, *CW* 3.

automaton-like conformity, which would mean that our conception of the truth or the good is "doing nothing for [our] mind or heart, except standing sentinel over them to keep them vacant."[45] Authoritative teaching is the effort to make us "weak and orthodox" rather than "strong with freedom of thought."[46] Just as a man can be treated as morally free insofar as "his habits or his temptations are not his masters, but he theirs: who even in yielding to them knows that he could resist,"[47] he can be thought to possess the "power of self-formation" insofar as he can reflect critically on his beliefs and values, and insofar as further experience or deliberation could alter his mind or move his heart. In short, there is no *intrinsic* issue in being raised a *this* or *that* as long as you become a *thinking* this or *rational* that—as long as your beliefs and values are not held to be "more important than truth."[48]

Having thus softened this concern, we can address inheritance anew and clearly see that there are several prudential reflections that strongly advise against any tendency toward interference with this parental-communal influence. The first, and fatal, concern is the exercise of power that such oversight and intervention would make necessary. What we are dealing with here is the germ of a totalitarian nightmare. The powers that be would be authorized to invigilate not only the family but every aspect of society. Also, the levers of power would need to be pulled *only* by the enlightened "clerisy"[49] that Cowling warns of: what would or could guarantee this, and what would or could prevent these guardians (and *who* are they?) from becoming frighteningly corrupt and vindictive, is a question for dystopian dreamers.

Moreover, the "heavy-handed" nature of interference is unlikely to be the ideal or most efficient or enduring way to affect those parties who hold or inherit either incoherent or undesirable beliefs or practices: "More positive and subtle approaches, such as the provision of attractive alternatives or incentives, are more in keeping with the spirit of liberal pluralism and may well be more effective in any case."[50] By contrast, the preservation of an open society, in which families and communities are at liberty to act spontaneously (yet justly) within their natural and respective spheres of influence, is probably the most reliable way to strain or dilute those

45. Mill, *On Liberty*, 248.
46. Mill, "Whewell on Moral Philosophy," 168, *CW* 10.
47. Mill, *System of Logic*, 841.
48. Mill, "Whewell on Moral Philosophy," 168.
49. Cowling, *Mill and Liberalism*, chap. 6.
50. Crowder, "Two Concepts of Liberal Pluralism," 142.

influences that are *truly* dogmatic, for their continued potency typically depends precisely on the kind of institutionalized intolerance that society would be forced to exercise in order to hinder their continued transmission.

And finally, there is nothing more natural, or that sparks deeper passion, than the parental-communal desire to convey cherished beliefs or values to each succeeding generation. Thus, the societal effort to secure a starkly Millian upbringing to everyone—that is, the attempt to thwart the cultivation of anything other than an initial, high-minded agnosticism on contentious, debatable issues—is certain to be regarded as an insufferable intrusion into the parental-communal sphere, and will doubtless become a flash point that endangers the very survival of the ethos and culture that Mill would see prevail in society at large. Liberal society relies for its stability and vitality on what Rawls labels an *overlapping consensus*, where each citizen, representing a particular conception of the truth or the good (or *comprehensive doctrine*), has prepotent reasons internal to their own viewpoint to support the basic norms and institutions of the liberal order.[51] Of course, Mill's practical philosophy *is* a comprehensive doctrine; yet, as we have seen, the overlapping consensus upon which its realization and success hinges depends on it not always *acting* like one.

Again, those are all *prudential* reasons. However, what I want to do now is to offer several *principled* reasons (all to varying degrees inspired by Mill) as to why society ought not to interfere (pro tanto) with our parental-communal inheritance. The first one comes out of *On Liberty*. Having just proclaimed Humboldt's doctrine of individuality, Mill then rebalances the scale: "On the other hand, it would be absurd to pretend that people ought to live as if nothing whatever had been known in the world before they came into it; as if experience had as yet done nothing towards showing that one mode of existence, or of conduct, is preferable to another. Nobody denies that people should be so taught and trained in youth, as to know and benefit by the ascertained results of human experience." But this just begs the question: *What* experience? According to *whom*? Which "traditions and customs" are we talking about?[52] In a pluralistic society, an indefinite plurality of answers will be given to the question: what beliefs or practices, beyond the rudimentary ones, can we ascertain as truthful or valuable given the long history of human experience and deliberation? And thus, in a pluralistic society, there will be an

51. See Rawls, *Political Liberalism*, II.4.
52. Mill, *On Liberty*, 262.

indefinite plurality of fallible but legitimate theories as to the nature and content of the supplementary teaching and training that children ought to receive.

Moreover, Mill is explicit in saying that certain desirable aspects of human nature, like our capacity for sympathy and altruism, while not innate, are natural, and thus ought to be cultivated via association or other educative approaches. He also has a positive vision for what education should ultimately produce: "Whatever it teaches, it should teach as penetrated by a sense of duty; it should present all knowledge as chiefly a means to worthiness of life, given for the double purpose of making each of us practically useful to his fellow-creatures, and of elevating the character of the species itself, exalting and dignifying our nature."[53] But, again, all this just begs the question: What *other* desirable aspects of human nature—what virtues or qualities—are likewise not innate but natural, and thus require cultivation? And what particular beliefs, doctrines, values, or practices should be encouraged as "exalting and dignifying our nature"? As before, there is bound to be a multiplicity of valid responses.

Similarly, Mill says that certain characteristics or dispositions—such as the "executive" virtues of self-discipline and self-control—are constitutive of what it means to be an autonomous, self-forming individual: "none but a person of confirmed virtue is completely free."[54] But, once more, this just begs the question: what *else* might be integral to a person being "completely free"? There are myriad philosophies and traditions that each offer their own distinctive understanding of what personal freedom involves and demands. Mill, for his part, affirms what ought to be foundational to *any* theory of personal freedom: the capacity to reflect critically, act intentionally, and overcome impulse or indolence. However, it is thus an open question as to what might *also* be required: A particular anthropology? Sociology? Psychology? Theology? Phenomenology? A particular account of practical reason? The will or the soul? Human history? Human consciousness?

But, with all that, we might ask: why, then, does Mill not make such observations explicitly? Well, notice that in discussing each "principled" case, Mill is narrowly focused on what is essential to his practical philosophy: first, what he calls the "results of human experience" probably refers to general rules of prudence, and perhaps to the qualitative superiority of the higher pleasures; second, he invokes association because it

53. Mill, "Inaugural Address Delivered to the University of St. Andrews," 248.
54. Mill, *System of Logic*, 841.

is needed to awaken and foster our affinity for social life and capacity for moral action; and third, he outlines those basic attributes of freedom that are vital to protecting us from despots, both internal and external. Thus, we might surmise that Mill's attention is simply confined to the functioning and flourishing of the liberal order, which, presumably, ought to be receptive to "social pluralism and parental freedom"[55] as long as they neither advocate harm nor inescapably cut people off from the pluralism of the wider society, which, for Mill, is *the* great liberating antidote for dogmatists of all persuasions. Obviously, the public square cannot *eliminate* dogmatism; but, again, dogmatism cannot be targeted in the home or community via legal or social interference without flouting Nietzsche's warning: "Whoever fights with monsters should see to it that in the process he does not become a monster."[56]

Too Communitarian?

In chapter 3 of *Utilitarianism*, Mill tackles a perennial inquiry: "What is [the] sanction [of morality]? what are the motives to obey it? or more specifically, what is the source of its obligation? whence does it derive its binding force?"[57] In short, the question is: *Why be moral?* What is Mill's account of moral motivation?

Apart from the sanctions of "legislation and religion," Bentham locates the moral motive in what *he* imagines to be the *egoistic* pleasures of sociality: "The only interests which a man at all times and upon all occasions is sure to find *adequate* motives for consulting, are his own. Notwithstanding this, there are no occasions in which a man has not some motives for consulting the happiness of other men. In the first place, he has, on all occasions, the purely social motive of sympathy or benevolence: in the next place, he has, on most occasions, the semisocial motives of love of amity and love of reputation."[58] As I remarked in chapter 1, it was *the* educative project of the Philosophical Radicals to establish an indissoluble association between the expected happiness of individuals and the general happiness.

As far as this goes, Mill agrees: "The whole force therefore of external reward and punishment, whether physical or moral, and whether proceeding from God or from our fellow men . . . become available to enforce the utilitarian morality, in proportion as that morality is recognised; and

55. Baum, "J. S. Mill on Freedom and Power," 208n62.
56. Nietzsche, *Beyond Good and Evil*, §146.
57. Mill, *Utilitarianism*, 227.
58. Bentham, *Principles of Morals and Legislation*, 143–144, W 1.

the more powerfully, the more the appliances of education and general cultivation are bent to the purpose." Mill accepts carrots and sticks, with their (limited) power of association, as a first and last resort. But he also expects many people to act morally out of a nonegoistic altruism. And usually, these motives work in tandem: "the smallest germs of the feeling are laid hold of and nourished by the contagion of sympathy and the influences of education; and a complete web of corroborative association is woven round it, by the powerful agency of the external sanctions." Sociality gives a "firm foundation" to the *moral* "ought," for having an impartial regard for the good of others is *the* most basic aspect of sociality: "The deeply-rooted conception which every individual even now has of himself as a social being, tends to make him feel it one of his natural wants that there should be harmony between his feelings and aims and those of his fellow creatures."[59]

However, beyond the power of laws, gods, habits, and desires, Mill's "ultimate" moral motivation is our sentimental reverence for the fact that some principles of conduct are *intrinsically* binding: "The internal sanction of duty, whatever our standard of duty may be, is one and the same—a feeling in our own mind; a pain, more or less intense, attendant on violation of duty, which in properly-cultivated moral natures rises, in the more serious cases, into shrinking from it as an impossibility." While our social nature gives us a deep-seated attraction to morality, what makes us truly *moral* is the same for Mill as for any genuine moralist: "the conscientious feelings of mankind." The *moral* reason to be moral is the "mass of feeling" surrounding morality itself: "This feeling, when disinterested, and connecting itself with the pure idea of duty," is "the essence of Conscience."[60]

One might retort that this motive is "entirely subjective, having its seat in human consciousness only." True, Mill says, but irrelevant. While the moral motive has its "seat" in the mind, what *takes* this "seat" is an objective fact, as observed by the mind's eye: the integrity or iniquity of human activity. Indeed, *whatever* the doctrine, our moral motive cannot *not* be subjective: "No one's belief that Duty is an objective reality is stronger than the belief that God is so; yet the belief in God, apart from the expectation of actual reward and punishment, only operates on conduct through, and in proportion to, the subjective religious feeling." A "belief in God" inspires piety only insofar as the believer is moved by a "subjective" love or fear of the Lord. We can ask "Need I obey God?" just as clearly as "Need

59. Mill, *Utilitarianism*, 233.
60. Ibid., 228–229.

I obey my conscience?" If the response in either case is "Yes, for otherwise you will be punished," then we have already forsaken the *moral* motive anyway: "Those whose conscientious feelings are so weak as to allow of their asking this question, if they answer it affirmatively, will not do so because they believe in the transcendental theory, but because of the external sanctions."[61]

Mill's moral theory includes a full array of motivational forces, including an authentically *moral* motivation: the "pure idea of duty."[62] In short, there are many reasons to be moral, the highest, for Mill, being a "high enthusiasm for ideal nobleness,"[63] what Kant dubs a "good will."[64] Those persons possessed of a good will do the right thing *because* it is the right thing to do; they find in morality *itself* a decisive reason for action. It is unclear to what extent Mill expected the average person to live up to this lofty standard of moral character. Mill repeatedly speaks of moral virtue as something quasi-heroic; and, in *Utilitarianism*, he seems to regard sociality as the most reasonable or realistic ideal for most individuals. Nonetheless, the aspiration is there for noble souls, wherever they are found.

Now, as Mill remarks, one could reply that he too readily dismisses the critical importance of the Transcendent: "There is, I am aware, a disposition to believe that a person who sees in moral obligation a transcendental fact, an objective reality belonging to the province of 'Things in themselves,' is likely to be more obedient to it."[65] Indeed, in a purely practical sense, one could argue that Mill is too cavalier about forgoing the Transcendent as it appears in traditional religion,[66] and too bullish or naïve about making do instead with something like the Religion of Humanity. And yet, Mill *could* concede this point without altering his theory: "If it be a true belief that God desires, above all things, the happiness of his creatures, and that this was his purpose in their creation, utility is not only not a godless doctrine, but more profoundly religious than any other."[67] Again, Mill finds philosophy and spirituality united.

However, the more pressing concern one might have is that Mill's moral theory fails to account for our moral experience *as divorced* from

61. Ibid., 229–230.
62. Ibid., 228.
63. Mill, *Autobiography*, 113, *CW* 1.
64. Kant, *Groundwork of the Metaphysics of Morals*, chap. 1.
65. Mill, *Utilitarianism*, 229.
66. Mill is more sympathetic to this point in "Theism," 483–488, *CW* 10.
67. Mill, *Utilitarianism*, 222.

the community. Consider Ivan's challenge to Alyosha from *The Brothers Karamazov*:

> Tell me straight out, I call on you—answer me: imagine that you yourself are building the edifice of human destiny with the object of making people happy in the finale, of giving them peace and rest at last, but for that you must inevitably and unavoidably torture just one tiny creature, that same child who was beating her chest with her little fist, and raise your edifice on the foundation of her unrequited tears—would you agree to be the architect on such conditions? Tell me the truth.

While Ivan is impressing upon Alyosha the problem of evil, we can also interpret this passage as fashioning a hypothetical scenario where we ourselves are actually given this option. And I believe that Mill, like so many of us, would, like Alyosha, "softly" reply, "No, I would not agree."[68] But the question is *why*, and the problem is that Mill's account of moral motivation is ultimately contingent on what is requisite to the general happiness. Can our reluctance "to torture just one tiny creature" be brought under this rubric? Well, we might appeal to the rule-based judgment of the impartial observer and say that torturing a child would be verboten. And yet, this judgment is associated with our community of interest: What if the child was not part of our community? What if her tears, imbued with magical, utopia-giving properties, were shed separate and apart from our community, in another dimension even? Well, we might instead appeal to the fact that such an act would brutalize the community and make it more likely that such things would happen again for specious reasons. And yet, what if the torture were carried out, but then the perpetrators drank potions that wiped their memories of the event?

Outlandish hypotheticals aside, the point is that there is *always* a way, in theory, to dissociate at least *certain* irreducibly moral sentiments from the general happiness, and that at *some point* our reluctance to torture an innocent being—*whatever* the promised reward—*must* come down to the naked, innate wickedness of the proposition. Indeed, Mill's moral theory sinks the whole of our moral experience into what the general interest recommends, impartially considered; but the issue is that not *all* of our moral sentiments—our feelings of *must*—can be thusly distilled. Mill captures the morality of the individual as a member of the community, but what about as an individual human being *full stop*? A victim on the rack may beseech their torturers with "You are debasing your souls!" or

---

68. Dostoevsky, *Brothers Karamazov*, II.5.4.

"Can you not see the civic injustice of this?" But may they not *also* simply damn the brute moral evil of inflicting such pain? And might not their cries elicit from us a distinctively *moral* sympathy regardless of the general happiness?

Mill is certainly not blind to such considerations—recall his appeal in *Utilitarianism* to the golden rule. But the fact of the matter is that Mill the moralist is, at core, a purely social-political philosopher. His moral theory resides in the oikos and the agora, and travels to the city limits; it is concerned *first* and *last* with how we must behave as constituents of a free community. Mill's Utilitarianism is the proper morality of the individual *citizen*; but it does not speak directly to moral experiences (feelings of *must*) that cannot be fully or best explained in Utilitarian terms. Of course, the question is: *are there* any such experiences *really*? Mill thinks not: where the general happiness is not implicated, he believes that all we have are *aesthetic* experiences; namely, variably intense feelings of *ought*. But Mill declines to consider whether at least *some* aesthetic sentiments can morph, naturally and indelibly, into moral sentiments for intelligible, *supra*-Utilitarian reasons. I believe this does not undermine Mill but merely underlines the horizon of his moral vision.

Fin

At core, Mill's practical philosophy is united by an all-embracing vision of balance and harmony between individuality and sociality. Mill's theory is that this balance and harmony ought to prevail *for* the happy individual; *between* moral individuals; in the individual liberty that is *granted*; and in the individual freedom that is *guaranteed*. His whole practical philosophy is *one* holistic picture of the good, moral, and free life, where all three of these ideals are mutually supportive and constitutive of individual and social flourishing.

In studying Mill, I kept coming back to a line from Walt Whitman: "Produce great persons, the rest follows."[69] Mill is dedicated above all to the idea that the chief and most significant solution to any of the ills that we face as human beings in society is the general cultivation of deep feeling and high aspirations. And more than anything else, Mill's thought is a spur to feeling for and aspiring to human excellence.

Harmony. Mill holds that the good life and the good society will be marked by a sense of harmony in all things. Individuals will not be divided

---

69. Whitman, "By Blue Ontario's Shore."

against themselves or society: like Plato's charioteer, their higher faculties will be at the reins, working in tandem to pursue an individuality that benefits society, and to pursue a sociality that benefits themselves. Individuality enhances the value of society, and a flourishing society expands and enhances the opportunities for higher activity. Intellectual and ethical liberty are the bread and butter of this scheme: like *yin* and *yang*, Mill sees a harmony of opposites between the basic sociality that morality entails and the absolute liberty that fills its empty spaces.

Liberality. More than being an advocate of liberalism, Mill promotes a general liberality of mind, heart, and soul. Capaciousness. Openness. Broadness. While penetrating a subject or question with one eye, Mill would have our other eye look eagerly for what we do not know or do not understand. Mill was bursting at the seams with tension-riddled wisdoms; but better that than a false simplicity or dogmatic satedness.

Moderation. Mill always sought the higher mean between extremes. Not an unsatisfying or indecisive centrism, but a passionate and deliberate attention to the deeper union of opposites. Not pleasure *or* perfection; not utility *or* duty; not individuality *or* sociality; not progress *or* conservation—but *both*, always both. One-sided ideologies are mere flatterers and dissemblers: they give clear direction and total confidence, but they always fail to account for complexity, experience, and limitation. Mill gives clear direction and total confidence, too—not toward any particular end state, but in the fervent pursuit of wholeness.

Community. Mill envisions community in the best sense of the word: not as the subjugation of the individual to the group but as a true *communion* of separate persons. Alone, the individual is shrunken and distorted; but in a community *of individuals*, each can achieve the full height of their individuality. The important thing is to maintain a strong, thriving collective while forever reaffirming the fundamental social and political significance of the individual personality. Hence Mill's republican ethic: there is nothing more individualistic and liberating than a truly *moral* and *just* society.

Kinship. Mill champions a society in which individuals are encouraged and enabled to follow through on the courage of their convictions: to speak openly and freely in good faith and good will, knowing that others, in good faith and good will, will assume their *mutual* good faith and good will, and will offer considerations and criticisms not as hostile enemies, but as friends who will the good for one another. A setting in which individuals are cowed by the power and vitriol of factions or mobs is a setting in which a horizontal *dominus* still holds the reins, and in which things will only get worse for all parties concerned until all sides make a mutual effort to give one another the benefit of the doubt—to extend to one another the same leeway and sympathy accorded to friends and family.

Humility. We are each of us only a tiny fraction of all the things a human being can think, feel, say, do, and experience. Thus, it would behoove each of us to maintain the Socratic ignorance of knowing how little we know, and always to hold out for the possibility that our most settled convictions, beliefs, and sentiments may be complexified or altered by life's surprises or by the testimony of other persons. And it is absolutely essential for us to avoid the unbridled arrogance and immaturity that goes along with the notion that *we* uniquely have the bull's-eye bead on things; that we are not exaggerating a half-truth; blindly following our partialities, passions, or prejudices; or just thinking or behaving in lockstep with our class, our creed, our tribe.

Allow me to conclude with a few thoughts on how we should approach Mill going forward. In keeping with his many-sidedness, Mill has been consistently claimed by a diverse array of philosophical schools and political outlooks as one of their own. For starters, I think it ought to be clear by now that Mill cannot be reduced to any one-sided doctrine or ideology; his allegiances are of the broadest, most capacious variety. Indeed, his Utilitarianism does not exclude, but actually elevates, the likes of Aristotle; and his liberalism need not immediately rankle even the most conservative member of the larger liberal tradition. Conservatives, so often framing Mill as the overflowing font of the absolute worst of modern liberalism, have routinely denounced and demeaned his philosophical output: Mill's "peculiar brand of utilitarianism—a cake of Benthamite hedonism glazed with Wordsworthian sentimentality—has proved to be irresistible for the multitudes susceptible to that sort of confection."[70] Rest assured, there is plenty of daylight between Mill and thinkers like Fitzjames Stephen, let alone Burke or Kirk. However, Mill offers something far more salubrious than a sentimental hedonism; and his alleged excesses—like his lingering affection for the Religion of Humanity—are largely peripheral to his fundamental thought. In short, there is no reason why conservatives cannot sit down at Mill's table over dessert.

At the same time, those liberals who find themselves on Mill's side of the aisle have often been reluctant to throw in with him, given his supposed incoherence, illogic, and inconsistency. Mill has long been liberalism's greatest apostle, in that his work rouses the soul and expresses the

70. Kimball, "Conservative Icons."

ethos and spirit of liberalism in ways that neither Locke nor Rawls can so easily manage. And yet, his perceived philosophical pitfalls have often kept him sidelined, whereas, in reality, his philosophy is nothing if not coherent, logical, and consistent, as well as strikingly lucid and robust. Naturally, there will be those who are apprehensive about the fact that Mill grounds his practical philosophy on a rather thick notion of happiness; but I think it is becoming increasingly apparent that just such a thick notion is exactly what is needed if the liberal philosophy is to survive and thrive.

In other words, I believe what we have in Mill is the once and future wellspring of liberalism, in its healthiest and hardiest form. In Mill's value theory, we have a conception of happiness that integrates the objectivity of human nature and the human good with the subjectivity of human individuality. In Mill's moral theory, we have a conception of duty that integrates an ultimate appeal to happiness with the deep, felt need for moral absolutism. In Mill's liberal theory, we have a conception of the good and moral society that harmonizes the just claims of the individual with the just claims of society at large. And in Mill's republican theory, we have a conception of the good and moral polity that buttresses and enriches that which makes for a just, flourishing community. Admittedly, it is a rather lofty ideal; but one well worth striving for, now and always.

REFERENCES

Anderson, Elizabeth. "John Stuart Mill and Experiments in Living." *Ethics* 122, no. 1 (1991): 4–26.

Annas, Julia. *The Morality of Happiness*. Oxford: Oxford University Press, 1993.

Anschutz, R. P. *The Philosophy of J. S. Mill*. London: Oxford University Press, 1963.

Aristotle. *Metaphysics*. Translated by C. D. C. Reeve. Indianapolis: Hackett, 2016.

———. *Nicomachean Ethics*. Translated by David Ross. Oxford: Oxford University Press, 1980.

———. *Physics*. Translated by C. D. C. Reeve. Indianapolis: Hackett, 2018.

———. *Politics*. Translated by Benjamin Jowett. New York: Barnes & Noble, 2005.

Ayer, A. J. *Language, Truth, and Logic*. Mineola, N.Y.: Dover, 1952.

Bain, Alexander. *J. S. Mill: A Criticism*. London: Longmans, Green, 1882.

Barker, Chris. *Educating Liberty: Democracy and Aristocracy in J. S. Mill's Political Thought*. Rochester, N.Y.: University of Rochester Press, 2018.

Baum, Bruce. "J. S. Mill on Freedom and Power." *Polity* 31, no. 2 (1998): 187–216.

Beaumont, Tim. "J. S. Mill on Calliclean Hedonism and the Concept of Pleasure." *Dialogue* 58, no. 3 (2019): 553–578.

Bell, Duncan. "John Stuart Mill on Colonies." *Political Theory* 38, no. 1 (2010): 34–64.

Bentham, Jeremy. *Theory of Legislation*. Translated by R. Hildreth. London: Trübner, 1864.

———. *The Works of Jeremy Bentham*. Edited by John Bowring. Edinburgh: William Tait, 1838–1843.

Berger, Fred. *Happiness, Justice, and Freedom: The Moral & Political Philosophy of John Stuart Mill*. Berkeley: University of California Press, 1984.

Berlin, Isaiah. *The Crooked Timber of Humanity: Chapters in the History of Ideas*. Edited by Henry Hardy. Princeton: Princeton University Press, 2013.

———. *Freedom and Its Betrayal: Six Enemies of Human Liberty*. Edited by Henry Hardy. Princeton: Princeton University Press, 2014.

———. "John Stuart Mill and the Ends of Life." In *Liberty*, edited by Henry Hardy, 218–251. Oxford: Oxford University Press, 2007.

———. "Two Concepts of Liberty." In *Liberty*, edited by Henry Hardy, 166–217. Oxford: Oxford University Press, 2007.

Bloom, Harold. *Shakespeare: The Invention of the Human*. New York: Riverhead Books, 1998.

Bradley, F. H. *Ethical Studies*. Oxford: Oxford University Press, 1988.

Brandt, R. B. "Utilitarianism and Moral Rights." *Canadian Journal of Philosophy* 14, no. 1 (1984): 1–19.

Brink, David. "Millian Principles, Freedom of Expression, and Hate Speech." *Legal Theory* 7, no. 2 (2001): 119–157.

———. "Mill's Deliberative Utilitarianism." *Philosophy & Public Affairs* 21, no. 1 (1992): 67–103.

———. *Mill's Progressive Principles*. Oxford: Oxford University Press, 2013.

Brown, D. G. "The Harm Principle." In *A Companion to Mill*, edited by Christopher Macleod and Dale E. Miller, 409–424. Malden, Mass.: Wiley-Blackwell, 2017.

———. "Mill's Moral Theory: Ongoing Revisionism." *Politics, Philosophy & Economics* 9, no. 1 (2010): 5–45.

Butler, Joseph. *Fifteen Sermons & Other Writings on Ethics*. Edited by David McNaughton. Oxford: Oxford University Press, 2017.

Carlyle, Thomas. *Latter-Day Pamphlets*. London: Chapman and Hall, 1898.

———. *Sartor Resartus*. London: Grant Richards, 1902.

Carnap, Rudolf. *Philosophy and Logical Syntax*. London: Kegan Paul, Trench, Trübner, 1935.

Carritt, E. F. *The Theory of Morals: An Introduction to Ethical Philosophy*. Oxford: Oxford University Press, 1952.

Christman, John. "Liberalism and Individual Positive Freedom." *Ethics* 101, no. 2 (1991): 343–359.

Constant, Benjamin. "The Liberty of Ancients Compared with That of Moderns." *Online Library of Liberty*. 1819. https://oll.libertyfund.org/titles/constant-the -liberty-of-ancients-compared-with-that-of-moderns-1819.

Cowling, Maurice. *Mill and Liberalism*. Cambridge: Cambridge University Press, 1990.

Crisp, Roger. "Hedonism Reconsidered." *Philosophy and Phenomenological Research* 73, no. 3 (2006): 619–645.

———. *Mill on Utilitarianism*. London: Routledge, 1997.

———. *Reasons and the Good*. Oxford: Oxford University Press, 2006.

Crowder, George. "Two Concepts of Liberal Pluralism." *Political Theory* 35, no. 2 (2007): 121–146.

Dalberg-Acton, John. *Acton-Creighton Correspondence*. Edited by John Neville Figgis and Reginald Vere Laurence. London: Macmillan, 1906.

Deneen, Patrick. *Why Liberalism Failed*. New Haven, Conn.: Yale University Press, 2018.

Donner, Wendy. *The Liberal Self: John Stuart Mill's Moral and Political Philosophy*. Ithaca, N.Y.: Cornell University Press, 1991.

Donner, Wendy, and Richard Fumerton. *Mill*. Malden, Mass.: Wiley-Blackwell, 2009.

Dostoevsky, Fyodor. *The Brothers Karamazov*. Translated by Richard Pevear and Larissa Volokhonsky. New York: Farrar, Straus and Giroux, 2002.

Duncan-Jones, Austin. *Butler's Moral Philosophy*. London: Penguin, 1952.

Dworkin, Ronald. *Justice for Hedgehogs*. Cambridge, Mass.: Belknap, 2011.

Dyzenhaus, David. "John Stuart Mill and the Harm of Pornography." *Ethics* 102, no. 3 (1992): 534–551.

Eggleston, Ben. "Mill's Moral Standard." In *A Companion to Mill*, edited by Christopher Macleod and Dale E. Miller, 358–373. Malden, Mass.: Wiley-Blackwell, 2017.

Feagin, Susan L. "Mill and Edwards on the Higher Pleasures." *Philosophy* 58, no. 224 (1983): 244–252.

Feinberg, Joel. "Psychological Egoism." In *Ethical Theory: An Anthology*, edited by Russ Shafer-Landau, 183–195. Malden, Mass.: Blackwell, 2007.

Feldman, Fred. *Pleasure and the Good Life: Concerning the Nature, Varieties, and Plausibility of Hedonism*. Oxford: Oxford University Press, 2004.

Finlay, Graham. "Mill on Education and Schooling." In *A Companion to Mill*, edited by Christopher Macleod and Dale E. Miller, 504–517. Malden, Mass.: Wiley-Blackwell, 2017.

Fletcher, Guy. "Mill's Art of Life." In *A Companion to Mill*, edited by Christopher Macleod and Dale E. Miller, 297–312. Malden, Mass.: Wiley-Blackwell, 2017.

Frankena, William K. "Sidgwick and the History of Ethical Dualism." In *Essays on Henry Sidgwick*, edited by Bart Schultz, 175–198. Cambridge: Cambridge University Press, 2002.

Frankl, Viktor E. *Man's Search for Meaning*. Boston: Beacon, 1959.

Fumerton, Richard. "Mill's Epistemology." In *A Companion to Mill*, edited by Christopher Macleod and Dale E. Miller, 192–206. Malden, Mass.: Wiley-Blackwell, 2017.

Galston, William. *Liberal Purposes: Goods, Virtues, and Diversity in the Liberal State*. Cambridge: Cambridge University Press, 1991.

George, Robert. "John Stuart Mill and John Henry Newman on Liberty and Conscience." *Saint Anselm Journal* 10, no. 2 (2015): 40–46.

Gray, John. "John Stuart Mill: Traditional and Revisionist Interpretations." *Literature of Liberty* 2, no. 2 (1979): 7–37.

———. *Mill on Liberty: A Defence*. London: Routledge, 1996.

Gregg, Samuel. "John Stuart Mill's Intolerant Faith and the Religion of Liberalism." *Public Discourse*, June 19, 2017. www.thepublicdiscourse.com/2017/06/19529/.

Halldenius, Lena. "Locke and the Non-arbitrary." *European Journal of Political Theory* 2, no. 3 (2003): 261–279.

Hamburger, Joseph. *John Stuart Mill on Liberty and Control*. Princeton: Princeton University Press, 1999.

Hansson, Sven Ove. "Mill's Circle(s) of Liberty." *Social Theory and Practice* 41, no. 4 (2015): 734–749.

Harman, Gilbert, *Reasoning, Meaning, and Mind*. Oxford: Oxford University Press, 1999.

Helvétius, Claude Adrien. *De l'espirit; or Essays on the Mind and Its Several Faculties*. Translated by Uncredited. London: Thomas Davidson, 1825.

———. *A Treatise on Man; His Intellectual Faculties and His Education*. Vol. 1. Edited by W. Hooper. London: Albion Press, 1810.

Himmelfarb, Gertrude. "Liberty: 'One Very Simple Principle?'" *American Scholar* 62, no. 4 (1993): 531–550.

Hoag, Robert W. "Happiness and Freedom: Recent Work on John Stuart Mill." *Philosophy & Public Affairs* 15, no. 2 (1986): 188–199.

———. "J. S. Mill's Language of Pleasures." *Utilitas* 4, no. 2 (1992): 247–278.

———. "Mill's Conception of Happiness as an Inclusive End." *Journal of the History of Philosophy* 25, no. 3 (1987): 417–431.

Holbrook, Daniel. *Qualitative Utilitarianism*. Lanham, Md.: University Press of America, 1988.

Humboldt, Wilhelm von. *The Limits of State Action*. Edited by J. W. Burrow. Cambridge: Cambridge University Press, 2009.

Hume, David. *An Enquiry Concerning the Principles of Morals*. Edited by J. B. Schneewind. Indianapolis: Hackett, 1983.

———. "Of the Original Contract." In *Essays: Moral, Political, and Literary*, edited by Eugene F. Miller, 465–487. Indianapolis: Liberty Fund, 1987.

———. *A Treatise of Human Nature.* Edited by Ernest C. Mossner. New York: Penguin, 1985.

Hutcheson, Francis. *An Inquiry into the Original of Our Ideas of Beauty and Virtue.* Edited by Wolfgang Leidhold. Indianapolis: Liberty Fund, 2008.

———. *A System of Moral Philosophy.* Vol 1. Glasgow: R. and A. Foulis, 1755.

Jacobson, Daniel. "Mill on Freedom of Speech." In *A Companion to Mill*, edited by Christopher Macleod and Dale E. Miller, 440–453. Malden, Mass.: Wiley-Blackwell, 2017.

———. "Mill on Liberty, Speech, and the Free Society." *Philosophy & Public Affairs* 29, no. 3 (2000): 276–309.

———. "Utilitarianism without Consequentialism: The Case of John Stuart Mill." *Philosophical Review* 117, no. 2 (2008): 159–191.

Jenkins, Joyce. "Desire and Human Nature in J. S. Mill." *History of Philosophy Quarterly* 14, no. 2 (1997): 219–234.

Kant, Immanuel. *Groundwork of the Metaphysics of Morals.* Edited by Mary Gregor and Jens Timmermann. Cambridge: Cambridge University Press, 2012.

Kateb, George. "A Reading of *On Liberty*." In *On Liberty: Rethinking the Western Tradition*, edited by David Bromwich and George Kateb, 28–68. New Haven, Conn.: Yale University Press, 2003.

Kelly, P. J. *Utilitarianism and Distributive Justice: Jeremy Bentham and the Civil Law.* Oxford: Oxford University Press, 1990.

Kenny, Anthony. *A New History of Western Philosophy.* Oxford: Oxford University Press, 2010.

Kimball, Roger. "Conservative Icons: James Fitzjames Stephen." *The Conservative*, September 3, 2017. https://theconservative.online/article/conservative-icons-james-fitzjames-stephen.

King, John T., and Mark A. Yanochik. "John Stuart Mill and the Economic Rationale for Organized Labor." *American Economist* 56, no. 2 (2011): 28–34.

Laertius, Diogenes. *Lives of Eminent Philosophers.* Books 6–10. Translated by R. D. Hicks. Cambridge, Mass.: Harvard University Press, 1931.

Larsen, Timothy. *John Stuart Mill: Secular Life.* Oxford: Oxford University Press, 2018.

Locke, John. *Second Treatise of Government.* Edited by C. B. Macpherson. Indianapolis: Hackett, 1980.

Loizides, Antis. "Mill on Happiness: A Question of Method." *British Journal for the History of Philosophy* 22, no. 2 (2014): 302–321.

Long, Roderick T. "Mill's Higher Pleasures and the Choice of Character." *Utilitas* 4, no. 2 (1992): 279–297.

Lukianoff, Greg, and Jonathan Haidt. *The Coddling of the American Mind: How Good Intentions and Bad Ideas Are Setting Up a Generation for Failure.* London: Penguin, 2019.

Lyons, David. *In the Interest of the Governed: A Study in Bentham's Philosophy of Utility and Law.* Oxford: Oxford University Press, 1991.

———. *Rights, Welfare, and Mill's Moral Theory.* Oxford: Oxford University Press, 1994.

MacIntyre, Alasdair. *After Virtue: A Study in Moral Theory.* Notre Dame, Ind.: University of Notre Dame Press, 2007.

Macleod, Christopher. "John Stuart Mill." In *The Stanford Encyclopedia of Philosophy*, September 12, 2021. https://plato.stanford.edu/entries/mill/.

———. "Was Mill a Noncognitivist?" *Southern Journal of Philosophy* 51, no. 2 (2013): 206–223.

Macleod, Christopher, and Dale E. Miller. "Preface." In *A Companion to Mill*, edited by Christopher Macleod and Dale E. Miller, xvi–xviii. Malden, Mass.: Wiley-Blackwell, 2017.

Martí, José Luis, and Philip Pettit. *A Political Philosophy in Public Life: Civic Republicanism in Zapatero's Spain*. Princeton: Princeton University Press, 2010.

Martin, Rex. "Mill's Rule Utilitarianism in Context." In *John Stuart Mill and the Art of Life*, edited by Ben Eggleston, Dale E. Miller, and David Weinstein, 22–39. Oxford: Oxford University Press, 2011.

Marwah, Inder. "Complicating Barbarism and Civilization: Mill's Complex Sociology of Human Development." *History of Political Thought* 32, no. 2 (2011): 345–366.

McGlynn, Clare, and Ian Ward. "Would John Stuart Mill Have Regulated Pornography?" *Journal of Law and Society* 41, no. 4 (2014): 500–522.

Melville, Herman. *Moby-Dick; or, The Whale*. 1851. Reprint, London: Penguin, 2002.

Mill, James. *Analysis of the Phenomena of the Human Mind*. Vol. 2. London: Baldwin and Cradock, 1829.

———. "Essay on Government." In *Political Writings*, edited by Terence Ball. Cambridge: Cambridge University Press, 1992.

Mill, John Stuart. *The Collected Works of John Stuart Mill*. Edited by John M. Robson. Toronto: University of Toronto Press, 1963–1991.

Miller, Dale E. "John Stuart Mill's Civic Liberalism." *History of Political Thought* 21, no. 1 (2000): 88–113.

———. *J. S. Mill: Moral, Social, and Political Thought*. Cambridge: Polity, 2010.

Milligram, Elijah. "Liberty, the Higher Pleasures, and Mill's Missing Science of Ethic Jokes." *Social Philosophy and Policy* 26, no. 1 (2009): 326–353.

———. "Mill's Epiphanies." In *A Companion to Mill*, edited by Christopher Macleod and Dale E. Miller, 12–29. Malden, Mass.: Wiley-Blackwell, 2017.

Moore, G. E. *Principia Ethica*. Edited by Thomas Baldwin. Cambridge: Cambridge University Press, 2000.

Morales, Maria. "Rational Freedom in John Stuart Mill's Feminism." In *J. S. Mill's Political Thought: A Bicentennial Reassessment*, edited by Nadia Urbinati and Alex Zakaras, 43–65. Cambridge: Cambridge University Press, 2007.

Nietzsche, Friedrich. *Beyond Good and Evil*. In *Basic Writings of Nietzsche*, translated by Walter Kaufmann, 179–436. New York: Random House, 2000.

———. *The Twilight of the Idols*. Translated by Duncan Large. Oxford: Oxford University Press, 1998.

Northup, Solomon. *Twelve Years a Slave*. Vancouver: Engage Books, 2014.

Nozick, Robert. *Anarchy, State, and Utopia*. New York: Basic Books, 1974.

Nussbaum, Martha. "Mill between Aristotle & Bentham." *Daedalus* 133, no. 2 (2004): 60–68.

Pettit, Philip. "The Instability of Freedom as Non-interference." *Ethics* 121, no. 4 (2011): 693–716.

———. *Just Freedom: A Moral Compass for a Complex World*. New York: Norton, 2014.

———. "Keeping Republican Freedom Simple." *Political Theory* 30, no. 3 (2002): 339–356.

——. *On the People's Terms: A Republican Theory and Model of Democracy*. Cambridge: Cambridge University Press, 2012.

——. *Republicanism: A Theory of Freedom and Government*. Oxford: Oxford University Press, 1997.

Pitkin, Hannah. "Obligation and Consent." *American Political Science Review* 59, no. 4 (1965): 990–999.

Pitts, Jennifer. "Legislator of the World? A Rereading of Bentham on Colonies." *Political Theory* 33, no. 2 (2003): 200–234.

Plato. *The Republic of Plato*. Translated by Allan Bloom. New York: Basic Books, 2016.

Pullam, Mark. "A Victorian Case for Ordered Liberty." *Law & Liberty*, May 15, 2018. https://lawliberty.org/classic/victorian-case-ordered-liberty-equality-fraternity -james-fitzjames-stephen/.

Quincy, H. Keith. "The Higher Pleasures & Their Quantification." *Polity* 12, no. 3 (1980): 457–480.

Rashdall, Hastings. *The Theory of Good and Evil: A Treatise on Moral Philosophy*. Vol. 1. Oxford: Clarendon, 1907. Facsimile printed by Elibron Classics, 2004.

Rawls, John. *Political Liberalism*. Cambridge, Mass.: Harvard University Press, 2005.

——. *A Theory of Justice*. Cambridge, Mass.: Harvard University Press, 1999.

Rees, J. C. *John Stuart Mill's* On Liberty. Oxford: Oxford University Press, 1985.

——. "A Re-reading of Mill on Liberty." *Political Studies* 8, no. 2 (1960): 113–129.

Reeves, Richard. "Mill's Mind: A Biographical Sketch." In *A Companion to Mill*, edited by Christopher Macleod and Dale E. Miller, 3–11. Malden, Mass.: Wiley-Blackwell, 2017.

Riley, Jonathan. "Interpreting Mill's Qualitative Hedonism." *Philosophical Quarterly* 53, no. 212 (2003): 410–418.

——. *Mill on Liberty*. London: Routledge, 1998.

Rosenblum, Nancy. *Another Liberalism: Romanticism and the Reconstruction of Liberal Thought*. Cambridge, Mass.: Harvard University Press, 1987.

Rothbard, Murray. *Classical Economics: An Austrian Perspective on the History of Economic Thought*. Auburn: Edward Elgar, 1995.

Rousseau, Jean-Jacques. *The Social Contract and Other Later Political Writings*. Edited by Victor Gourevtich. Cambridge: Cambridge University Press, 1997.

Ryan, Alan. *J. S. Mill*. London: Routledge & Kegan Paul, 1975.

——. "J. S. Mill on Education." *Oxford Review of Education* 37, no. 5 (2011): 653–667.

——. *The Making of Modern Liberalism*. Princeton: Princeton University Press, 2012.

——. *The Philosophy of John Stuart Mill*. Hampshire: Macmillan, 1987.

Saunders, Ben. "J. S. Mill's Conception of Utility." *Utilitas* 22, no. 1 (2010): 52–69.

Schmidt-Petri, Christoph. "On an Interpretation of Mill's Qualitative Hedonism." *Prolegomena* 5, no. 2 (2006): 173.

Sen, Amartya, and Bernard Williams. "Introduction: Utilitarianism and Beyond." In *Utilitarianism and Beyond*, edited by Amartya Sen and Bernard Williams, 1–22. Cambridge: Cambridge University Press, 1982.

Seth, James. "The Alleged Fallacies in Mill's 'Utilitarianism.'" *Philosophical Review* 17, no. 5 (1908): 469–488.

Sharp, F. C. *Ethics*. New York: Appleton-Century, 1928.

Sidgwick, Henry. *The Methods of Ethics*. Indianapolis: Hackett, 1991.

Skorupski, John. *Why Read Mill Today?* London: Routledge, 2006.

Smith, Adam. *The Theory of Moral Sentiments.* Edited by Ryan Patrick Hanley. London: Penguin, 2010.

Snare, Francis. *Morals, Motivation, and Convention: Hume's Influential Doctrines.* Cambridge: Cambridge University Press, 2002.

Sober, Elliot. "Hedonism and Butler's Stone." *Ethics* 103, no. 1 (1992): 97–103.

Sosa, Ernest. "Mill's *Utilitarianism.*" In *Mill's* Utilitarianism: *Text and Criticism*, edited by James M. Smith and Ernest Sosa, 154–172. Belmont, Calif.: Wadsworth, 1969.

Spector, Horacio. "Four Conceptions of Freedom." *Political Theory* 38, no. 6 (2010): 780–808.

Stanley, Jason. *How Fascism Works: The Politics of Us and Them.* New York: Random House, 2018.

Stephen, James Fitzjames. *Liberty, Equality, Fraternity.* Carmel, Ind.: Liberty Fund, 1993.

Sturgeon, Nicholas L. "Mill's Hedonism." *Boston University Law Review* 90 (2010): 1705–1729.

Taylor, Harriet. "On Marriage." In *The Complete Works of Harriet Taylor Mill*, edited by Jo Ellen Jacobs and Paula Harms Payne. Bloomington: Indiana University Press, 1998.

Ten, C. L. *Mill on Liberty.* Oxford: Clarendon, 1980.

———. "Mill's Defence of Liberty." In *On Liberty in Focus*, edited by John Gray and G. W. Smith, 212–238. London: Routledge, 1991.

———. "Reviewed Work: The Liberal Self: John Stuart Mill's Moral and Political Philosophy by Wendy Donner." *Canadian Journal of Philosophy* 24, no. 2 (1994): 327–335.

Tercheck, Ronald J. "The Limits of Mill's Tolerance." Review of *John Stuart Mill on Liberty and Control*, by Joseph Hamburger. *Review of Politics* 62, no. 3 (2000): 583–585.

Thompson, Dennis. *John Stuart Mill and Representative Government.* Princeton: Princeton University Press, 1976.

Threet, Dan. "Mill's Social Pressure Puzzle." *Social Theory and Practice* 44, no. 4 (2018): 539–565.

Tocqueville, Alexis de. *Democracy in America.* Translated by Harvey Mansfield and Delba Winthrop. Chicago: University of Chicago Press, 2000.

Tunick, Mark. "Tolerant Imperialism: John Stuart Mill's Defense of British Rule in India." *Review of Politics* 68, no. 4 (2006): 586–611.

Turner, Piers Norris. "The Absolutism Problem in *On Liberty.*" *Canadian Journal of Philosophy* 43, no. 3 (2013): 322–340.

———. "'Harm' and Mill's Harm Principle." *Ethics* 124, no. 2 (2014): 299–326.

———. "Mill and Modern Liberalism." In *A Companion to Mill*, edited by Christopher Macleod and Dale E. Miller, 567–582. Malden, Mass.: Wiley-Blackwell, 2017.

———. "Rules and Right in Mill." *Journal of the History of Philosophy* 53, no. 4 (2015): 723–745.

Urbinati, Nadia. "The Many Heads of the Hydra." In *J. S. Mill's Political Thought: A Bicentennial Reassessment*, edited by Nadia Urbinati and Alex Zakaras, 66–97. Cambridge: Cambridge University Press, 2007.

———. *Mill on Democracy: From the Athenian Polis to Representative Government*. Chicago: University of Chicago Press, 2002.

Urmson, J. O. "The Interpretation of the Moral Philosophy of J. S. Mill." *Philosophical Quarterly* 10, no. 3 (1953): 33–39.

Varouxakis, Georgios. "Mill on Democracy Revisited." In *A Companion to Mill*, edited by Christopher Macleod and Dale E. Miller, 454–471. Malden, Mass.: Wiley-Blackwell, 2017.

Waldron, Jeremy. *The Harm in Hate Speech*. Cambridge, Mass.: Harvard University Press, 2012.

———. "Mill on Liberty and on the Contagious Diseases Act." In *J. S. Mill's Political Thought: A Bicentennial Reassessment*, edited by Nadia Urbinati and Alex Zakaras, 11–42. Cambridge: Cambridge University Press, 2007.

Weinstein, David. "Interpreting Mill." In *John Stuart Mill and the Art of Life*, edited by Ben Eggleston, Dale E. Miller, and David Weinstein, 44–63. Oxford: Oxford University Press, 2011.

West, Henry. *An Introduction to Mill's Utilitarian Ethics*. Cambridge: Cambridge University Press, 2004.

———. "Mill's Proof of the Principle of Utility." In *The Blackwell Guide to Mill's Utilitarianism*, edited by Henry R. West, 174–183. Malden, Mass.: Blackwell, 2006.

Whitman, Walt. "By Blue Ontario's Shore." In *The Complete Poems*, edited by Francis Murphy, 362–377. London: Penguin, 2004.

Williams, Geraint. "The Greek Origins of J. S. Mill's Conception of Happiness." *Utilitas* 8, no. 1 (1996): 5–14.

Wordsworth, William. *The Major Works*, edited by Stephen Gill. Oxford: Oxford University Press, 2008.

Zakaras, Alex. "John Stuart Mill, Individuality, and Participatory Democracy." In *J. S. Mill's Political Thought: A Bicentennial Reassessment*, edited by Nadia Urbinati and Alex Zakaras, 200–220. Cambridge: Cambridge University Press, 2007.

Zuk, Peter. "Mill's Metaethical Non-cognitivism." *Utilitas* 30, no. 3 (2018): 271–293.

INDEX

acedia (sloth), 36

Acton, Lord, 237

Act Utilitarianism, 10, 127–33, 151

aesthetics/art: creative process of, 41; as domain of human action/value, 92–93, 97–98; as higher pleasures, 35; liberty for expression of, 181; Mill's experience of, 2, 35, 181, 240; science contrasted with, 93, 96, 98

akrasia (weakness of will), 20, 38, 71

altruism: associationist explanations of, 63–64; Benthamite philosophy and, 101–2; egoistic explanations of, 59–60; happiness in relation to, 57–58; and motivation to morality, 281

Ancients vs. Moderns, 244–45

Aristotle: causal theory of, 53; conception of happiness, 10, 33–34; on hierarchy in human nature, 248; and higher pleasures, 31–32; on human flourishing, 57, 67, 69–70, 261; on intellectual and moral virtue, 263; *Nicomachean Ethics*, 21; value theory of, 21

art. *See* aesthetics/art

Art of Life (moral, aesthetic, sympathetic/expedient domains), 46, 92–99

associationism, 47–53, 63–64

Athenian democracy, 257, 259

autonomy, 153, 200, 216, 227, 279

Bacon, Francis, 38

Bain, Alexander, 13

barbarians/children, 32, 199, 204, 215, 225, 242, 251, 258, 266

Beatles, 267

Bentham, Jeremy: *Deontology*, 99; godfather to Mill, 2, 29; intellect downplayed by, 168; Mill's philosophical use of, 6, 28–29, 82. *See also* Benthamite philosophy

Benthamite philosophy: desire, 39–40; empiricism of, 38; felicific/hedonic calculus, 108–9, 117, 128–29, 146; general criticisms of, 99; the good, 13–14;

happiness, 10, 67, 99–107; hedonism, 16–17; interference with liberty, 146, 157–58; liberty, 11, 143–44, 218–19; Mill's criticisms of/departures from, 14, 16–17, 23, 29, 36, 44–47, 52, 58–59, 61, 65, 69, 93, 95, 99–107, 123, 136, 168; moral theory, 59, 72, 74–77, 82, 99–107; motivations to morality, 280; "ought" statements in, 54, 93–95; pleasure, 16–17, 19, 23, 39–40; in practice, 100–102; in principle, 103–7; psychological egoism, 58–59; psychological hedonism, 49–50; quantitative hedonism, 14, 23

Berger, Fred, 129

Berlin, Isaiah, 52, 56n195, 142, 207–8, 216–18

Blakey, Robert, 95–96

Bloom, Harold, 3, 206

Bradley, F. H., 43–45

Brandt, Richard, 128

Breaking Bad (television series), 123

Brink, David, 83, 132

Brutus, Lucius Junius, 112–13

Burke, Edmund, 218

Butler, Joseph, 41–43, 45, 60–61

Carlyle, Thomas, 16, 54, 71, 95, 101, 104

character: diversity of, 184; happiness associated with, 67, 68–69. *See also* self; virtue

checks on power, 209–10, 221, 223, 224, 234–35

childrearing, 275–80

children. *See* barbarians/children

Christianity, 34, 170, 175, 238, 261, 269, 272–74

Church of England, 275

Cicero, 171

civic humanism, 106, 256–60

civic participation, 11

civility, 188–98

Classical Utilitarianism, 72–74

cognitivism, 94–98

A NOTE ON THE TYPE

THIS BOOK has been composed in Miller, a Scotch Roman typeface designed by Matthew Carter and first released by Font Bureau in 1997. It resembles Monticello, the typeface developed for The Papers of Thomas Jefferson in the 1940s by C. H. Griffith and P. J. Conkwright and reinterpreted in digital form by Carter in 2003.

Pleasant Jefferson ("P. J.") Conkwright (1905–1986) was Typographer at Princeton University Press from 1939 to 1970. He was an acclaimed book designer and AIGA Medalist.

The ornament used throughout this book was designed by Pierre Simon Fournier (1712–1768) and was a favorite of Conkwright's, used in his design of the *Princeton University Library Chronicle.*